EMPLOYMENT LAW
CHECKLISTS 2009

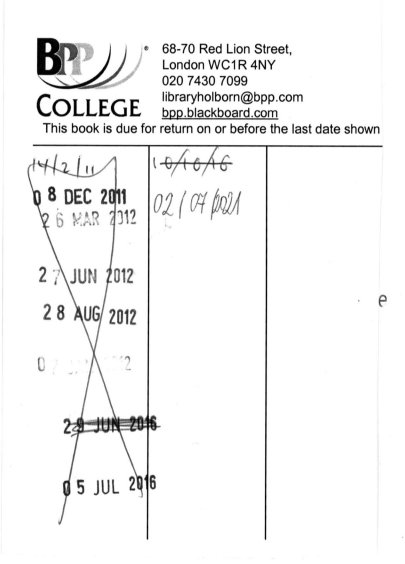

EMPLOYMENT LAW CHECKLISTS 2009

Julia Palca

Catherine Taylor

OXFORD

UNIVERSITY PRESS

OXFORD
UNIVERSITY PRESS

Great Clarendon Street, Oxford OX2 6DP

Oxford University Press is a department of the University of Oxford.
It furthers the University's objective of excellence in research, scholarship,
and education by publishing worldwide in

Oxford New York

Auckland Cape Town Dar es Salaam Hong Kong Karachi
Kuala Lumpur Madrid Melbourne Mexico City Nairobi
New Delhi Shanghai Taipei Toronto

With offices in

Argentina Austria Brazil Chile Czech Republic France Greece
Guatemala Hungary Italy Japan Poland Portugal Singapore
South Korea Switzerland Thailand Turkey Ukraine Vietnam

Oxford is a registered trade mark of Oxford University Press
in the UK and in certain other countries

Published in the United States
by Oxford University Press Inc., New York

First published 1993 by Blackstone Press Ltd
Fourth edition published 2009 by Oxford University Press

British Library Cataloguing in Publication Data
Data available

Library of Congress Cataloging in Publication Data
Data available

ISBN 978–0–19–954747–0

1 3 5 7 9 10 8 6 4 2

Typeset by Cepha Imaging Private Ltd., Bangalore, India
Printed by MPG Books Group in the UK

PREFACE

Employment Law Checklists is a book designed to assist lawyers who do not profess to be experts in employment law and non-lawyers such as human resources managers who deal on a day-to-day basis with employment and industrial relations issues. This book is intended to be practical, guiding the reader on the appropriate steps which need to be taken and the facts which need to be considered before employment decisions are reached.

The latest edition of the book has been revised and updated to deal with the arrival of protection from age discrimination and the new transfer of undertaking regulations as well as all the developments in legislation and case law in the other areas of the book. Generally, the book cites the most important statutory provisions and case law. However it does not include all relevant statute or case references. In certain areas, where the law is particularly developed, in particular Chapters 2, 7, 8, and 9 which deal with discrimination, unfair dismissal, redundancy, and the transfer regulations respectively, in addition to the checklists separate commentary on the law has been included to assist the reader.

Employment law continues to change (albeit not quite at the same pace as we have seen in previous years) and the final chapter of this book contains brief details of the most important anticipated legislative changes.

In most chapters of the book, save those relating to sex discrimination and maternity rights, we have used masculine pronouns, but of course in all sections the contents of the book apply equally to both sexes.

We should like to thank in particular several of our present and former colleagues at Olswang who have assisted us in producing this edition of Employment Law Checklists as follows: Nicola Cordran who originally wrote the chapter on data protection and privacy; Sophia Moore for helping us in our quest to ensure the book is up to date and in relation to Chapter 12 in particular; and Davina Pereira and Dawn Malling for their help and support in producing the book.

Julia Palca
Catherine Taylor
Olswang
October 2008

CONTENTS

Contents

Contents

ABBREVIATIONS

ACAS	Advisory, Conciliation, and Arbitration Service
CAC	Central Arbitration Committee
CBI	Confederation of British Industry
CRE	Commission for Racial Equality
DDA 1995	Disability Discrimination Act 1995
DPA 1998	Data Protection Act 1998
DRC	Disability Rights Commission
DTI	Department of Trade and Industry
EA 2002	Employment Act 2002
EAT	Employment Appeal Tribunal
EDT	Effective date of termination
EEAR 2006	Employment Equality (Age) Regulations 2006
EHRC	Equality and Human Rights Commission
EOC	Equal Opportunities Commission
EqPA 1970	Equal Pay Act 1970
ERA 1996	Employment Rights Act 1996
ERA 1999	Employment Relations Act 1999
EWC	Expected week of childbirth
HRA	Human Rights Act
I&C Committee	Information and Consultation Committee
ITEPA 2003	Income Tax (Earnings and Pensions) Act 2003
MAPLE Regulations 1999	Maternity and Parental Leave etc Regulations 1999
NWMA 1998	National Minimum Wage Act 1998
PAL Regulations 2002	Paternity and Adoption Leave Regulations 2002
PILON	Payment in lieu of notice provision
RBR 2003	Employment Equality (Religion or Belief) Regulations 2003
RRA 1976	Race Relations Act 1976

SAP	Statutory adoption pay
SDA 1975	Sex Discrimination Act 1975
SMP	Statutory maternity pay
SOR 2003	Employment Equality (Sexual Orientation) Regulations 2003
SSCBA 1992	Social Security Contributions and Benefits Act 1992
TUC	Trade Union Congress
TULR(C)A 1992	Trade Union and Labour Relations (Consolidation) Act 1992
TUPE 1981	Transfer of Undertakings (Protection of Employment) Regulations 1981
TUPE 2006	Transfer of Undertakings (Protection of Employment) Regulations 2006

1

EMPLOYEE STATUS AND THE CONTRACT OF EMPLOYMENT

A. Introduction

This chapter considers the contract of employment, which is the agreement **1.01** between the individual and employer, overlaying the statutory rights an individual enjoys. Specific aspects of the contract are considered and, in particular, those contractual terms which are determined by statute, such as working time, at least as far as an employer's minimum obligations are concerned. The chapter also considers the status of the individual and what rights the individual will enjoy depending on this status as this underpins the employee's rights and employer's obligations in relation to the contract of employment and other rights described in the remainder of this book. As this topic is fundamental to employment rights and underpins the contractual position it is dealt with first.

1

B. Employee Status

1.02 Why is an individual's employment status important? It determines an individual's rights other than his contractual rights. In particular, an individual's status will determine how many additional statutory rights he enjoys over and above those in the contract and the tax treatment of his earnings. So, for example, a true independent contractor will enjoy very few statutory rights. A 'worker' who may not be an employee, but something in between that and an independent contractor will enjoy some but not all employment rights. Agency workers will also enjoy lesser rights unless a court determines that they do in fact have an employment relationship with one of the parties to the agency relationship. The tax treatment of earnings also varies according to status; those who are traditional employees are taxable under Schedule E, are subject to PAYE provisions, and are entitled to receive social security benefits. Workers and individual contractors are more likely to be taxable under Schedule D and it is only in exceptional cases that tax will be deducted at source. Finally, whether an employer is vicariously liable for the acts of its employee will also require a determination of the individual's status. This section will concentrate primarily on the tests applicable for determining what rights an individual enjoys.

1.03 What approach do the courts take to determine an individual's employment status? Whilst there are clear rules to be applied in determining this question, it is a question of fact and degree in each case. The courts will look at the whole picture, and no one item is conclusive evidence either way. The test to be applied has been determined by a number of cases, including *Ready-Mixed Concrete (South East) v Minister of Pensions and National Insurance* [1968] 2 QB 497. Further, different statutes apply different tests in determining which individuals are entitled to benefit from the protection under their terms. The tests set out below are the common law tests which will be applied to determine whether an employee satisfies the definition under the relevant legislation. However, case law relevant to each separate piece of legislation should also be considered.

Employees

1.04 What are the key questions in determining whether an individual is employed under a contract of employment?

(a) Is there a contract between the working person and the alleged employer? There should be. For example, an agency worker may not have a contract with the entity to which he or she provides services on a day-to-day basis (but see para **1.14** below as to where a contract may be implied).

(b) If there is a contract, under its terms, there must be mutuality of obligation. Does the working person undertake to provide his or her services *personally* in return for remuneration and is there *sufficient degree of control* to enable the worker to be called a servant? There should be.

(c) If both the above tests are satisfied, are there any factors inconsistent with the existence of a contract of employment? There shouldn't be (see para **1.08** below).

What constitutes mutuality of obligation? This means both the employee and the **1.05** employer must be under legal obligations to one another, usually the obligation on the employee to work and on the employer to pay for that work (*Carmichael v National Power plc* [2000] IRLR 43).

What does the provision of services personally mean? The individual must be **1.06** obliged to provide the services him- or herself. Freedom to do a job by his own hands or by another's (ie to subcontract work) is inconsistent with an employment contract (*Express and Echo Publications Ltd v Tanors* [1999] IRLR 367; *James v Redcats (Brands) Limited* [2007] IRLR 296).

What factors will determine whether there is a sufficient degree of control? **1.07** Whether the employer decides how and when the task is to be done, the means to be employed, and where it will be done (*Ready-Mixed Concrete (South East) Ltd v Minister of Pensions and National Insurance* [1968] 2 QB 497, at 515).

What factors will be inconsistent with the existence of a contract of **1.08** employment?

(a) The individual is not obliged to work for the employer even if the employer so requests.
(b) The individual owns his own tools.
(c) The individual hires his own helpers.
(d) The individual may substitute someone else to do a particular task commissioned by the employer.
(e) The individual has responsibility for investment and management.
(f) The individual works for a number of other employers.
(g) The fact that the arrangement is not intended to be that of employer and employee including the fact that the individual charges VAT for his services and receives no benefits, such as pension and/or health insurance, which employees of that employer do receive.

How are employees taxed? Employers are obliged to deduct income tax and **1.09** National Insurance contributions due from their employees at source and pay employer's National Insurance contributions under PAYE regulations.

Workers

1.10 Who is a worker? The test for who is a worker is derived from statute and is wider than that for an employee.

(a) Does the individual work under a contract, whether express or implied (and, if it is express, whether oral or in writing)? They should.

(b) Is the contract a contract of employment? It could be.

(c) If not, does the individual undertake to do or perform personally any work or services for another party under the contract where the other party to the contract, whose status by virtue of the contract is *not a* client or customer of any profession or business undertaking carried on by the individual? They should do so.

(See, for example, TULR(C)A 1992, s 296; ERA 1996, s 230(3); Working Time Regulations 1998, reg 2(1); Part-time Workers (Prevention of Less Favourable Treatment) Regulations 2000, reg 1(2))

1.11 What does the 'profession or business undertaking' exception referred to at para **1.10(c)** above mean?

(a) Is the individual genuinely 'self-employed'? Then they will not be a worker.

(b) Does the individual have a sufficiently arm's length and independent arrangement with any third party to be treated as working for themselves? Then they will not be a worker.

(c) Does the individual actively market his services as an independent person to the world in general? Then they will not be a worker.

(See *Byrne Bros (Farmwork) Ltd v Baird* [2002] IRLR 96; *Wright v Redrow Homes (Yorkshire) Ltd* [2004] IRLR 720; *Cotswold Developments Construction Ltd v Williams* [2006] IRLR 181)

[Note that the test used in the discrimination legislation is slightly different. All the discrimination legislation refers to 'employment' throughout, but the definition of employment is wider than the test described above at para **1.04**. The test is 'employment under a contract of service or of apprenticeship or a contract personally to execute any work or labour' (see, for example, SDA 1975, s 82(c); RRA 1976, s 78(1) and para **2.20** below). Thus, the profession or business exception is omitted.]

1.12 What employment rights does a 'worker' enjoy? In addition to rights under any contract and in tort (for example, to claim in respect of a personal injury) workers enjoy limited statutory employment rights as follows:

(a) the right for a part-time worker not to be treated less favourably than a comparable full-time worker, under the Part-time Workers (Prevention of Less Favourable Treatment) Regulations 2000 (see para **4.61** below);

(b) the right to claim unlawful deductions from wages under the ERA 1996 (see para **1.41** et seq);

(c) the right not to suffer detriment or be dismissed as a result of a protected disclosure (whistle-blowing) under the ERA 1996 (see para **7.95** below);

(d) the right to receive the National Minimum Wage (see para **1.05** above);

(e) the right to be accompanied at grievance or disciplinary meetings and not to suffer detriment, nor to be unfairly dismissed, in relation to that right, under ss 10–12 of the Employment Relations Act 1999;

(f) rights under the Working Time Regulations 1996 (see para **1.62** below);

(g) rights under the discrimination legislation—for example, the sex, race, disability, and age discrimination legislation (see Chapter 2);

(h) the right not to suffer deductions of unauthorized union subscriptions and the right to take part in lawful picketing under the Trade Union and Labour Relations (Consolidation) Act 1992 (TULR(C)A 1992) (see Chapter 5 below).

How are workers taxed? Most workers will be taxed under Schedule D (although **1.13** worker status and Schedule E tax treatment is possible). Schedule D means the worker will submit an invoice and charge value added tax if their earnings in any year are sufficiently high. The worker will then account directly to the Inland Revenue for tax and National Insurance contributions on these sums. The employer has no obligation to deduct PAYE or employee's National Insurance contributions and no obligation to pay employer's National Insurance contributions.

Agency Workers

Who is an agency worker? The test for an agency worker is again derived from **1.14** statute (see, for example, National Minimum Wage Act 1998, s 34 and Working Time Regulations 1998, reg 36). Note that the definition in the discrimination legislation is different from that set out below (see, for example, SDA 1975, s 9 in relation to contract workers) but case law has held it should be given a wide construction to cover a wide category of workers.

(a) Is the individual supplied by a person ('the agent') to do work for another ('the principal') by an arrangement between the agent and the principal?

(b) Is there any contract between either the principal and the individual or agent and the individual in relation to that work?

(c) Is either the agent or principal a client or customer of any profession or business undertaking carried on by the individual?

If the answer to the first question is yes and to the two following questions is no, the worker is an agency worker.

1.15 What employment rights does an agency worker enjoy? An agency worker who complies with the strict definition above has very few employment rights, namely only the following:

(a) the right to receive the National Minimum Wage (see para **1.50** below);

(b) the right to be accompanied at grievance and disciplinary meetings and not to suffer detriment nor to be unfairly dismissed, in relation to that right, under ss 10–12 of the Employment Relations Act 1999;

(c) the right not to suffer detriment or be dismissed related to a protected disclosure (whistle-blowing) under the ERA 1996 (see para **7.95** below);

(d) rights under the Working Time Regulations 1996 (see para **1.62** below);

(e) rights under the discrimination legislation—for example the sex, race, disability, and age discrimination legislation (see Chapter 2).

1.16 How may an agency worker be able to establish that there exists an employment contract (or worker's contract) with the agent or principal? The worker will need to develop the concept of an implied contract of employment arising between the worker and the agent or principal as appropriate and must show that it is necessary to do so to reflect the reality of the relationship between the parties. In particular, the worker will need to show the requisite degree of control and mutuality of obligation by the agency or principal (see paras **1.05** to **1.07** above). The length of time an agency worker has worked for a principal will be a factor to be taken into account but not determinative (*Frank v Reuters Ltd* [2003] IRLR 423; *Dacas v Brook Street Bureau (UK) Ltd* [2004] IRLR 358; *Bunce v Posworth Ltd (t/a Skyblue)* [2005] IRLR 557; *Cable & Wireless plc v Muscat* [2006] IRLR 354; *James v Greenwich London Borough Council* [2008] IRLR 302, CA; *Consistent Group Ltd v Kalwak and Others* [2008] EWCA Civ 430, CA) (see also para **7.55** below).

1.17 If an agency worker can establish a contract of employment (or worker's contract) with the agent or principal, what additional rights will he enjoy? See above at para **1.12** for rights enjoyed by workers and the rest of this book for rights enjoyed by employees.

1.18 How are agency workers taxed? This will depend, usually, on the type of contract between the agency worker and agent.

C. The Contract of Employment—Overview

Contents of the Contract

1.19 Do general principles of contract law apply to a contract of employment? Generally, yes. So, for example, a contract of employment is created just like other contracts, by an offer by one party which is accepted by the other, with both parties intending to create legal relations. However, there is some specific case law relating to contracts of employment and, in particular, its termination. Also, a contract of employment's terms are affected by statute more than some other forms of contract.

Express Terms

What forms can express terms take? They may be written or oral. The main examples are job offers and written statements of terms, which are dealt with below. There is no formal requirement that a job offer should be in writing.   **1.20**

What should an employer consider in relation to a job offer? Before confirming a job offer, it is wise for the employer to institute the following checks: **1.21**

(a) That the job offer will not start until the employee's notice period with his former employers expires (by agreement or effluxion of time).

(b) That the employee is not bound by post-termination restrictions that prevent him from performing his duties.

(c) That the employee can produce a document which satisfies the Immigration, Asylum and Nationality Act 2006. The relevant documents are set out in Home Office guidance ('Prevention of Illegal Working—Immigration, Asylum and Nationality Act 2006') which can be accessed at <http://www.bia.homeoffice.gov.uk>. Failure to obtain such a document may be a criminal offence resulting in fines or imprisonment.

(d) That all legal/regulatory requirements are met (eg regarding driving passenger or heavy goods vehicles, regulatory body rules).

(e) That the employee's references are valid and satisfactory.

What are the requirements in relation to a written statement? An employer must give each employee who has been employed for more than a month (but not workers), within two months of the commencement of employment, a written statement containing certain particulars of the terms of employment. It must set out the date (being not more than seven days before the notice is given) on which the relevant terms apply (ERA 1996, s 1).   **1.22**

What if the particulars of employment are varied? If there is any variation in the particulars of employment, the employer must give the employee a complete amended statement within one month, unless the variation relates only to the name of the employer or identity of employer. In that case the notice need only inform the employee of the change of name or identity (ERA 1996, s 4). Where the Transfer of Undertakings (Protection of Employment) Regulations 2008 apply, see Chapter 9.   **1.23**

1.24 What methods of giving particulars can be adopted by the employer?

(a) By giving the employee a contract of employment incorporating the relevant particulars;

(b) By giving the employee a copy of a written statement setting out the particulars;

(c) For certain particulars indicated by an asterisk(*) below, by referring, in a contract or statement of particulars, to another document to which the employee can gain access, which sets out relevant details.

1.25 What particulars must be included in the written statement? The particulars must set out contractual provisions relating to the following matters (and if there are no relevant provisions, the statement must say so):

(a) identity of employer;

(b) identity of employee;

(c) the date when employment began;

(d) whether any previous service counts as being continuous with the present contract, and if so the date when continuous employment began;

(e) job title or brief job description;

(f) place of work (or, if more than one, stating that, and giving the employer's address);

(g) scale or rate of remuneration, or the method of calculating remuneration;

(h) the intervals at which remuneration is paid (for example, weekly or monthly);

(i) normal hours of work;

(j) entitlement to public and other holidays and holiday pay;

(k) *provision for sickness and injury, including sick pay;

(l) *pension rights, and whether a contracting-out certificate has been given under the Pension Schemes Act 1993;

(m) notice period, or if the contract is a fixed-term contract, the date the fixed term expires;

(n) *details of any collective agreements (whether specific to the employer or made with an employer federation) which affect the employee's terms;

(o) if an employee is posted outside the UK for more than one month:
  • the period of the posting;
  • the currency in which he will be paid;
  • any additional pay or benefits;
  • any terms and conditions relating to the employee's return to the UK;

(p) the person to whom the employee should apply with any grievance.

(ERA 1996, ss 1–3)

What is the effect of particulars provided in a written statement? The contents of **1.26** a written statement of particulars are express terms and as such are the main, but not conclusive, evidence of the terms of the contract. If no particulars are given, or if the particulars which are given are wrong, an employment tribunal may determine what the particulars should have contained, or what amendments should be made. No sanction, however, may be imposed upon an employer who fails to give the particulars. It is, however, advisable for an employer to provide the appropriate particulars, not just because it is sound business practice, but also because in employment tribunal proceedings the tribunal will not look kindly upon an employer who has ignored these obligations (ERA 1996, ss 11–12).

What other express contractual terms would be expected to appear in a contract **1.27** of employment? Whilst certain terms will be implied into a contract, other topics which may be of relevance to employment are not automatically incorporated by implication into the contract of employment. If the parties therefore wish the contract to refer to these matters, they must do so expressly. Such topics include:

(a) Whether the employee is obliged to work overtime and if so to what extent and on what pay.

(b) Whether the employee is able to take up other employment outside working hours (see also para **1.31(f)** below).

(c) Whether the employee should have more onerous confidentiality obligations than are implied by law (see para **1.31(f)** below).

(d) Whether the employee consents to certain deductions being made from wages. If no such consent is given, in general no deductions can be made. The employer might want the ability to make deductions for outstanding sums owed by the employee on termination if any fine is imposed pursuant to a disciplinary procedure, or if there are till or stock shortages (see ERA 1996, ss 13 to 27 and para **1.41** below).

(e) Whether the employer is entitled to institute lay-off or short-time working on no pay or on reduced pay. The employer has no right to impose lay-off or short-time working without pay unless there is an express contractual provision to that effect or this is an established custom and practice (see ERA 1996, ss 28 to 35 and para **1.55** below).

(f) A 'garden leave' clause, enabling an employer to suspend an employee from performing work, usually on full pay and benefits. Such a clause will only be enforced by the courts by way of injunction if there is a significant risk to the employer's confidential information or goodwill, and so long as the employee continues to receive full pay and benefits. This clause may assist an employer whose employee has given notice where the employee has confidential information regarding, for example, current contracts with customers, pricing policy, or a strong customer connection, which will become less valuable to the employee's future employer if the employee is not allowed access to it for a period of time (*Provident Financial Group plc and Whitegates Estate Agency Ltd v Hayward* [1989] IRLR 84) (see also paras **1.110(b)** and **1.112** below).

(g) What duties the employee may be required to perform: it is in the employer's interest for the contract to be flexible so that the employer can, under the contract, require the employee to perform a variety of tasks (for example, 'the employee shall perform such duties as may from time to time be [reasonably required]').

(h) Express terms regarding the ownership of all rights in the product of the employee's work, whether written, artistic, or scientific. In the absence of contractual assignments of copyright or patent rights, the statutory position is as follows:

- the employer is the first owner of the copyright in any work created by the employee in the normal course of work for the employer (the Copyright, Designs and Patents Act 1988, s 11(2));
- a patent in any invention made by the employee in the normal course of duty will belong to the employer. The employee is always entitled to such a fair share of profits from any invention as is reasonable in all the circumstances (Patents Act 1977, ss 39–41).

[Note: These provisions do *not* apply to the self-employed (which may include some categories of workers), who are generally first owners of intellectual property rights of their own creations.]

(i) A provision requiring the return of all company property (including documents, whether paper or electronic) on demand and certainly on termination of employment.

(j) A provision for the suspension on full pay of any employee during the investigation of a disciplinary issue.

1.28 For more senior employees or employees with access to confidential information, key customer/suppliers or with influence over other employees, employers should also consider the imposition of post-termination restrictions. These must not be in restraint of trade, nor must they be penal. They must do no more than protect the employer's legitimate interests in its business. They must be reasonable both in extent and duration. Post-termination restrictions normally limit the following aspects of an ex-employee's activities:

(a) The geographical area in which the employee can compete with the employer and/or the sections of the employer's business with which the employee can compete for a particular period after termination (such a covenant should be limited in duration and will only be valid in certain circumstances depending on the legitimate interests to be protected).

(b) Solicitation of the employer's customers with whom the employee has had an established connection or has had contact, for a particular period after termination.

(c) Dealings, either direct or indirect, with any of the employer's customers with whom the employee has an established connection for a particular period after termination. This is a wider covenant than that in para **1.28(b)** above and includes circumstances where customers have sought out the former employee of their own accord. The period of the restriction should therefore never be longer than the period of a non-solicitation covenant at para **1.28(b)** above.

(d) Not enticing away the employer's other senior employees for a particular period after termination. Note that an absolute prohibition on employing employees of the former employer who have decided to leave of their own volition is unlikely to be enforceable.

(e) Another useful provision for senior employees is a provision which requires the automatic resignation of all directorships and other offices on termination of employment.

1.29 The employer may also wish to be able to terminate the employee's contract of employment with immediate effect and pay him a particular sum, for example, the remuneration which he would have received, for the balance of the contract period (a 'payment in lieu' clause). If so, an express clause should be included in the contract. Any sums payable pursuant to this clause will be taxed under normal Schedule E provisions and so the tax break usually applicable to such payments will not be available. The main reason for incorporating such a provision is to allow flexibility and to preserve post-termination restrictions in a contract: if the employer terminates the contract without giving due notice (even if it pays in lieu of that notice), a breach of the contract will have been committed as a result of which the employer may no longer be able to enforce any of the post-termination restrictions contained in the contract (see also para **1.117** and para **7.21(c)** in relation to wrongful dismissal below).

Implied Terms

1.30 What are the main means by which terms will be implied into a contract of employment? Terms may be implied into the contract:

(a) by the *conduct* of the parties (for example, if the parties have always behaved in a particular way which must have been anticipated by them when the contract was entered into, or by variation at a later stage (*Quinn v Calder*

Industrial Materials [1996] IRLR 126; *Duke v Reliance Systems* [1982] IRLR 347; *Albion Automotive Ltd v Walker* [2002] IRLB 702));

(b) by *custom and practice* (which must be reasonable, certain, and generally well known (*Sagar v H Ridehalgh & Son Ltd* [1931] 1 Ch 310));

(c) because terms are *necessary* to give efficacy to the agreement. One test is whether, if at the time the contract was entered into, an officious bystander were to ask whether a particular point was contained in the contract, the parties to the contract would have turned to him and have said 'of course' (*Shirlaw v Southern Foundries (1926) Ltd* [1939] 2 KB 206; *Lister v Romford Ice and Cold Storage Co Ltd* [1957] AC 555; *Deeley v British Rail Engineering Ltd* [1980] IRLR 147);

(d) because they are *characteristic* of the employment relationship: ensuring that the parties behave in a reasonable, but not excessively onerous, manner towards each other. A prime example of this type of implied term is the term of trust and confidence (*Malik v Bank of Credit and Commerce International SA* [1997] IRLR 462).

1.31 What are the most common obligations on an employee implied into the contract of employment? Implied duties on the part of the employee include:

(a) The duty not to be negligent in performance of duties.

(b) The duty to be reasonably competent to do the job.

(c) The duty to cooperate with the employer in the performance of the job.

(d) The duty to carry out reasonable instructions of the employer.

(e) The duty to adapt to a new working environment or system, if reasonably introduced by the employer after proper training.

(f) The duty of fidelity, for example:

- the duty to behave honestly and so not to make secret profits during the course of employment, such as personal commissions, kickbacks, or bribes. Such a profit could include a holiday for the employee. An employee offered such a 'perk' by a client or supplier of the employer should obtain the employer's consent before accepting;

- the duty to disclose misdeeds on the part of others in certain circumstances (but not necessarily on their own part unless they are a director) (*Bell v Lever Bros* [1932] AC 61; *Sybron Corporation v Rochem Ltd* [1983] IRLR 253; *Item Software (UK) Ltd v Fasshi* [2005] ICR 450);

- the duty not to take away the employer's property after termination of employment;

- the duty to keep information confidential during the course of employment and trade secrets confidential after the termination of employment (*Faccenda Chicken Ltd v Fowler* [1986] IRLR 69) although see para **7.95** below on the protection for those who make certain public disclosures; and

- the duty not to compete, nor to set up an operation which competes with the employer, whilst still employed. Employees can, however, take certain steps to prepare to compete, such as arranging financing or finding premises (*Balston Ltd v Headline Filters Limited* [1990] FSR 385).

(g) not without reasonable and proper cause to act in a manner likely to destroy the relationship of trust and confidence between employer and employee (*Western Excavating (ECC) Ltd v Sharp* [1978] QB 761; *Malik v BCCI* [1997] IRLR 462, HL).

An employee who fails to honour these obligations will be in breach of his **1.32** contract and may be disciplined by the employer. Any of the duties may be modified or extended by an express term dealing with the relevant topic subject to the rules relating to restraint of trade (see para **1.28** above).

What are the most common rights of an employee implied into the contract of **1.33** employment? There are two types of implied rights; those which are implied by statute and those which are not. In relation to rights implied by statute, much of the remainder of this book deals with these rights but those set out below are particularly relevant to the contract of employment.

(a) The right to equal pay and to equal terms and conditions (see Chapter 2).
(b) The right to a minimum level of pay (see para **1.50** below).
(c) The right to minimum notice periods (see para **1.107** below).
(d) The right to 'guaranteed pay' during non-working periods. This is a small daily sum, to be paid for a maximum of five days during any three-month non-working period (see para **1.55** below).
(e) The imposition of a maximum number of working hours per week and breaks in working time together with restrictions on night work (see para **1.62** below).
(f) The right to four weeks' paid holiday (see para **1.80** below).
(g) The right to receive statutory sick pay; maternity pay; paternity pay; adoption pay (see Chapters 3 and 4).
(h) The right to inspect and, upon payment, to receive copies of personnel records (see Chapter 10).

For implied rights of the employee which may not be based on statute, see para **1.34** below in relation to an employer's obligations.

What are the most common obligations on an employer implied into the contract **1.34** of employment? Duties and obligations imposed upon the employer include:

(a) To pay the employee (see para **1.40** below).

Employee Status and the Contract of Employment

(b) To behave towards the employee with good faith. This can be subdivided into the following obligations:
  - not without reasonable and proper cause to act in a manner likely to destroy the relationship of trust and confidence between employer and employee (*Western Excavating (ECC) Ltd v Sharp* [1978] QB 761; *Malik v BCCI* [1997] IRLR 462, HL);
  - not to treat the employee arbitrarily, capriciously, or inequitably regarding pay and other matters (*Clark v Nomura International plc* [2000] IRLR 766; *Commerzbank AG v Keen* [2007] IRLR 132);
  - not to undermine the authority of senior staff over their subordinates;
  - not falsely to accuse the employee of dishonesty or other misconduct.

(c) To behave reasonably towards the employee, eg to give him reasonable notice before exercising a right to require the employee to move jobs; not to put excessive pressure on the employee so that his mental or physical health will suffer.

(d) To treat staff with dignity (where breaches of this general provision constitute harassment on discriminatory grounds, the employee may also be able to complain of discrimination on that basis (see Chapter 2 below)).

(e) Not to expect the employee to work in intolerable conditions and to take reasonable care for the safety of the employee, for example, in the selection of proper staff, the provision of adequate working materials, and the provision of a safe system of working (*Wilsons and Clyde Coal Co Ltd v English* [1938] AC 57, later translated into a contractual duty).

(f) Although there is no general duty upon employers to provide work for their employees, there is a duty to provide work for:
  - skilled or professional workers who need to work to maintain their skills (for example, scientists, doctors, and other technicians);
  - employees who are paid partly by commission, such as members of a sales force, or by piece work;
  - trainees; and
  - those who need publicity to enhance their careers such as actors or presenters (*William Hill Organisation Ltd v Tucker* [1998] IRLR 313).

(g) To provide training for any employee required to operate new machinery or undertake new working practices.

(h) If any reference is given (and an employer is not obliged to do so) the employer must exercise reasonable care and skill to ensure that it is accurate and fair, and presented in such a way so as to not be misleading (*Spring v Guardian Assurance plc and Others* [1994] ICR 596) (see para **1.114** below).

(i) *Sunday trading*: Not to force people who do not want to do so to work on Sunday. This means:

- protected shopworkers (those in employment on 25 August 1994 who were not 'Sunday-only' workers) can only be required to work on Sundays if they sign an 'opting-in' notice agreeing to work on Sundays, and have not subsequently retracted it by signing an 'opting-out' notice;
- opted-out shopworkers (those employed after 26 August 1994, who are not 'Sunday-only' workers, who have signed an 'opting-out' notice saying that they object to working on Sunday) cannot be forced to work on Sunday unless they subsequently sign an 'opting-in' notice;
- treating protected or opted-out workers in a discriminatory fashion (eg by dismissing them, selecting them for redundancy, or failing to promote them on this ground) is an automatically unfair dismissal.

If the employer is in serious breach of any of the obligations set out above, the **1.35** employee may resign, claim constructive dismissal, and both sue for damages for wrongful dismissal and claim compensation for unfair dismissal (see Chapter 7). These damages may include damages for 'personal injury' for breaches of para **1.34(d)** and **(e)** but only if the damage was a reasonably foreseeable one as a result of the employer's failure to provide a safe place of work (see also paras 7.322 *et seq*).

Incorporated Terms

What are incorporated terms? Certain terms in other documents may be incorpo- **1.36** rated into the contract of employment, either expressly or by implication. Such documents include a collective agreement between the employer and a trade union of which the employee is a member; works rules; staff handbooks; or office manuals. Where incorporation is by express reference to the relevant document it should if at all possible make it clear which parts of the document are incorporated.

How is it determined what terms are incorporated? Where the whole document **1.37** is incorporated by express reference, usually only those terms directly relating to the employee's contract, such as pay, benefits, hours, and duties are incorporated in the contract (*Keeley v Fosroc International* [2006] IRLR 961). Provisions in collective agreements concerning the conduct of the relationship between employer and union, such as collective bargaining rights or disputes procedures, will generally not be incorporated into the employee's contract of employment (*National Coal Board v National Union of Mineworkers* [1086] IRLR 439).

A 'no strike clause' in a collective agreement can only be incorporated into the **1.38** employee's contract of employment if:

(a) the collective agreement is in writing;

(b) the collective agreement contains an express statement that the clause is incorporated into individual contracts;

(c) the collective agreement is reasonably accessible in the workplace during work hours;

(d) each trade union which is a party to the collective agreement is independent; and

(e) the employee's contract of employment expressly or impliedly incorporates the collective agreement.

(TULR(C)A 1992, s 180)

1.39 Can terms be incorporated by implication? If there is no incorporation by express reference, provisions in works rules, staff handbooks, and office manuals will only be incorporated into contracts of employment where they are always followed by custom and practice (*Henry v London General Transport Services* [2002] IRLR 472) or where the parties must have intended them to have been included, for example benefits and sick pay schemes. The following factors indicate whether documents which are not expressly incorporated into any contract of employment are impliedly incorporated:

(a) the nature of the document;

(b) the methods used to bring the document to the employee's attention;

(c) whether the document came into existence before or after the contract of employment began.

D. Pay and Minimum Wage

1.40 What determines what an employee will be paid? An employee's entitlement to be paid, when, and how much is generally governed by the contract of employment. Statute intervenes in the following ways:

(a) an employer's right to make certain deductions from salary is circumscribed by statute, mainly the ERA 1996, ss 13–27 (see para **1.41** below);

(b) by prescribing a minimum level of pay (see para **1.50** below);

(c) by not differentiating between men and women as to pay (see Chapter 2).

Deductions from Pay

1.41 What deductions can be made from pay by an employer? During the course of employment the employer can only make the following deductions from an employee's wages:

(a) deductions required or authorized to be made by a statutory provision such as PAYE and National Insurance contributions (ERA 1996, s 13(1)(a));

(b) any deduction required or authorized to be made by virtue of a relevant provision of the worker's contract (ERA 1996, s 13(1)(a));

(c) any deduction to which the employee has consented in writing prior to it being made (ERA 1996, s 13(1)(b));

(d) any payment to a third party to which the employee has consented in writing (ERA 1996, s 14(4));

(e) any deductions made for reimbursement of previous overpayments of wages or expenses (ERA 1996, s 14(1));

(f) any deduction made as a consequence of any disciplinary proceedings if those proceedings were held by virtue of a statutory provision (ERA 1996, s 14(3));

(g) any deductions made on account of an employee's participation in industrial action (including not only pay but also any damages suffered by the employer as a result of the industrial action) (ERA 1996, s 14(5));

(h) any payments the employer is required by statute to make to a public authority following an appropriate order (ERA, s 14(3));

(i) any sums the employer is required to pay pursuant to an attachment of earnings order made by the court (ERA 1996, s 14(6)).

Who benefits from these protections, employees only or the wider category of **1.42** workers? The protections apply to workers as well.

What is meant by 'pay' in this context? Pay is wages which is very widely defined **1.43** and includes fees, bonuses including a non-contractual bonus, commissions and holiday pay, statutory sick pay, statutory maternity, paternity and adoption pay, as well as some more esoteric statutory payments (ERA 1996, s 27(1)). It will not usually include pay in lieu of notice (*Delancey v Staples* [1992] ICR 483) or payments under a bonus scheme which were incapable of quantification (*Coors Brewers v Adcock* [2007] IRLR 440). Pay expressly does not include:

(a) advances on loans;

(b) payments for expenses;

(c) any payment by way of a pension, allowance, or gratuity in connection with the worker's retirement or as compensation for loss of office;

(d) any payment referable to redundancy;

(e) any payment to the employee other than in his capacity as a worker.

(ERA 1996, s 27(3))

What is meant by a 'relevant provision' of an employee's contract? It should be a **1.44** provision of the contract comprised:

(a) in one or more written terms of the contract of which the employer has given the worker a copy on an occasion prior to the employer making the deduction in question; or

1

(b) one or more terms of the contract (whether express or implied and, if express, whether oral or in writing) the existence and effect, or combined effect, of which in relation to the employee, the employer has notified to the worker in writing on such an occasion.

(ERA 1996, s 13(2))

1.45 What is prior written consent? The consent must precede not only the deduction itself but also the event giving rise to the deduction (*Potter v Hunt Contracts Ltd* [1992] ICR 337).

1.46 What is a deduction? Broadly any deficiency in what is properly payable to the worker, except where the deficiency arises from an error of computation (ERA 1996, s 13(3)(4)).

1.47 Are there any industries where workers are given further protection? Special provisions apply in the retail industry, where, even if the employee has consented in writing to deductions being made, deductions in any period to compensate for stock deficiencies or cash shortages (or any payments the employee is required to make as a result of deficiencies or shortages) cannot exceed 10 per cent of the employee's gross wages for the relevant period (ERA 1996, ss 17 to 22).

1.48 What remedies are available to an employee whose employer makes an unlawful deduction? If the employer wrongfully makes deductions from pay or makes no payment whatsoever, the employee may complain to an employment tribunal within three months of the relevant deduction, or of the last deduction in the series, seeking an order for payment of the sums due (ERA 1996, s 23). Before doing so, the employee must bring a grievance (EA 2002, s 32 and Sch 4; see also paras **7.81** and **7.83**). The employee may also, if he so wishes, bring proceedings in a county court or High Court for damages for breach of contract, but cannot recover more then once in respect of any particular deduction. If the employer fails to make a payment which the employment tribunal then orders it to make, the employer will be unable to recover the payment from the worker subsequently, even where the employer was right to recover it (ERA 1996, s 259(4)).

1.49 What documentation is an employee entitled to receive in relation to their pay? The employer must also give an employee (but not a worker) an *itemized pay statement* showing gross pay; all deductions such as those for tax, National Insurance contributions, pension payments, or any trade union subscription; and the net amount receivable (ERA 1996, ss 8–12).

National Minimum Wage

1.50 Who can benefit?

(a) A worker (see para **1.10** above) including an agency worker or home worker,

(b) A person who is working or ordinarily works in the United Kingdom under the contract,

(c) A person who has ceased to be of compulsory school age,

(d) but excluding, amongst others, au pairs, apprentices, voluntary workers, and those who work in a family business.

(National Minimum Wage Act 1998 (NMWA 1998), ss 43, 44, 44A, 45; National Minimum Wage Regulations 1999, reg 2(2))

What is the National Minimum Wage rate? **1.51**

(a) The standard rate increased to £5.73 per hour in October 2008.

(b) For 18–21 year olds the rate increased to £4.77 in October 2008.

(c) For 16-17 year olds who are above the compulsory school leaving age the rate increased to £3.53 per hour in October 2008.

(National Minimum Wage Regulations 1999, regs 11 and 13)

How do you calculate wages for the purposes of the National Minimum Wage? **1.52**

(a) The relevant period for the calculation is one month or in the case of a worker who is paid by reference to a shorter period than one month, that period (National Minimum Wage Regulations 1999, reg 10(1)).

(b) Payments made in that period and later periods (if relevant to that period) are taken into account, but it is only money payments, not benefits in kind (National Minimum Wage Regulations 1999, regs 30–37).

(c) Other sums which are excluded from the calculation include loans or advances; pension or other retirement scheme payments; settlement payments; redundancy payments (National Minimum Wage Regulations 1999, regs 30–37).

(d) Certain reductions will then be made, for example, premiums paid for work; eg shift premiums or premiums for work on bank holidays; tips or service charges which are *not* paid through the payroll (National Minimum Wage Regulations 1999, regs 30–37).

(e) The type of working arrangement a worker enjoys (ie salaried; piece work) will then determine the method of calculation of the National Minimum Wage and whether travelling or 'on call' working time will be relevant to the calculation (National Minimum Wage Regulations 1999, reg 14).

(f) For certain types of piece working arrangements, it may be possible to enter into a 'fair estimate' agreement, which estimates the number of hours it will take the employee to do the work.

Are there any other obligations on the employer? **1.53**

(a) The employer must maintain records—in practice since it is for the employer to prove compliance with the National Minimum Wage, they would be wise to do so anyway (National Minimum Wage Regulations 1999, reg 38).

(b) The employer must allow the worker access to these records if the worker believes he or she has not been paid the National Minimum Wage in any period (NMWA 1998, s 10).

1.54 How can an employee claim entitlements under the legislation?

(a) An employee may bring a claim under the contract of employment in the High Court or county court, which could include asking the court to declare that a particular part of the legislation applies (NMWA 1998, s 17).

(b) Relevant officers who are appointed to ensure compliance with the National Minimum Wage can issue enforcement orders and penalty notices under the Act. The employer may appeal the enforcement notice (NMWA 1998, ss 19–22).

(c) An employee who is not allowed access to records can apply to an employment tribunal and if upheld, the tribunal can award the worker a sum equivalent to 80 times the hourly amount of the minimum wage.

(d) It is a criminal offence to refuse to pay the National Minimum Wage, to obstruct compliance officers, or not to keep proper records. Fines for these offences can be up to £5,000.

1.55 What other payment obligations are there on an employer?

(a) Guarantee payments (ERA 1996, ss 28–35)
  - In certain circumstances, an employee who is given no work to do during his normal working hours on any day may be entitled to a minimum fallback payment or guarantee payment;
  - An employee who qualifies is entitled to a maximum payment of £20.40 per day (as from 1 February 2008) for a maximum of five days in a three-month period.

(b) Pay during medical suspension (ERA 1996, ss 64–65)
  - An employee who is suspended from work on certain medical grounds may also be entitled to minimum pay during his suspension (see also para **3.09** below in relation to suspension for maternity-related grounds);
  - The medical grounds relate mainly to those engaged in lead or other dangerous chemical process or radiation hazards.

E. Pensions

1.56 Pensions are an extremely complex area, not least due to the terminology adopted. What are the main different types of pension?

(a) *Occupational pension*—a pension administered by the employer and pension trustees. It is subject to the terms of the Pension Act 1995 which impose duties on both the employer and the trustees. An occupational pension scheme may or may not require contributions by the employee.

(b) *Personal pension*—a personal pension is a retirement scheme which operates in a tax efficient manner. It will usually not be administered by the employer, although the employer may provide access to the scheme, in which case it may be called a Group Personal Pension. Schemes are provided by certain regulated institutions. There are limits on the contributions which can be made by an employee if the employee wishes to maximize the tax efficiency of the scheme. A personal pension scheme may or may not require contributions from the employer.

(c) *Stakeholder pension*—a type of personal pension scheme which complies with the requirements of the Welfare Reform and Pensions Act 1999 (see para 1.57 below).

(d) *Money Purchase Scheme*—a type of pension scheme where the amount of benefit that is provided on retirement is determined by the value of the scheme's investments at that time. Most personal pension schemes operate on this basis.

(e) *Final Salary Scheme*—a type of pension scheme where the amount of benefit that is provided on retirement is determined by the employee's salary on retirement. Final salary schemes are becoming rarer as they are expensive.

What are the minimum obligations with which an employer must comply **1.57** in relation to pensions? In 2001, the Government imposed a minimum obligation on employers to allow its employees access to a personal pension scheme which complies with certain requirements (Welfare Reform and Pensions Act 1999).

Which employers are subject to this minimum obligation? Excluded employers **1.58** include:

(a) those who employ four or fewer employees;
(b) where the employer already contributes at least 3 per cent of its employees' pensionable salary to a contractual personal pension scheme which meets certain minimum requirements.

Which employees are entitled to the rights? Employees only and not workers are **1.59** entitled (see para 1.02 et seq). Excluded employees include:

(a) an employee who qualifies for an occupational pension scheme, irrespective of whether in fact the employee took up that right;

(b) an employee who has been employed for less than three months;

(c) an employee whose earnings fall below the National Insurance lower limit for earnings in any one week in a three-month period.

1.60 What are an employer's duties? Employers should:

(a) ensure there is a stakeholder pension scheme available to relevant employees which satisfies the relevant legislation and that it is registered;

(b) consult with employees and relevant organizations before designing the scheme;

(c) provide the name and address of the designated scheme;

(d) allow representatives of the designated scheme access to the relevant employees for the purposes of supplying them with information about the schemes;

(e) if so requested, deduct contributions from an employee's remuneration and pay them to the trustees or manager of the scheme; subsequently change or stop the contributions;

(f) keep records of all deductions.

1.61 What if an employer fails to comply? There are civil penalties under the Pensions Act 1995 and criminal penalties where the employer is concerned with the fraudulent evasion of direct pay arrangements.

F. Working Time

1.62 What determines the terms relating to working time as between an employer and an employee? The number of hours an employee works is a contractual matter to be determined between the employee and employer. However, the Working Time Regulations 1998 introduced some minimum obligations on employers in respect of hours, work at night, and the breaks (as well as annual leave) to which an employee is entitled. It implements Council Directive 93/104/EC on working time and (in part) Council Directive 94/33/EC on the protection of young people at work. In the case of limits on the number of hours an employee can work in any week, these are implied into the contract with the employee (*Barber v RJB Mining (UK) Limited* [1999] IRLR 308, HC). Whilst throughout this section the references are to employees, in fact the rights apply to 'workers' (Working Time Regulations 1998, reg 2(1)).

1.63 What is the maximum number of hours an employee can work? An employee's working time, including overtime, in any reference period must not exceed an average of 48 hours in any seven-day period (Working Time Regulations 1998, reg 4).

What is the reference period for the purposes of calculating average working **1.64** time? The reference period for these purposes is:

(a) 17 weeks; or
(b) the period of employment, if shorter; or
(c) 52 weeks where there is agreement in a collective agreement or work-force agreement that it should be extended for objective or technical reasons; or
(d) 26 weeks if one of the following 'special cases' set out below applies:
- where the employee lives far from his or her workplace;
- where the employee works in security or surveillance;
- where there is a requirement for continuity, eg in hospitals, residential institu-tions, and prisons; docks and airports; press, radio, TV, and cinematographic production; postal, telecoms, and protection services; gas, water, and electric-ity production; refuse collection; industries which cannot be interrupted on technical grounds; research and development activities; agriculture;
- where there is a foreseeable surge in activity, eg in agriculture, tourism, and postal services;
- where the employee's activities are affected by unforeseen or exceptional events beyond the employer's control or an accident or imminent risk of an accident.

(Working Time Regulations 1998, regs 4(3)(5), 21, and 23(b))

What is working time for these purposes? Working time means: **1.65**

(a) any period during which the employee is working, at the employer's disposal, and carrying out his activity or duties;
(b) any period during which the employee is receiving relevant training;
(c) any other period which is agreed to be treated as working time under the terms of a workforce agreement, collective agreement, or other agreement (Working Time Regulations 1998, reg 2).

How is the definition of working time interpreted? In *Sindicato de Médicos* **1.66** *de Asistencia Publica (SIMAP) v Conselleria de Sanidad y Consumo de la Generalidat Valenciana* C-303/98 [2000] IRLR 845, the European Court held that all three elements (working, at the employer's disposal, and carrying out his activity) must be satisfied, and that in that case, which related to doctors on call, the three elements would be satisfied if the doctors had to be present at the Health Centre, but not if their presence was not required and they were simply required to be contactable or 'on call'. See also *Landeshaupstadt Kiel v Dr Med Norbert Jaeger* C-151/02 ECJ 9/9/2003 (unreported).

1.67 How is working time calculated? The formula to determine working time within each seven-day period is:

$$\frac{A+B}{C}$$

where:

A is the total number of hours that the worker has worked during the reference period;

B is the total number of hours that the worker has worked in the period beginning immediately after the end of the reference period and ending when the number of days in that subsequent period equals the number of excluded days during the reference period; and

C is the number of weeks in the reference period.

(Working Time Regulations 1998, reg 4(6))

1.68 'Excluded Days' are:

(a) any period of annual leave taken by the worker in accordance with the Working Time Regulations 1998;

(b) any period of sick leave;

(c) any period of maternity, paternity, parental, or adoption leave; and

(d) any period during which an opt-out agreement applies to the employee (see para **1.70** below).

(Working Time Regulations 1998, reg 4(7))

1.69 Is the employee very senior? If the employee is very senior, he may come within an exception where some or all of the employee's time is treated as 'unmeasured' (Working Time Regulations 1998, reg 20). To satisfy the test the employer must show that on account of the specific characteristics of the activity in which the employee is engaged, the duration of his working time is not measured or predetermined or can be determined by the worker himself, as may be the case for managing executives or other persons with autonomous decision-taking powers. The Department of Trade and Industry (DTI) has indicated this will only apply in the case of the most senior executives, although there has been no case law dealing with this issue. In addition, family workers and workers officiating at religious ceremonies may come within this definition.

1.70 Has the employee opted out of the limit on working time? An employee can agree in writing with his or her employer to disapply the 48-hour limit on working time. The agreement may relate to a specified period or apply indefinitely. There is a default provision which allows an employee to terminate it on seven days' notice; otherwise a notice period of up to three months may be specified.

Usually such a provision is simply included in the contract of employment of the employee (Working Time Regulations 1998, reg 5).

1.71 What are the limits on night working? An employee who works at night time must not in any reference period work on average more than eight hours in any 24-hour period (Working Time Regulations 1998, reg 6(1)). In practice an employer will comply with this requirement if it complies with the 48-hour limit on working hours. The reference period is the same as for other working time (see para **1.64** above) save that the extension of the reference period to 52 weeks by a collective or workforce agreement will not apply.

1.72 An employee who works at night time and whose work involves special hazards or heavy physical or mental strain must not work more than eight hours in any 24-hour period. Work of this kind will either be agreed to be such or designated as such after a health and safety risk assessment (Working Time Regulations 1998, reg 6(7)).

1.73 'Night time' for these purposes means a period which is not less than seven hours which includes the period between midnight and 5 am. To be a 'night worker', the employee must work for at least three hours during night time on the majority of days when the employee works.

1.74 What other obligations apply to night workers? An employer must ensure the employee can have a free health assessment when the employee switches to night working and at regular intervals whilst the employee is doing it (Working Time Regulations 1998, reg 7).

1.75 What exemptions apply? The limits on working time will not apply to an employee who can come within the following exemptions, where:

(a) the unmeasured time exemption, described above at para **1.69** applies;
(b) the 'special cases' exemption described at para **1.64(d)** above applies;
(c) where a collective agreement or workforce agreement contains an agreement to that effect (Working Time Regulations 1998, reg 23).

1.76 What are the minimum obligations on an employer in relation to breaks?

(a) Daily rest—the employer must allow an employee to take 11 consecutive hours rest in any 24-hour period (Working Time Regulations 1998, reg 10).
(b) Weekly rest period—the employer must allow the employee to take an uninterrupted rest period of 24 hours in each seven-day period or 48 hours in any 14-day period (Working Time Regulations 1998, reg 11).
(c) Rest breaks—the employer must allow a minimum period of 20 minutes in a period of work longer than six hours to be taken away from the employee's work station (Working Time Regulations 1998, reg 12).

(d) The obligation on the employer is to facilitate the breaks and the onus is then on the employee to actually take them.

1.77 What exemptions apply? The breaks obligations will not apply to an employee who can come within the following exemptions:

(a) The unmeasured time exemption described above at para **1.69**.

(b) The special cases exemptions described above at para **1.64(d)**.

(c) Where a collective agreement or workforce agreement contains an agreement to that effect (Working Time Regulations, reg 23).

(d) There are also certain exemptions which apply to shift workers, giving the employer more flexibility (Working Time Regulations, reg 22).

(e) In the latter three cases the employer must wherever possible allow the employee to take an equivalent period of compensatory rest, unless it is not possible for objective reasons when other steps must be taken to safeguard the employee's health and safety.

1.78 How would an employee enforce these rights?

(a) Where the right is the failure to honour a 'limit', for example on working hours or night working, an employee makes a complaint to the Health and Safety Executive or local authority. The limit is then enforced by the Health and Safety Executive or the local authority, depending on the type of business. If the complaint is upheld it is a criminal offence, punishable by a fine, which can be unlimited in amount (Working Time Regulations, regs 28 and 29).

(b) Where an employee has been prevented from exercising a right, for example, rest breaks or annual leave (see below at para **1.80**) the employee may complain to an employment tribunal. The usual three-month time limit applies to such a claim (Working Time Regulations, reg 30).

(c) An employee who has suffered detriment or been dismissed on the grounds that or by reason of the fact that the employee has relied on rights under the Working Time Regulations will also have a claim in respect of the detriment or dismissal (ERA 1996, ss 45A and 101A).

In the case of (b) and (c) above an employee must first bring a grievance before claiming in the Tribunal (EA 2002, s 32 and Sch 4; see also paras **7.81** and **7.83**).

1.79 Are there any other rights? An employee may take advantage of whichever of the contractual rights and the rights under the Regulations are the more favourable to the employee (Working Time Regulations, reg 17).

G. Holidays

What is the minimum obligation on an employer in relation to holiday? **1.80**

(a) The employer must, from 1 April 2009, allow an employee to take 5.6 weeks' annual leave in each leave year (28 days if the employee works a five-day week). From 1 October 2007 until 30 March 2009, the entitlement is to 4.8 weeks. Complicated pro-rating will be required in respect of holiday entitlements prior to 1 April 2009 (Working Time Regulations, regs 13, 13A). Guidance in relation to this can be found at <http://www.berr.gov.uk/employment/holidays/index.html>.

(b) The employer must also pay the employee in respect of any period of annual leave at the employee's normal weekly rate of pay. Where the rates of pay vary, a formula based on the average weekly pay over a 12-week period is adopted (Working Time Regulations 1998, reg 16).

Practically, how does the right to take the entitlement to leave in the leave year **1.81** work? The first issue is to determine when the leave year starts. The leave year commences on:

(a) 1 October 1998, (if the employment commenced prior to that date and there is no agreement otherwise);

(b) the date the employment commences; or

(c) a date agreed in a contract of employment, collective agreement, or a workforce agreement (Working Time Regulations 1998, regs 13(3), 13A(4)).

When does the employee become entitled to leave? The right accrues from day **1.82** one of employment. If the employment commences part way through the leave year, the employee receives a pro rata amount. In the first year of employment, leave is deemed to accrue at the rate of 1/12th of that entitlement on the first day of each month but see the guidance in relation to pro-rating leave at para **1.80** below. In this case, any fractions of a day will be rounded up to a half day if they are less than a half day and a whole day, if they are more than a half day (Working Time Regulations 1998, reg 15A).

So how much leave is an employee entitled to? If an employee works five days a **1.83** week, from 1 April 2009, the employee with a leave year commencing on that date will be entitled to 28 days' leave. If the employee works three days a week, from 1 April 2009, the employee with a leave year commencing on that date will be entitled to 17 days' leave and so on. There is no express provision dealing with how entitlement to leave (as opposed to pay) is calculated, where an employee's hours vary from week to week and an employee wishes to take a part week off. Bank holidays taken by the employee count to satisfy the entitlement to annual leave (*Campbell and South Construction Group Ltd v Greenwood* [2001] IRLR 588, EAT).

1.84 What notice requirements are there? Both the employer and employee may give notice as to when the leave should (or should not) be taken. Notice can be in relation to some or all the holiday to be taken, must specify the date(s) on which the holiday is (or is not) to be taken, and must be given to the employer or employee within certain prescribed time limits. However, as these provisions can be varied by the contract of employment, collective agreement, or workforce agreement, they are usually superseded (Working Time Regulations 1998, reg 15).

1.85 Can an employee carry over any leave entitlement? An employee must take four weeks of the leave in the leave year in respect of which it accrues and no payment in lieu of untaken but accrued leave can be made by the employer except on termination (Working Time Regulations 1998, reg 13(9)). Any days over the four weeks of leave and contractual leave may still be carried forward (Working Time Regulations 1998, reg 13A(6)). Leave does not continue to accrue during a period of long-term sick leave (*Commissioners of the Inland Revenue v Ainsworth and Others* [2005] IRLR 465). The same applies during maternity leave (see paras **3.17(e)** and **3.19(c)** below). However, this finding has been challenged in *Stringer and Others v HM Revenue and Customs* (Case C-520/06) which is the Attorney General's opinion on *Ainsworth* as a result of an appeal to the House of Lords who then referred the matter to the European Court of Justice. Under that opinion, employees will accrue holiday but not be able to take it during long-term sick leave. A separate opinion of the Attorney General in *Schultz-Hoff v Deutsche Rentenversichering Bund* (Case C-350/06) recommends that employees should be able to carry over such holiday and take it on their return to work. Further, should their employment terminate, they should be paid in lieu of it. The judgments of the ECJ are awaited to clarify the position.

1.86 What right does the employee have to receive holiday pay during employment? An employee is entitled to be paid in respect of any period of annual leave at the rate of a week's pay in respect of each week of leave (Working Time Regulations, reg 16(1)).

1.87 An employer *cannot modify* this obligation in the following ways:

(a) unilaterally reducing the hourly pay of its employees (*Davies v MJ Wyatt (Decorators) Ltd* [2000] IRLR 759, EAT);

(b) from 15 March 2006, 'rolling up' holiday pay into salary and then expressly excluding the employer's liability for holiday pay or failing to specify the amount of the salary which relates to holiday pay (*Robinson Steele v RD Retail Services, Clarke v Frank Seddon Ltd; Caulfield and Ors v Hanson Clay Ltd (formerly Marshalls Clay Products Ltd)* [2006] IRLR 386).

Otherwise, however, any contractual payment of remuneration made in respect of **1.88** a period of leave goes towards any liability of the employer to make payments under the Regulations and vice versa (Working Time Regulations 1998, reg 16(4)(5)).

What right does the employee have to receive holiday pay on termination of **1.89** employment?

(a) If an employee has taken less holiday than their entitlement under the Regulations, then the employer must pay the employee an amount as specified in a contract of employment, collective agreement, or workforce agreement (which can be a token amount) or an amount calculated in accordance with the rules set out below (Working Time Regulations 1998, reg 14(2)).

(b) If the latter, the following formula will be applied:

$$(A \times B) - C$$

where:

A is the period of leave to which the employee is entitled under the Regulations; B is the proportion of the employee's leave year which expired before the termination date; and C is the period of leave taken by the employee between the start of the leave year and the termination date (Working Time Regulations 1998, reg 14(3)).

(c) An employer can provide that if an employee exceeds their holiday entitlement under the Regulations, the employee must repay the holiday pay or undertake additional work. Such provision can appear in a contract of employment, collective agreement, or workforce agreement (Working Time Regulations 1998, reg 14(4)).

What exemptions apply to the entitlement to annual paid leave? In respect of any **1.90** entitlement to leave over the four weeks of leave specified in reg 13A of the Regulations, a specific exemption applies (Working Time Regulations, reg 26A). Broadly, if an employer is already contractually obliged, as at 1 October 2007, to allow the employee to take the maximum total of leave (5.6 weeks) whether by way of bank holidays or otherwise, then, subject to certain other conditions, the employer shall not be obliged to comply with the Regulations in relation to the additional leave. However, it is quite finely balanced as to whether this gives any real advantage to the employer. No other exemptions apply to the right to annual leave under the Regulations.

How would an employee enforce these rights? The same rights of enforcement **1.91** apply to annual leave as apply to other rights under the Working Time Regulations 1998, namely action via the Health and Safety Executive or local authority and a direct claim to the employment tribunal (see para **1.78** above). In addition, an employee may take advantage of whichever of the contractual rights and the rights under the Working Time Regulations are more favourable to the employee (Working Time Regulations, reg 17).

H. Fixed-term Contracts

1.92 What is a fixed-term contract? A contract which is due to end when a specified date is reached, a specified event does or does not happen, or a specified task has been completed. Employees employed on fixed-term contracts enjoy additional protections (Fixed-term Employees (Prevention of Less Favourable Treatment) Regulations 2002). The Regulations implement Council Directive 99/70 and the framework agreement on fixed-term working embodied therein. The Regulations do not cover apprentices or agency workers (Fixed-term Employees Regulations 2002, regs 19 and 20).

1.93 What protections do they enjoy? The right not to be treated less favourably than those on permanent contracts as regards the terms of their contract, or by being treated to their detriment by the employer by any act or deliberate failure to act (Fixed-term Employees Regulations 2002, reg 3(1) and (2)). The right includes the right not to be less favourably treated in relation to length of service qualification, training, and opportunities for permanent employment. It is possible to justify such treatment on objective grounds (Fixed-term Employees Regulations 2002, reg 3(3)(b)) (see also para **2.56** below). However unlike other discrimination it is possible to take an overall view when looking at the contract of a fixed-term contract employee as compared to a permanent employee.

1.94 Employers are restricted as to how often and for how long they can extend a fixed-term contract. Broadly any contract for periods of longer than four years will automatically become a contract of indefinite duration (Fixed-term Employees Regulations 2002, reg 8). Longer periods can be objectively justified or agreed in a collective or workforce agreement.

1.95 Employers must inform their fixed-term employees of permanent vacancies in their organization (Fixed-term Employees Regulations 2002, reg 3(6)).

1.96 An employee who believes his rights have been infringed under the Regulations can apply to the employment tribunal. The employee will also be protected from detriment or dismissal for relying on their rights under the Regulations in a similar way to those who enjoy family rights (Fixed-term Employees Regulations 2002, regs 6 and 7). There is no requirement that a grievance be raised prior to submission of a complaint. See also paras **7.17** and **7.18** below.

I. Varying Contract Terms

What should an employer consider first in relation to varying terms and conditions? **1.97**
The employer should check to see whether the terms of the present contract are sufficiently flexible to allow it lawfully to make the required changes. This may either
involve a widely drafted provision which allows the variation or it may be an express
variation provision. However, such clauses should be treated with caution. If any of
the following is a concern, the route set out in para **1.99** below should be followed:

(a) Is the clause drafted in very general terms, for example 'the employer reserves
the right to vary any of the terms and conditions of employment on reasonable
notice as it reasonably sees fit …'? If so, unless the change is relatively minor,
this type of clause will not give the employer an unfettered right to vary the
employee's contractual terms, as the courts construe such provisions restric-
tively (*Wandsworth LBC v Da Silva* [1998] IRLR 193, CA; *Securities and
Facilities Division v Hayes* [2001] IRLR 81). Consider also what will be reasonable notice.

(b) Is the variation, even if expressly provided for in the contract of employment,
likely if exercised to breach the implied term of mutual trust and confidence?
For example, an express mobility clause, if exercised without consideration
of the effect on the employee, is likely to do this (*United Bank v Akhtar*
[1989] IRLR 507).

(c) Clauses which allow the variation of benefits, such as health insurance or car
allowances, on notice are very common. Are they enforceable? Only if the
variation does not breach the term of mutual trust and confidence.

(d) Would the variation be discriminatory? An example of this would be a variation of shift pattern which may be indirectly discriminatory against women
as working mothers. Equally, a relocation clause may discriminate indirectly
on a similar basis (see paras **2.39** and **2.51** below).

(e) Is the variation expressly forbidden by some other provision of law, for exam-
ple, the prohibition on contracting out of statutory rights (see for example,
ERA 1996, s 203(1)); the shopworkers' legislation (see para **1.47** above);
National Minimum Wage legislation (see para **1.50** above)?

What should the employer do if there is no provision in the contract allowing **1.98**
for the variation of its terms? If there is no effective clause providing for the variation of the contract, the employer should seek the consent of the employee to any
variation. Consent may be express or implied. Express consent may be oral or in
writing. The latter is obviously preferable because it makes for certainty. Implied
consent may be inferred if the employee continues to work, adopting the changes,

without protest for a reasonable period. However, such implied consent should be treated with caution, especially where the changes are ones which will not immediately affect the employee (*Jones v Associated Tunnelling Co Limited* [1981] IRLR 477, EAT). To assist in obtaining consent, the employer should consider 'buying out' unwanted terms by paying the employee to agree to contractual variations.

1.99 If agreement cannot be reached on any variation, and provided the employer has a pressing business need to implement a variation, the employer should proceed as follows:

(a) Consider the disadvantages caused to the employees by the change to the contract of employment.

(b) Formulate reasonable new contract terms within the context of the employer's pressing business requirements; in doing so, the interests of the employee cannot be ignored, so the employer should not seek to impose totally draconian new terms.

(c) Consult with the employee, explaining the pressing business need which makes the variation necessary, and what terms are proposed. This consultation should also comply with the requirements of a Step 1 meeting under the statutory disciplinary procedure (see para **8.83** below in relation to redundancy; similar issues apply in relation to this process).

(d) If a trade union or other employee representatives are involved, consult with them and try to obtain their agreement to the changes (see para **1.102** below).

(e) If the employee will still not consent to the change, terminate the old contract by giving proper notice, and in this regard the employer should comply with the statutory disciplinary procedure, the contractual provisions relating to consultation or warnings of impending terminations, the obligation to consult collectively, and the general obligation to behave reasonably before dismissal.

(f) Offer the employee a new contract of employment including the varied terms to commence immediately on the termination of the old contract.

1.100 An employee who does not wish to accept any variations may, if *variations are material and wrongfully imposed* by the employer:

(a) work under protest and bring proceedings against the employer for damages for breach of contract or for sums due under the contract (*Rigby v Ferodo Ltd* [1987] IRLR 516; *Burdett-Coutts v Hertfordshire CC* [1984] IRLR 91); or

(b) resign, claim constructive dismissal, and sue for damages for wrongful and, if appropriate, unfair dismissal (see Chapter 7); or

(c) if variation consists of deduction from wages, bring a claim for unlawful deduction of wages in the employment tribunal (see para **1.41** above).

If the *employer has acted correctly* in accordance with the provisions of para **1.99** above:
1.101

(a) accept the new job; or

(b) accept the new job under protest, argue that the changes imposed cannot be justified by any pressing business reason of the employer, and claim compensation for having been unfairly dismissed by the termination of the original contract and the restoration of the original contract terms (*Hogg v Doner College* [1990] ICR 39, EAT); or

(c) refuse to accept the new job, argue that the proposed new terms could not be justified by a pressing business need, and claim unfair dismissal.

A dismissal or potential dismissal as the result of a variation of contract of employment may be a dismissal which triggers the obligation to consult with employee representatives where there may be 20 or more dismissals in a 90-day period (see para **8.43** below).
1.102

An employer has a duty to notify individual employees of any changes to the contract of employment, such as changes negotiated by the employer with the employee's trade union (see para **1.23** above).
1.103

On a transfer of undertaking, different rules apply (see paras **9.37** and **9.45**).
1.104

J. Breach of Contract

If the *employee* breaches the contract of employment the employer may:
1.105

(a) if the breach is sufficiently material to constitute a repudiatory breach of contract, dismiss the employee;

(b) sue the employee for damages for breach of contract. Given that most employees have limited financial resources to pay damages, this tactic is normally only employed as a counterclaim to any claim for wrongful dismissal brought by the employee;

(c) refuse to pay the employee the whole of the wages due for any period during which the employee takes industrial action or does not perform part or all of his duties;

(d) obtain an injunction restraining future breaches of the contract if the employer can show that such breaches are likely to recur, that damages are an inadequate remedy, that he will suffer loss as a result of the breaches, and that the balance of convenience is in favour of granting the injunction.

1.106 If the *employer* is in breach of contract the employee may:

(a) protest at the breaches but continue to work and bring proceedings against the employer for sums due under the contract or for damages for breach of contract;

(b) if sufficiently serious, resign, claim constructive dismissal, and damages and compensation for wrongful and/or unfair dismissal (see Chapter 7);

(c) in exceptional circumstances, obtain an injunction restraining breaches of contract by the employer. Such injunctions are only granted very rarely (for example, where the employer fails properly to follow disciplinary procedures) and will not be granted if a court is convinced that the relationship of trust and confidence between employer and employee has irretrievably broken down (*Irani v Southampton and South-West Hampshire Health Authority* [1985] IRLR 203).

K. Termination of Contract

Notice Periods

1.107 What notice must be given to terminate a contract of employment? If no notice period is expressed in the contract of employment, the court will imply a reasonable notice period. For manual or semi-skilled workers, that notice period is likely to be between one week and one month either way; for middle-ranking employees, the notice period will be between one and three months; and for senior employees, the notice period will be between three months and, say, one year. The precise notice period will be determined by the tests set out in para **1.30** above.

1.108 In addition, there are statutory minimum notice periods which override lesser contractual provisions:

(a) once an employee has been employed for one month, he is obliged to give at least one week's notice of termination of his employment;

(b) once an employee has been employed for one month, he is entitled to receive a minimum notice period of one week during the first two years of his employment, and thereafter is entitled to one week's notice for each completed year of employment up to a maximum of 12 weeks.

(ERA 1996, s 86)

1.109 *Example*: An employee with a contractual notice period of one month from either party has been employed for seven and a half years. The employee is entitled to receive seven weeks' notice of dismissal and must give one month's notice of resignation.

What are an employee's obligations once notice has been given? An employee is **1.110** obliged not to leave his employment before the expiry of his notice period, unless the employer agrees. An employee who resigns without giving notice:

(a) cannot be forced to return to work;

(b) may be restrained by an injunction obtained by the employer from joining a rival, provided that there is a provision in the contract of employment stating that during the notice period the employee can be required not to work ('garden leave'), or that there is an express provision in the contract restraining competition during employment, and that the employer will actually suffer damage if the employee leaves early, for example, if the employee proposes to join a competing business (*Provident Financial Group plc and Whitegates Estate Agency Ltd v Hayward* [1989] IRLR 84).

What obligations are there on an employer in respect of a notice period? If an **1.111** employer terminates an employee's contract of employment without giving due notice, the employee may bring an action against the employer for wrongful dismissal to recover the sums he would have received during the balance of the notice period. The employee usually has an obligation to mitigate his loss (for the position on wrongful dismissal see para **7.03**). The employee may also allege that any post-termination restrictions are unenforceable and that the dismissal was unfair.

What if an employer wishes to rely on a garden leave provision? If the employer **1.112** wishes to rely on the garden leave provision, it must undertake to provide the employee with full contractual remuneration and benefits for the entire notice period, and must satisfy the court that all the other preconditions for the grant of interlocutory injunctions exist (see para **5.52(c)**). An injunction will not be granted (or may only be granted for a limited period) if the employee is subject to a long notice period and can satisfy the court that relevant skills he possesses will atrophy if he cannot exercise them during the notice period.

What are the main methods of termination of the contract? **1.113**

(a) By consent of both parties (although if the employer forces the employee to consent, this would be construed as a dismissal).

(b) By either party giving the requisite notice to the other (see para **1.107** above). Even if the employer gives the employee proper notice, there may still be grounds for the employee to claim compensation for unfair dismissal or redundancy.

(c) By expiry of a fixed-term contract. Such expiry can be an unfair dismissal or redundancy. If the contract continues after its expiry, it will continue on the same terms as before save for the term, and will be terminable on reasonable notice.

(d) By frustration—if it becomes impossible for the parties to perform the contract at all or in substantially the same way as was envisaged when the contract was entered into (*FC Shepherd & Co v Jerrom* [1986] IRLR 358). Examples include the absence of the employee because of long-term ill health (*Marshall v Haxland and Wolff Ltd* [1972] IRLR 90) or imprisonment, or because a material work permit expires or cannot be transferred from a previous employer.

(e) By dismissal by the employer. This may be in breach of or in accordance with the contract and may be fair or unfair (see Chapter 7).

(f) By the employee resigning following a repudiatory breach of contract by the employer and claiming constructive dismissal (see para 7.67).

(g) Following a pregnancy or adoption, if an employee who has the right to return does not exercise that right or if the employer refuses to allow the employee to return (see Chapter 3 below). Such a refusal will normally amount to an unfair dismissal and sex discrimination.

(h) By operation of law, for example, if a statute is passed rendering further performance impossible.

References

1.114 An employer is not obliged to give any employee a reference. If the employer does give a reference, the reference must be fair and accurate and made without malice. If it is not:

(a) A subsequent employer may sue the original employer for negligent/ fraudulent misstatement, if the reference is inaccurate and he can show that the employer must have known this, or did not take care to ensure that it was accurate.

(b) The employee may sue the employer:
   • for negligence if the reference is inaccurate and he can show that the employer must have known this, or did not take care to ensure it was in fact accurate (*Spring v Guardian Assurance plc and Others* [1994] IRLR 460);
   • for defamation (even though a reference is usually given on an occasion of qualified privilege) if he can show the employer was acting maliciously, ie that it knew the reference was false, or was reckless as to whether or not it was true or false;
   • if the employee is still employed at the time the reference is given, for breach of the implied term of mutual trust and confidence if the reference given is misleading (*TSB Bank plc v Harris* [2000] IRLR 157, EAT);
   • for discrimination, if the reference was tainted by discrimination (see Chapter 2).

L. Other Miscellaneous Contractual Issues

Long-term Disability Benefits

What are the issues in relation to the provision of long-term disability benefit? **1.115** Long-term disability benefit is a benefit which is increasingly provided and is popular with employers and employees. The benefit involves an employer agreeing to pay an employee a salary replacement, usually a percentage of salary, where an employee is unable to perform their job due to ill health. Usually the benefit only applies after a waiting period of three or six months and applies until the employee recovers, reaches retirement age, or dies. Typically the employer underwrites the benefit by an insurance policy. There have been a number of cases in relation to this benefit, not least because it is a very valuable benefit for an employee. Usually the employee has a directly enforceable contractual right against the employer to receive the reduced pay if he satisfies the criteria set out by the employer. This can lead to a number of potential problems for the employer who is relying on the insurance policy to cover the payments.

What should an employer do to guard against these problems? An employer **1.116** should:

(a) as far as possible, ensure that the employee is only entitled to the benefit if the insurer pays out under the policy—this requires careful drafting;

(b) as most long-term disability insurance policies will only pay benefits where the employee remains in employment, the employer should not dismiss an employee who may benefit or is benefiting from long-term disability benefit. An exception to this may be a summary dismissal for cause or a genuine redundancy situation, but even then the employer should attempt to ensure that the insurer keeps paying benefit to the employee (*Aspden v Webbs Poultry and Meat Group (Holdings) Ltd* [1996] IRLR 521);

(c) if the insurer refuses benefit, the employer must take all reasonable steps to ensure that the employee receives the benefit which may include litigation, especially if the employee agrees to indemnify the employer for costs (*Marlow v East Thames Housing Group Ltd* [2002] IRLR 792).

Payments in Lieu of Notice

What are the issues in relation to payment in lieu of notice? Many employers **1.117** include in their contracts of employment a clause which allows the employer, at its option, to pay the employee an amount equivalent to the salary (and sometimes benefits) that the employee would have earned during their notice period. The advantages of such a provision are that it gives an employer flexibility in the termination process, allowing it to remove an employee from the workplace, where otherwise the working out of notice would be a painful process for both parties. More cynically, it allows an employer to terminate employment on a certain date and so prevent the employee from becoming entitled to certain benefits or rights, for example, the one-year qualifying period to claim unfair dismissal. It also allows the employer to terminate employment with immediate effect, without it affecting the enforceability of the post-termination restrictions.

1.118   There are, however, two disadvantages to such a provision, as follows:

(a)   The clause must be carefully drafted to ensure it gives the employer only the option of paying in lieu of notice, so that it remains the employer's choice as to whether it does or not. Otherwise it may give the employee the right to a liquidated sum on termination, rather than the usual claim for damages which are subject to reduction for mitigation (*Abrahams v Performing Rights Society* [1995] IRLR 486).

(b)   Payments up to £30,000 on termination of employment may be paid without deduction of tax if certain conditions are met. However, the Inland Revenue has made it clear that payments in lieu of notice made pursuant to a provision in the contract of employment (and sometimes even where they are not) will attract tax.

Share Options and the Employment Contract

1.119   What are the issues in relation to share options? One area which has attracted attention in recent years is the interaction between an employee's rights under a share option scheme and the termination of the contract of employment. The question is whether an employee can claim damages for losses under a share option scheme where such losses are caused by a wrongful or unfair dismissal. The answer to this question will be yes (assuming that the employee would have had rights that the employee could exercise during the notice period and that the options are worth something).

1.120   What should an employer do to guard against this liability? An employer can attempt to exclude such liability by including an express provision to that effect in the share option scheme itself, or in the contract of employment. Such clauses are usually known as 'Micklefield' clauses, after the leading case (*Micklefield v SAC Technology Ltd* [1990] IRLR 218, Ch D). Such clauses should not be relied on absolutely, first because they may fall foul of the Unfair Contract Terms Act 1977 (especially if Scottish law applies). Also, they are likely to be void in terms of preventing a statutory claim for unfair dismissal or other statutory rights because they constitute an invalid attempt to contract out of statutory rights (ERA 1996, s 203 and equivalent provisions).

Discretionary Bonuses

What are the issues in relation to discretionary bonuses? Over the years, the ques- **1.121** tion of how discretionary a discretionary bonus actually is has been debated by the courts. Additionally, certain drafting which employers have included in the terms and conditions relating to bonuses has also been considered. Employers should bear the following in mind:

(a) Although an employer's discretion is very wide, it must exercise it in a way that is reasonable and not irrational or perverse. However, the burden of proof is on an employee to establish that the employer has been irrational or perverse and it is a high one (*Horkulak v Cantor Fitzgerald International* [2004] IRLR 942; *Commerzbank AG v Keen* [2007] IRLR 132).

(b) An employee cannot rely on the Unfair Contract Terms Act 1977 to argue that the terms of a bonus scheme are unenforceable (for example, where the terms provide that a bonus will only be payable if the employee continues to be employed by the employer (*Commerzbank AG v Keen* [2007] IRLR 132)). However, in certain circumstances, the implied term of mutual trust and confidence may override the express terms of the contract (*Reda v Flag Ltd* [2007] IRLR 247; *Takacs v Barclay Services Jersey Limited*, (2006) IDS Employment Law Brief No 819).

(c) As part of the implied term of mutual trust and confidence, an employer should, however, inform the employee of how it reached its decision (*Commerzbank AG v Keen* [2007] IRLR 132).

2

EQUAL PAY AND DISCRIMINATION

A. Introduction

Employers who adopt discriminatory practices do so at their peril. The Equal Pay **2.01** Act 1970 (EqPA 1970), the Sex Discrimination Act 1975 (SDA 1975), the Race Relations Act 1976 (RRA 1976), the Disability Discrimination Act 1995 (DDA 1995), the Employment Equality (Religion or Belief) Regulations 2003, SI 2003/1660 (RBR 2003), the Employment Equality (Sexual Orientation) Regulations 2003, SI 2003/1661 (SOR 2003), and the Employment Equality (Age) Regulations 2006, SI 2006/1031 (EEAR 2006) between them provide that employers cannot discriminate between people of different sexes and races, against those who intend to undergo, are undergoing or who have undergone gender reassignment, against those who suffer from a disability, against employees because of their religion or belief or sexual orientation or age in their selection procedures, contractual terms, and treatment of employees. In addition, Article 141 (formerly Article 119) of the EC Treaty, and the Equal Treatment Directive (76/207/EEC [1976] OJ L39/40, as amended by Directive 2002/73/EC [2002] OJ L269/15) give additional protection to employees who are discriminated against on grounds of sex. There is also protection from discrimination of those who are or are not trade union members (see para **6.23**), take up other offices as part of their employment or who are whistle-blowers (see para **7.94**), those who work part-time (see paras **4.61–4.68**), and those who work under fixed-term contracts (see paras **1.92** above and **7.114** below).

B. Equal Pay

CHECKLIST

2.02 Is the complainant employed under a contract of service or of apprenticeship or a contract personally to execute any work or labour? If not he may not have a claim under EqPA 1970 (EqPA 1970 s 1(6)(a) and see para **2.20** below).

2.03 Does the complainant work wholly outside Great Britain? If so, he will not be able to bring a claim under EqPA 1970, although there may be an exception for those who are posted abroad where the employee was ordinarily resident in Great Britain when he was recruited or at some point during the employment and the employer has a place of business at an establishment in Great Britain and the work the employee was doing was for the business at that establishment (SDA 1975, s 10 and see para **2.20** below).

2.04 Does the claim relate to a contractual term relating to:

(a) pay;
(b) bonuses;
(c) concessions and benefits in kind;
(d) terms in collective agreements;
(e) general contractual provisions such as those regarding holidays, sickness benefits, and hours?

If so, it will come within the terms of the EqPA 1970 (EqPA 1970, s 1(1) and see para **2.21** below).

2.05 Does the claim relate to:

(a) terms included in compliance with the law regarding the complainant's employment (EqPA 1970, s 6(1)(a)—to a large degree, such provisions have been removed from the statute book and so this exception is now very limited);
(b) terms affording special treatment to women in connection with pregnancy and childbirth (EqPA 1970, s 6(1)(b));
(c) terms relating to membership of or rights under occupational pension schemes, save that retirement ages must be the same and access to and benefits under occupational pension schemes must be equal (see EC Treaty, Article 141 (formerly Article 119), and the Pensions Act 1995) (EqPA 1970, s 6(1B))?

If so, the complainant will not have a claim under the EqPA 1970.

Was there a difference in terms and conditions of employment, for example, is **2.06** there a difference in:

(a) pay;
(b) hours of work;
(c) method of allocation of bonuses or size of bonuses;
(d) incentive payments;
(e) concessions and benefits in kind such as advantageous loans, mortgage repayment allowances, participation in insurance schemes or share option schemes;
(f) provisions in collective agreements, in respect of the above matters, incorporated into the contracts of employment;
(g) terms relating to holidays, sickness benefits, and other contractual provisions?

If so, the complainant may have a claim under the EqPA 1970 (see para **2.21** below).

Is there a comparator who is a genuine individual, and not a hypothetical com- **2.07** parator? There should be, other than in cases relating to pay during maternity leave (*Alabaster v Barclays Bank plc and Secretary of State for Social Security (No. 2)* [2005] IRLR 576 and EqPA 1970, ss 1(2)(e) and (2)(f); see also *Allonby v Accrington and Rossendale College and Others* [2004] IRLR 224 in relation to national laws). In non-maternity cases the complainant may, if he wishes, compare himself with his predecessor or his replacement (*MacCarthys Ltd v Smith* [1980] ICR 672; *Kellis v Pilkington plc* [2002] IRLR 693).

Is the comparator employed by the same employer or an associated employer and **2.08** working at the same establishment (EqPA 1970, s 1(6))? The employee should be. Whether the employee is working at the same establishment is a question of fact, depending upon the following factors:

(a) the degree of exclusive occupation of the premises;
(b) the degree of permanence of the arrangements;
(c) the organization of workers—whether they are organized as part of one group, or in separate and distinct entities;
(d) how the administration is organized—if there is central administration and the head office runs several sites, such as building sites, those sites are likely to be part of the same establishment. If each site is separately run, such as branches of a chain of shops, each site is likely to be a separate establishment.

(*Barley v Amey Roadstone Corp Ltd (No. 2)* [1977] IRLR 299, in the context of a protective award under TULR(C)A 1992, but applicable here.)

2.09 If the comparator (who is employed by the same employer or an associated employer) is not working at the same establishment, is he working at an establishment where broadly similar terms and conditions apply for the relevant class of employee? This must be the case, for example, where a collective agreement applies to both establishments (*Leverton v Clwyd County Council* [1989] ICR 33). Note that where the differences identified in the pay of workers performing like work or work of equal value cannot be attributed to a single source (even where the employer is the same), the claim does not come within the legislation (or Article 141) since there is no body which is responsible for the inequality and which could restore equal treatment (*Lawrence v Regent Office Care Ltd* [2002] IRLR 822; *Robertson and Others v Department for Environment, Food and Rural Affairs* [2005] IRLR 363; *Armstrong and Others v Newcastle-upon-Tyne NHS Hospital Trust* [2006] IRLR 124).

2.10 Was the comparator engaged upon like work? The employee will need to be engaged upon like work to claim. *Like work* means work of the same or a broadly similar nature and where the differences (if any) are not of practical importance in relation to the terms and conditions of employment. Regard should be had to the frequency with which any such differences occur in practice, as well as to the nature and extent of the differences (EqPA 1970, ss 1(2)(a) and 1(4)). This is a question of fact and the tribunal should not be too pedantic in its examination (*Capper Pass Ltd v Lawton* [1977] QB 852). The first issue is to examine the nature of the work done by the employee and what skill and knowledge are required to do it. Different training requirements may disqualify a job from being like work. The timing of the work will be irrelevant (*Dugdale v Kraft Foods* [1977] IRLR 368).

The second issue is to examine whether there are differences and, if so, their nature and extent and how frequently they operate? If they operate infrequently (for example, if occasionally a comparator is asked to undertake heavy work) or are minor (for example, where canteen ladies sometimes wait at tables whereas their male comparator does not) work will still be regarded as like (*Capper Pass* (above); *Dorothy Perkins Ltd v Dance* [1977] IRLR 226).

2.11 Was the complainant engaged on work *rated as equivalent*, that is, his job and the comparator's job have been given equal value in terms of the demands made on the worker under various headings (for instance, effort, skill, decision) (EqPA 1970, ss 1(2)(b) and 1(5))? To establish this, the employer must have carried out a job evaluation scheme and the two jobs identified by the complainant must be rated by that scheme as equivalent. If they are, yet terms and conditions of employment between people of opposite sexes are different, the employee will succeed (subject to a justification defence). If they are not rated as equivalent, an employee will only succeed in a claim for equal pay if he can show that discriminatory criteria were used in setting up the job evaluation scheme (*Rummler v Dato-Druck GmbH* [1987] IRLR 32), or that the scheme has not been put into effect and complied with. Note, however, there is no legal obligation on an employer to conduct a job evaluation scheme.

2.12 Was the complainant engaged in work of *equal value*, that is, work which would not fall within the tests for like work or work rated as equivalent, but which is, in terms of the demands made on him (for instance under such headings as effort, skill, and decision) of equal value to a comparator of the opposite sex in the same employment (EqPA 1970 s 1(2)(c)). If so, the complainant may apply to the employment tribunal which may proceed to determine the question or require a member of a panel or independent experts to prepare a report with respect to that question (see Employment Tribunals (Constitution and Rules) Regulations 2004, Sch 6 which contains the Employment Tribunals (Equal Value) Rules of Procedure, setting out the detailed procedure to be adopted by the employment tribunal in determining this question). However, if the employer has already conducted a job evaluation study of the two jobs, which has given the work of the complainant and the comparator different values, this will be a defence to a claim under this head (EqPA 1970, s 2A(2)). The exception to this is where the job evaluation scheme is deemed to be one which was made on a system which discriminates on grounds of sex or is otherwise unsuitable to be relied upon (EqPA 1970, ss 2A(2A) and (3) —see also *Neil and Others v Ford Motor Co Limited* [1984] IRLR 339).

2.13 Can the employer show that, even where the two individuals are engaged in like work, or if their work is rated as equivalent under a job evaluation scheme, where there is a variation between the complainant's contract and that of the comparator man that variation is genuinely due to a material factor which is not the difference of sex between the two cases? Such factor must be a material difference which causes the *whole* of the difference. If so, the complainant's claim will fail. If the difference only explains part of the variation, then the complainant's claim will succeed as to the unexplained part (EqPA 1970, s 1(3)(a)). Material factors include:

(a) qualifications or level of experience (*McGregor v General Municipal Boilermakers and Allied Trades Union* [1987] ICR 505);

(b) length of service (see *Cadman v Health and Safety Executive* [2006] ICR 1623, where the ECJ held that an employer does not need to specifically justify the use of length of service to determine pay, as long as there is no evidence which raises serious doubts that length of service is an appropriate means to attain the employer's objective with regard to that particular job);

(c) degree of skills acquired (*Tyldesley v TML Plastics Ltd* [1996] IRLR 395);

(d) place of employment (*Navy, Army and Air Force Institutes v Varley* [1976] IRLR 408);

(e) regional pay variations or that market forces have dictated that a later applicant is paid more (or less) than someone who is already established in the job (*Ratcliff v North Yorkshire Council* [1995] IRLR 439; *Rainey v Greater Glasgow Health Board* [1977] IRLR 26; *Enderby v Frenchay Health Authority and Secretary of State for Health* [1993] IRLR 591) but note that if the market or collective bargaining arrangements are tainted by sex, objective justification will be necessary (see para **2.15** below));

(f) different economic circumstances affecting the business itself where the comparator was working at a different time from the complainant (*Waddington v Leicester Council for Voluntary Services* [1977] IRLR 32);

(g) that the individuals are in differing levels in the grading structure (*Strathclyde Regional Council v Wallace* [1998] IRLR 146);

(h) part-time working—but this can only be a justification if the differential between part-time and full-time rates is objectively justifiable and will satisfy the Part-time Workers (Prevention of Less Favourable Treatment) Regulations 2000 (see paras **4.61–4.68** below);

(i) the comparator is a 'red circled' worker (ie where the comparator has been demoted but his pay has not been reduced) although the differential in pay should be phased out over time, and there should be no outsiders within the 'red circle' (*Snoxell and Davies v Vauxhall Motors Ltd* [1977] 3 All ER 770; *United Biscuits Ltd v Young* [1978] IRLR 15; *Home Office v Bailey* [2005] IRLR 757; see also *Sita UK Ltd v Hope* EAT/0787/04, where a simple assertion of 'red circling' is insufficient to establish a material factor defence).

2.14 Where an independent report has concluded that the complainant's work is of equal value to that of a comparator, where there is a variation between the complainant's contract and that of the comparator, is the variation genuinely due to a material factor which is not a difference of sex? If so, the employee's claim will fail (EqPA 1970, s 1(3)(b)). 'Factor' can encompass any issue, and not merely a material difference between the complainant's case and that of the comparator, and factors would include all those examples cited above. In particular, market forces will be construed widely so that, even where a lone individual demands, and receives, a higher wage, this may be a defence.

2.15 Could the genuine material factor be indirectly discriminatory? If so, the employer will need to objectively justify the difference (see para **2.22** below).

2.16 What remedy is available to the employee? Generally, six years in back pay equality to her comparator without cap and equality in the future (EqPA 1970, s 2ZB(3) and see para **2.23** below).

Has the complainant brought a grievance in relation to her claim? If not, the com- **2.17** plainant may not be able to bring a claim in the employment tribunal (EA 2002, s 32; the Employment Act 2002 (Dispute Resolution) Regulations 2004, reg 15 and see **2.25** below).

Has the complainant brought the claim in the employment tribunal or county **2.18** court during employment or within six months of the termination of the contract in relation to which the claim arises? If not, the complainant's claim will be time-barred unless the complainant has brought a grievance in relation to the inequality, in which case the time may be extended (see EA 2002, s 32 and the Employment Act 2002 (Dispute Resolution) Regulations 2004, reg 15; see also para **2.25** below).

Commentary

If an employee shows she does substantially similar work to a named member of **2.19** the opposite sex, or performs work which has been rated as equivalent work under a job evaluation scheme, or is of equal or greater value than work carried out by a named member of the opposite sex, and any element of the employee's contractual terms is worse than that of the chosen comparator, the EqPA 1970 operates (via a somewhat cumbersome route) to bring the worse contractual term up to the same level as the better one (EqPA 1970, s 1).

An employee for these purposes means one 'employed' under a contract of service **2.20** or of apprenticeship or a contract personally to execute any work or labour at an establishment in Great Britain (EqPA 1970, s 1(6)(a)). It does, therefore, cover a wider category of individuals than employees, but probably does not extend to the full range of 'workers' (*Quinnen v Hovells* [1984] IRLR 227; *Allonby v Accrington and Rossendale College* [2004] IRLR 224) (see also para **1.10** above). There can be no claim for equal pay where the complainant works wholly outside Great Britain. However, from October 2005, if the employer has a place of business at an establishment in Great Britain, the work the employee is doing is for the purposes of the business carried on at that establishment and the employee is ordinarily resident in Great Britain when she is recruited or at any time during the course of the employment, then she may be able to bring an equal pay claim (SDA 1975, s 10(1), (1A)).

The EqPA 1970 applies not only to wages but also to all contractual terms such **2.21** as bonus, holiday entitlement, car policies, and sickness benefits. Employees must be careful to claim under the correct act—SDA 1975, s 6(6) excludes all claims under that legislation relating to benefits consisting of the payment of money when the provision of those benefits is regulated by the woman's contract of employment (see also *Hoyland v Asda Stores Ltd* [2006] IRLR 468). Each element that makes up a contract of employment is looked at individually, and employers cannot rely upon a general balancing out of benefits under the contract as a whole although terms relating to pay of the same kind can be aggregated (*Hayward v Cammell Laird Shipbuilders Ltd* [1988] ICR 464; *Degnan and Others v Redcar and Cleveland Borough Council* [2005] IRLR 615).

2.22   Once an employee has shown that her job is substantially the same as or of equal value to the job of a member of the opposite sex, the employer's only excuse for any different contractual terms is that it is a material difference which is genuinely due to a material factor other than sex, such as length of service or degree of skill, which justifies the differential in pay or benefits (EqPA 1970, s 1(3)). If, however, this factor is found to be indirectly discriminatory, then the employer will be required to objectively justify the factor (*Glasgow City Council v Marshall* [2000] ICR 196). The variation to be objectively justified must be both 'appropriate' and 'necessary' and a test of proportionality must be applied (*Rainey v Greater Glasgow Health Board* [1987] IRLR 26; *Strathclyde Regional Council v Wallace and Others* [1998] IRLR 146). An employee may use a statistical approach to demonstrate indirect discrimination (*Bailey and Others v Home Office* [2005] IRLR 369; *Villalba v Merrill Lynch and Co Inc and Others* [2006] IRLR 437; *Middlesborough Borough Council v Surtees & Others* [2008] ICR 349). Note that an employer may have difficulties in relying on cost as a ground for objective justification (*Cross and Others v British Airways plc* [2005] IRLR 423; *Grundy v British Airways plc and other appeals* UKEAT/0676/04RN). (See also *Sharp v Caledonian Group Services Ltd* [2006] IRLR 4 and *Villalba v Merrill Lynch & Co Inc and Others* [2006] IRLR 437. In the former, the EAT accepted the principle laid out in *Brunnhofer v Bank der Österreichischen Postparkasse AG* [2001] IRLR 571 that all material factors must be objectively justified, not just those which are shown to be discriminatory. In the latter, the EAT stayed with the established position that only those which are indirectly discriminatory may be justified. Both cases were subject to appeal, but have now settled, so *Glasgow City Council v Marshall* (above), which states that only factors which are indirectly discriminatory need to be justified, remains the leading authority.)

2.23   The employee who is successful in her claim is entitled in future to remuneration and benefits on the higher level enjoyed by her comparator, and (generally) to have the difference refunded for the period starting six years before the court or tribunal application was made (EqPA 1970, s 2ZB(3)). There is no cap on the amount that may be recovered (EqPA 1970, s 2(5)). Interest can be ordered on these sums (Employment Tribunals (Interest on Awards in Discrimination Cases) Regulations 1996, SI 1996/2803). There is no power for the tribunal to award compensation for injury to feelings and/or aggravated damages (*Newcastle Upon*

Tyne City Council v Allan; Degnan and Others v Redcar and Cleveland Borough Council [2005] IRLR 504).

The EqPA 1970 applies Article 141 (formerly Article 119) of the EC Treaty and **2.24** the Equal Treatment Directive (76/207/EEC). Article 141 can be used by an employee to extend her rights under the EqPA 1970. The Equal Treatment Directive works in a similar way, but only for employees of public authorities, for example local authorities or the health service. Further, as the ambit of Article 141 is in some ways wider than that of the EqPA 1970, many cases have been brought to highlight the incompatibility between the two. For example, under Article 141, the two-year time limit on claims has been held to be unenforceable leading to amendments to the EqPA 1970. The main exception to this principle is that Article 141 applies only to 'pay' and this has been construed more narrowly under Article 141 than under the EqPA 1970.

The complainant may bring a claim in the employment tribunal, but must do so **2.25** during employment or within six months of the termination of the contract in relation to which the claim arises (EqPA 1970, s 2(4)). This time limit has been considered to be compatible with European law (*Preston v Wolverhampton Healthcare NHS Trust* [2000] ICR 961; see also *Cumbria County Council v Dow* [2008] IRLR 91 and 109 for guidance in relation to a variation and termination of contract in these circumstances). Prior to bringing a claim the employee must raise a grievance under the statutory dispute procedures or she will be barred from bringing a claim (EA 2002, s 32). The grievance, to be valid, must specify a comparator (*Highland Council v TGWU/Unison* EAT 0020/07; see also paras **7.81–7.83** below). If the employee does bring a grievance, the six-month time limit will be extended (Employment Act (Dispute Resolution) Regulations 2004, reg 15).

Equal pay questionnaires. A person who considers he may have or has a complaint **2.26** under the EqPA 1970 may ask questions via a statutory form of questionnaire to establish whether in fact there are grounds. The response to the questionnaire will stand as evidence in any subsequent proceedings. A failure to respond at all or to do so within an eight-week time limit will lead to an adverse inference by the tribunal (EqPA, 1970, s 7B and the Equal Pay (Questions and Replies) Order 2003) (see also *Barton v Investec Henderson Crosthwaite Securities Limited* [2003] ICR 1205, EAT).

Code of practice. The Equality and Human Rights Commission (formerly the Equal **2.27** Opportunities Commission (EOC)) first issued a code of practice in 1997 aimed at tackling disparity in pay in the workplace. It was updated, expanded, and re-issued with effect from 1 December 2003. The application of this code or failure to apply it can be taken into account when an equal pay claim is being considered by the employment tribunal (SDA 1975, s 56A; Code of Practice on Equal Pay (2003)).

2.28 Equality of pay and contractual provisions for those undergoing or who have undergone gender reassignment, those who are discriminated against on grounds of marital status, those of different races, those who are disabled, those who are discriminated against on grounds of their religion or belief, sexual orientation, or age are not dealt with under separate legislation but under the SDA 1975, RRA 1976, DDA 1995, RBR 2003, SOR 2003, and EEAR 2006, respectively.

C. Sex Discrimination Act 1975, Race Relations Act 1976 and Discrimination on the Grounds of Religion or Belief or Sexual Orientation

CHECKLIST

2.29 Is the complainant employed under a contract of service or of apprenticeship or a contract personally to execute any work or labour? If not, he or she may not have the protection of the legislation (SDA 1975, s 82(1); RRA 1976, s 78; RBR 2003, reg 2(3); SOR 2003, reg 2 and see also paras **2.20** above, **2.45** (sex), **2.68** (race), and **2.79** (religion and sexual orientation) below as the same points will apply).

2.30 Do any of the genuine occupational qualification defences apply? If so, the complainant will not have a claim (see paras **2.55** (sex), **2.70** (race), and **2.79** and **2.80** (religion and sexual orientation) below).

2.31 Does the complainant work wholly outside Great Britain? If so, he will not have a claim although there may be an exception for those who are posted abroad where the employee was resident in Great Britain when he was recruited or at some point during the employment and the employer has a place of business at an establishment in Great Britain and the work is for the purposes of the business carried out at that establishment (see paras **2.45** (sex), **2.68** (race), and **2.79** (religion and sexual orientation) below).

2.32 If claiming sex discrimination, is the complainant a minister of religion, claiming in relation to accommodation facilities, a prison officer, claiming about special treatment to women in connection with pregnancy and childbirth? If so, she may be excluded from claiming (see para **2.46** below; see also paras **2.59** and **2.60** in relation to gender reassignment specifically).

2.33 If claiming race discrimination, is the complainant employed in a private household, claiming in relation to sports representation and competitions, claiming in relation to acts safeguarding national security? If so, the complainant may be prevented from claiming (see para **2.71** below).

If claiming discrimination based on religion or belief or sexual orientation, is the **2.34** claim in relation to acts safeguarding national security, and (sexual orientation only) benefits dependent on marital status or status as a civil partner? If so, the complainant may be prevented from claiming (see para **2.81** below).

Is the complainant an employee, temporary worker, supplied by an employment **2.35** agency, or a worker and claiming sex discrimination or race discrimination or discrimination based on religion or belief or sexual orientation in respect of the areas listed below?

(a) Arrangements for recruitment (whether or not anyone is in fact recruited) (SDA 1975, s 6(1)(a); RRA 1976, s 4(1)(a); RBR 2003 and SOR 2003, reg 6(1)(a)).
(b) Recruitment advertisements (SDA 1975, s 38; RRA 1976, s 29).
(c) Contractual benefits, but only where discrimination is on grounds other than sex (see paras **2.21** and **2.28** above).
(d) Non-contractual benefits (see paras **2.21** and **2.28** above).
(e) Occupational pension schemes (race, marital status, gender reassignment, religion or belief, sexual orientation only) (see also para **2.19** et seq in relation to sex).
(f) Opportunities for promotion and transfer (SDA 1975, s 6(2)(b); RRA 1976 s 4(2)(b); RBR 2003 and SOR 2003, reg 6(2)(b)).
(g) Training opportunities (save in a case where positive training of particular groups is allowed) (SDA 1975, s 6(2)(b); RRA 1976, s 4(2)(b); RBR 2003 and SOR 2003, reg 6(2)(b); see also SDA 1975, ss 47 and 48; RRA 1976, ss 37 and 38; RBR, reg 25; SOR, reg 26).
(h) Harassment (see para **2.50** below).
(i) Grounds for dismissal.
(j) Claims by employees in relation to their treatment after the termination of employment as long as the act complained of arose from the employment relationship or was closely connected with it (*Rhys-Harper v Relaxion Group Plc* [2003] IRLR 484; SDA 1975, s 20A; RRA 1976, s 27A; RBR, reg 21; SOR, reg 21).

If so, the complainant could have a claim under the relevant discrimination legislation.

Would the employee have received the same treatment from the employer or **2.36** potential employer but for his or her own sex, marital or civil partnership status, race, the fact he intends to undergo, is undergoing, or had undergone a gender reassignment, religion or belief, or sexual orientation? If so, and the employee can convince the Tribunal on the balance of probabilities that this is the case the employee concerned may have a claim for direct discrimination (see para **2.49** below).

2.37 Can the employer show on the balance of probabilities that sex, marital or civil partnership status, race, the fact he intends to undergo, is undergoing or had undergone a gender reassignment, religion or belief, or sexual orientation are not the reason for its less favourable treatment? If not, the employer may not be able to defend an allegation of direct discrimination (see paras **2.49** and **2.53** below).

2.38 Has the complainant been subject to unwanted conduct which has the purpose or effect of violating another person's dignity or creating an intimidating, hostile, degrading, humiliating, or offensive environment for them on the grounds of the person's sex, marital or civil partnership status, race, the fact he intends to undergo gender reassignment, religion or belief, or sexual orientation? If so, the complainant may have a claim of harassment (see para **2.50** below).

2.39 Is the complainant subject to a provision, criterion, or practice which is applied to everyone but which disadvantages a class of people, the majority of whom are one sex or race or married, or of the same religion or sexual orientation and does the employee who is claiming suffer that disadvantage? If so, the employee concerned may have a claim for indirect discrimination (see paras **2.51**, **2.52**, and **2.68** below).

2.40 To prove whether a provision, criterion, or practice amounts to indirect discrimination (which obligation is on the claimant SDA 1975, s 63A and *Nelson v Carillion Services Ltd* [2003] IRLR 428; RRA 1976, s 54A):

(a) identify the criteria for selection;
(b) identify the relevant pool of potential candidates;
(c) divide the pool into those who satisfy the criteria and those who do not and consider whether the members of the minority group are under-represented in the group which satisfies the criteria in comparison with the statistics and over-represented in the group which does not satisfy the criteria;
(d) does the group which is over-represented suffer disadvantage as a result of the imposition of the provision, criteria, or practice, and does the employee complaining suffer that disadvantage? If so, it is potentially discriminatory.

2.41 Can the employer show that the conditions which have been imposed are a proportionate means of achieving a legitimate aim? If so, the employer may have a defence to a claim of indirect discrimination (see paras **2.56** and **2.68** below).

2.42 Has the complainant been treated less favourably than others because that person threatens to bring proceedings, to give evidence or information, to take any action or to make any allegations concerning the employer under the discrimination legislation? If so, the complainant may have a claim of victimization as long as the allegation was made in good faith (see para **2.57** below).

If the complainant is an employee, did the employee bring a grievance in relation **2.43** to her claim? If not, the claimant may not be able to bring a claim in the employment tribunal (EA 2002, s 32 and Employment Act 2002 (Dispute Resolution) Regulations 2003, reg 15; and see paras **2.66,** and **2.82** below).

Has the complainant brought the claim in the employment tribunal during em- **2.44** ployment or within three months of the act complained of? If not, the complainant's claim is likely to be out of time, unless the complainant is an employee and has brought a grievance in relation to the deduction, in which case the time may be extended (see EA 2002, s 32 and Employment Act 2002 (Dispute Resolution) Regulations 2004, reg 15; see also paras **2.66,** and **2.82** below).

Commentary

Sex Discrimination Act 1975

The EqPA 1970 and the SDA 1975 complement each other. While the EqPA **2.45** 1970 deals with contractual terms, the SDA 1975 deals with all other aspects of employment, from recruitment, through career structure to dismissal. In order to bring a claim for sex discrimination, an employee must be employed under a contract of service or apprenticeship or any other contract to personally execute any work or labour (SDA 1975, s 82(1)). This is the same test as described at **2.20** above, but see also *Mingley v Pennock & Ivory* [2004] IRLR 373. There can be no claim for sex discrimination (including by reason of marital status, civil partnership, and gender reassignment) where an employee works wholly outside Great Britain (SDA 1975, ss 6 and 10). However, from October 2005, if the employer has a place of business at an establishment in Great Britain, the work the employee is doing is for the purposes of the business carried on at that establishment and the employee is ordinarily resident in Great Britain when she is recruited or at any time during the course of the employment, then she may have a claim (SDA 1975, s 10(1), (1A)). As the provisions relating to race discrimination and discrimination on grounds of religion or belief or sexual orientation are substantially the same as those relating to sex discrimination, the substantive tests are not set out separately in the sections which deal with these claims and the statements of law made here will apply to those claims. The appropriate references to the RRA 1976 only are included below. Equally, cases relating to race discrimination are quoted as authority for the general propositions they support where appropriate.

There can be no claim for sex discrimination in the following cases: **2.46**

(a) ministers of religion (SDA 1975, s 19);
(b) arrangements regarding the provision of certain accommodation facilities (SDA 1975, ss 46 and 47);

(c) prison officers (SDA 1975, s 18) (although the blanket exception only applies to requirements that people should be of a particular height);

(d) special treatment afforded to women in connection with pregnancy and childbirth (SDA 1975, s 2(2)).

2.47 The SDA applies not only to direct acts of discrimination, where an employee can show that a member of the opposite sex has been treated more favourably on any particular matter, but also to indirect discrimination, victimization, and harassment.

2.48 The basic test is whether the individual would have received the same treatment from the employer or potential employer but for his or her own sex, the fact he intends to undergo, is undergoing, or has undergone a gender reassignment or his or her marital or civil partnership status (SDA 1975, ss 1(1), 2A, 3). For the remainder of this section, the term 'sex' shall also refer to discrimination on the basis of marital or civil partnership. Gender reassignment is dealt with at para **2.58** below.

2.49 Direct discrimination occurs when a person is receiving less favourable treatment on account of his or her sex (SDA 1975, ss 1(2)(a), 3; RRA 1976, s 1(1)(a)). Usually, this involves the identification of an actual comparator but it is also open to the claimant to base the claim on a 'hypothetical' comparator (*Shamoon v Chief Constable of the Royal Ulster Constabulary* [2003] ICR 337). The exception to this is where a pregnant woman is claiming. Case law has held that in this situation, no comparator is necessary as this is a gender-specific situation (*Dekker v Stichting VJV-Centrum Plus* [1992] ICR 325, ECJ; *Webb v EMO Air Cargo (UK) Ltd* [1994] ICR 770) (but now enshrined in statute rather than simply being a product of case law (SDA 1975, s 3A)). In all other cases, there are two key questions, as follows:

(a) Has the complainant been less favourably treated? Unreasonable treatment alone is not enough, if everyone else is being treated unreasonably; there has to be some differential (*Glasgow City Council v Zafar* [1998] ICR 120, HL). Equally, different treatment is not enough; it has to be less favourable (*Smith v Safeway plc* [1996] ICR 868, CA). At this stage, the burden of proof is on the complainant (SDA 1975, s 63A; RRA 1976, s 54A). The claimant must prove the fact of less favourable treatment on a prescribed ground on the balance of probabilities. Inferences can be drawn from the primary facts and evasive or equivocal responses to a statutory questionnaire by the respondent employer can be taken into account (*Igen Ltd v Wong* [2005] IRLR 258; *Anya v University of Oxford* [2001] IRLR 377; *Barton v Investec Henderson Crosthwaite Securities Limited* [2003] ICR 1205, EAT; *Madarassy v Nomura International plc* [2007] IRLR 246).

(b) Was the less favourable treatment on the ground of the person's sex, marital status, civil partnership, or gender reassignment? Motive is generally irrelevant (*James v Eastleigh Borough Council* [1990] IRLR 288 HL). At this stage the burden of proof transfers to the respondent employer and the employer must prove that he did not commit and is not to be treated as committing that act. The test is on the balance of probabilities, but the tribunal will normally require cogent evidence (SDA 1975, s 63A; RRA 1976, s 54A; *Igen Ltd v Wong* [2005] IRLR 258; *Anya v University of Oxford* [2001] IRLR 377; *Barton v Investec Henderson Crosthwaite Securities Limited* [2003] ICR 1205, EAT: *Madarassy v Nomura International plc* [2007] IRLR 246).

[Note that the burden of proof in relation to claims of discrimination on grounds of nationality or colour and victimization under RRA 1976 is different and reflects the common law test of burden of proof as outlined in *King v Great Britain— China Centre* [1992] ICR 516 (see *Oyarce v Cheshire County Council* [2007] IDS Law Brief No 835; *Okonu v G4S Security Services (UK) Ltd* [2008] ICR 598).]

Sexual or racial harassment can take the form of unwelcome sexual attention, a **2.50** suggestion that sexual activity or its refusal may help or hinder a career, sustained obscene or lewd language or behaviour, or sexually offensive material. There is also a self-standing claim of harassment in the statutes, which is where on the grounds of sex or race or ethnic or national origins a person engages in unwanted conduct which has the purpose or effect of violating another person's dignity or creating an intimidating, hostile, degrading, humiliating, or offensive environment for her (SDA 1975, s 4A(1)(a); RRA 1976, s 3A(1)). Additionally, for sex discrimination only, there will be harassment if on the grounds of her sex, a person engages in any form of unwanted verbal, non-verbal, or physical conduct of a sexual nature that has the purpose of violating another person's dignity or creating an intimidating, hostile, degrading, or humiliating environment for her and/or on the ground of her rejection of or submission to unwanted conduct of this kind, a person treats her less favourably than the person would treat her had she not rejected, or submitted, to the conduct (SDA 1975, s 4A(1)(b) and (c)). Conduct will only be regarded as having this effect if, having regard to all the circumstances, including, in particular, the perception of the victim, it would be reasonably considered as having that effect (SDA 1975, s 4A(2); RRA 1976, s 3A(2)).

The SDA 1975 also applies where a provision, criterion, or practice is applied to **2.51** everyone, but which subtly discriminates against a class of people, the majority of whom are of one sex, and detriment is suffered by the complainant who is part of that group of people. Married people and those in civil partnerships can also complain of indirect discrimination, but those undergoing gender reassignment cannot. The test is that the treatment puts or would put a woman at a particular disadvantage when compared with a man and which puts her at that disadvantage (SDA 1975, s 1(2)(b); RRA 1976, s 1(1)(b) and 1(1)(c) but see also para **2.68** below in relation to slight differences under RRA 1976).

2.52   Although the test for indirect discrimination must be applied in each case, examples of indirect discrimination include:

(a)   a requirement or policy that people should be a certain height;

(b)   treatment that disadvantages workers with young children (which may also discriminate on the grounds of marital status) in particular, inflexibility in relation to flexible working, for example, part-time and home working, or job sharing (*Bilka-Kaufhaus GmbH v Weber von Hartz* [1987] ICR 110; *Clymo v Wandsworth Borough Council* [1989] ICR 250; *Robinson v Oddbins Ltd* [1996] 27 DCLD 1; *Lockworth v Crawley Warren Group Ltd* [2001] IDS Employment Law Brief, No 680, EAT);

(c)   a requirement or practice that candidates should have a long period of previously uninterrupted working—which tends to exclude women who have taken time off work to look after children;

(d)   a requirement or practice that applicants should be aged 25 to 35 (which excludes many women with young children) (*Price v Civil Service Commission and the Society of Civil and Public Servants* [1978] IRLR 3);

(e)   a requirement that employees should work long and uncertain hours (*London Underground Ltd v Edwards (No 2)* [1998] IRLR 364).

2.53   Defence to direct discrimination claim: once an employee can show direct discrimination in that she is being treated less favourably than a named person, or even that she is being treated less favourably than a hypothetical member of the opposite sex and the employer has been unable to show that the reason for the treatment was something other than her sex, the employer has two possible defences: that it was an employee's actions, not the employer's, which were discriminatory and that the employer did everything reasonably practicable to prevent those actions (SDA 1975, s 41(3); RRA 1976, s 32(3)), or that gender was a genuine occupational qualification for the job (SDA 1975, s 7(2)).

2.54   Usually it is very difficult for an employer to avoid a claim of discrimination on the grounds that it is not vicariously liable for it (SDA 1975, s 41(1)). In particular, an argument that the employee was not acting in the course of her employment when he did the discriminatory act will not succeed (*Jones v Tower Boot Co Ltd* [1997] IRLR 168) although this becomes more blurred at work-related social events (*Chief Constable of the Lincolnshire Police v Stubbs* [1991] IRLR 81; *Sidhu v Aerospace Composite Technology Ltd* [2000] IRLR 602). The exception to this is where the employer took such steps as were reasonably practicable to ensure that the act or type of act was proscribed (SDA 1975, s 41(3)). The employee or agent himself or herself may, however, still be liable.

The genuine occupational qualification defence applies to claims for sex discrim-   **2.55**
ination (but not marital/civil partnership discrimination or discrimination against those undergoing gender reassignment—in the latter case, see para **2.59** below) in relation to arrangements made for filling a job; refusal of a job; denial of opportunities for promotion, transfer, or training for the job in question; or that there is a genuine need for a position to be filled by a person of a particular sex, for example:

(a) Physiology and authenticity in entertainment matters, for example, models and actors.
(b) Requirements of decency or privacy, for example, lavatory attendants.
(c) Jobs in a single-sex establishment such as a prison.
(d) Work abroad which can only be done by a man, for example, certain types of work in the Middle East.
(e) A job which is one of two to be done by a married couple.
(f) A job which requires personal services towards the welfare and education of others which can most effectively be done by a person of the same sex.
(g) A job which is likely to involve the holder living in or working in a private home with a degree of physical or social contact with other persons living there or involving intimate details of such persons' lives, such as a private nurse or companion.
(h) A job where the employee would have to live in, and there are no separate sleeping or toilet arrangements between the sexes.

(SDA 1975, s 7(2))

Defence to indirect discrimination claim: The defences to an allegation of indi-   **2.56**
rect discrimination used to be that the conditions which have been imposed are justifiable on reasonable, non-sexual grounds, or grounds not related to marital status, for example because of economic or administrative reasons, safety, hygiene, or management experience. In establishing these grounds, the employer must conduct a balancing exercise between the real business need dictating the imposition of the provision, criterion, or practice and the impact the imposition will have on the woman (*Rainey v Greater Glasgow Health Board* [1987] ICR 129; *Allonby v Accrington and Rossendale College* [2000] IRLR 364, CA). Now, the statutory test requires that the business reason for the imposition of the provision, criterion, or condition is a proportionate means of achieving a legitimate aim (SDA 1975, s 1(2)(b)(iii); RRA 1976, s 1(1A)(b)(iii) but see para **2.68** in relation to the differences in the tests in the SDA 1975 and RRA 1976). However, most commentators believe that the employer would be wise to consider both the old and the new tests.

2.57 Victimization arises if an employer treats any person less favourably than others because that person threatens to bring proceedings, to give evidence or information, to take any action or to make any allegations concerning the employer with reference to SDA 1975 (or EqPA 1970) (SDA 1975, s 4(1); RRA 1976 s 2(1)). The allegation must be made in good faith to obtain the protection (SDA 1975, s 4(2); RRA 1976, s 2 (2)). The test involves comparing the victimized person against someone who has not performed a protected act and looking at the subjective reasons for the employer's actions. There is no need for conscious motivation connected with the discrimination legislation (*Nagarajan v London Regional Transport* [1999] IRLR 572, HL; *Chief Constable of West Yorkshire Police v Khan* [2001] IRLR 830, HL).

2.58 SDA 1975 also protects against direct and indirect discrimination on grounds of marital status and gender reassignment:

(a) *Marital discrimination*—Marital discrimination applies where there is direct or indirect discrimination by reason of a person's marital status or civil partnership (SDA 1975, s 3). The tests are identical to those relating to sex discrimination.

(b) *Gender reassignment*—The test for discrimination on the grounds of gender reassignment is different. A person (A) will discriminate against a person (B) where A treats B less favourably and does so because B intends to undergo, is undergoing, or has undergone gender reassignment. 'Less favourably' has a specific meaning where it relates to absence from work for vocational training—it means either that the person is treated less favourably than he would be if the absence was due to sickness or injury or less favourably than he would be if the absence was due to some other cause and, having regard to the circumstances of the case, it is reasonable for him to be treated no less favourably (SDA 1975, s 2A).

2.59 It will be a defence to a claim for discrimination on grounds of gender reassignment in relation to arrangements made for filling a job; refusal of a job; the terms on which employment is offered; denial of opportunities for promotion, transfer, or training for the job in question; or where the employee is dismissed from it or subjected to detriment as a result of it, that being a man or woman is a genuine occupational qualification and the employer can show that the treatment was reasonable in view of the relevant circumstances (SDA 1975, s 7A).

2.60 Relevant circumstances are all of those listed under para **2.55** above and additionally (but in relation to certain aspects of discrimination only) where:

(a) the job involves the holder of the job being liable to perform intimate searches under statutory powers;

(b) the job is in a private home and may result in objections due to the degree of physical or social contact with the person in the private home or the knowledge of the intimate details of such a person's life;

(c) the job involves living on the work premises and others may object to sharing premises with someone undergoing gender reassignment and no reasonable alternative arrangements can be made;

(d) the job involves the provision of personal services to vulnerable individuals and no cover can be provided while the gender reassignment is being done.

(SDA 1975, s 7B)

2.61 Remedies for sex discrimination include a declaration and unlimited compensation to put the employee in the position as if the discrimination had not taken place. The employee can also recover compensation for injury to feelings, aggravated and exemplary damages (although awards in the latter two categories are rare). Please see Chapter 12—Table of Recent Tribunal Awards in Discrimination Cases for more detail on this and examples of recent awards.

2.62 Again, there is a European aspect to sex discrimination which works in broadly the same way as in relation to equal pay, as both Article 141 and the Equal Treatment Directive provide for equal treatment of men and women.

2.63 An employee may submit a questionnaire under the SDA 1975 (in prescribed form) asking the employer to confirm or deny certain facts. The employer must answer the questionnaire within eight weeks and any failure to answer, or an inaccurate or evasive answer, may be taken into account by any employment tribunal considering the issue of discrimination at a later date and it may draw adverse inferences from such answers or failure to answer (SDA 1975, s 7).

2.64 Individuals who feel they may have been subject to discrimination may ask the Equality and Human Rights Commission (EHRC) (formerly the EOC) either to conduct an official investigation on their behalf or to assist in the conduct of any claim.

2.65 If the EHRC gives notice that it intends to conduct a formal investigation, the employer must supply all information requested. Fines are imposed for falsifying evidence. In addition, the employer should comply with any non-discrimination notice that may be sent following the investigation. An appeal against the notice must be made to an employment tribunal within six weeks of the notice being served (SDA 1975, s 57).

2.66 Prior to bringing a complaint, the employee must raise a grievance under the statutory dispute procedures or she will be barred from bringing a claim (EA

2002, s 32 and see paras **7.81–7.83** below). Any complaint to the employment tribunal must be brought within three months of the act complained of (SDA 1975, s 76(1)) unless the tribunal thinks it just and equitable to extend the period (SDA 1975, s 76(5)) or the employee does bring a grievance in which case the three-month time limit will be extended (Employment Act (Dispute Resolution) Regulations 2004, reg 15). Continuing discrimination ends only when the practice ceases to be discriminatory. There is a distinction between a single act with continuing effect (where that single act will start the three-month time limit) and the constant repetition of discriminatory acts (where the last discriminatory act may start the time limit running, but all of the previous acts may also be in time too) (SDA 1975, s 76 (6)(b)).

2.67   The EHRC has issued a code of practice pursuant to its power to do so (SDA 1975, s 56A; Code of Practice on Sex Discrimination, Equal Opportunity Policies, Procedures and Practices in Employment (1985)). A failure to abide by the code will not render an employer liable to proceedings, but the code will be admissible in any employment tribunal proceedings.

Race Relations Act 1976

2.68   Employers must not discriminate on the grounds of colour, race, nationality, or ethnic or national origins against any person of either sex. Legislation to this effect has been in force in the UK since 1976. However, in 2000 a Council Directive (2000/43/EC) implementing the principle of equal treatment between persons irrespective of racial or ethnic origin came into force. The race discrimination legislation must now be construed in accordance with this Directive. This applies not only to recruitment policies, treatment during employment and career structures, and dismissal, but also to contractual terms. In order to bring a claim for race discrimination an employee must be employed under a contract of service or of apprenticeship or a contract to personally execute any work or labour (RRA 1976, s 78) (see paras **2.20** and **2.45** above). There can be no claim for race discrimination where an employee works wholly outside Great Britain unless, if the employer has a place of business at an establishment in Great Britain, the work the employee is doing is for the purposes of the business carried on at the establishment and the employee is ordinarily resident in Great Britain when he is recruited or at any time during the course of the employment (RRA 1976, ss 4 and 8) when the employee may be able to claim. The provisions relating to race discrimination are substantially the same as those relating to sex discrimination in terms of the definitions of direct and indirect discrimination, victimization and harassment, the defences available, and the burden of proof, and are therefore not dealt with separately in this book (although the relevant references to the RRA 1976 are included in the section on sex discrimination at para **2.45**

et seq above). However, note that the test for indirect discrimination under RRA 1976 is twofold:

(a) where the discrimination relates to the employee's racial group, the test is whether the application of a 'requirement or condition' (as opposed to the wider 'provision, criterion or practice') leads to the indirect discrimination and justification is not subject to the 'legitimate aim/proportionate means' requirement (RRA 1976, s 1(1)(b)); and

(b) where the indirect discrimination is on grounds of race, ethnic, or national origins, the test is the same as indirect sex discrimination (see paras **2.52** and **2.56** above (RRA 1976, s 1(1A)).

Generally as the test under RRA 1976, s 1(1A) is regarded as easier to satisfy most claims will now be brought under this section (see para **2.74** below).

2.69

Examples of indirect race discrimination include:

(a) special treatment of workers from a particular area with a predominantly ethnic population;

(b) imposition of language tests which would exclude large numbers from ethnic minority groups.

There is a genuine occupational qualification defence to a race discrimination claim so that it will be a defence to a claim for race discrimination in relation to arrangements made for filling a job; refusal of a job; denial of opportunities for promotion, transfer, or training for the job in question, that there is a genuine need for a position to be filled by a person of a particular race. For example:

2.70

(a) To provide authenticity in entertainment (for example, acting).

(b) Jobs requiring personal services towards the welfare of others which can most effectively be done by a person of a particular race (for example, community officers).

(c) Jobs in establishments which require the maintenance of a particular ambience, for example, in an ethnic bar or restaurant.

(RRA 1976, s 5)

There can be no claim for race discrimination in the following cases:

2.71

(a) Employment in a private household (RRA 1976, s 4(3)).

(b) Selection for sports representation and competitions (RRA 1976, s 39).

(c) Acts safeguarding national security (RRA 1976, s 42).

An employee may submit a questionnaire in the same way as it is possible to do so in respect of sex discrimination claims (RRA 1976, s 69). The position in

2.72

relation to grievances, remedies and the timing of claims is the same as described at para **2.66** above (see also RRA 1976, s 68).

2.73 The Commission for Racial Equality (CRE) has now been replaced by the EHRC, but continues to fulfil broadly the same role.

2.74 Note that segregation of individuals on racial grounds will always be discriminatory, even where it does not involve less favourable treatment. 'Racial grounds' for this and other purposes means colour, race, nationality, or ethnic or national origins (RRA 1976, s 3(1)). 'Ethnic origins' requires there to be a segment of the population distinguished from others by a sufficient combination of shared customs, beliefs, traditions, and characteristics derived from a common or presumed common past, even if not drawn from what, in biological terms, was a common racial stock (*Mandla v Dowell Lee* [1983] ICR 385). Sikhs, Jews, and those of the Romany race are all ethnic groups; Rastafarians are not. English and Scottish people are separate national groups. An employee will be discriminated against on 'racial grounds' if he is treated less favourably on the basis he refuses to implement a racially discriminatory policy or is affected by that policy irrespective of that person's race (*Redfearn v Serco Ltd* [2006] IRLR 623, CA).

2.75 The CRE (now the EHRC) first issued a Code of Practice in 1983 which has been recently updated (RRA 1976, s 47; Commission for Racial Equality; Code of Practice Racial Equality in Employment (1983)). A failure to abide by the code will not render an employer liable to proceedings, but the code will be admissible in any employment tribunal proceedings.

Discrimination on the Grounds of Religion or Belief or Sexual Orientation

2.76 Employers must not discriminate on grounds of religion or belief or sexual orientation under RBR 2003 and SOR 2003. These regulations implement Council Directive (2000/781/EC) establishing a framework for equal treatment in employment and occupation. The Regulations must be construed in accordance with the Directive. The provisions relating to this type of discrimination are substantially the same as those which apply to sex and race discrimination claims (although the test for indirect discrimination is the same as sex discrimination and RRA 1976, s 1(1A) (see para **2.68** above)).

2.77 Religion or belief means any religion, religious belief, or philosophical belief or a lack of religion or belief (RBR 2003, reg 2(1)). The definition of 'religion' is broad and includes all those religions widely recognized in this country (see also *Hussain v Bhullar Bros (t/a BB Supersave)* (ET Case No 1806638/04)). 'Religious belief' may include other beliefs founded on religion. A philosophical belief must be a profound belief affecting a person's way of life, or perception of the world, such as atheism and humanism. Rastafarianism is a philosophical belief (*Harris v NKL Automotive Ltd* EAT/0134/07).

Sexual orientation means orientation towards people of the same sex, the opposite sex, or both (SOR 2003, reg 2(1)). **2.78**

There can be no claim for this kind of discrimination unless the employee comes within the category of 'worker' described in paras **2.20** and **2.45** above. Equally, where an employee works wholly outside Great Britain, he will not be able to bring a claim unless the employee is resident in Great Britain at some point during his recruitment or employment and the employer is based at an establishment in Great Britain (RBR 2003, reg 9(1) and (2)). There will also be a genuine occupational qualification defence to allegations in relation to religion or belief discrimination where having regard to the nature of the employment or the context in which it is carried out, being of a particular religion or belief is a genuine and determining occupational requirement and it is proportionate to apply that requirement and either the person to whom the requirement is applied does not meet it or the employer believes they do not meet it. This exception will also apply slightly less strictly where the employer has an ethos based on religion or belief, when the employer should apply the same test but religion or belief should be a genuine occupational requirement for the job (RBR 2003, reg 7). **2.79**

There is also a genuine occupational qualification defence for sexual orientation. Where the employment is *not* for the purposes of organized religion, it is that being of a particular sexual orientation is a genuine and determining occupational requirement, that it is proportionate to apply that requirement in this case, and that the person does not satisfy the requirement or the employer believes they do not. Where the employment is for the purposes of organized religion, it is that the requirement relating to sexual orientation is applied so as to comply with the doctrines of the religion or because of the nature of the employment and the context in which it is carried out, so as to avoid conflicting with the strongly held religious convictions of a significant number of the religious followers and the person to whom the requirement is applied does not satisfy it or the employer believes they will not satisfy it (SOR 2003, reg 7). **2.80**

There are exceptions under both sets of Regulations where the acts relate to matters of national security (reg 24 in both) and under SOR 2003 for benefits dependent on marital status (reg 25). **2.81**

Employees may submit questionnaires in relation to their claim of discrimination in the same way they can for a sex or race discrimination claim (RBR 2003, reg 33; SOR 2003, reg 33). The position in relation to grievances, remedies, and the timing of claims is the same as described at para **2.66** above. **2.82**

D. Disability Discrimination Act 1995

CHECKLIST

2.83 Is the complainant employed under a contract of service or of apprenticeship or a contract personally to execute any work or labour? If not, he will not have the protection of the legislation (see para **2.96** below).

2.84 Is the complainant a member of the armed forces, an employee who works outside Great Britain (although there may be an exception for those who are posted abroad where the employee was resident in Great Britain when he or she was recruited or at some point during the employment and the employer has a place of business at an establishment in Great Britain and the work the employee is doing is for the business at that establishment), or an employee who works on a ship, aircraft, or hovercraft? If so, he will probably not have a claim (see paras **2.96** and **2.113** below).

2.85 Does the complainant have a disability, ie a physical or mental impairment which has substantial and long-term adverse effect on the employee's ability to carry out his normal day-to-day activities? If so, he will be able to bring a claim under the DDA. (See paras **2.97** et seq below.)

2.86 Does the employee suffer from alcoholism, drug or nicotine addiction, hay fever, pyromania, kleptomania, exhibitionism, a tendency to physical or sexual abuse of other persons, or voyeurism? If so, these will not qualify as a disability and so the complainant will not have a claim (Disability Discrimination (Meaning of Disability) Regulations 1996, SI 1996/1455 and para **2.98** below).

2.87 Has the complainant been treated less favourably by someone than he treats or would treat a person not having that particular disability whose relevant circumstances, including his abilities, are the same as or not materially different from, those of the disabled person? If so, the complainant may have a claim of direct discrimination (DDA 1995, s 3A(5) and para **2.106** below).

2.88 Has the complainant received less favourable treatment for a reason relating to disability? If so, the complainant may have a claim of disability-related discrimination (DDA 1995, s 3A(1) and para **2.105** below).

2.89 Has the employer complied with its duty to take such steps as are reasonable to prevent substantial disadvantage to a disabled person? If not, the complainant will have a claim (DDA 1995, s 3A(2) and paras **2.107** and **2.108** below).

2.90 Can the employer justify its treatment of the complainant by showing a reason for it which is material to the particular circumstances of the case and substantial?

If so, the employer may have a defence, but not if the claim is one of direct discrimination and it will have to show that it has complied with the duty to make reasonable adjustments as well (DDA 1995, s 3A(3)(5)(6) and para **2.109** below).

Has the complainant been treated less favourably than others because that **2.91** person has brought proceedings against another person under DDA 1995, given information or evidence in relation to such a claim, otherwise done anything under DDA 1995 in relation to the employer, or alleged that the employer has breached DDA 1995 or believes the employer intends to do so? If so, the complainant may have a claim for victimization, as long as the allegation was made in good faith (DDA 1995, s 55 and para **2.110** below).

Has the complainant been subject to unwanted conduct which has the purpose **2.92** or effect of violating another person's dignity or creating an intimidating, hostile, degrading, humiliating, or offensive environment for them? Can the conduct, having regard to all the circumstances, including, in particular, the perception of the victim, reasonably be considered as having that effect? If so, the complainant may have a claim of harassment on grounds of disability (DDA 1995, s 38) and para **2.111** below).

Is the employer unaware of the disability? This may be a defence to a claim for **2.93** disability-related discrimination and the duty to make reasonable adjustments but caution should be exercised (DDA 1995, s 4A(3) and para **2.112** below).

If the complainant is an employee, did the employee bring a grievance in relation **2.94** to his claim? If not, the complainant may not be able to bring a claim in the employment tribunal (EA 2002, s 32 and the Employment Act 2002 (Dispute Resolution) Regulations 2004, reg 15; see also para **2.115** below).

Has the complainant brought the claim in the employment tribunal during **2.95** employment or within three months of the act complained of? If not, the complainant's claim is likely to be out of time unless the complainant is an employee and has brought a grievance in relation to the deduction, in which case the time may be extended (see EA 2002, s 32 and the Employment Act 2002 (Dispute Resolution) Regulations 2004, reg 15; see also para **2.115** below).

Commentary

Statute also provides that it is unlawful to discriminate against employees on **2.96** grounds of their disability. UK legislation has been in place since 1995; however, Council Directive (2000/78/EC) establishing a framework for equal treatment in employment and occupation led to amendments in 2003. The DDA 1995 must now be construed in accordance with the Directive and see para **2.106** for an example of where the DDA 1995 was amended. An employee for these purposes means 'employed' under a contract of service or of apprenticeship or a contract personally to execute any work or labour (DDA 1995, s 68; see paras 2.20 and 2.45 above). There can be no claim for disability discrimination where the complainant works wholly outside Great Britain. However, if the employer has a place of business at an establishment in Great Britain, the work the employee is doing is for the purposes of the business carried on at that establishment, and the employee is ordinarily resident in Great Britain when he is recruited or at any time during the course of the employment, then he may have a claim (DDA 1995, s 68(2) and (2A)).

2.97 A person has a disability if he has a mental or physical impairment which has a substantial and long-term adverse effect (ie at least 12 months) on his ability to carry out normal day-to-day activities (DDA 1995, s 1(1), Sch 1).

2.98 Physical or mental impairment includes any physical or mental illness, but does not include such conditions as alcoholism, drug or nicotine addiction, hay fever, pyromania, kleptomania, voyeurism (DDA 1995, Sch 1, para 1; Disability Discrimination (Employment) Regulations 1996, SI 1996/1455). With effect from December 2005, the requirement that a mental illness be clinically well recognized was removed. Further, a person who has cancer, HIV infection, or multiple sclerosis is to be deemed to have a disability and hence to be a disabled person (DDA 1995, Sch 1, para 6A). However, more recently the tribunals have been concentrating on effects of the disability rather than the precise cause of it (*Millar v The Board of the Inland Revenue* [2006] IRLR 112).

2.99 The disability must actually affect the employee's ability to carry out normal day-to-day activities and must be long-term, that is, likely to last more than 12 months (even though its onset may only be in the future) (DDA 1995, Sch 1, paras 2 and 8).

2.100 An impairment may be taken to affect normal day-to-day activities only if it affects one of the following:

(a) mobility;
(b) manual dexterity;
(c) physical coordination;
(d) continence;
(e) the ability to lift, carry, or otherwise move everyday objects;
(f) speech, hearing, or eyesight;
(g) memory or ability to concentrate, learn, or understand; or
(h) perception of the risk of physical danger.

(DDA 1995, Sch 1, para 4(1))

However, the fact that the activities which are impaired are not ones which appear in the above list does not exclude a finding of disability: a broader approach should be taken (*Hewett v Motorola Ltd* [2004] IRLR 545; EAT). Severe disfigurement is deemed to have a substantial effect on the ability of the person concerned to carry out normal day-to-day activities (DDA 1995, Sch 1, para 3).

The adverse effect must be substantial. Substantial means 'more than minor or **2.101** trivial' rather than 'very large' (guidance on the Definition of Disability (2006), para B1—see para **2.103** below). The employment tribunal can take into account the fact that medication may reduce those affects.

Each case must be assessed on the facts and the available medical evidence. So, for **2.102** example, stress or anxiety will not amount to a disability in every case and medical evidence will be important (although the employment tribunal has been known to take a more relaxed approach) (*Morgan v Staffordshire University* [2002] IRLR 190, EAT). Full guidance as to how to approach the issue of whether there is a disability on the basis of the questions set out above was given in *Goodwin v The Patent Office* [1999] IRLR 4.

The Government has also issued guidance as to the definition of disability **2.103** ('Guidance on matters to be taken into account in determining questions relating to disability' (2006), issued pursuant to DDA 1995, s 3(9)). The Guidance came into force from 1 May 2006 replacing previous Guidance issued in 1996. The Guidance must be taken into account by the employment tribunal (DDA 1995, s 3(3)). Case law has also stressed that this must be taken into account when considering claims under DDA 1995. Ultimately, an employer should look at all the circumstances but concentrate on those actions which the employee *cannot* do (*Goodwin v The Patent Office* [1999] IRLR 4; *Leonard v Southern Derbyshire Chamber of Commerce* [2001] IRLR 19).

Once the fact of disability has been established, there are a number of tests relat- **2.104** ing to disability discrimination: disability-related discrimination; direct discrimination; non-compliance with duty to make reasonable adjustments; justification; victimization; knowledge of the disability; and harassment.

Disability-related discrimination. This is where, for a reason which relates to the **2.105** disabled person's disability, the employer treats the complainant less favourably than he treats or would treat others to whom the reason does not or would not apply (DDA 1995, s 3A(1)). The correct comparator was until recently someone who does not have any disability or show any symptoms of it, for example, someone who has not been absent as a result of their disability (*Clark v Novacold Ltd* [1999] ICR 951). However the House of Lords in *Mayor and Burgesses of the London Borough of Lewisham v Malcolm* [2008] UKHL 43 has overturned this test and disapproved *Clark* in favour of a test which says the comparator is someone who is not disabled but has shown the same symptoms and so, for example, has been absent from work. One note of caution in relation to this decision is that it was not given in the employment context; however it seems likely that it will be followed in future employment cases. The decision narrows significantly the category of employees which come within the definition of this type of discrimination.

2.106   *Direct discrimination.* A person directly discriminates against a disabled person if, on the ground of the disabled person's disability, he treats the disabled person less favourably than he treats or would treat a person not having that particular disability whose relevant circumstances, including his abilities, are the same as or not materially different from, those of the disabled person (DDA 1995, s 3A(5) and DRC Code of Practice: Employment and Occupation (2004) para 4.37). [Note that direct discrimination (and also harassment on grounds of disability) may also include direct discrimination because an employee is associated with a person who is disabled (*S. Coleman v Attridge Law and Steve Law* [2008] All ER 245).]

2.107   *Failure to implement adjustments.* An employer also discriminates against a disabled person if he fails to comply with a duty to make reasonable adjustments (DDA 1995, s 3A(2)). Where a provision, criterion, or practice applied by an employer, or any physical feature of premises occupied by an employer places the disabled person concerned at a substantial disadvantage which is personal to him, it is the duty of the employer to take such steps as is reasonable for him to take, in all the circumstances of the case, in order to prevent the provision, criterion, practice, or feature having that effect (DDA 1995, s 4A(1) and *O'Hanlon v Commissioners for HM Revenue & Customs* [2007] IRLR 404). Failure to take such steps will be a breach of DDA 1995. Examples of such adjustments would be the alteration of working hours, the provision of training, the modifying of instruction or reference manuals, and the modification of premises. What is reasonable will be determined by taking into account all the circumstances (DDA 1995, s 4(A)). The employment tribunal will judge this objectively (*Morse v Wiltshire County Council* [1998] ICR 1023). Examples of reasonable adjustments are:

(a)   making adjustments to premises;
(b)   allocating some of the disabled person's duties to another person;
(c)   transferring him to fill an existing vacancy;
(d)   altering his working hours;
(e)   assigning him a different place of work;
(f)   allowing him to be absent during working hours for rehabilitation, assessment, or treatment;
(g)   giving him, or arranging for him to be given, training;

(h)   acquiring or modifying equipment;
(i)   modifying instructions or reference materials;
(j)   modifying procedures for testing or assessment;
(k)   providing a reader or interpreter;
(l)   providing supervision.

(Disability Rights Commission (DRC) Code of Practice: Employment and Occupation 2004)

In looking at whether it is reasonable for an employer to take a particular step, a **2.108** court will consider the effectiveness of the step in preventing the disadvantage, the practicability of the step, the financial and other costs of the adjustment, and the extent of any disruption involved, the extent of the employer's financial or other resources, the availability to the employer of financial or other assistance to help make the adjustment, the nature of the employer's activities, and the size of his undertaking and, in relation to private households, the extent to which taking the step would disrupt the household or disturb any person residing there (DRC Code of Practice: Employment and Occupation 2004). An employer may well be required to spend some money on the reasonable adjustments (*Ross v Ryanair Ltd and Stansted Airport Ltd* [2004] EWCA Civ 1751). The House of Lords has also given a wide interpretation to the duty—'arrangements' appear to encompass almost anything which puts the disabled person at a disadvantage and steps include transferring the disabled person to a new role, not simply giving him an opportunity to apply for it (*Archibald v Fife Council* [2004] IRLR 197). However, it will rarely be a reasonable adjustment to pay an employee who is off sick full pay where they would not otherwise be entitled to full pay (*O'Hanlon v HMRC* [2007] IRLR 404).

Justification. An employer can rely on a defence of justification in relation to disabil- **2.109** ity-related discrimination (see para **2.105** above) and the failure to make reasonable adjustments (but not discrimination by reason of disability). The defence will not apply in relation to disability-related discrimination where the employer had a duty to make reasonable adjustments and failed to do so, unless he can show the justification would have applied even if he had made the reasonable adjustments (DDA 1995, s 3A(6)). For discrimination to be justified, the reason for it must be both material to the circumstances of the particular case and substantial (DDA 1995, s 3A(3)). When looking at whether the grounds are material and substantial, an employment tribunal should not substitute its own view, but consider whether the employer has established that they are reasonable and substantial, and then whether the employer's response was within a range of reasonable responses (*Jones v Post Office* [2001] ICR 805; *Williams v J Walter Thompson Group Ltd* [2005] IRLR 376).

Victimization. A person (A) discriminates against another person (B) if he treats **2.110** B less favourably and does so because B has brought proceedings against A or any other person under DDA 1995, given evidence or information in relation to such a claim, otherwise done anything under DDA 1995 in relation to A, or alleged that A has breached DDA 1995 or where A believes B intends to do so (DDA 1995, s 55). Any allegation must be made in good faith and must not be false (DDA 1995, s 55(4)).

2.111 *Harassment.* A person subjects a disabled person to harassment where for a reason which relates to the disabled person's disability he engages in unwanted conduct which has the purpose or effect of violating the disabled person's dignity or creating an intimidating, hostile, degrading, humiliating, or offensive environment for him (DDA 1995, s 3B(1)). Conduct shall only be regarded as having this effect if having regard to all the circumstances, including, in particular, the perception of the victim, it should be reasonably considered as having that effect (DDA 1995, s 3(B)(2)).

2.112 *Knowledge of disability.* The position used to be that lack of knowledge of the disability is no defence (*H J Heinz Co Ltd v Kenrick* [2000] IRLR 144; *London Borough of Hammersmith and Fulham v Farnsworth* [2000] IRLR 691) except possibly in relation to the obligation to make reasonable adjustments (DDA 1995, s 4A(3)(b) and see *Jama v Alcohol Recovery Project* (EAT 0602/06). See also the Disability Rights Commission Code of Practice: Employment and Occupation at para 4.11). Lack of knowledge did not prevent the employer from putting forward a defence of justification (*Quinn v Schwarzkopf* [2002] IRLR 602). However since the decisions in *Taylor v OCS Group Ltd* [2006] ICR 1602 and most recently in *Mayor and Burgesses of the London Borough of Lewisham v Malcolm* [2008] UKHL 43 where the House of Lords has held (albeit not in the employment context) that knowledge is necessary in the context of disability-related discrimination under s 3A(1), the previous decisions are therefore overturned in this regard.

2.113 There can be no claim for disability discrimination in the following cases:

(a) members of the armed forces (DDA 1995, s 64(7));
(b) employees who work wholly outside Great Britain (DDA 1995, s 68(2)) (unless they are resident in Great Britain and the employer is resident in Great Britain (s 68(2A));
(c) employees who work on board ships, aircraft, or hovercraft (DDA 1995, s 68(2C)).

2.114 An employer is responsible for a discriminatory act carried out by an employee or agent or in some circumstances other persons in the control of the employer. If the employer took such steps as were reasonably practicable to ensure that the act or type of act did not occur, the employer itself will not be found guilty of discrimination (DDA 1995, s 58) (see also para **2.54** in relation to the similar provisions which appear in the SDA 1975).

Individuals who feel they may have been subject to discrimination may ask the **2.115** EHRC (formerly the DRC) either to conduct an official investigation on their behalf or to assist in the conduct of any claim. The EHRC has additional powers where it can require a discriminatory body to enter into a written undertaking which is enforceable by the courts. If the complainant wishes to bring a claim on an individual basis, he must apply to the employment tribunal. However, the complainant must, prior to bringing a claim, raise a grievance under the statutory dispute procedures or he will be barred from bringing a claim (EA 2002, s 32). The normal time limit for bringing a claim is three months from the act complained of (DDA 1995 Sch 3, Part 1, para 3(1)) unless the Tribunal thinks it is just and equitable to extend the time limit (DDA 1995, Sch 3, Part 1 para 3(2) and see also paras **7.81–7.83** below). However, if the employee does bring a grievance, the three-month period will be extended (Employment Act (Dispute Resolutions) Regulations 2004, reg 15).

It is also possible to submit a DDA questionnaire in a similar way to the other **2.116** discrimination legislation (DDA 1995, s 56(2), (4); Disability Discrimination (Questions and Replies) Order 2004). The position in relation to remedies is the same as set out in para **2.61** in relation to sex discrimination.

E. Discrimination on the Grounds of Age

CHECKLIST

Is the complainant employed under a contract of service or of apprenticeship or a **2.117** contract personally to execute any work or labour? If not, he or she may not have the protection of the legislation (EEAR 2006, reg 2 and see paras **2.20** and **2.45** above for a similar test).

Does the employee work wholly outside Great Britain? If yes, he will not have **2.118** a claim although there may be an exception for those who are posted abroad where the employee was resident in Great Britain when he was recruited or at some point during the employment and the employer has a place of business at an establishment in Great Britain and the work was for that establishment (EEAR 2006, reg 10; see also para **2.130** below).

Is the complainant doing service in any of the naval, military, or air forces, as an **2.119** unpaid office holder or an unpaid volunteer? If so, they will not be covered by the legislation (see para **2.131** below).

Is the complainant claiming age discrimination about one of the areas below: **2.120**

(a) arrangements for recruitment (EEAR 2006, reg 7(1)(a));
(b) contractual and non-contractual benefits (including occupational pension schemes);

(c) opportunities for promotion and transfer and training (EEAR 2006, reg 7(2)(b) but see also reg 29 in relation to positive action);

(d) harassment (see para **2.138**);

(e) grounds for dismissal (EEAR 2006, reg 7(2)(d) but see also para **7.236** et seq in relation to the specific rules governing dismissals);

(f) claims by employees in relation to their treatment after the termination of employment as long as the act complained of arose from the employment relationship or was closely connected with it (EEAR 2006, reg 24);

(g) vocational training (EEAR 2006, reg 20).

2.121 Would the employee have received the same treatment from the employer or potential employer but for his age (or apparent age)? If so, the employee concerned may have a claim for direct discrimination (see para **2.133** below).

2.122 Is the complainant subject to a provision, criterion, or practice which is applied to everyone but which disadvantages those in a specific age group and does the employee who is claiming suffer that disadvantage? If so, the employee concerned may have a claim for indirect discrimination (see para **2.134** below).

2.123 Can the employer show that the direct or indirect discrimination is a proportionate means of achieving a legitimate aim? In considering this, the employer will need to ask the following questions:

(a) What is a legitimate aim?
  (i) economic factors such as business needs and efficiency;
  (ii) the health, welfare, and safety of the individual;
  (iii) the particular training requirements of the job;
(b) Does the legitimate aim correspond with a real need of the business? It should do and not simply be cheaper.
(c) What is proportionate?
  (i) it must actually contribute to the legitimate aim;
  (ii) the discriminatory effect should be significantly outweighed by the importance and benefits of the legitimate aim;
  (iii) the employer should have no reasonable alternative to the action it is taking.

(ACAS Age Guide; see also para **2.137** below)

2.124 Has the complainant been subject to unwanted conduct which has the purpose or effect of violating another person's dignity or creating an intimidating, hostile, degrading, humiliating, or offensive environment on grounds of their age? If so, the employee may have a claim for harassment (EEAR 2006, reg 6).

2.125 Has the complainant been treated less favourably than others because that person threatens to bring proceedings, to give evidence or information, to take any action, or to make any allegations concerning the employer under EEAR 2006?

If so, the complainant may have a claim for victimization as long as the allegation was made in good faith (EEAR 2006, reg 4).

Does one of the other exceptions to liability under EEAR 2006 apply? The excep- **2.126** tions are as follows:

(a) The act was done in order to comply with a requirement of a statutory provision (EEAR 2006, reg 27).

(b) A person (who is an employee as defined in ERA 1996, s 230(1)) is recruited whose age is greater than the employer's normal retirement age or, if the employer does not have a normal retirement age, 65, or would be within a six-month period (EEAR 2006, reg 7(4)).

(c) A person (who is an employee as defined in ERA 1996, s 230(1)) is dismissed at or over the age of 65 where the reason for the dismissal is retirement (EEAR 2006, reg 30(2) and see also paras **7.236** et seq below).

(d) The act is done for the purposes of safeguarding national security (EEAR 2006, reg 28 and see also para **2.131** below).

(e) The act prevents or compensates for disadvantages linked to age suffered by persons of that age or age group doing the work concerned (EEAR 2006, reg 29). Usually this will cover access to certain types of training or work. It will not, however, excuse positive discrimination, which will still need to be objectively justified.

(f) An exception to allow different rates of pay under NMWA 1998 for employees of different ages (EEAR, reg 31).

(g) An exception to allow certain benefits to be based on length of service (EEAR 2006, reg 32). An employee with a length of service of five years or less cannot bring a claim in relation to certain benefits. Where an employee has more than five years' service, he may be able to bring a claim in relation to benefits which place him at a disadvantage, unless the provider of the benefits can show that the provision of benefits in this way fulfils a business need of his undertaking (for example, by encouraging the loyalty or motivation or rewarding the experience, of some or all of his workers) (EEAR 2006, reg 32(2)). For this purpose, benefit does not include any benefit awarded to a worker by virtue of his ceasing to work for the employer (EEAR 2006, reg 32(7)). The ACAS Age Guide makes it clear that an employer must be able to produce evidence to support the justification described above.

(h) An exception which allows enhanced redundancy to be paid on the basis of age as long as the terms of the scheme mirror the terms of the statutory scheme, save that the cap on weekly pay need not apply and the multiplier may be more than one (EEAR 2006, reg 33). Also, those who take voluntary redundancy and have less than two years' service may take the benefit of enhanced redundancy as long as it mirrors the statutory scheme (EEAR 2006, reg 33(2)).

(i) An exception in relation to the provision of life assurance cover applies to retired workers. It will not be age discrimination where an employer arranges for life assurance cover to cease on the early retirement of the employee or when they reach age 65 (EEAR 2006, reg 34). Note, however, this exception does not apply to other benefits and where these cease at a certain age, this will need to be objectively justified, which may be difficult as cost alone will usually be an insufficient justification.

(j) There are exceptions in relation to pension schemes. Generally, it will be unlawful to discriminate against a member or prospective member of a pension scheme (EEAR 2006, reg 11(1)). However, this will not apply to:

    (i) rights accrued or benefits payable in respect of periods of service prior to the coming into force of the EEAR 2006 (EEAR 2006, reg 11(1));

    (ii) certain parts of occupational pension schemes (see EEAR 2006, reg 11(3) and Schedule 2, Part 1).

2.127 If the complainant is an employee, did the employee bring a grievance in relation to their claim? If not, the complainant may not be able to bring a claim in the employment tribunal (EA 2002, s 32 and Employment Act 2002 (Dispute Resolution) Regulations 2003, reg 15; see also para **2.140** below).

2.128 Has the complainant brought the claim in the employment tribunal during employment or within three months of the act complained of? If not, the complainant's claim is likely to be out of time, unless the complainant is an employee and has brought a grievance in relation to the deduction, in which case the time may be extended (see EA 2002, s 32 and Employment Act 2002 (Dispute Resolution) Regulations 2004, reg 15; see also para **2.140** below).

Commentary

2.129 After an extensive period of consultation, the Employment Equality (Age) Regulations 2006 (EEAR 2006) came into force on 1 October 2006. The Regulations implement the last remaining strand of the Equal Treatment Framework Directive (No 2000/78) and in accordance with the other legislation, must be construed in accordance with this legislation. The implementation is currently being challenged in several regards (including the use of a compulsory retirement date) in the *Heyday* case (*R (on the application of the Incorporated Trustees of the National Council of Ageing) v Secretary of State for Trade and Industry* [2007] EWHC 3090), and the decision of the ECJ is awaited although as a result of the decision is *Palanos v Cortfield Servicios SA* [2007] IRLR 989, the challenge to the compulsory retirement date is unlikely to be successful. The Regulations are supported by the ACAS Guide 'Age and the Workplace' (the 'ACAS Age Guidance'). This is currently the only official DTI guidance on EEAR 2006 and will, no doubt, be referred to in the Employment Tribunal (although note EEAR 2006 contains no specific provision for the issuance of Codes of Practice; cf the other discrimination legislation). At the time of writing, there are no relevant EAT cases to provide further guidance. EEAR 2006 introduces the concepts of direct and indirect discrimination, but also a new 'fair' means of dismissal (in relation to which, see para 7.236 below). This chapter will deal only with the claim of age discrimination, defences to that claim, and exceptions.

In order to bring a claim for age discrimination, an employee must be employed   **2.130**
under a contract of service or apprenticeship or a contract personally to do work (EEAR 2006, reg 2; see also paras **2.20** and **2.45** above). There can be no claim for age discrimination unless the employment of the employee is regarded as being at an establishment in Great Britain. This will be the case only where the employee does his work wholly or partly in Great Britain (EEAR 2006, reg 10(1)(a)). If he works outside Great Britain, he may still be covered if the employer has a place of business at an establishment in Great Britain, the work is for the purposes of the business carried on at that establishment, and the employee is ordinarily resident in Great Britain when he is recruited or at any time during the course of employment (EEAR 2006, reg 10(2)).

Employees in almost all professions will be able to bring a claim for age discrimi-   **2.131**
nation. There are no exemptions for the police, prison officers etc, although see the general exemptions at para **2.126** above. However, those doing service in any of the naval, military, or air forces (EEAR 2006, reg 28), unpaid office holders (EEAR 2006, reg 10(8)), and unpaid volunteers (unless they are in an employment relationship or gaining vocational work experience) will not be protected.

EEAR 2006 outlaws both direct and indirect discrimination, discrimination by   **2.132**
victimization, and harassment. However, unlike the other discrimination legislation it is possible to put forward a defence of objective justification for both direct *and* indirect discrimination. There is also a much more significant number of exceptions.

Direct discrimination occurs when on the grounds of a person's age, they receive   **2.133**
less favourable treatment than other persons (EEAR 2006, reg 3(1)(a)). This test is the same as the test in the other discrimination legislation (see para **2.49** above). In relation to comparators, see EEAR 2006, reg 3(2) and para **2.49** above.

Indirect discrimination also mirrors the test in SDA 1975 (see para **2.51** above).   **2.134**
Indirect discrimination will occur when an employer applies a provision, criterion, or practice to an employee which he would apply equally to persons not in the same age group as that employee, but which puts or would put people in the

same age group as that employee at a disadvantage and does actually put that employee at a disadvantage (EEAR 2006, reg 3(1)(b)).

2.135   For these purposes 'age' includes a person's apparent age, so a mistaken belief as to an individual's age which leads to discrimination will be no defence (EEAR 2006, reg 3(3)(b)). For the purposes of the definition of indirect discrimination, 'age group' is defined as being 'a group of persons defined by reference to age, whether by reference to a particular age or a range of ages' (EEAR 2006, reg 3(3)(b)). There is currently no further guidance as to what this will mean in practice.

2.136   There will be a defence to a claim for direct and/or indirect discrimination where there is a genuine occupational requirement. This may apply where possessing a characteristic related to age is a genuine and determining occupational require-ment and it is a proportionate requirement in the particular case (EEAR 2006, reg 8(2)).

2.137   There will also be a defence to both direct and indirect discrimination where the employer's actions can be justified. Justification requires the employer to show that the otherwise discriminatory actions are a proportionate means of achieving a legitimate aim (EEAR 2006, reg 3(1)). The ACAS Age Guide suggests that a justification defence may be made out where it is necessary to fix a maximum age for the recruitment or promotion of employees in order to reflect the training requirements of the post or the need for a reasonable period of employment before retirement. It also points out that an employer will need clear evidence to support his defence, mere assertion will not be enough. This defence will not, however, apply to claims of victimization or harassment.

2.138   The tests for harassment and victimization are the same as the tests in the rest of the discrimination legislation (EEAR 2006, regs 4 and 6 and see paras 2.50 and 2.57). Equally, the position in relation to vicarious liability for acts of employees is the same as that in the SDA 1975 (EEAR 2006, reg 25(3) and para 2.54).

2.139   EEAR 2006 also contains certain other exceptions relating to statutory authority, national security, positive action, retirement, national minimum wage, length of service, enhanced redundancy, and life insurance. See para 2.126 above in rela-tion to this.

2.140   The remedies for age discrimination are broadly the same as sex discrimination (EEAR 2006, reg 38). Equally there are similar provisions relating to burden of proof, questionnaires, grievances, and the time limits for claims (EEAR 2006, regs 37, 41, and 42 and paras 2.61, 2.63, and 2.66 above).

3

RIGHTS ON MATERNITY AND ADOPTION

A. Introduction

On 6 April 2003, as part of the UK Government's 'family-friendly' initiative, **3.01** simplified and enhanced rights relating to maternity came into force. At the same time, a completely new set of rights, relating to adoption, were introduced. The scheme of the new rights relating to adoption follows the existing maternity scheme closely. These rights were improved in 2006 in relation to employees whose expected week of childbirth begins on or after 1 April 2007. So employees on both childbirth and adoption are entitled to receive a minimum period of 52 weeks' leave. Over and above those basic rights, the employee will have other rights subject to the employee having sufficient length of employment. These rights include the right to receive maternity or adoption pay for up to 39 weeks and to return to work (although the specific terms of that right will still depend on the length of the leave taken). This chapter will cover all of these rights as well as the connected rights relating to antenatal care and the suspension from work for maternity-related reasons.

B. Antenatal Care

3.02 Is the employee entitled to be paid at her normal hourly rates to attend antenatal care? Yes, as long as she complies with certain requirements in terms of proof (ERA 1996, ss 55–57 and see para **3.03** below).

3.03 Is there any service or other eligibility requirement? There is no service requirement; any pregnant employee is eligible who has on the advice of a registered medical practitioner, midwife, or nurse made an antenatal appointment (ERA 1996, s 55(1)). An employee for these purposes is an individual as defined in s 230 of ERA 1996, that is an individual who works or worked under a contract of employment (defined as a contract of service or apprenticeship, whether express or implied and (if it is express) whether oral or in writing). Those who benefit from the right to take adoption leave are not covered as these provisions are derived from health and safety concerns which will not apply to those taking adoption leave. Nor is the partner of the pregnant employee who wishes to accompany their partner to appointments.

3.04 Is this the first antenatal appointment for the employee? If so, the employee is entitled to be paid at her normal hourly rate to attend an antenatal appointment, unless the employer reasonably refuses to do so (ERA 1996, s 55(3) and see para **3.07** below).

3.05 Is it the employee's second or subsequent appointment? If so, the employee must supply the employer, if the employer so requests, with a certificate of pregnancy signed by a registered doctor, midwife, or nurse, together with an appropriate appointment card in order to qualify for paid antenatal leave (ERA 1996, S 55(2)).

3.06 How is the employee's pay to be calculated? For those on a weekly or monthly salary, this is not an issue—they will be paid as normal. For those on hourly pay, the calculations are set out in s 56 ERA 1996 by reference to their working hours (or where these differ from week to week, an average of them based on the last 12 weeks).

3.07 Can an employer refuse a request because:

(a) the employee could make arrangements to attend antenatal care outside her normal working hours;

(b) the employee wishes to take off an unreasonably long time to attend the appointment;

(c) the employee has already had numerous appointments?

Although there is no case law on these specific points as they relate to the right to take time off and be paid in relation to antenatal appointments, an employer should be cautious in refusing on this basis given the protection afforded under the SDA 1975 (see *Gilbank v Miles* [2006] IRLR 538).

Has the employer unreasonably refused the employee's request to take time off **3.08** or failed to pay her in accordance with the legislation? If so, the employee may apply to the employment tribunal within three months of the appointment date for an order that the employer pay her what she would have earned during the time taken attending the appointment, including travelling and waiting time (ERA 1996, s 57). The employee may also have a claim under the SDA 1975. Note there is no requirement to bring a grievance under the statutory dispute procedures before a claim is brought under the ERA 1996 (EA 2002, s 32 and Sch 4).

C. Right to be Paid During a Suspension on Maternity Grounds

Is an employer obliged to conduct a risk assessment in relation to the health of a **3.09** pregnant employee as a result of pregnancy? Yes. In addition to the general obligation on employers to conduct health and safety risk assessments, when an employer receives written notification that an employee is pregnant or that she has given birth in the previous six months or is breastfeeding, then the employer should conduct a risk assessment, taking into account advice provided by the employee's GP or midwife (Management of Health & Safety at Work Regulations 1999, SI 1999/3242, regs 16 and 18(1)). However, a failure to do so where there is no actual risk to the mother's health will not be sex discrimination (*Madarassy v Nomura* EAT [2007] ICR 867; see also *New Southern Railway Ltd v Quinn* [2006] IRLR 266).

Does the employer reasonably suspect that it is medically impossible for the **3.10** employee to continue carrying out her duties due to pregnancy, the fact that she has recently given birth, or is breastfeeding and that if she does it will breach legislation? If so, it should check whether continuing to employ the employee will breach a statutory requirement, or a recommendation contained in a relevant provision of a Health and Safety at Work Act 1974 code of practice (ERA 1996, s 66). In practice, this usually means an order of the Secretary of State and the current ones relate to suspension of employees to avoid risk from any processes or working conditions, or physical, biological, or chemical agents (Management of Health & Safety at Work Regulations 1999, SI 1999/3242, reg 16).

If the employee continuing to work is likely to breach the above legislation, what **3.11** should the employer do?

(a) obtain appropriate medical evidence;

(b) if medical evidence confirms the employer's suspicions, the employer should see if there is any way of altering the employee's duties to avoid the risk

(Management of Health & Safety at Work Regulations 1999, SI 1999/3242, reg 16(2) and (3)) or, if not, if there are any suitable alternative posts which the employee can safely fill and offer them to her (ERA 1996, s 67(1));

(c) 'suitable' here means suitable for the employee to do and appropriate for her to do in all the circumstances. If the terms and conditions of the offer are different from her previous terms, they must be no less favourable (ERA 1996, s 67 and see also *British Airways (European Operations at Gatwick) Ltd v Moore* [2000] ICR 678);

(d) if the employee refuses the offer, or if there is no alternative, the employee may be suspended and the employee will be entitled to be paid her remuneration throughout the suspension unless she has been offered suitable alternative employment and unreasonably refused it (ERA 1996, s 67). 'Unreasonably' should be interpreted in a similar way to the way it is interpreted for the purposes of redundancy.

3.12 Has the employer failed to pay the employee? The employee can complain to the employment tribunal for her remuneration during a period of suspension, such complaint to be brought within three months of the day to which the failure to pay relates. An employee can also complain about a failure to offer suitable alternative work; the three-month time limit then runs from the first day of suspension. Note that there is no requirement to bring a grievance under the statutory dispute procedures before a claim is brought (EA 2002, s 32 and Sch 4).

3.13 What if the employer dismisses the employee rather than suspending her? If the employer dismisses the employee rather than suspending her, the employee will probably have a claim for automatically unfair dismissal for a reason connected with pregnancy (ERA 1996, s 99 and Maternity and Parental leave etc Regulations 1999 (MAPLE Regulations 1999), reg 20(3)(c) and (eee) and see para **3.34** below) and may also have a claim under SDA 1975.

D. Maternity Leave

Relevant Terms and Dates

3.14 What are key terms and dates which relate to maternity leave and pay?

(a) **'Expected Week of Childbirth' (EWC).** This is the week beginning with midnight between Saturday and Sunday in which it is expected that the baby will be born. The beginning of this week will therefore be a Sunday and the end of it a Saturday (MAPLE Regulations 1999, reg 2).

(b) **Key Dates.** There are two key dates. These are:
- the end of the 15th week before the EWC. This will be a Saturday.
- the beginning of the 11th week before the EWC. This will be a Sunday.

Who can benefit from statutory maternity leave? Any pregnant employee, irre- **3.15** spective of her length of service or the number of hours she works. An employee for these purposes is as defined in s 230(1) and (2) ERA 1996 and see para **3.03** above.

What is an employee's basic right to maternity leave? An employee is entitled **3.16** to a 52-week period of maternity leave provided she complies with certain notification requirements and provided her EWC is after 7 April 2007 (MAPLE Regulations 1999, reg 7(1)). The first 26 weeks of this period are known for some purposes as ordinary maternity leave. The 26 weeks which follow the period of ordinary maternity leave are known as additional maternity leave. Different rights exist during these two periods.

Ordinary Maternity Leave

What rights is an employee entitled to during ordinary maternity leave? During **3.17** ordinary maternity leave, the employee is entitled to the benefit of the terms and conditions of employment which would be applicable to her if she had been at work, except for contractual remuneration and is bound by any obligations under those terms and conditions (ERA 1996, s 71(4) and MAPLE Regulations 1999, reg 9). Terms and conditions of employment are defined to include matters connected with an employee's employment whether or not they arise under the employee's contract of employment. However, this cannot be looked at in isolation and the employee's rights under the SDA 1975 and the EqPA 1970 must also be taken into account. This means:

(a) the employee is entitled to receive contractual benefits in kind, for example, provision of health insurance, life insurance, disability insurance, company pension scheme, health club membership, staff canteen, and also company car and mobile telephone (unless provided strictly for business use);

(b) the employee should not be entitled to salary or other entitlements as a result of terms and conditions about remuneration such as contractual monetary allowances, for example, a company car allowance or a clothing allowance (ERA 1996, s 71(5)(b), MAPLE Regulations 1999, reg 9(2) and (3)) (see below in relation to pensions);

(c) an employee may be entitled to a payment under a bonus scheme and it should be considered carefully on its terms (*GUS Home Shopping Ltd v Green and McLaughlin* [2001] IRLR 75; *Hoyland v Asda Stores Ltd* [2006] IRLR 468);

(d) pensionable service will continue to accrue, although there will be no entitlement to payments under a pension scheme other, perhaps, than an 'occupational' pension scheme, ie company-run, company contribution pension scheme where contributions may have to continue depending on the terms of the scheme;

(e) contractual and statutory entitlements to holiday will continue to accrue during ordinary maternity leave and the holiday will usually be available to take at the end of the maternity leave;

(f) the employee will be entitled to and subject to any variations of terms and conditions applicable to employees of similar position and status to her, or which are introduced generally to the workplace during her ordinary maternity leave on her return to work. This will include any increase in remuneration during the ordinary maternity leave or the right to receive a pay rise.

However, the effect of SDA 1975 and EqPA 1970 on the above should be considered carefully, particularly in relation to bonuses (see cases referred to above and also *Land Brandenburg v Sass* [2005] IRLR 147 and *Equal Opportunities Commission v Secretary of State for Trade and Industry* [2007] IRLR 327).

3.18 What right to return will the employee have if she returns to work during or at the end of ordinary maternity leave? The employee will be entitled to return to work during or at the end of ordinary maternity leave to the same job, with her seniority, pension rights, and similar rights as they would have been if she had not been absent and on terms and conditions no less favourable than those which would have applied if she had not been absent (subject to any express contractual provision which allows the variation of her terms and conditions and/or her job being made redundant) (MAPLE Regulations 1999, regs 10, 18(1), and 18A(1)). If she is made redundant, the employer must offer her any job which is suitable alternative employment (see para **3.32** below).

Additional Maternity Leave

3.19 What rights is an employee entitled to during additional maternity leave? An employee has more limited rights during additional maternity leave. Whilst the contract of employment continues during additional maternity leave to a limited degree, practically this means that, unless agreed otherwise between the employer and the employee (whether expressly or implicitly) and subject to the points made in relation to the application of SDA 1975 and EqPA 1970 (see para **3.17** above):

(a) there is no obligation for the employer to pay remuneration although the position in relation to bonuses remains unclear (see para **3.17** above);

(b) the obligation to pay contributions into a pension scheme (occupational or otherwise) will depend on the terms of the scheme;

(c) only holiday pursuant to the Working Time Regulations 1998 continues to accrue, such that the employee can take it on their return to work. The rules as to what would happen to that accrued holiday should the employee only return to work in the next holiday year, are currently being considered in the context of long-term sickness absence by the European Court of Justice in *Stringer v HM Revenue and Customs* (Case C-520/06), although at the time of writing it seems likely that an employee's entitlements will be preserved (see para **1.85** above).

Otherwise, only the following limited terms and conditions of employment will survive: **3.20**

(a) the employer's implied obligation of trust and confidence and the reciprocal implied obligation on the employee of good faith;
(b) obligations on the employer in relation to notice of termination; compensation in the event of redundancy; disciplinary or grievance procedures;
(c) obligations on the employee (express or implied) in relation to notice of termination; disclosure of confidential information; acceptance of gifts or other benefits; participation in any other business.

(MAPLE Regulations 1999, reg 17)

What right to return will the employee have if she returns to work during or at **3.21**
the end of additional maternity leave? The employee will be entitled to return to work during or at the end of the additional maternity leave to the job in which she was employed before her absence or, if it is not reasonably practicable for the employer to permit her to return to that job, to another job which is both suitable for her and appropriate for her to do in the circumstances, with her seniority, pension rights, and similar rights preserved as if they were continuous with the period before the additional maternity leave commenced and on terms and conditions no less favourable than those which would have been applicable had she not been absent (MAPLE Regulations 1999, reg 18(2) and 18A(1)). The definition of job in which she was employed before her absence has been considered in the case of *Blundell v St Andrew's Catholic Primary School* [2007] UKEAT 329/06, where the same job for a returning primary school teacher did not include returning to teach the same level of class.

Timing and Notification of Leave

What is the earliest date on which ordinary maternity leave can begin under the **3.22**
statutory scheme? The timing is at the election of the employee, but the earliest is the beginning of the 11th week before the EWC. Any period of additional maternity leave will commence immediately after the ordinary maternity leave (MAPLE Regulations 1999, regs 4(2)(b) and (6)).

Rights on Maternity and Adoption

3

3.23 Can the start of ordinary maternity leave commence automatically for any reason? Other than on suspension for health and safety reasons (see para **3.10** above) the earliest date on which the ordinary maternity leave will commence automatically is on the first day of absence wholly or partly because of the pregnancy which occurs after the beginning of the fourth week before the EWC, even if this is earlier than the date elected by the employee. The exception to this is where the day on which childbirth occurs is before this date, when leave will commence on this date (MAPLE Regulations 1999, regs 6(1)(b) and (2)). The employee is then required to notify the employer as soon as is reasonably practicable of the commencement of the maternity leave period (MAPLE Regulations 1999, regs 4(3) and (4)).

3.24 Has the employee complied with notification requirements? No later than the end of the 15th week before the EWC, the employee must give written notice to her employer of:

(a) her pregnancy;

(b) the EWC; and

(c) the date on which she intends her ordinary maternity leave period to start.

(MAPLE Regulations1999, regs 4(1)(a) and 2)

3.25 If requested to do so by her employer, she must also produce for inspection a certificate from a registered medical practitioner or a registered midwife (Mat B1) stating the EWC (MAPLE Regulations 1999, reg 4(1)(b)).

3.26 How does the employee vary the period or date on which she notified the commencement of her maternity leave, other than where the automatic commencement provisions apply (see para **3.23** above)? An employee must notify her employer of the variation at least 28 days before the date varied or 28 days before the new date, whichever is the earliest, or, if that is not reasonably practicable, as soon as is reasonably practicable (MAPLE Regulations 1999, reg 4(1A)).

3.27 Does the employer need to notify the employee of anything? An employer who receives a notification from an employee must, within 28 days of receipt of that notification, inform the employee of the date on which her additional maternity leave will end (MAPLE Regulations 1999, reg 7(6) and (7)).

3.28 Can an employee come straight back to work after the birth? An employee is prohibited by law from returning to work until two weeks after the birth and an employer who allows her to do so will be subject to a fine. Therefore, the maternity leave period will be extended automatically if the employee has not given birth by the end of the maternity leave period (ERA 1996, s 72; MAPLE Regulations 1999, reg 8).

Does the employee have to tell the employer she is returning to work after mater- **3.29** nity leave? There is no requirement on the employee to notify an employer of whether she is going to return at the end of maternity leave, whether ordinary or additional, although this does not prevent the employer from asking her to give some indication.

What if the employee wishes to return early, ie before the end of the maximum **3.30** period of leave? If the employee wishes to return before the end of her maternity leave period, she must notify the employer eight weeks before her proposed return date. If she does not, as long as the employer has notified the employee of her additional maternity leave period in accordance with MAPLE Regulations 1999, reg 7(6) and (7), the employer can postpone her return date by eight weeks (as long as that does not take her return date outside the maximum ordinary or additional maternity leave period) and the employer is under no obligation to pay her in the intervening period (MAPLE Regulations 1999, reg 11).

What happens if the employee is ill when she is due to return from maternity **3.31.** leave? There is no provision for extending the maternity leave period due to the illness of the employee. However, since the assumption must be that the employee's contract of employment continues in existence during the maternity leave period, the employee will be entitled to sick absence and contractual sick pay (although not always statutory sick pay) in accordance with her contract. See also *Halfpenny v IGE Medical Systems Ltd* [2001] ICR 73 in relation to the court's likely reaction to an employee who fails to return on the date notified due to ill health (albeit this case relates to the position under the pre-1999 legislation which did not provide for the continuation of the contract of employment during leave).

Redundancy

What happens to an employee who is made redundant whilst on maternity leave? **3.32** If the job of an employee who is on ordinary or additional maternity leave becomes redundant, she has the right to be offered a suitable alternative vacancy with her employer or a company associated with her employer before that employment is terminated, so that the new job commences on the termination of the old job. This is compared to the normal situation where it is up to the employer whether to offer such a vacancy and thus cancel any liability for a redundancy payment (MAPLE Regulations 1999, reg 10(2) and (3)). Note that the employer will under reg 10(1) have to show that it is not practicable by reason of redundancy for it to continue to employ her. Clearly, if the reason she is selected for redundancy is her pregnancy, she will have claims of unfair dismissal (MAPLE Regulations 1999, reg 20(2)) and sex discrimination (see para **3.34** below).

3.33 What is a 'suitable alternative vacancy'? A vacancy will be deemed a suitable alternative if it is suitable in relation to the employee, appropriate for her to do in the circumstances, and the terms and conditions are not substantially less favourable to her than if she had continued to be employed under the previous contract (MAPLE Regulations 1999, reg 10(3)).

Dismissal and Detriment

3.34 Can an employer dismiss an employee because she is pregnant? Generally, it will be automatically unfair to dismiss the employee because she is pregnant or for certain reasons connected with her pregnancy and the employee will have the right to claim unfair dismissal irrespective of her length of service (ERA 1996, ss 99 and 108(3)(b) and MAPLE Regulations 1999, reg 20; see also para **7.112** below) as well as a claim under SDA 1975, s 3A.

3.35 Can an employer treat an employee to her detriment because she is pregnant? Generally, if an employee is treated to her detriment because she is pregnant or for certain reasons connected with her pregnancy, then the employee will have the right to claim in respect of that detriment, irrespective of her length of service (ERA 1996, s 47C; MAPLE Regulations 1999, reg 19; SDA 1975, s 3A). However, she will not have a claim in respect of the failure to pay her remuneration or comply with her terms and conditions during additional maternity leave as long as the employer is acting in accordance with the statutory scheme (SDA 1975, s 6A and see para **3.19** above).

3.36 What does pregnancy or a reason connected with pregnancy mean?

(a) pregnancy itself and/or the fact that the employee has given birth to a child;

(b) the fact that she was suspended for health and safety reasons;

(c) the fact that she has gone on maternity leave or availed herself of any of the benefits of maternity leave;

(d) the fact that she failed to return after a period of leave, where her employer did not give her the notification described in para **3.27** above and she reasonably believed that the period had not ended or her employer gave her less than 28 days' notice of the end of the leave and it was not reasonably practicable for her to return.

(MAPLE Regulations 1999, regs 19 and 20)

The definition would also cover miscarriages and pregnancy-related illnesses (although not those undergoing IVF treatment). Employees would obviously enjoy other rights under SDA 1975 as well (see Chapter 2).

3.37 Does an employee have any additional rights in relation to dismissal? The employee who is dismissed at any time while she is pregnant or who is dismissed at the end of her maternity leave period is entitled to be given written reasons for her dismissal on request, irrespective of her length of service (ERA 1996, s 92(4)).

3.38 What remedies are available to the employee? Remedies for unfair dismissal and sex discrimination are dealt with in Chapters 2, 7 and 12. The remedy for a claim in respect of detriment as described in para **3.35** above should be brought in the employment tribunal before the end of the period of three months beginning with the date of the detriment (ERA 1996, s 48). A claim in respect of a failure to provide a written statement should be brought within three months of the date of dismissal (ERA 1996, s 93). The employee will be required to raise a grievance in respect of such a claim other than where it relates to a failure to provide written reasons (EA 2002, s 32 and Sch 4 and see also paras **7.81–7.83**).

'Keeping in Touch' Days

3.39 Can the employee work at all during the maternity leave period? Save for the compulsory leave period of two weeks (see para **3.28** above) the employee is allowed with the employer's consent (but cannot be required) to carry out up to 10 days' work for her employer during the statutory maternity leave period without bringing her maternity leave period to an end (MAPLE Regulations 1999, reg 12A(1)(5)(6)). Work can cover training and keeping in touch and any time worked during a day shall constitute a whole working day (MAPLE Regulations 1999, reg 12A(2)(3)). In addition, reasonable contact from time to time, for example, to discuss the employee's return to work, shall not bring the leave period to an end (MAPLE Regulations 1999, reg 12A(4)).

3.40 Will the employee be paid for this work? See para **3.66** below.

E. Adoption Leave

Relevant Terms for Adoption Leave and Pay

3.41 What are key terms and dates which relate to adoption leave and pay?

(a) Is the person an adopter? A person will only be an adopter if he or she has been matched with the child for adoption by an adoption agency. If two people are adopting jointly, one of them must elect to be the adopter for these purposes (Paternity and Adoption Leave Regulations 2002 (PAL Regulations 2002), reg 2(1)).

(b) Has a person been 'matched' with a child? This occurs when an adoption agency decides that a person would be a suitable adoptive parent for the child, either individually or jointly. Matching takes place on the date that person receives notification of the agency's decision (PAL Regulations 2002, reg 2(4)).

(c) What is the date of placement? This is the date the child takes up permanent residence with the adopter.

Basic Right and Eligibility

3.42 What is an employee's basic right to adoption leave? An employee who satisfies certain eligibility requirements is entitled to:

(a) a 26-week ordinary adoption leave period (PAL Regulations 2002, reg 18(1)); and

(b) a period of additional adoption leave of a further 26 weeks (PAL Regulations 2002, reg 20(2)).

An employee for these purposes is as defined in s 230(1) and (2) ERA 1996 and see para **3.03** above.

3.43 What are the eligibility requirements which must be satisfied?

(a) the employee must have been 'matched' with a child for adoption and, if the adoption is joint, elected to be the adopter;

(b) the employee must have been continuously employed for a period of not less than 26 weeks, ending with the week in which the employee was notified of having been matched with the child;

(c) the employee must have notified the agency of agreement to the placement of the child and the date of placement;

(d) the employee must have complied with the notice requirements set out in PAL Regulations 2002, reg 17 (see para **3.46** below).

(PAL Regulations 2002, reg 15)

Additionally, the employee must not be taking paternity leave in relation to the adoption (PAL Regulations 2002, reg 8(2) and 15(2)).

Ordinary Adoption Leave and Additional Adoption Leave

3.44 What rights will an employee have during adoption leave? The same rights which apply during ordinary maternity leave and additional maternity leave will apply (see paras **3.17** and **3.19** above respectively).

Timing and Notification of Leave

3.45 What is the earliest date on which ordinary adoption leave can begin under the statutory scheme?

(a) the date on which the child is placed with the adopter for adoption; or

(b) a date which is no more than 14 days before that date of placement.

(PAL Regulations 2002, reg 16)

3.46 Has the employee complied with the notification requirements? An employee must within seven days of being notified of matching, give notice of his/her intention to take ordinary adoption leave in respect of a child, specifying:

(a) the date on which the child is expected to be placed with the employee for adoption;

(b) the date on which the employee has chosen that the period of leave should begin.

(PAL Regulations 2002, reg 16(1))

3.47 Does the employee have to provide any further evidence? If requested to do so by the employer, the employee must also provide the employer with evidence in the form of a document issued by the adoption agency that matched the employee with the child, of the following details:

(a) the name and address of the agency;

(b) the date on which the employee was notified that he/she had been matched with a child;

(c) the date on which the agency expects to place the child with the employee.

(PAL Regulations 2002, reg 17(3))

3.48 How does an employee vary the period or date on which the employee wishes the ordinary adoption leave to commence? The date of commencement of the leave may be varied by 28 days' notice (to be given in writing if the employer so requests) at least 28 days before or, if it is not reasonably practicable, as soon as is reasonably practicable (PAL Regulations 2002, reg 17(4) to (6)).

3.49 Does the employer have to notify the employee of anything? An employer who receives a notification from an employee must, within 28 days of receipt of that notification, inform the employee of the date on which either the ordinary adoption leave or, if he/she is entitled to both ordinary and additional adoption leave, the additional adoption leave, will end (PAL Regulations 2002, reg 17(7)). Failure to do so may affect the employer's rights at the end of the adoption leave period.

Minimum Duration of Adoption Leave

3.50 Does the employee need to tell the employer she is returning to work after adoption leave? There is no requirement on the employee to notify an employer of whether he/she is going to return at the end of adoption leave (as opposed to during the period of leave) whether ordinary or additional, although this does not prevent the employer from asking the employee to give some indication.

3.51 What if the employee wishes to return early? If the employee wishes to return before the end of the adoption leave period, the employee must notify the employer eight weeks before the proposed return date. If the employee does not, the employer can postpone the return date by eight weeks (as long as that does not take the return date outside the maximum ordinary or additional adoption leave period) and the employer is under no obligation to pay the employee in the intervening period (PAL Regulations 2002, reg 25).

3.52 What if the adoption is disrupted by death or for some other reason? Different rules apply where the placement is disrupted, for example, by reason of death or where the placement ends for another reason. In that case the leave will usually end eight weeks later (PAL Regulations 2002, reg 22).

Right to Return After Ordinary Adoption Leave and Additional Adoption Leave

3.53 The rights are identical to those in relation to return after ordinary maternity leave and additional maternity leave (see PAL Regulations 2002, reg 27 and paras **3.18** and **3.21** above).

3.54 What happens to an employee who is made redundant whilst on adoption leave? The rights are identical to those where an employee is made redundant on maternity leave (see PAL Regulations 2002, reg 23 and para **3.32** above).

Dismissal and Detriment

3.55 Can an employer dismiss an employee because the employee takes adoption leave? Generally, it will be automatically unfair to dismiss the employee because the employee takes adoption leave or for certain reasons connected with the adoption leave and the employee will have the right to claim unfair dismissal, irrespective of the employee's length of service (ERA 1996, s 99; PAL Regulations 2002, reg 29).

3.56 Can an employer treat an employee to the employee's detriment because the employee takes adoption leave? Generally, if an employee is treated to their detriment because the employee takes adoption leave or for certain reasons connected with the adoption leave, then the employee will have the right to claim in respect of that detriment, irrespective of the length of service of the employee (ERA 1996, s 47C; PAL Regulations 2002, reg 28).

3.57 What does adoption or a reason connected with adoption leave mean?

(a) the employee took or sought to take adoption leave;

(b) the employer believed the employee was likely to take adoption leave;

(c) the employee undertook, considered undertaking, or refused to undertake work in accordance with the provisions relating to 'keeping in touch days';

(d) the employee failed to return after a period of leave, where the employer did not give the employee the notification described in para **3.49** above and the employee reasonably believed that the period had not ended or the employer gave the employee less than 28 days' notice of the end of the leave and it was not reasonably practicable for the employee to return.

(PAL Regulations 2002, reg 29(3))

3.58 The employee who is dismissed at any time while the employee is on adoption leave or who is dismissed at the end of the adoption leave period is entitled to be given written reasons for the dismissal on request, irrespective of the employee's length of service (ERA 1996, s 92(4A)).

3.59 What remedies are available to the employee? Remedies for unfair dismissal are dealt with in Chapter 7. The remedy for a claim in respect of detriment as described in para **3.56** above should be brought in the employment tribunal before the end of the period of three months beginning with the date of the detriment (ERA 1996, s 48). A claim in respect of a failure to provide a written statement should be brought within three months of the date of dismissal (ERA 1996, s 93). The employee will be required to raise a grievance in respect of such a claim other than where it relates to a failure to provide written reasons (EA 2002, s 32 and Sch 4 and see also paras **7.81–7.83**).

'Keeping in Touch' Days

3.60 Can the employee work at all during the adoption leave period? The employee is allowed with the employer's consent (but cannot be required) to carry out up to 10 days' work for her employer during the statutory adoption leave period without bringing her adoption leave period to an end (PAL Regulations 2002, reg 21A(1)(5)(6)). Work can cover training and keeping in touch and any time worked during a day shall constitute a whole working day (PAL Regulations 2002, reg 21A(2)(3)). In addition, reasonable contact from time to time for example to discuss the employee's return to work shall not bring the leave period to an end (PAL Regulations 2002, reg 21A(4)).

F. Statutory Maternity and Adoption Pay

3.61 What must an individual show to qualify for maternity or adoption leave pay? An employee who is pregnant and who has been employed for *less* than 26 weeks immediately before the 14th week before the EWC is entitled to receive a maternity allowance but not SMP. The maternity allowance is paid by the DSS. An employee who is an adopter who has been employed for *less* than 26 weeks immediately before the notification of matching is not entitled to any specific benefit and should refer to their adoption agency or local authority. Any other employee is generally entitled to SMP or SAP as appropriate. Employee for these purposes means a person gainfully employed under a contract of service or an office (SSCBA 1992, s 171(1) and s 171ZS(2)).

3.62 What conditions must be met before SMP is payable?

(a) either the employee must have been employed for at least 26 weeks immediately before the 14th week before her EWC whether or not she has actually been working throughout this period; or

(b) the employee *would* have been employed for at least 26 weeks immediately before the 14th week before her EWC had she not been suspended for maternity-related grounds (see para **3.10**); and

(c) the employee must still be pregnant at the 11th week before the EWC or have had the baby by that time; and

(d) the employee must, when she worked normally, have had average weekly earnings not less than the National Insurance contributions lower earnings limit.

(SSCBA 1992, s 164(1))

3.63 What conditions must be met before SAP is payable? The employee:

(a) is a person with whom a child is, or is expected to be, placed for adoption under the law of any part of the United Kingdom; and

(b) must have worked continuously for the same employer for at least 26 weeks before the week in which they are notified of having been matched with a child; and

(c) have ceased to perform any work for the employer; and

(d) must, when she worked normally, have had average weekly earnings, not less than the National Insurance contributions lower earnings limit; and

(e) elected to receive statutory adoption pay (rather than statutory paternity pay).

(SSCBA 1992, s 171ZL)

3.64 What notice must the employee give the employer of the start of her maternity or adoption pay? The employee must give her employer 28 days' notice of the date on which she expects liability to pay her to begin. This notice must be given in writing if the employer so requests. If it is not reasonably practicable for 28 days' notice to be given (for example, where the baby is born before the employee goes on maternity leave) the employee must give the employer notification as soon as it is reasonably practicable for her to do so (SSCBA 1992, s 164(4) or s 171ZL(6)).

3.65 The employee must provide the employer with evidence of the pregnancy and EWC or adoption and the employer must not pay SMP/SAP until the employee does. Appropriate evidence includes a certificate from a doctor or midwife or adoption agency (Statutory Maternity Pay (General) Regulations 1986, reg 22 and Statutory Paternity Pay and Adoption Pay Regulations 2002, reg 24).

3.66 The employee should not be working during any week when SMP or SAP is being paid other than as prescribed (SSCBA 1992, s 165(4) and s 171ZN(3)). Keeping in touch days (see para **3.39** above) will not disentitle the employee to the receipt of SMP or SAP.

Period of SMP and SAP

3.67 How long will the employee be paid and when will it start?

(a) The maximum statutory period during which SMP or SAP is payable is 39 weeks.

(b) SMP or SAP will start when ordinary maternity or adoption leave starts.

3.68 What happens if the employee returns to work before the end of her maximum permitted SMP or SAP period? SMP or SAP will cease to be payable on her return to work.

3.69 What happens if an employee does not return to work at the end of the leave period—does the employee have to repay? No, the employee does not have to repay.

(SSCBA 1992, ss 165 and 171ZN)

Amount of SMP and SAP

3.70 What are the rates of SMP?

(a) For the first six weeks of the maternity pay period, 90 per cent of her normal weekly earnings (earnings for these purposes meaning any payment from which National Insurance contributions are deducted). If there is a pay rise during this period, this must be taken into account in calculating SMP (see also paras **3.17** and **3.19** above).

(b) For any subsequent weeks, the lower of 90 per cent of her normal weekly earnings and a rate set by the Government, which was set in April 2008 at £117.18 per week.

3.71 What are the rates of SAP? The lower of the employee's normal weekly earnings and a rate set by the Government, which was set in April 2008 at £117.18 per week.

3.72 SMP or SAP is treated as if it were the normal income of an employee. Tax and National Insurance contributions should be deducted from it and the employer must account to HM Revenue & Customs for employer's and employee's National Insurance contributions.

General Considerations

3.73 Has the employer failed to pay SMP or SAP? If so, the employee may request written reasons for this refusal and, if not satisfied, may refer the issue to the Commissioners for HM Revenue & Customs. Failure to pay SMP or SAP which is due is a criminal offence (Finance Act 2001, Sch 6, Part 1).

3.74 The employer must keep records of SMP and SAP payments for three years (Statutory Maternity Pay (General) Regulations 1986, reg 26, Statutory Paternity Pay & Adoption Pay (Admin) Regulations 2002, reg 9).

3.75 Who pays for SMP and SAP? The Government. Employers may recover all or part of any SMP and SAP payments made by deducting the amount of the payments (including the employer's National Insurance contributions in respect of the SMP and SAP) from National Insurance contributions they make on behalf of their employees in general. Small employers can recover 100 per cent of SMPs and SAPs, plus 5 per cent. All other employers will only be able to recover 92 per cent of payments made (SSCBA 1992, s 167 and EA 2002, s 7; SSCBA 1992, s 171ZM).

G. Contracting Out

3.76 Can an employer contract out of its obligations in relation to maternity or adoption? No and an employee can take advantage of whichever provisions (contractual or statutory) are the most beneficial to the employee (MAPLE Regulations 1999, reg 21; PAL Regulations 2002, reg 30; SSCBA 1992, Sch 13, para 3 and s 171Z0).

4

FAMILY FRIENDLY RIGHTS

A. Introduction

In addition to the rights on maternity and adoption described in the previous **4.01** chapter, there are a whole range of additional rights available to those who are parents or who take parental responsibility for a child. These rights derive from a mixture of European Directives (Parental Leave; Time off for Dependants; Part-Time Workers' Rights) and the Government's 'family friendly' initiative (Paternity Leave; the right to request flexible working which now extends to those responsible for other family members as well as children).

B. Right to Paternity Leave and Pay

What is the basic right? An employee who satisfies certain eligibility requirements **4.02** is entitled to take two weeks' leave around the date of their child's birth or adoption for the purposes of caring for the child or supporting the child's mother. The leave can be two consecutive weeks, or one week only. An employee has no statutory right to take two non-consecutive single weeks of leave (ERA 1996, ss 80A and 80B and the PAL Regulations 2002, reg 4 et seq).

What are the eligibility requirements which must be satisfied? **4.03**

(a) The employee must have been employed for 26 weeks ending with the week immediately preceding the 14th week before the EWC or, where the child is being adopted, 26 weeks ending with the week in which the adopter is notified that they have been matched with the child for the purposes of adoption. Employed means an individual who has entered into or works or worked under a contract of service or apprenticeship, whether express or implied, and (if it is express) whether oral or in writing (PAL Regulations 2002, reg 2).

(b) The employee must expect to have responsibility for the upbringing of the child.

(c) The employee must be the biological father of the child or be married to, the civil partner, or the partner of the child's mother or, in the case of adoption, be either married to, the civil partner, or the partner of the child's adopter.

(PAL Regulations 2002, regs 4(2) and 8(2))

4.04 What rights does an employee have during paternity leave? During paternity leave, an employee is entitled to the benefit of all of the terms and conditions of employment (other than remuneration) which would have applied if the employee had not been absent and bound by any obligations arising under those terms and conditions (PAL Regulations 2002, reg 12).

4.05 What does this mean practically? As the employee will only be away for a maximum period of two weeks, in most cases the employer will treat the leave like holiday and all benefits will continue. See paras **4.10** and **4.11** below, however, for issues which may arise should an employer not take this approach.

4.06 On what date can paternity leave commence?

(a) Leave must commence on or after the birth.

(b) Leave must be taken within 56 days of the birth.

(c) Otherwise the employee can choose one of the following options for the commencement date:
- the date of the birth or placement of the child on adoption;
- a certain number of days after the birth or placement;
- a pre-determined date which must fall after the EWC or the date placement is expected to happen.

(PAL Regulations 2002, regs 5 and 9)

4.07 Has the employee complied with the notification requirements? No later than the 15th week before the EWC (or the notification of matching in the case of adoption) the employee must give notice (in writing if requested) to the employer of:

(a) the EWC (or the date of matching and the expected date of placement of the child on adoption);

(b)   the length of the leave;

(c)   the date it will commence.

(PAL Regulations 2002, regs 6 and 10)

Are there any other evidential requirements? If requested, and/or if the employee **4.08** wishes to claim Statutory Paternity Pay, the employee must also give the employer a declaration signed by the employee to the effect that the leave is for the purpose of caring for a child or supporting the child's mother and that the employee satisfies the eligibility requirements set out in para **4.03** above. The employee must also give the employer further notice (in writing, if requested) as soon as is reasonably practicable after the child's birth, of the date on which the child was born (PAL Regulations 2002, regs 6 and 10).

How does the employee vary the date of commencement of paternity leave? An **4.09** employee must notify the employer of the variation at least 28 days before the new date, whichever is the earliest, or, if that is not reasonably practicable, as soon as is reasonably practicable (PAL Regulations 2002, regs 6 and 10).

What rights does an employee have who returns after paternity leave? The right **4.10** to return after paternity leave is the right to return to the job in which the employee was employed before the absence as long as the paternity leave was an isolated period of leave and was not combined with a period of additional maternity or adoption leave or parental leave of more than four weeks (PAL Regulations 2002, reg 13(1)).

Otherwise the employee is entitled to return to the job in which the employee was **4.11** employed before the absence, or, if that is not reasonably practicable, to another job which is both suitable for the employee and appropriate (PAL Regulations 2002, reg 13(2)).

The employee must also return with seniority, pension rights, and similar rights **4.12** as they would have been if the employee had not been absent in the case of the situation in para **4.10** above and continuous with the previous rights in the case of para **4.11** above, and in both cases on terms and conditions not less favourable than those which would have applied if the employee had not been absent (PAL Regulations 2002, regs 14(1)).

Can an employer dismiss an employee because the employee is taking paternity **4.13** leave? Generally it will be automatically unfair to dismiss an employee because the employee took or sought to take paternity leave (ERA 1996, s 99; PAL Regulations 2002, reg 29).

Can an employer treat an employee to the employee's detriment because the **4.14** employee takes paternity leave? Generally, if the employee is treated to the employee's detriment because the employee took or sought to take paternity leave, the employee will have a claim irrespective of their length of service (ERA 1996, s 47C; PAL Regulations 2002, reg 28).

4.15 What claims can the employee bring? Claims in relation to unfair dismissal and the remedies available are dealt with in Chapter 7. Claims in relation to detriment and refusal must be brought within three months of the employer's act. The employee will be required to raise a grievance in respect of such a claim (EA 2002, s 32 and Sch 4 and see also paras **7.81–7.83**). Remedies available are a declaration and compensation.

4.16 What are the rates of paternity pay? The lower of 90 per cent of the employee's normal weekly earnings and a rate set by the Government, which was set in April 2008 at £117.18 per week.

4.17 Who pays for Statutory Paternity Pay? The Government. Employers may recover all or part of any Statutory Paternity Pay by deducting the amount of the payments from National Insurance contributions they make on behalf of their employees in general. Small employers can recover 100 per cent of Statutory Paternity Pay plus 5 per cent. All other employers will only be able to recover 92 per cent of payments made.

(SSCBA 1992, ss 171ZC–171ZE and the Statutory Paternity Pay and Statutory Adoption Pay (General) Regulations 2002).

Commentary

4.18 The Government is planning to extend the right to paternity leave but only where the mother chooses to return from maternity leave early. In that case the other carer for the child could take up to six months' additional paternity leave. The leave is likely to be unpaid unless the mother returns to work prior to the exhaustation of the statutory maternity/adoption pay period, currently 39 weeks. At the time of writing, consultation as to these proposals is ongoing. The Government has stated that they will not be implemented before April 2010.

C. Right to Parental Leave

4.19 What is the basic right? An employee who satisfies certain eligibility requirements is entitled to 13 weeks (18 weeks where the child is disabled) of unpaid leave for the purposes of caring for a child. Unless otherwise agreed, the leave must be taken in one week blocks and no more than four weeks can be taken in any one year. Different rules apply to the parents of disabled children (ERA 1996, ss 76–80; MAPLE Regulations 1999).

4.20 What are the eligibility requirements which must be satisfied by the employee?

(a) Continuous employment for a period of not less than a year.
(b) Parental responsibility for the child.

(MAPLE Regulations 1999, reg 13)

Employment for these purposes means an individual who has entered into or works or worked under a contract of service or apprenticeship, whether express or implied, and (if it is express) whether oral or in writing (MAPLE Regulations 1999, reg 2).

4.21 When must the leave be taken? The parental leave must be taken prior to the child's fifth birthday, or the fifth anniversary of placement where the child is adopted or the date of their 18th birthday where the child is disabled (whichever is earlier) (MAPLE Regulations 1999, reg 15).

4.22 Is it possible for an employer to agree its own parental leave policy with the employee? Yes it is, either in a collective agreement, workforce agreement, or individually with the employee (MAPLE Regulations 1999, reg 16). However, the employee is still entitled to take advantage of whichever of the statutory and contractual rights is more favourable (MAPLE Regulations 1999, reg 21(2)).

4.23 What happens if no agreement is reached? The statutory fallback provisions set out in Schedule 2 to MAPLE Regulations 1999 which are described in the remainder of this section will apply (MAPLE Regulations 1999, reg 16).

4.24 What rights is an employee entitled to during parental leave? An employee's rights during parental leave are limited to those which apply during additional maternity leave (see para **3.19** above and MAPLE Regulatons 1999, reg 17).

4.25 What period of leave is an employee entitled to take? Thirteen weeks' leave in respect of any individual child (or 18 weeks in respect of a child who is entitled to a disability allowance) (MAPLE Regulations 1999, reg 14 (1) and (1A)).

4.26 How much leave can be taken at once? An employee taking parental leave can take four weeks in any year, to be taken in week long blocks (*Rodway v New Southern Railways Ltd* [2005] ICR 1162). The year for parental leave will run from the date the employee became entitled to take the leave, although it is possible to agree a different year, for example, the holiday year. Those taking parental leave to care for a disabled child may take the leave in blocks of less than one week (MAPLE Regulations 1999, Sch 2, paras 7–9).

4.27 Has the employee complied with the notification requirements? At the employer's request, the employee must produce the following evidence for inspection by the employer, such evidence as may be reasonably required of:

(a) the employee's responsibility or expected responsibility for the child;
(b) the child's date of birth or placement;

   (c) if relevant, evidence of the child's disability.

(MAPLE Regulations 1999, Sch 2, para 2)

4.28 Are there any other requirements?

   (a) If the notice relates to parental leave to be taken on the birth or placement of a child, the notice must also include the expected week of childbirth or placement.

   (b) The employee must give notice of the commencement of leave at least 21 days before the date on which the employee wishes the leave to commence.

(MAPLE Regulations 1999, Sch 2, paras 3–5)

4.29 Can the employer postpone a period of leave? Generally an employer can postpone the leave if:

   (a) the leave is *not* being taken on birth or placement; if it is, the employer cannot postpone;

   (b) the employer considers that the operation of his business would be unduly disrupted if the employee took the leave at the time notified;

   (c) the employer agrees to permit a later period of leave of the same duration and to take place no more than six months later; and

   (d) the employer gives the employee notice of the postponement, setting out the reasons for it and specifying the new date for the leave, within seven days of the date the leave was previously due to commence.

(MAPLE Regulations 1999, Sch 2, para 6)

4.30 What rights does an employee have who returns after parental leave? The right to return after a period of parental leave is the right to return to the job in which the employee was employed before the absence or, if it is not reasonably practicable for the employer to permit the employee to return to that job, to another job which is both suitable for the employee and appropriate for the employee to do in the circumstances (MAPLE Regulations 1999, reg 18(2)). This right is a right to return with the seniority, pension rights, and similar rights as they would have been if she had not been absent and on terms and conditions not less favourable than those which would have applied if the employee had not been absent (MAPLE Regulations, reg 18A(1)) unless the parental leave has been combined with a period of additional maternity or adoption leave when the lesser rights set out at para **3.19** will apply.

4.31 Can an employer dismiss or treat an employee detrimentally because the employee took or sought to take parental leave? Generally, if the employer does an employee will have a claim, irrespective of the length of service of the employee (ERA 1996, ss 47C and 99; MAPLE Regulations 1999, regs 19 and 20). Claims in relation to unfair dismissal and the remedies available are dealt with in Chapter 7. Claims in relation to detriment must be brought within three months of the employer's act (ERA 1996, s 48). The employee will be required to raise a grievance in respect of such a claim (EA 2002, s 32 and Sch 4 and see also paras **7.81–7.83**). Remedies available are a declaration and compensation.

Can an employee claim because the employer was unreasonable in postponing a **4.32** period of leave or prevented or attempted to prevent the employee from taking the leave? Generally, an employee will be able to claim for a declaration and compensation irrespective of the length of service of the employee (ERA 1996, s 80). Any claim must usually be brought within three months of the matter complained of (ERA 1996, s 80(2)) but it is not necessary to bring a grievance.

There is no right to remuneration during parental leave. See para **4.30** above for **4.33** other rights during parental leave.

D. Right to Time Off for Dependants

What is the basic right to time off for dependants? An employee who satisfies **4.34** certain eligibility requirements is entitled to a reasonable time off work to deal with certain unexpected or sudden emergencies and to make necessary longer term arrangements (ERA 1996, s 57A).

What are the eligibility requirements which must be satisfied? **4.35**

(a) There is no qualifying period of employment but the individual must be an employee. Employee for these purposes means an individual who has entered into or works or worked under a contract of service or apprenticeship, whether express or implied, and (if it is express) whether oral or in writing (ERA 1996, s 230).
(b) The emergency must come within the statutory definition (see When can the right be exercised? at para **4.37** below).
(c) If the time off relates to a 'dependent' they must also come within the statutory definition.

Who is a dependent? A dependent is: **4.36**

(a) the husband, wife, civil partner, child, or parent of the employee; or
(b) someone who lives in the same household as the employee, for example, an elderly relative (but not a tenant, boarder, or lodger); or
(c) someone who relies on the employee for assistance, even if they do not live with the employee, were they to fall ill, be injured or assaulted, or to make arrangements for the provision of care in the event of illness or injury.

(ERA 1996, s 57A (3) and (4))

4.37 When can the right be exercised? It can be exercised:

(a) if a dependent falls ill, or has been injured or assaulted;

(b) when a dependent is having a baby;

(c) to make longer term arrangements for a dependent who is ill or injured;

(d) to deal with the death of a dependent, for example, to make funeral and other arrangements (but it would not cover sick leave as a result of bereavement) (*Forster v Cartright Black Solicitors* IDS Brief 765, September 2004);

(e) to deal with an unexpected disruption or breakdown of care arrangements for a dependent;

(f) to deal with an unexpected incident involving the employee's child during school hours.

(ERA 1996, s 57A(1))

4.38 What are the employee's obligations? An employee's obligations are as follows:

(a) to tell the employer the reason for the absence as soon as reasonably practicable;

(b) to tell the employer how long the employee expects to be absent (ERA 1996, s 57(2));

(c) only to take a reasonable period of leave (see para **4.39** below).

4.39 What is a reasonable period of leave? In considering this, an employer should take into account the individual circumstances of the employee seeking the leave, but in the vast majority of cases it will be no more than a few hours or, at the most, one or possibly two days. An employer can take into account previous absences of the employee. The disruption to the employer's business is not relevant when considering this (*Miss J Qua v John Ford Morrison, Solicitors* [2003] ICR 482; see also *MacCulloch & Wallis Limited v Moore* IDS Brief 740, September 2003).

4.40 An employer's only obligation is to allow the employee to take the leave. In particular, there is no obligation to pay the employee unless the contract of employment provides for it.

4.41 Can an employer dismiss or treat detrimentally an employee because an employee took or sought to take time off for dependants? Generally an employee will have a claim, irrespective of the length of service of the employee (ERA 1996, ss 47C and 99). Claims in relation to unfair dismissal and the remedies available are dealt with in Chapter 7. Claims in relation to detriment and refusal must be brought within three months of the employer's act. The employee will be required to raise a grievance in respect of such a claim (EA 2002, s 32 and Sch 4 and see also paras **7.81**–**7.83**). Remedies available are a declaration and compensation.

Can an employee claim because the employer unreasonably refused to permit **4.42**
him to take the time off for dependants? Generally, an employee will be able
to claim for a declaration and compensation irrespective of the length of service
of the employee (ERA 1996, s 57B). Any such claim must be brought within
three months of the refusal, but no grievance is necessary before the claim is
brought.

E. Right to Request Flexible Working

What is the basic right? An employee who satisfies certain eligibility requirements **4.43**
is entitled to request a contractual variation to the hours the employee is required
to work, the length of time he is required to work or, as between the home and
place of business, the place where he is required to work. If the request is in the
correct form, an employer must respond to it in a prescribed manner either agreeing the request or refusing it. In the latter case, a refusal can only be on certain
statutory grounds and an employee may appeal. If an employer fails to comply
with the processes, fails to put forward a statutory ground, or relies on incorrect
facts, the employee can bring a claim in the employment tribunal for an order
that the employer reconsider the request or for compensation (ERA 1996,
ss 80F to 80I; various regulations).

What are the eligibility requirements which must be satisfied by the employee? **4.44**
The employee must:

(a) on the date of the application, have 26 weeks' continuous employment;
(b) either:
  • be the mother, father, adopter, guardian, special guardian, or foster parent
    of the child, or married to, the civil partner, or the partner of the person
    within the above category and living with the child;
  • have or expect to have responsibility for the upbringing of the child;
  • make the application before the child in respect of whom the application
    is made reaches the age of 6 (or, if disabled, 18).

(Flexible Working (Eligibility, Complaints and Remedies) Regulations 2002,
reg 3, 3A)

(c) or:
  • in respect of a person who is aged 18 or more, is or expects to be caring for
    a person in need of care who is either married to or the partner or civil
    partner of the employee, or a relative of the employee or living at the same
    address as the employee.

(Flexible Working (Eligibility, Complaints and Remedies) Regulations 2002,
reg 3B)

Employment for these purposes means where an individual who has entered into or works or worked under a contract of service or apprenticeship, whether express or implied, and (if it is express) whether oral or in writing (Flexible Working (Eligibility, Complaints and Remedies) Regulations 2002, reg 2).

4.45 What in general terms is involved in the process?

(a) The process involves an application by the employee, a meeting, and an appeal.

(b) The process takes up to 12 weeks as follows:

Day 1	Request in prescribed form
Day 28	Meeting
Day 42	Employer's response
Day 56	Employee's appeal
Day 70	Appeal meeting
Day 84	Response on appeal.

(c) The time limits can be extended by agreement between the employer and employee or where the person who would ordinarily consider the application is absent from work on annual leave or on sick leave on the day the application is made.

(d) All stages of the process are recorded in writing. Email can be used for this purpose.

(e) The employee has the right to be accompanied to the meeting or appeal meeting by a work colleague chosen by the employee, who can address the meeting and confer with the employee but not answer questions on behalf of the employee.

(Flexible Working (Procedural Requirements) Regulations 2002. See also the Government's guidance note (PL520) which is accessible via <http://www.dti. gov.uk>, contains very useful guidance on all stages of the process and forms for both the employer and the employee to complete.)

4.46 What must an employee do to apply? An employee must:

(a) apply in writing;

(b) state that the application is being made under the statutory right to request a flexible working pattern;

(c) confirm the eligibility requirements;

(d) explain what effect, if any, the employee thinks the proposed change would have on the employer and how, in their opinion, any such effect may be dealt with;

(e) specify the flexible working pattern applied for;

(f) state the date on which the proposed change should become effective;

(g) state whether a previous application has been made to the employer and, if so, when;

(h) date the application.

(ERA 1996, s 80F(2))

Are there any restrictions on the timing of the application? The application must **4.47** be the only application to that employer made under the process in the previous 12 months (ERA 1996, s 80F(4)).

What should the employer do on receipt of the form? **4.48**

(a) There is no legal requirement for the employer to acknowledge the form but best practice would dictate that the employer will do so.

(b) The employer should decide who will consider the request.

(c) Unless the employer immediately agrees to the request, within 28 days of the application, the employer must hold a meeting (Flexible Working (Procedural Requirements) Regulations 2002, reg 3).

What happens at the meeting? **4.49**

(a) There are no legal requirements in respect of the meeting. However, the DTI guidance stresses it is an opportunity for the employee and employer to discuss the issues face to face.

(b) Other suggestions are an agenda and even allowing an external adviser to attend if that might help.

When should the employer respond to the request? The employer's response **4.50** must be given within 14 days of the meeting (Flexible Working (Procedural Requirements) Regulations 2002, reg 4).

How should the employer respond if it wishes to agree? **4.51**

(a) Think carefully about what is being agreed. Any agreement is permanent. Therefore build in some flexibility for the future. For example, make part of the agreement that the employer can end the flexible working arrangement after a certain minimum period.

(b) The agreement must be in writing, detail the new working pattern, and state the date when it will start (Flexible Working (Procedural Requirements) Regulations 2002, reg 3(2) and (3)). If a meeting has been held, it should also be dated (Flexible Working (Procedural Requirements) Regulations 2002, reg 5(c)).

How should the employer respond if it wishes to reject the request? An employer **4.52** can only reject a request on one of the statutory grounds (Flexible Working (Procedural Requirements) Regulations 2002, reg 5(b)).

4

Family Friendly Rights

4.53 What are the statutory grounds? The statutory grounds are:

(a) the burden of additional costs;

(b) detrimental effect on the ability to meet customer demand;

(c) inability to reorganize work amongst existing staff;

(d) inability to recruit additional staff;

(e) detrimental impact on quality;

(f) detrimental impact on performance;

(g) insufficiency of work during the periods the employee proposes to work;

(h) planned structural changes.

(ERA 1996, s 80G(1)(b))

4.54 What must the notification of rejection set out? The notification of rejection must:

(a) be in writing;

(b) state the business reasons for refusing the application;

(c) provide sufficient explanation as to why the business reasons for refusal apply in the circumstances;

(d) provide details of the employee's right of appeal;

(e) be dated.

An employer must, when setting out the reasons for the refusal, bear in mind an employee's right to claim sex discrimination. This means that the explanation should deal with why the business reason is a good reason and also take into account the impact on the employee (see para **2.51** for further detail and also *Starmer v British Airways* [2005] IRLR 862).

(Flexible Working (Procedural Requirements) Regulations 2002, reg 5 and the Government's Guidance Note (see para **4.45** above))

4.55 How does the employee appeal a refusal of a request?

(a) The employee must notify an appeal within 14 days of the notification of the refusal.

(b) The notification should set out the grounds of appeal and be dated.

(c) The employer must then hold an appeal meeting within 14 days of the appeal notification.

(d) There are no legal requirements as to who should hear the appeal and what should happen at the meeting. However, the DTI guidance suggests it should be someone more senior than the person who made the original decision.

(e) Within 14 days of the appeal meeting, the employer must notify its decision.

(f) If the appeal is upheld or refused, the employer must set out the agreement or refusal as described above.

(Flexible Working (Procedural Requirements) Regulations 2002, regs 6, 7, 8, 9, and 10)

4.56 If an employee believes that the employer has not complied with the process, what claims can the employee bring? The employee can bring:

(a) a claim that the employer has failed to comply with the process in terms of a failure to hold the meeting to discuss the application within the time limits, or a failure to provide all the necessary information;
(b) a claim that the employer has failed to put forward one of the statutory grounds;
(c) a claim that the employer has relied on incorrect facts.

4.57 What remedies are available to the employee? The remedies available are:

(a) an order to the employer to reconsider the request;
(b) an order for compensation of up to eight weeks' pay, but with weekly pay capped at £320 per week.

(ERA 1996, ss 80H and 80I)

4.58 What is the remedy if an employer dismisses or treats an employee detrimentally because the employee made a request to work flexibly? A dismissal will be automatically unfair (ERA 1996, s 104C and see para 7.113 below). A refusal of flexible working has been held to be grounds for a claim for constructive dismissal if it was also discriminatory (*Shaw v CCL Limited* [2008] IRLR 284). See also para 4.59 below.

4.59 Can an employee bring a claim for sex discrimination where an employer refuses a request for flexible working?

(a) If the grounds given do not satisfy the objective justification defence, a woman may have a claim for indirect sex discrimination although the test for indirect discrimination is more likely to be made out where the employee makes the request in order to look after her children;
(b) If a request from a man is refused where in similar circumstances that of a woman would be accepted, the man may have a claim for direct sex discrimination.

(See paras 2.51 and 2.49)

Commentary

4.60 The Government announced in November 2007 that it will consider extending the right to flexible working to some or all children aged between 6 and 18.

Consultation will take place but no timetable for implementation has been announced at the time of writing.

F. Rights of Part-time Workers

4.61 What is the basic right? Part-timers have the right not to be treated less favourably in their contractual terms and conditions than comparable full-timers. Less favourable treatment can be justified on objective grounds which the Government defines as where 'it can be shown it is necessary and appropriate to achieve a legitimate business objective' (Employment Relations Act 1999, s 19; Part-time Workers (Prevention of Less Favourable Treatment) Regulations 2000). The Regulations implement Council Directive 97/81/EC concerning the Framework Agreement on part-time work. Note that individuals may also have claims under EqPA 1970 and SDA 1975, especially if the claimant is a woman (see Chapter 2 above).

4.62 Who is eligible for this protection? The right applies to workers—that is both employees and those who have entered into another form of contract whereby the individual undertakes to perform personally any work or services for another party to the contract whose status is not by virtue of the contract that of a client or customer of any profession or business undertaking carried on by the individual (see Part-time Workers (Prevention of Less Favourable Treatment) Regulations 2000, reg 1(2) and see para **1.02** above in relation to the definition of 'worker').

4.63 Who qualifies as a part-timer? Part-timers are those who currently work fewer hours than full-timers, those who vary their terms and conditions to work part-time, and those that return to part-time working after maternity leave (Part-time Workers (Prevention of Less Favourable Treatment) Regulations 2000, regs 2, 3, and 4). Only part-timers employed on the same type of contract as full-timers will benefit from the Regulations subject to the exceptions identified later in this paragraph. Regulation 2(3) specifies four categories of contract which will be treated as different, including a catch-all category at reg 2(3)(d) 'any description of worker that it is reasonable for the employer to treat differently from other workers on the ground that workers of that description have a different type of contract'. This was held by the House of Lords to apply only if the type of contract did not come within on of the three other categories of contract specified in reg 2(3) (*Matthews and Others v Kent and Medway Towns Fire Authority and Others* [2006] ICR 365). As such the contracts should be examined on the basis of the type of contract in accordance with reg 2(3) rather than individual terms and conditions of employment. Additionally, the part-time workers must be engaged in the same or broadly similar work (Part-time Workers (Prevention of Less Favourable Treatment) Regulations 2000, reg 2(4)(a)(ii)). Again, this will be a question of fact and the court should not concentrate on the differences but should ensure that equal weight is given to the similarities (*Matthews and Others v Kent and Medway Towns Fire Authority and Others* [2006] ICR 365). The exception to these rules are where an employee becomes part-time as the result of a variation of contract when the full-time terms he previously enjoyed can form the basis of the comparison (Part-time Workers (Prevention of Less Favourable Treatment) Regulations 2000, reg 3(2)). Equally where an employee who previously worked under full-time terms and conditions returns to work after a period of absence to part-time work, as long as the period of absence is not more than 12 months, she can compare the new terms to the full-time terms she enjoyed before her absence (Part-time Workers (Prevention of Less Favourable Treatment) Regulations 2000, reg 3(2)). This is the case even if the contract under which she returns is of a different type. Finally the part-time worker and the full-time worker must be based at the same establishment unless there is no full-time worker comparator at the same establishment, when such a comparator who satisfies the other requirements for a comparator is based at a different establishment.

How might the terms and conditions of part-time workers be affected detrimentally? **4.64**

(a) Part-time workers must enjoy the same chances of promotion and access to training as full-time workers.

(b) Pay must be at the same basic rate as full-time workers. However, performance-related variations may be allowed.

(c) Part-timers will only be entitled to overtime payments when they have worked the same number of hours as a full-time worker.

(d) Part-timers must be given access to profit sharing and share option schemes.

(e) Part-timers must not be treated less favourably than full-time workers in terms of calculating the rate of sick pay or maternity pay, the length of service required to qualify for payment, and the length of time for which payments will be received.

(f) Part-timers should be allowed benefits such as health insurance, subsidized mortgages, staff discounts, company cars, although they can be provided on a pro rata basis. The fact that they cannot be provided pro rata is no excuse for failing to provide them.

(g) Holiday entitlement needs to be pro rata for part-time workers. Care needs to be taken when looking at the issue of paid bank holidays (although see *McMenemy v Capita Business Services* [2007] IRLR 400).

(Part-time Workers (Prevention of Less Favourable Treatment) Regulations 2000, regs 5 and 7). See in particular reg 5(3) which states that in determining whether a part-time worker has been treated less favourably the pro rata principle shall be applied unless it is inappropriate.

4.65 Sections 19 and 20 of the ERA 1999 provide that a Code of Practice can be issued. No Code of Practice has yet been issued. However, Guidance Notes and a 'Law and Best Practice Guide' has been issued and are available on the DBERR website. They have no legal status.

4.66 Is there any defence to a claim under the Regulations? The defences available are that the treatment was not due to the worker being part-time (see *McMenemy v Capita Business Services* [2007] IRLR 400) and/or that the treatment could be objectively justified (Part-time Workers (Prevention of Less Favourable Treatment) Regulations 2000, reg 5(2)). There is no case law on what constitutes objective justification in relation to the Part-time Workers (Prevention etc) Regulations 2000.

4.67 However, the test of objective justification, identified in *Bilka Kaufhaus GmbH v Karin Weber von Hartz* [1986] ECR 1607 will apply, namely, that the treatment is:

(a) to achieve a legitimate aim, for example, a genuine business objective;

(b) necessary to achieve that objective; and

(c) an appropriate way to achieve the objective.

(*BR Matthews and Others v Kent and Medway Towns Fire Authority and Others* IDS Brief 743, October 2003)

4.68 What claims can an employee bring where an employer has breached a part-time worker's rights?

(a) A worker can request a written statement from the employer where the employee believes the employer has infringed his rights. The employer must provide the statement within 21 days of the request. If the employer fails to provide a statement or is evasive or equivocal in it, the employment tribunal can draw what inference it considers appropriate, including an inference that the employer has infringed the rights in question (Part-Time Workers (Prevention etc) Regulations 2000, reg 6).

(b) An employee can bring a claim to the employment tribunal that the employee's rights as a part-time worker have been infringed. The remedies available are a declaration, compensation, and an order that the employer take steps for the purposes of obviating and reducing the adverse effect on the complainant (Part-Time Workers (Prevention etc) Regulations 2000, regs 5 and 8(7)). Any claim must be brought within three months of the less favourable treatment or detriment complained of (Part-Time Workers (Prevention etc) Regulations 2000, reg 8(2)) but it is not necessary for the worker to bring a grievance.

(c) The employee will also have a claim if the employer dismisses the employee or treats the employee detrimentally for a reason connected with a claim in relation to the rights of that employee as a part-time worker (Part-Time Workers (Prevention etc) Regulations 2000, reg 7). Claims must be brought within three months of the dismissal, or the detriment, (Part-Time Workers (Prevention etc) Regulations 2000, reg 8(2)) but it is not necessary for the worker to bring a grievance before bringing a claim. Note that there is no direct right to bring a claim for automatically unfair dismissal if the dismissal is connected with a breach of the Regulations (cf ERA 1996, s 99).

4

Family Friendly Rights

5

INDUSTRIAL ACTION

A. Introduction

The law relating to trade disputes is extremely complex and therefore what follows is very much an outline of the relevant principles. The law is primarily enshrined in TULR(C)A 1992. There are also two applicable Codes of Practice, Code of Practice: Picketing (1992) and Code of Practice: Industrial Action Ballots and Notice to Employers (2005). **5.01**

What is the basic position where there is a trade dispute, ie where an employee **5.02** withdraws their labour in protest? No employee in England has a right to withdraw his labour with impunity. Any industrial action, whether it involves only a refusal to comply with some contractual requirements or a complete withdrawal of labour, is a breach of the individual's contract of employment. The right to strike is recognized by the European Convention on Human Rights as part of the right to freedom of association at Article 11 (*Unison v United Kingdom* [2002] IRLR 497). However, in principle, any third party (for example, a trade union) who encourages employees to take industrial action, whether by breaching their employment contracts or by forcing a breach of a contract which their employer has with a customer or supplier, commits the tort of inducing a breach of contract. Other so-called 'industrial torts' include interference with the employer's business by unlawful means, intimidation, and conspiracy. There is a great deal of case law as to what constitutes such a tort which is beyond the scope of this book.

5.03 Notwithstanding the above and in accordance with the European Convention on Human Rights, in certain circumstances, independent trade unions may be immune from liability if they commit an industrial tort (TULR(C)A) 1992, s 219). The circumstances have been gradually narrowed by legislation during recent years. First, any industrial action encouraged by a trade union must fall within the 'golden formula' (set out in TULR(C)A 1992, s 244 and para **5.05** below), ie it must be in contemplation or furtherance of a 'legitimate trade dispute'. Second, no industrial action can be taken unless it is supported by a majority vote in a properly held ballot, details of which are notified to the employer (see para **5.09** et seq below). The DTI has issued a Code of Practice on balloting for industrial action which sets out good practice, but a breach does not of itself lead to civil or criminal sanction (TULR(C)A 1992, s 207). Third, the first element in any industrial action must take place within 28 days of the announcement of the result of the strike ballot. There are additional rules in relation to individual liability in industrial action situations and picketing which are also summarized in this chapter.

B. Legitimate Trade Dispute

5.04 See Flow Chart on page 117.

What is a Legitimate Trade Dispute? Even where a trade union's actions would otherwise constitute an industrial tort, unions can seek the benefit of trade union immunity, but only if the industrial action which they are encouraging is genuinely undertaken in the belief that it will gain the union some advantage in connection with a trade dispute and is within the golden formula of categories (TULR(C)A 1992, s 219). To come within this provision, a trade union must show the following:

(a) that the dispute is one which comes within the definition of 'trade dispute' (see TULR(C)A 1992, s 244(1) and para **5.05** below);

(b) that it is not a dispute which is automatically unlawful or unprotected (see para **5.06** below);

(c) that the action is in contemplation or furtherance of a trade dispute (see para **5.07** below).

The type of acts described in TULR(C)A 1992, s 219 covers most but not all economic torts which would be involved in industrial action. However, the trade dispute, in respect of which immunity is sought, must be between an employer and its own workers (TULR(C)A 1992, s 244(1). See para **5.05** below for the definition of worker). Note that the immunity protects only the trade union and not the individual employee, who can still be sued for breach of contract (see para **5.41** et seq below).

What is a trade dispute for these purposes? Legitimate trade disputes within the **5.05** golden formula are set out in TULR(C)A 1992, s 244(1)—that is, they relate wholly or mainly to one of the following issues:

(a) terms and conditions of employment (including a dispute about the manner in which the terms are applied *P v NASUWT* [2001] IRLR 532, CA) or a dispute relating wholly or mainly to the job employees are being required to do. So, for example, *In re P* [2003] IRLR 307, HL a dispute over requiring teachers to teach a boy who had been excluded from the school did come within the golden formula;

(b) physical conditions in which any worker is required to work;

(c) the engagement, non-engagement, termination, or suspension of employment or the duties of employment of one or more workers;

(d) demarcation disputes;

(e) general disputes regarding allocation of work and duties of employment;

(f) disciplinary matters;

(g) a worker's membership or non-membership of a trade union;

(h) facilities for officials of trade unions;

(i) machinery for negotiation or consultation;

(j) recognition or representation disputes involving only the employer company.

The test is an objective test (*NWL Ltd v Woods* [1979] ICR 867). For the purposes of the above test, the term 'workers' means not only employees but also self-employed people who have agreed personally to perform any work or services for the employer, where the employer is not a client (TULR(C)A 1992, s 244(5)). The definition therefore includes casual workers. However, it does not include prospective workers (*University College London Hospital NHS Trust v UNISON* [1999] IRLR 31, CA), or past workers (unless the worker was sacked in connection with the current dispute).

Are there any disputes which will mean that industrial action will be automati- **5.06** cally unlawful or unprotected?

(a) Any dispute which has as one of its reasons (whether or not the major one) a conflict concerning:
  • imposition or retention of a closed shop (TULR(C)A 1992, s 222);
  • the dismissal of an employee for taking unofficial industrial action (TULR(C)A 1992, s 223);

- a third party employer's failure to recognize, negotiate with, or consult a union ('blacking') (TULR(C)A 1992, s 225); or
- action to enforce a union labour only clause (TULR(C)A 1992, s 222(3)) will automatically lose trade union immunity.

(b) Any secondary action (affecting an employer who is not a party to the trade dispute, even if the affected employer is an associated employer) or sympathy action, (where employees of another employer take action to support the dispute) has no trade union immunity (TULR(C)A 1992, s 224).

(c) Any action committed by an unlawful picket (TULR(C)A 1992, s 219(3)) (see para **5.50** below for what constitutes a lawful picket) is never protected.

5.07 Other disputes outside the golden formula include:

(a) any dispute between workers and workers (eg about a closed shop);
(b) any inter-union dispute (eg over recognition); and
(c) politically-motivated action (eg to protest against government policy).

5.08 When is an act in contemplation or furtherance of a trade dispute? This should be judged subjectively (*Express Newspapers Ltd v McShane* [1980] ICR 42; *Duport Steels Ltd v Sirs* [1980] IRLR 116); therefore, honest belief on the part of the trade union is sufficient.

C. The Ballot

5.09 What is the significance of the ballot? If the trade union immunity is to apply to protect the union, industrial action must be supported by a validly conducted ballot (TULR(C)A 1992, s 226(1)). If there has been an official call for industrial action before the ballot is held, the action will be unlawful. Each stage of the ballot process (that is, ballot paper, notice to employer, the vote itself, and the notification of the result) is prescribed by statute and dealt with below.

5.10 What are the requirements in relation to the ballot paper?

(a) Does the ballot paper state, without qualification, 'If you take part in a strike or other industrial action, you may be in breach of your contract of employment. However, if you are dismissed for taking part in a strike or other industrial action which is called officially and is otherwise lawful, the dismissal will be unfair if it takes place fewer than twelve weeks after you started taking part in the action, and depending on the circumstances may be unfair if it takes place later'? It should do.

(b) Does the ballot paper ask the question, requiring the person to answer yes or no, whether the individual is prepared to take part (or continue to take part)

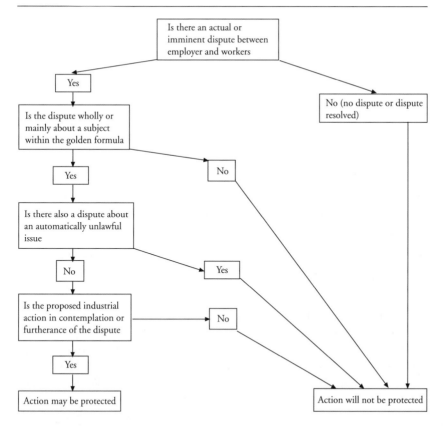

in a strike, and/or (as the case may be) does the ballot paper ask the question, requiring the person to answer yes or no, whether the individual is prepared to take part (or continue to take part) in action short of a strike? Are any additional questions strictly separated from these two questions? It should do.

(c) Does the ballot paper specify:
- the name of the independent scrutinizer appointed by the union to report on the conduct of the ballot? (Note: no scrutinizer is required where 50 or fewer workers are entitled to vote);
- who is authorized (by name or job title) to call upon members to take part in the industrial action? The authorized person must be someone with power to bind the union.

It should do.

(d) Is the ballot paper marked with its own serial number? Does the ballot paper state the address to which, and the date by which, it must be returned? It should be.

(If any of the elements described above are missing the ballot is invalid (TULR(C)A 1992, s 229, Code of Practice: Industrial Action Ballots and Notice to Employers (2005) paras 29 to 33).

    (e) Does any message on the ballot paper detract from any of the required statements? Might a message influence the way a member votes? If so, the ballot may be invalid (Code of Practice: Industrial Action Ballots and Notice to Employers, para 31).

5.11 Has the union given the employer notice of the ballot, received not later than one clear week before the first voting day (ie notice on or before Monday for action starting on the following Monday) so that the employer can know the identity of those intending to take action? It should have done (TULR(C)A 1992, s 226A(1)).

5.12 What are the requirements for the notice? The notice must be in writing and:

    (a) state that the union intends to hold a ballot;

    (b) specify the anticipated voting day or first voting day;

    (c) describe, so that the employer can readily ascertain them, the identity of those who will be balloted by reference to:

        • the categories of employees (including the number of employees in each category);

        • the workplaces at which they work (including the number at each workplace);

        • the total number of employees concerned; and

        • which employees pay trade union dues by deduction from salary.

The notice need not name the individual workers, but it must be as accurate as reasonably practicable, given the information in the trade union's possession at the relevant time (TULR(C)A 1992, s 226A).

5.13 Has the union sent the employer specimen ballot papers of each type to be used by its employees in connection with the dispute to arrive at least three days before the first day of the ballot (ie specimen received on or before Friday for action starting following Monday)? It should have done (TULR(C)A 1992, s 226A(1)(b)). If not, the trade dispute immunities will fail to protect the union as against that particular employer.

5.14 Who is entitled to vote in the ballot? It should be only those members of the trade union employed by the employer with whom there is a dispute who it is reasonable, at the time the ballot papers are sent out, for the union to believe will be asked to take part in industrial action (TULR(C)A 1992, s 227(1)) plus (according to a much-criticized Court of Appeal decision) any who it reasonably expects to take sympathetic action *(NURMTW v Midland Mainline Ltd* [2001] IRLR 813, CA but see also *P (a minor) v National Association of School Masters/Union of Women Teachers* [2003] ICR 386)). Overseas members may be ignored.

Is there anyone who is entitled to vote who is not given the opportunity to vote? **5.15** If so, the ballot may be unlawful.

Is there anyone who was not given the opportunity to vote who is nevertheless **5.16** being induced to go out on strike? If so, the ballot may be unlawful. Note: new members who were not members of the union at the time the ballot was conducted can be induced to take action once they join without falling foul of this provision (*London Underground Ltd v National Union of Rail, Maritime and Transport Workers* [1996] ICR 170). Also, accidental errors which do not have a significant effect on the result of the ballot will not invalidate the ballot (TULR(C)A 1992, s 232B).

If more than 50 people may vote in the ballot, has an appropriately qualified **5.17** *independent scrutinizer* been appointed by the union? The scrutinizer may be an independent solicitor holding a practising certificate, an accountant qualified to be an auditor of trade unions, or Electoral Reform Ballot Services Ltd, the Industrial Society, or Unity Security Balloting Services Ltd. The scrutinizer must be instructed to ensure the ballot is lawfully and properly conducted. If no scrutinizer is appointed, and more than 50 people may vote, the ballot will be invalid (TULR(C)A 1992, ss 226B and 226C).

When should the ballot take place? The union must comply with certain notice **5.18** requirements as set out in para **5.11** and this will dictate when the ballot should take place.

Is there a separate ballot for each workplace? This is necessary except: **5.19**

(a) where more than one workplace is affected by the same dispute; or
(b) where a union ballots *all* members of a particular job category (eg all joiners) employed by one employer; or
(c) where a union ballots *all its* members employed by any number of employers with whom the union is in dispute (TULR(C)A 1992, ss 228, 228A).

Have the ballot papers been distributed by post? They must be sent to those **5.20** required to vote by post at their home address or at any other address they may have nominated (TULR(C)A 1992, s 230(2)).

Have members been given a convenient opportunity to vote by post? They should **5.21** be (TULR(C)A 1992, s 230(2)).

Is the ballot secret, free, open, and fair? It should be. **5.22**

5.23 Is any voter required to incur direct cost in voting or has a stamped addressed envelope been supplied? No cost should be incurred by the voter (TULR(C)A 1992, s 230(1)).

5.24 In summary, if the ballot is not conducted secretly, normally with separate ballots at each workplace, by post, with all potential voters given a reasonable opportunity to vote without cost to themselves, it is likely to be invalid.

5.25 Has the union informed all persons entitled to vote in the ballot of the total number of votes cast, the number of 'yes' votes, the number of 'no' votes, and the number of spoiled papers (TULR(C)A 1992, s 231)? These details should be separated out (i) for national and overseas votes, if any overseas members voted in the ballot, and (ii) for each workplace. Ideally, the number of voting papers issued should also be announced.

It should announce these figures:

(a) to those entitled to vote in the ballot; and

(b) as soon as reasonably practicable, to the employer (TULR(C)A 1992, s 231A).

Failure to inform any relevant employer invalidates the whole ballot.

5.26 What was the result of the ballot? Was there a majority in favour of any of the questions specified on the ballot paper? If not, any industrial action thereafter will be unlawful.

5.27 Was a scrutinizer required to be appointed in accordance with para **5.17** above? If so, within four weeks of the end of the ballot, and preferably before industrial action begins, the scrutinizer must produce a report stating whether he is satisfied that the ballot was lawful and secret, and whether he was able to carry out his duties without interference and if not, why not (TULR(C)A 1992, s 231B). If either the employer or any person entitled to vote in the ballot requests a copy within six months of the date of the report, the union must supply it, free or at modest charge (TULR(C)A s 231B(2)).

D. Industrial Action

5.28 Who called for industrial action? Is it the person who is specified on the ballot paper or someone directly delegated by this person to make the call (*Tanks & Drums Ltd v TGWU* [1991] IRLR 372) (see para **5.10(c)**)? If not, the action will be unlawful.

Is the purpose of industrial action in contemplation or furtherance of a dispute **5.29** within the golden formula (see paras **5.04** et seq above)? If not, the action will be unlawful.

Is the industrial action for an automatically unfair reason (see para **5.06** above)? **5.30** If it is, the action will be unlawful.

Has the employer been given at least seven days' formal notice of intention to begin **5.31** or resume industrial action? If not, the action will be unprotected (TULR(C)A 1992, s 234A). The notice must contain the following information:

(a) describe number, category, and workplace of the 'affected employees' whom the union intends to call on to take industrial action in the same way as it does in the notice of ballot (see para **5.12(c)** above);

(b) say whether the industrial action is to be continuous (in which case, giving the start date and time if not at the commencement of a shift) or discontinuous (in which case, setting out the relevant dates and times if not to last for the whole day) (TULR(C)A 1992, s 234A(3)).

If the dates specified for discontinuous action change, or new ones are added, or **5.32** should continuous action stop for a period, a new seven-day notice needs to be given to the employer before further action can take place. This means it must be given by, say, a Monday for action to begin on the following Monday. This is not necessary if the only reason the action ceased was as a result of a court order or undertaking given to the court. If notice is not given there is no protection. If partial notice is given (eg specifying only some of the employees due to strike) there is only partial protection (TULR(C)A 1992, s 234(6), (7), (7A), (7B)).

When does the call for industrial action take place? Has there been any authoriza- **5.33** tion or endorsement of industrial action before the relevant ballot has ended? If so, the ballot will be invalid (TULR(C)A 1992, s 233 (3)(a)).

Who is called by the union to take industrial action? It must be only those union **5.34** members who were given the right to vote in the ballot (unless any error is accidental and insignificant) (TULR(C)A 1992, s 232A and s 232B), and only where there was a vote in favour of the relevant type of action. For example, if two workplaces were balloted in separate ballots, and only one voted in favour of industrial action, then only workers employed at that workplace can take the relevant action. No one who was deliberately denied the right to vote can be called out to take action (whether or not he accepts the call). Insignificant, accidental omissions may not be fatal (*P v NASUWT* [2001] IRLR 532).

Has the first authorization or endorsement of industrial action been given within **5.35** 28 days of the last day of voting, and does the industrial action itself start within that time (eg if a ballot ends on a Friday, action must start before midnight on the

Thursday four weeks later)? If it does not, the ballot will have become ineffective. The employer and union may agree, or the court may order an extension to this period (on a union application made up to eight weeks from the end date of the ballot) for any period up to a maximum of eight weeks (if extended by agreement) or 12 weeks (if extended by court order) from the last voting day of the ballot (TULR(C)A 1992, s 234).

5.36 What if the industrial action is suspended by agreement? If action has begun within the appropriate time frame, and is then temporarily suspended (for example because the parties are discussing settlement) no new ballot is necessary, but appropriate notice for the resumption of the action must be given (see para **5.32** above).

E. Repudiation

5.37 What is the signficance of 'repudiation'? Even if employed officials of a trade union have not authorized or endorsed industrial action, the union may still be regarded as responsible if the action has been authorized or endorsed by any committee of the union or any of the officials of the union (whether employed by it or not), and in those circumstances the union can only escape liability by repudiating the industrial action. If a dispute concerning a closed shop is one of the reasons for industrial action, then the trade union immunity will automatically cease, whatever other reasons there may be for the action.

5.38 Is industrial action threatened or taking place without the sanction of a valid ballot? Is strike action being proposed when the ballot only endorsed action short of a strike, or vice versa? If so, in each of these cases and if it is action authorized or endorsed by a union official (see TULR(C)A 1992, s 20 for what this means) and not repudiated by the union (see TULR(C)A 1992, s 21 and para **5.39** below for the meaning of this) either all individuals taking industrial action may be dismissed (although all must be treated equally from the date of dismissal for a period of three months, in that there must be no selective re-engagement in this period) or the union and others calling the action may be restrained by injunction from pursuing action.

5.39 Has the industrial action been repudiated by the principal executive committee or the general secretary of the union both to the chapel, its stewards, and to the union members, to the employer, and (on request) to any interested contractor (TULR(C)A 1992, s 21)? For repudiation to be effective, the union must:

(a) give written notice of repudiation as quickly as possible to those authorizing the strike and also to every member of the union who might take part in the strike and his or her employer, including the statement, in full: 'Your union has repudiated the call (or calls) for industrial action to which this notice relates and will give no support to unofficial industrial action taken in response to it (or them). If you are dismissed while taking unofficial industrial action, you will have no right to complain of unfair dismissal' (TULR(C)A 1992, s 21(2) –(4)); and

(b) not behave inconsistently with the repudiation (TULR(C)A 1992, s 21(5)).

What happens if the trade union does not repudiate the industrial action? If the action has been called in the union's name, is not repudiated, and is unlawful, the union will be responsible for any damage suffered as a result of the action (see para **5.45(d)** below). If the action is unofficial, or has been repudiated by the union, the employer may dismiss any individuals taking industrial action, and is not obliged to treat all such individuals equally in order to avoid applications for unfair dismissal (see para **5.44** below). **5.40**

F. Individual Liability of Employees and Trade Unions

What is the employee's basic position? If strike or other industrial action is taken by an employee, he is likely to be in breach of his contract of employment, either of an express term, such as attending for work or performing particular duties, or of the implied term of the duty to give faithful service. As a result of this implied term, even an employee's actions which might not on their face seem a breach of his contract, such as working to rule, or possibly even a voluntary overtime ban may be regarded as industrial action because their purpose is to disrupt the employer's business (*Ticehurst & Thompson v BT plc* [1992] IRLR 219). **5.41**

Is the employee in breach of contract because they have taken part in industrial action? Before an employer can take action against an employee who is taking part in some form of industrial action, he must establish that the employee is in breach of contract, either by taking strike action, or action short of a strike. Strike action is likely to constitute a breach of contract. Action short of a strike may constitute such a breach but it depends on the circumstances. **5.42**

What is meant by strike action or action short of a strike? **5.43**

(a) *Strike action*—means, in essence, a failure to attend ready for work during the individual's normal working hours.
(b) *Action short of a strike*—which is in breach of contract includes:
  • refusing to undertake certain normal duties which the employee is contractually obliged to perform;
  • obstructive withdrawal of cooperation;

- compulsory overtime ban (TULR(C)A 1992, s 229(2A)) (and possibly voluntary overtime ban, but only if employees refuse to carry out pre-assigned overtime (*Burgess v Stevedoring Services Ltd* [2002] IRLR 811, PC));
- go-slow;
- work-to-rule (if it involves a breach of contract). When reviewing whether a work-to-rule is a breach of contract, consider:
  - are the employees contractually obliged to work in a particular way?
  - is the employee given a discretion how to perform—in which case, he probably has an implied duty to cooperate in pursuing the employer's business (*Sim v Rotherham Metropolitan Borough Council* [1986] IRLR 391)?
  - is the employee deliberately exercising a judgement or discretion to disrupt the employer's business?

  In all these cases, the work-to-rule will be a breach of contract;
- blacking a third party's goods or services by actively refusing to deal with them.

5.44 What are the employer's possible remedies if the employee is in breach of his contract? If the employee is in breach of his contract of employment, either because he goes on strike or takes action short of a strike by committing a material breach of his contract of employment, the employer has the following remedies:

(a) It may *refuse to pay* the employee for the period when he has been taking industrial action. If an employee takes industrial action in the form of refusing to perform only one of several tasks, and the employer makes it clear it does not accept partial performance of duties, the employer may still refuse to pay the employee any pay for the entire duration of the industrial action unless the industrial action represents a specific identifiable period of non-work, in which case pay should be deducted only for that period. If the employer indicates it will accept partial performance of the contract it should pay the employee a rateable proportion of the normal wages covering those duties which the employee has actually performed (*Sim v Rotherham Metropolitan Borough Council* [1987] ICR 897; *Miles v Wakefield Metropolitan District Council* [1987] ICR 368; *Wiluszynski v Tower Hamlets LBC* [1989] ICR 493).

(b) It may sue *the employee for the losses* which it has suffered as a result of breaches of his contract of employment. This may be difficult to quantify, and any such action would not assist harmonious industrial relations once the dispute has ended. Further, the individuals sued may not have sufficient funds to be worth suing.

(c) The employer may itself operate a 'lock-out' to prevent employees entering its premises to perform any work at all where disruptive action short of a strike is being taken. However, before proceeding down this route an employer should exercise caution or it will risk being in repudiatory breach of contract (*Express Star Ltd v Bunday* [1986] IRLR 477).

(d) If the dispute is one which has been authorized by the relevant union, is protected by immunity under TULR(C)A 1992, s 219, and the industrial action has been underway for at least 12 weeks, it may *dismiss* the employee for taking industrial action in breach of his contract of employment. However, in doing so, it should proceed with caution. More precisely, where the dismissal is during or after protected industrial action, as specified within TULR(C)A 1992, s 238A, then if the reason for that dismissal is the employee's participation in the industrial action, the employer will only be able to dismiss fairly if:

- the dismissal takes place after the first 12 weeks of the industrial action; and
- provided the employee had not stopped taking part in the industrial action during its first 12 weeks; and
- provided the employer has taken such procedural steps as are reasonable to resolve the dispute (TULR(C)A 1992, s 238A).

(e) Where the industrial action is unofficial, the employer can dismiss any employee taking part in that action and the employee will have no claim for unfair dismissal (TULR(C)A 1992, s 337);

(f) Where the dismissal is during the course of other industrial action, ie excluding unofficial industrial action or industrial action which comes within s 238A of TULR(C)A 1992, an employer shall not be deemed to have dismissed unfairly, unless it does not dismiss all the employees taking part in the industrial action, or does so but then re-engages some but not all of them in the three-month period after the dismissals (TULR(C)A 1992, s 338);

(g) An employee who is absent from work through sickness or on holiday should not be dismissed unless the employer is satisfied that he is taking part in the industrial action:

- in respect of employees who are sick, employers should, if only a few people are sick, visit each employee's home during normal working hours to ascertain whether or not the employee would, if well, be on strike. If a substantial number of employees are sick, the employer may write to the employees. The letter should ask the employees whether, if they had not been sick, they would have worked normally on specified dates, and whether the individual is prepared to undertake to return to work normally immediately following recovery. These questions should require the answer yes or no. If either of the questions is answered in the negative this would be sufficient to constitute 'taking part' in industrial action;

5

Industrial Action

- in respect of those employees on holiday, if they can be contacted easily, they should be visited to ascertain whether or not they would, if not on holiday, be on strike. If there are a large number of them, they should be written to and asked whether, if they had not been on holiday, they would have worked normally on a specified date and whether they are prepared to undertake to return to work normally as soon as their holiday period ends. The individuals should be required to answer yes or no to both questions. If either of the questions is answered in the negative, this would be sufficient to constitute 'taking part' in industrial action. If employees cannot be contacted, action should not be taken against them unless and until they have demonstrated, following their return, an intention to take part in industrial action.

(h) An employer must also consider whether the employee's contract may be terminated summarily or whether notice must be given so as to avoid a contractual claim. An employer cannot obtain an order for specific performance of the contract (TULR(C)A 1992, s 236).

5.45 What remedies will the employer have against the trade union? The employer will also have the following remedies against a trade union which is not able to take advantage of the union immunities if the circumstances satisfy the following conditions:

(a) where an industrial tort has been committed and where the dispute is not a legitimate trade dispute within the golden formula (see below and para **5.04** above); or

(b) where a ballot has not been conducted or has been improperly conducted (see paras **5.09** et seq above);

(c) in each case the trade union has either authorized or endorsed the industrial action, or has refused to repudiate any industrial action called for by any committee or official of the union (whether employed or not, so including a shop steward; see paras **5.37** et seq above); and

(d) if, but only if the above conditions are satisfied and the industrial action involves any of the industrial torts, eg inducement to employees to breach their contracts of employment, inducement of third parties not to supply or buy from the employer, secondary action, intimidation, or any interference with the employer's business by unlawful means or conspiracy to do so, the employer may:

- seek an injunction against the union restraining breaches (see para **5.52** below); and/or
- claim damages against the union for any losses proved to have been suffered by the employer as a result of the industrial action. The maximum

sum of damages which can be awarded on any one claim against the union depends upon the number of members the union has:

- if the union has fewer than 5,000 members, the maximum is £10,000;
- if the union has between 5,000 and 24,999 members, the maximum is £50,000;
- if the union has between 25,000 and 99,999 members, the maximum is £125,000;
- if the union has 100,000 or more members, the maximum is £250,000. (TULR(C)A 1992, s 22(2). Interest may be awarded on top of the damages limit.)

What remedies may a third party have? An individual member of the public in **5.46** respect of whom actual or threatened industrial action may prevent or delay the supply of goods or services or reduce the quality of those goods or services (even if he has no contractual right to receive them) may apply to the High Court if the action is unlawful for an injunction restraining further disruption (TULR(C)A 1992, s 235A). A member of the relevant trade union who is affected by the dispute and likely to be induced to take part in industrial action has a statutory right to restrain unballoted action (TULR(C)A 1992, s 62).

G. Picketing

What is the general rule in relation to secondary action (ie industrial action taken **5.47** by workers where the real dispute is not between themselves and their own employer)? The general rule is that all secondary action is prohibited. The sole exception to this rule is picketing, which is the only possible form of legitimate secondary industrial action, but even so the manner in which pickets can be conducted is severely limited.

What should an employer do if it believes a criminal offence is being committed in **5.48** the course of a picket? If an employer believes that any criminal offence is being or is about to be committed, the employer should contact the police to request them to take appropriate preventative action. Pickets may be guilty of the following crimes:

(a) obstructing the highway, by wilfully obstructing free passage along a public highway or pavement;
(b) obstructing a police constable in the execution of his duty;
(c) assault, provided the individual has the capacity to carry into effect an intention to commit some physical injury, however slight;
(d) offences under the Public Order Act 1986, including:
- when an individual makes (orally, in writing, or via pictures) threatening or abusive or insulting comments or actions towards another with the

intention or the likely consequence that the individual believes he is likely
to be the subject of immediate unlawful violence, and/or

- unlawful assembly, where three or more people use or threaten violence as a result of which people might fear for their personal safety, and/or
- affray, violent disorder, and riot;

(e) public nuisance, for example, by obstructing the public in the exercise or enjoyment of a right of way;

(f) offences under TULR(C)A 1992, s 241 including doing the following without legal authority:

- using violence towards or intimidating another, his spouse, or children, or injuring his property,
- persistently following another from place to place,
- hiding any tools, clothes, or other property owned or used by other people, or depriving them or hindering them in their use,
- watching or besetting a person's residence or place of employment, or the approach to either place,
- following another person with two or more others in a disorderly manner in or through any street or road, in each case without legal authority;

(g) refusing to obey conditions imposed on a public assembly (Public Order Act 1986);

(h) harassing individuals by repeating actions(s) which distress the victim (Protection from Harassment Act 1997).

5.49 What other unlawful wrongs could those on picket lines commit? In addition, pickets may be found to have committed civil wrongs including:

(a) trespass upon the employer's property;

(b) interference with contracts to which the employer is a party (for example, by preventing the employer fulfilling its contracts, preventing employees from entering work, or preventing suppliers delivering supplies to the employer);

(c) private nuisance (for example, by blocking an access route to an employer's premises); or

(d) defamation.

5.50 When will a picket be lawful? A picket is only lawful in the following circumstances (TULR(C)A 1992, s 220):

(a) The only people who are on a picket are workers picketing at or near their own place of work, or trade union officials accompanying their members. If the place of work is on a private industrial estate, workers may picket at the nearest element of public land to that estate. If employees work at more than one place of work or if it is impossible for them to picket at that place, they can picket any place they work or the administrative headquarters of their employer. A person dismissed during the industrial dispute in question may picket his former place of work; and

(b) The picket must be in contemplation or furtherance of a legitimate trade dispute (see paras **5.04** et seq above); and

(c) The only activities pickets can lawfully conduct are peacefully to obtain or communicate information or peacefully to persuade any person to work or abstain from working (see *Broome v DPP* [1974] ICR 84 which relates to a predecessor but similar piece of legislation); and

(d) There is no specific restriction on the number of people at any picket, although a mass picket is generally regarded as an obstruction of the highway or intimidation. The 1992 Code of Practice on Picketing recommends that in general there should be no more than six pickets at any entrance.

If these conditions are all satisfied, then the trade union and those participating in the picket will be immune from liability in tort. Coming within the golden formula set out at TULR(C)A 1992, s 219, is not enough on its own (TULR(C)A 1992, s 219(3)). However, s 220 of TULR(C)A 1992 does not provide a defence to a criminal offence.

What are the remedies where a picket is unlawful? If any picket is not conducted **5.51** properly in accordance with para **5.50** above, an employer can seek an injunction banning any picket other than one restricted to, say, six people per entrance acting peacefully. The injunction may be directed against any union or individual which or who is authorizing or endorsing an unlawful picket and against any individuals taking part in an unlawful picket. Criminal proceedings could be brought against the picketers, or police could be required to move the picketers on if they reasonably anticipate a breach of the peace (see para **5.49** above).

H. Injunctions

What will an employer be required to show where an injunction is sought? It will **5.52** be necessary for the employer to demonstrate to the court, by witness statement evidence, the following facts:

(a) For industrial action injunctions:
- the nature of the industrial action taken, and a brief history of the events leading up to the union's involvement in those events;
- whether the industrial action is within the golden formula;

- whether the ballot has been properly held;
- whether notice has been properly given;
- that the industrial action involves employees breaching their contracts of employment, or the commission of some other industrial tort.

(b) For picketing injunctions:
- a brief history of the facts leading to the dispute about which individuals are picketing;
- the identity of those on the picket line (where possible), including whether any picket is a union official (whether paid or unpaid);
- whether the picketing is in contemplation of a trade dispute which is within the golden formula;
- the activities of those on the picket line.

(c) For both types that:
- the employer will suffer serious damage as a result of the industrial action or picketing;
- there is a serious issue to be tried;
- damages would not be an adequate remedy, either because the potential loss is unquantifiable or because the damage suffered would be in excess of the relevant union's maximum damage limits (see para **5.45(d)** above) or because the likely damage to the employer goes beyond the immediate loss of business;
- the balance of convenience is in favour of maintaining normal production, and preserving the status quo;
- should an injunction be awarded and the employer be required to undertake to compensate the union for any damage suffered by the union in the event that the injunction was wrongly granted in the first place, the employer can afford to pay any such damages (a 'cross-undertaking in damages').

5.53 Should the employer give the trade union notice of the injunction? The employer should seek to give the union or, if known, the union's normal solicitors, notice of the intention to apply for an injunction if the trade union is likely to raise the defence that the action taken was in contemplation or furtherance of a trade dispute (TULR(C)A 1992, s 221(1)).

5.54 Can the injunction order the employees back to work? Not usually—the purpose of the injunction is to restrain the defendants from, for example, inducing others to breach their contracts or trespassing; the court will not specifically order strikers or picketers back to work. The court may, too, require a union to take particular steps to ensure:

(a) that there is no, or no further inducement of people to take part in industrial action; and/or

(b) that no person engages in any conduct after the injunction as a result of any pre-injunction inducements.

(TULR(C)A 1992, s 20(6))

Is an injunction only concerned with obtaining a civil remedy? No, there can be **5.55** criminal sanctions. If the injunction is granted it should be endorsed with a penal notice, informing those upon whom it is served that any breach will be a contempt of court, and served personally upon all the defendants. If the injunction is ignored, the trade union itself or any of its officers who can be shown to have knowledge of the injunction but who have, nevertheless, ignored it may be committed for contempt of court. The application for committal may be made by the employer upon motion to the court. If there has been a contempt, any individual found to be in contempt may be fined or imprisoned, and the union may be fined or its assets may be sequestrated until the union has purged its contempt. Sequestration will only be granted if disobedience to the original injunction has been deliberate.

5

Industrial Action

6

UNION RECOGNITION

A. Introduction

One of the innovations which the Labour Government introduced to UK indus- **6.01** trial relations, in 1999, was a mechanism by which an independent union could require employers to recognize it for certain minimum collective bargaining purposes. The Employment Relations Act 1999, via TULR(C)A 1992, s 70 and Sch A1 introduced the relevant legislation. The process governing union recognition is policed by the Central Arbitration Committee (CAC). It is tortuous and complicated, almost as if it were designed to encourage the parties to reach a recognition agreement voluntarily, rather than go through all the hoops. Indeed the CAC positively encourages voluntary union recognition agreements. In this chapter, we summarize the process in checklists and flowcharts, but given the complexity of the process this summary should only be regarded as an outline of the likely steps and ultimately recourse must be had to the detailed provisions of Sch A1 of TULR(C)A 1992 for the definitive position.

Recognition generally implies that a union has a right to negotiate over a selected **6.02** set of matters. Often, those matters are agreed between employer and union.

133

However, if there is no agreement, and if, broadly speaking, a majority of the relevant employment unit supports union recognition, then a union will acquire recognition for a minimum of three years.

6.03 Stripped down to its essentials, a union which cannot agree voluntary recognition with an employer makes an application to the CAC. If the CAC accepts the application, it then goes on to determine, in default of agreement, the relevant bargaining unit. Once this has been determined, CAC will look at union membership within the unit to see whether over 50 per cent of the workers in the unit are members of the relevant union. If they are, CAC will order recognition without a ballot. If more than 10 per cent of the workers are union members, CAC will order a ballot of the workforce in the bargaining unit. To succeed, not only must the majority of those who vote favour recognition, but that majority must itself represent at least 40 per cent of all the workers in the unit. If the union succeeds in a ballot, then (again in default of agreement) the CAC will impose a structure for the conduct of the recognition, normally in the form of a collective agreement. If the union is recognized pursuant to this CAC process, then the recognition agreement is binding on the parties, unless they expressly agree otherwise. The agreement cannot be reversed (unless the bargaining unit is no longer an appropriate unit) for at least three years.

6.04 If the CAC has been involved in the recognition process in some way and three years have expired since the recognition agreement was finalized, either party, or indeed the relevant workers, can start a de-recognition process. If CAC accepts the de-recognition claim, it will review matters such as the appropriateness of the bargaining unit, the number of people working for the employers, and the number of union members within the unit and may, if it believes it appropriate, conduct a secret ballot in the same manner, and with the same result, as the recognition ballot. Therefore, if a ballot is held and a majority of those who vote (being at least 40 per cent of the eligible workers) elect to retain the union, then the union's recognition will be confirmed for another three years.

B. Recognition—The Concept

6.05 What are the general consequences of recognition? A union which is recognized pursuant to the statutory process is entitled absent other agreement to:

(a) certain information, as follows:
  - information in respect of items for which it is recognized for purposes of collective bargaining (TULR(C)A 1992, s 181) but not to other information unless specifically entitled by statute (*R v CAC, ex p BTP Tioxide Limited* [1982] IRLR 60, HC);

- information and consultation on TUPE (TUPE Regulations 2006, reg 13 and see para **9.48** below);
- information and consultation on redundancies where 20 or more employees may be asked to leave within ninety days (TULR(C)A 1992, s 188);
- information and consultation with safety representatives under the Health and Safety at Work etc Act 1974, s 2(4);
- information and consultation about occupational pension schemes (Pension Schemes (Consultation by Employers, etc) Regulations 2006);

(b) time off work for a union's representatives to conduct their union activities (TULR(C)A 1992, s 168);
(c) begin the process of establishing a European Works Council;
(d) insist on consultation about training (TULR(C)A 1992, s 70B);
(e) negotiate on issues regarding pay, hours, and holidays (TULR(C)A 1992, Sch A1, para 3);
(f) enjoy recognition for a minimum period of three years (subject to there being a change of circumstances).

Is the position different where the recognition is voluntary? Voluntary recognition will occur where there is recognition of the union by an employer to any extent for the purposes of collective bargaining (TULR(C)A 1992, s 178(3) and for the definition of collective bargaining see TULR(C)A 1992, s 178(1)(2)). See also *National Union of Gold, Silver and Allied Trades v Albury Bros Ltd* [1979] ICR 84. Where parties voluntarily agree that a union will be recognized, without going through the CAC process, the following applies: **6.06**

(a) The union will enjoy all of the rights described at para **6.05** above as long as it is an independent trade union.
(b) The collective agreement is not legally binding, unless it expressly states to the contrary (TULR(C)A 1992, s 179).
(c) The collective agreement can be terminated by either party at any stage.
(d) The parties can determine the issues over which the union is to have recognition rights. They may include:
    - terms and conditions of employment;
    - pay and pensions;
    - recruitment, suspension, and dismissal;
    - demarcation;
    - disciplinary and grievance issues;
    - trade union membership;
    - facilities for the union;
    - the negotiation machinery.
(e) A union may be granted:
    - full rights, giving it the power to enter into full negotiations with the employer leading to agreement; or

6

Union Recognition

- representational rights, allowing the union to represent members, for example at disciplinary and grievance hearings in relation to some or all of the range of issues which are agreed to be part of the collective bargaining arrangement.

(f) Under TULR(C)A 1992, a party can apply for a voluntary recognition agreement to be treated as an agreement for recognition under Sch A1 (TULR(C)A 1992, Sch A1, para 55). If such an application is successful, the union will enjoy protection in relation to the termination of the agreement, amongst other things.

C. Preliminary Statutory Requirements for Compulsory Recognition

(See flow charts at pp 144–6)

6.07 What must a trade union do to satisfy the preliminary statutory requirements for compulsory recognition? Before a union can make an application to the CAC, it should satisfy itself of the following:

(a) The trade union must be certified independent (under TULR(C)A 1992, s 6; TULR(C)A 1992, Sch A1, para 6).

(b) The employer must have at least 21 workers (either itself or with other companies controlled by the same group) either on the day the employer receives the request or on average over the previous 13 weeks. Workers comprise both employees and freelancers, full- and part-time: the key is whether an individual performs services personally for someone who is not a professional client (TULR(C)A 1992, s 296 and Sch A1, para 7).

(c) No other union should be recognized as representing all or part of the bargaining unit (TULR(C)A 1992, Sch A1, para 35 and *R (on the application of National Union of Journalists) v Central Arbitration Committee* [2006] ICR 1).

(d) The Union must be able to satisfy the 'ten per cent' test by showing that at least ten per cent of the workers in the proposed bargaining unit are already members of the union (TULR(C)A 1992, Sch A1, para 36).

(e) No other application for recognition should have been made by the trade union during the previous three years in respect of the same or broadly the same bargaining unit (TULR(C)A 1992, Sch A1, paras 39–40).

(f) The Union must then write to the employer requesting recognition and:
- identifying the union;
- identifying the proposed bargaining unit: this must be a clear and recognizable bargaining unit, but need not be absolutely precise. If the union's

description is inappropriate (for example because it does not fully appreciate the organizational structure of the proposed bargaining unit), then it would be wise to submit a fresh application to the employer at this stage, before making its submission to the CAC; and

- stating that the request for recognition is made pursuant to Schedule A1 of the Trade Union and Labour Relations (Consolidation) Act 1992.

(TULR(C)A 1992, Sch A1, paras 5 and 8)

How can the employer respond to the request? **6.08**

(a) By not agreeing to it within a 10-day period. More particularly, at least 10 working days must have elapsed, starting with the day after that on which the employer received the initial request, without the union and employer having agreed:
  - a bargaining unit; and
  - that the union is to be recognized as entitled to conduct collective bargaining on behalf of the unit.

  (TULR(C)A 1992, Sch A1, para 10). If no such agreement is reached an application can be made to the CAC. If, however, the employer does agree these points, no further steps need be taken under the procedure and the union will be voluntarily recognized (see para **6.06** above).

(b) By expressing willingness to negotiate (TULR(C)A 1992, Sch A1, para 10(2)(3)). More particularly, if, during the first 10 working day period, the employer informs the union that it does not accept the request but is willing to negotiate, then at least 30 working days must have elapsed (starting with the day after that on which the employer first received the request for recognition) without those negotiations having been fruitful and without the parties having agreed an extension to this time limit before an application can be made to the CAC. If, within the first 10 working days following receipt of the union's request, an employer who is negotiating proposes to the Union that ACAS be requested to assist in conducting the negotiations and the union has rejected or failed to accept the proposal within 10 working days starting from the day after that on which the employer made the proposal then the union is disbarred from making an application to the CAC (TULR(C)A 1992, Sch A1, para 12(5)). If, however, agreement is reached with the union in relation to the bargaining unit and recognition occurs as set out in para **6.06** above as a result of these negotiations within the 30-day period or such longer period as is agreed, no further steps need be taken under the procedure. In these checklists, we refer only to the union. However, more than one union may apply to the CAC.

  (See flow charts at pp 144–5)

(c) After the relevant time period has elapsed, by applying to the CAC. More particularly, at the conclusion of the initial 10 working day period or extended

6

Union Recognition

negotiation period, if the parties have not reached agreement, the union may apply to the CAC to decide either or both of:

- whether the union's proposed bargaining unit is appropriate or some other bargaining unit is appropriate;
- whether the union has the support of a majority of the workers constituting the appropriate bargaining unit.

(TULR(C)A 1992, Sch A1, para 12)

6.09 What will happen once an application has been made to the CAC?

(a) CAC must acknowledge the application and then determine whether it has jurisdiction to consider the claim, by considering the items in para **6.07** above. The CAC must in addition be satisfied that the union's members constitute at least 10 per cent of the workers in the relevant bargaining unit.

(b) Within 10 working days of receipt of the application, CAC must inform the union and employer whether it accepts the application. If the application is accepted, the union cannot withdraw it without the consent of the employer.

(c) Note that the CAC has the power to extend all time limits in the process.

(TULR(C)A 1992, Sch A1, para 13–15)

D. The Appropriate Bargaining Unit

(See flow charts at pp 144–5)

6.10 How will the CAC determine what is to be the appropriate bargaining unit?

(a) If the employer and union have not agreed on the appropriate bargaining unit within 20 working days after the date when CAC gives notice of acceptance of the application, CAC must decide the appropriate bargaining unit, within the next 10 working days. CAC must consider the following matters:

- the need for the unit to be compatible with effective management— this is the overriding issue; the other matters are relevant only so long as they do not conflict with this requirement;
- the views of the employer and of the union;
- existing national and local bargaining arrangements;
- the desirability of avoiding small fragmented bargaining units within an undertaking. CAC will consider issues such as whether there is an integrated management structure across sites, and whether the pay and benefits issues, performance reviews, and so on are established across sites or are on a site for site basis;
- the characteristics of workers falling within the proposed bargaining unit and of any other employees (*note—not workers*) of the employer whom the

CAC considers relevant. The unit can even include a section of the company in which, at the particular point in time, there happened to be no workers;
- the location of workers.

(TULR(C)A 1992, Sch A1, paras 18, 18A, 19, and 19A)

(b) The union will have put forward the first suggested bargaining unit in its initial application (see para **6.07** above). CAC will consider whether the proposed bargaining unit is appropriate. It must decide whether the union's proposed unit is compatible with effective management, taking into account the employer's arguments including its counter-proposals. If the union's proposal is appropriate, CAC does not need to enquire further or select the most appropriate bargaining unit (*R v CAC, ex p Kwik-Fit (GB) Limited* [2002] IRLR 395, CA). Accordingly, the union's proposed unit is likely to prevail in the substantial majority of cases, provided the proposed unit is easily definable and managerially effective, so that CAC can conclude that it is likely to assist in fair and efficient workplace practices and arrangements. The CAC will contemplate a multiple-employer bargaining unit. However, this is likely to apply only where the operation of two associated companies is so inextricably intertwined that in reality the two workforces are unified (*GPMU and Derry Print Limited and John Brown (Printers) Limited* (17.1.02 TUR1/113 and TUR1/115)).

(c) CAC must give notice of its decision to the parties.

(d) If the agreed or CAC-imposed bargaining unit is different from that in the original application, CAC must decide again whether the application is valid (using the criteria set out in para **6.07** above) within 10 working days from the date the new appropriate unit was agreed/declared. If CAC decides that the application is invalid by reference to the new bargaining unit (eg it fails the 10 per cent test, or another union is recognized for any area within the new bargaining unit) the recognition process ends (TULR(C)A 1992, Sch A1, paras 20, 43–50).

E. The Recognition Decision

(See flow charts at p 146)

6.11 Once a valid bargaining unit has been determined, when will recognition be automatic? If CAC receives evidence that more than 50 per cent of workers in the unit are already members of the union, it will normally issue a declaration that the union is recognized in relation to the unit. Exceptions are if:

(a) CAC is satisfied that a ballot should be held in the interests of good industrial relations; or

(b) a significant number of the union's members within the unit tell CAC they do not want the union to conduct collective bargaining; or

(c) membership evidence leads CAC to conclude that there are doubts whether a significant number of union members want the union to conduct collective bargaining (eg where a union has offered free membership to workers in the unit until it is recognized—*AEEU and Huntleigh Healthcare Ltd* (TUR1/19/00, 2001, CAC).

(TULR(C)A 1992, Sch A1, para 22)

6.12 What is the alternative to automatic recognition? If any of the exceptions in para **6.11** above applies, or if fewer than 50 per cent of workers in the unit are union members, CAC will announce a ballot.

6.13 What are the terms associated with the holding of a ballot?

(a) The union may, within 10 working days of the announcement of a ballot, withdraw from the process (effectively admitting defeat). Alternatively the parties may jointly agree to dispense with the ballot (normally because they have reached agreement).

(b) If there is a ballot, CAC appoints a scrutineer, with the ballot being held within 20 working days of the appointment. CAC decides the conduct of the ballot (voting at the workplace, by post, or (very rarely) both) looking at issues of fairness, cost, and practicality.
(TULR(C)A 1992, Sch A1, para 25)

(c) The employer has the following duties during the ballot period:
- to cooperate generally with the union and scrutineer;
- to allow the union reasonable access to the bargaining unit to lobby the workers. However, the employer has certain rights to be present at any meetings;
- to give CAC within 10 working days of the start of the ballot, where possible, names and home addresses of the workers in the bargaining unit (but not to duplicate this information if already provided and with an obligation to update for any joiners/leavers);
- to refrain from making any offer to the workers to induce them not to attend any meeting between the union and workers in the bargaining unit and which is not reasonable;
- to refrain from threatening any action against a worker on the basis he attended or took part in any such meeting.

CAC can order a recalcitrant employer to comply with these duties within a specific period. If the employer still fails, CAC may declare the union recognized, without any ballot (TULR(C)A 1992, Sch A1, paras 26 and 27).

(d) The schedule also provides that unfair practice must not be adopted by either of the parties and the repercussions if such practices are adopted (TULR(C)A 1992 Sch A1, paras 27A to 27C).

(e) The scrutineer:
- must pass through to the workers identified by the employer pursuant to para **6.13(c)** any canvassing information supplied by the union (TULR(C)A 1992, Sch A1, para 26(6));
- will send the employer and the union a demand for 50 per cent each of the gross costs of the ballot (TULR(C)A 1992, Sch A1, paras 28(2)(4)).

When will the union be recognized as a result of the ballot? The union will be **6.14** recognized if:

(a) a majority of those workers who vote select recognition; and
(b) those who support recognition form at least 40 per cent of the total number of workers in the bargaining unit.

In these circumstances CAC will issue a declaration that the union is recognized (TULR(C)A 1992, Sch A1, para 29(3)).

F. Consequences of Recognition

(See flow charts at p 146)

What are the consequences of recognition?   **6.15**

(a) Once a union has been declared as recognized, the parties have 30 working days to negotiate a collective agreement (all or part of this may be binding or not binding, according to the agreement) (TULR(C)A 1992, Sch A1, paras 30(1)–(4)).

(b) If the parties cannot agree, either one may ask CAC to mediate. Mediation will last 20 working days from the date a party asked CAC to mediate (TULR(C)A 1992, Sch A1, paras 30(3), 31).

(c) If there is no agreement during the CAC mediation period, CAC will impose a legally binding collective agreement (TULR(C)A 1992, Sch A1, para 31(3)).

(d) If the parties agree a collective agreement, but it is not working, either side may refer the matter to CAC who will then proceed to mediate (TULR(C)A 1992, Sch A1, para 32).

(e) The union will be recognized to represent workers in agreeing pay, hours, and holidays for all workers in the bargaining unit (see paras **6.05** and **6.06** above).

(f) The agreement can be terminated by the employer, but only:
- if the bargaining unit has ceased to exist (see para **6.17** below); or
- after three years has expired (see para **6.18** below).

(See flow charts at pp 144–5)

G. Varying the Recognition Arrangements

(See flow chart at p 148)

6.16 What happens if during the three-year period, the recognized bargaining unit changes materially?

(a) If the recognized bargaining unit changes materially, either party may apply to CAC for a declaration on whether the original unit is still an appropriate bargaining unit or whether some other unit is now appropriate. CAC will consider this application if there has been:
- a change in the organization or structure of the employer's business;
- a change in the employer's business activities;
- a substantial change in the number of workers in the original unit.
(TULR(C)A 1992, Sch A1, paras 66 and 67)

(b) CAC has 10 working days within which to decide whether, bearing in mind the issues in para **6.16(a)** above, it is likely that the original unit is no longer appropriate. If it thinks this is unlikely, then the application fails (TULR(C)A 1992, Sch A1, para 68).

(c) If CAC accepts the application, the parties then have 10 working days to agree on a different bargaining unit. If that bargaining unit encompasses a worker already covered by an outside bargaining unit (where another independent union is recognized), the procedure ends. If it does not, CAC will declare that the new business unit is recognized under the same terms as before (with any necessary modifications bearing in mind the change of the bargaining unit) (TULR(C)A 1992, Sch A1, para 69).

(d) If the parties cannot agree a new bargaining unit, CAC has 10 working days to decide finally whether the original bargaining unit is still appropriate (considering the issues in para **6.16(a)** above, ie, whether there have been changes in the employer's organization, structure, or activities, or significant changes in the number of workers employed in the unit) or whether some other bargaining unit is now appropriate. If CAC decides that the original unit is no longer appropriate, it must consider five issues in determining a new unit compatible with effective management. These are the same as those which it considered in creating the original unit (see para **6.10(a)** above) and are:

- the views of the employer and the union;
- existing national and local bargaining arrangements;
- the desirability of avoiding small fragmented bargaining units within an undertaking;
- the characteristics of workers falling within the original unit and of any other relevant employees (note, not workers) of the employer;
- the location of the workers.

(TULR(C)A 1992, Sch A1, para 70)

(e) If CAC decides a new bargaining unit is appropriate, it issues a declaration to that effect. The unit will be recognized on the same terms as before, subject to any modifications deemed necessary by the CAC as a result of the changed unit (see para **6.17** below) (TULR(C)A 1992, Sch A1, paras 72 and 82).

(See flow chart at p 148)

What happens if, during the three-year period, the recognized bargaining unit **6.17**
ceases to exist?

(a) Where the employer thinks the bargaining unit has ceased to exist, and wants to stop the bargaining arrangements, it gives the union a notice, copied to CAC:
- identifying the unit and the bargaining arrangements;
- stating the date;
- stating that the unit has ceased to exist;
- stating that the bargaining arrangements are to cease to have effect on a specified date at least 35 working days hence.

(TULR(C)A 1992, Sch A1, para 74)

(b) Once CAC has accepted the notice as valid, the union has 10 working days to put in an objection. If it does not do so, bargaining arrangements cease. If the union wants to object, it may apply to the CAC to decide whether the original unit has ceased to exist or whether it is no longer appropriate on the basis of changes in the employer's organization, structure, or activities, or a substantial change in the number of workers (see para **6.16(a)** above) (TULR(C)A 1992, Sch A1, para 75).

(c) If CAC accepts the employer's application it must give the employer and union an opportunity to comment on the issues and then decide within 10 working days:
- that the original unit has ceased to exist, in which case bargaining arrangements shall cease on the date specified in the employer's original notice (see para **6.17(a)** above) or on the day after CAC's decision, if later; or

6

Flow Chart: Union recognition flow chart

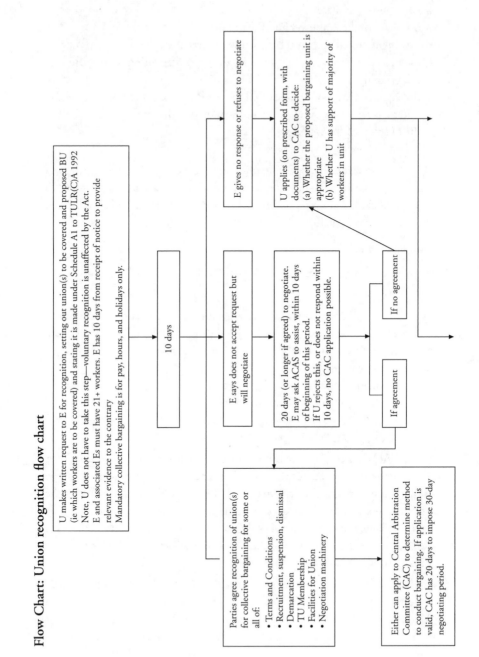

U makes written request to E for recognition, setting out union(s) to be covered and proposed BU (ie which workers are to be covered) and stating it is made under Schedule A1 to TULR(C)A 1992

Note, U does not have to take this step—voluntary recognition is unaffected by the Act.

E and associated Es must have 21+ workers. E has 10 days from receipt of notice to provide relevant evidence to the contrary

Mandatory collective bargaining is for pay, hours, and holidays only.

10 days

E says does not accept request but will negotiate

E gives no response or refuses to negotiate

20 days (or longer if agreed) to negotiate. E may ask ACAS to assist, within 10 days of beginning of this period.
If U rejects this, or does not respond within 10 days, no CAC application possible.

U applies (on prescribed form, with documents) to CAC to decide:
(a) Whether the proposed bargaining unit is appropriate
(b) Whether U has support of majority of workers in unit

If agreement

If no agreement

Parties agree recognition of union(s) for collective bargaining for some or all of:
• Terms and Conditions
• Recruitment, suspension, dismissal
• Demarcation
• TU Membership
• Facilities for Union
• Negotiation machinery

Either can apply to Central Arbitration Committee (CAC) to determine method to conduct bargaining. If application is valid, CAC has 20 days to impose 30-day negotiating period.

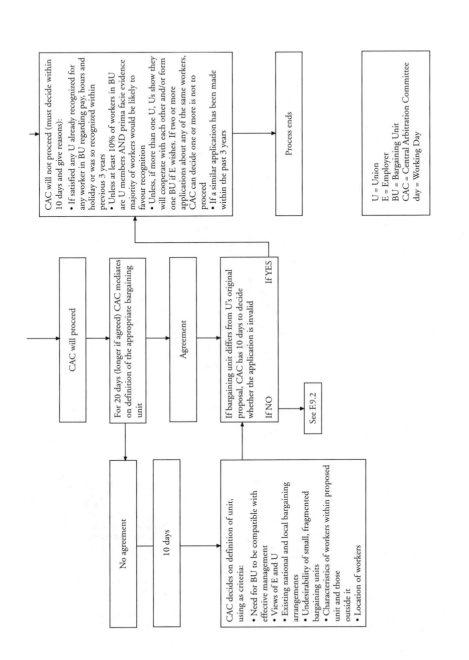

CAC will not proceed (must decide within 10 days and give reasons):
- If satisfied any U already recognized for any worker in BU regarding pay, hours and holiday or was so recognized within previous 3 years
- Unless at least 10% of workers in BU are U members AND prima facie evidence majority of workers would be likely to favour recognition
- Unless, if more than one U, Us show they will cooperate with each other and/or form one BU if E wishes. If two or more applications about any of the same workers, CAC can decide one or more is not to proceed
- If a similar application has been made within the past 3 years

Process ends

U = Union
E = Employer
BU = Bargaining Unit
CAC = Central Arbitration Committee
day = Working Day

CAC will proceed

For 20 days (longer if agreed) CAC mediates on definition of the appropriate bargaining unit

Agreement

If bargaining unit differs from U's original proposal, CAC has 10 days to decide whether the application is invalid

If YES

If NO

See F.9.2

No agreement

10 days

CAC decides on definition of unit, using as criteria:
- Need for BU to be compatible with effective management
- Views of E and U
- Existing national and local bargaining arrangements
- Undesirability of small, fragmented bargaining units
- Characteristics of workers within proposed unit and those outside it
- Location of workers

Flow Chart: Recognition process from ballot

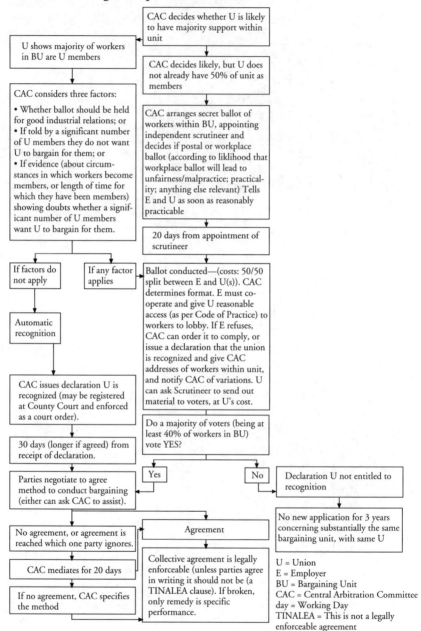

CAC decides whether U is likely to have majority support within unit

↓

CAC decides likely, but U does not already have 50% of unit as members

↓

CAC arranges secret ballot of workers within BU, appointing independent scrutineer and decides if postal or workplace ballot (according to likelihood that workplace ballot will lead to unfairness/malpractice; practicality; anything else relevant) Tells E and U as soon as reasonably practicable

↓

20 days from appointment of scrutineer

↓

Ballot conducted—(costs: 50/50 split between E and U(s)). CAC determines format. E must co-operate and give U reasonable access (as per Code of Practice) to workers to lobby. If E refuses, CAC can order it to comply, or issue a declaration that the union is recognized and give CAC addresses of workers within unit, and notify CAC of variations. U can ask Scrutineer to send out material to voters, at U's cost.

↓

Do a majority of voters (being at least 40% of workers in BU) vote YES?

Yes / No

U shows majority of workers in BU are U members

↓

CAC considers three factors:

• Whether ballot should be held for good industrial relations; or
• If told by a significant number of U members they do not want U to bargain for them; or
• If evidence (about circumstances in which workers become members, or length of time for which they have been members) showing doubts whether a significant number of U members want U to bargain for them.

If factors do not apply / If any factor applies

Automatic recognition

↓

CAC issues declaration U is recognized (may be registered at County Court and enforced as a court order).

↓

30 days (longer if agreed) from receipt of declaration.

↓

Parties negotiate to agree method to conduct bargaining (either can ask CAC to assist).

↓

No agreement, or agreement is reached which one party ignores.

↓

CAC mediates for 20 days

↓

If no agreement, CAC specifies the method

No → Declaration U not entitled to recognition

↓

No new application for 3 years concerning substantially the same bargaining unit, with same U

Agreement

↓

Collective agreement is legally enforceable (unless parties agree in writing it should not be (a TINALEA clause). If broken, only remedy is specific performance.

U = Union
E = Employer
BU = Bargaining Unit
CAC = Central Arbitration Committee
day = Working Day
TINALEA = This is not a legally enforceable agreement

- that the original unit has not ceased to exist but some other bargaining unit is more appropriate (in which case the procedure set out at paras **6.16(c)** and (**d**) above is followed for determining the new bargaining unit).
(TULR(C)A 1992, Sch A1, para 76)

(See flow chart at p 148)

What happens where, during the three-year period, a new bargaining unit is determined by CAC? **6.18**

(a) CAC must decide if any worker within the new unit is also covered by another bargaining unit, whether statutory (ie as declared by CAC) or voluntary (ie agreed between parties without CAC application). If there is an overlap with another statutory unit, recognition for both units must cease within 65 working days (TULR(C)A 1992, Sch A1, paras 82 and 83).

(b) If the overlap is with a voluntary unit, the voluntary unit remains but the original bargaining unit ceases to exist on a date specified by CAC (TULR(C)A 1992, Sch A1, para 84).

(c) If there is no overlap, CAC must assess whether the new unit is sufficiently different from the old unit as to question whether a majority would still be in favour of union recognition. If CAC decides that the two units are sufficiently similar that the quality of support does not need to be reassessed, it will declare that the union is recognized for the new bargaining unit on the same terms as before, subject to any modifications CAC deems necessary to take into account the change of the bargaining unit (TULR(C)A 1992, Sch A1, para 85).

(d) If CAC decides that the level of support does need to be reassessed, it will proceed exactly as it had done originally, once the original business unit was determined (see (TULR(C)A 1992, Sch A1, para 86 and paras **6.11–6.15** above).

6

Union Recognition

Flow Chart: Variation or Termination of Bargaining Unit

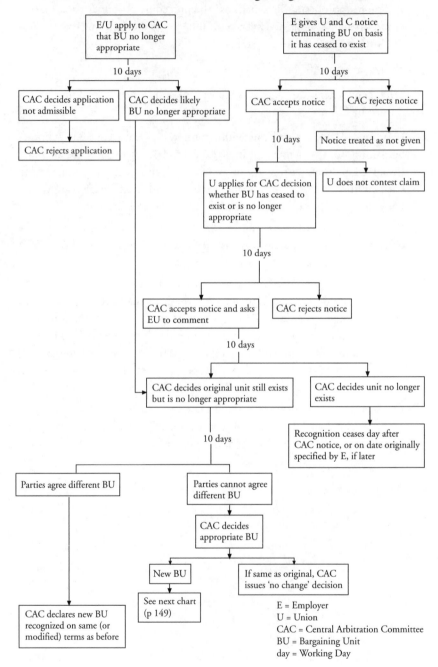

E/U apply to CAC that BU no longer appropriate

10 days

CAC decides application not admissible

CAC decides likely BU no longer appropriate

CAC rejects application

E gives U and C notice terminating BU on basis it has ceased to exist

10 days

CAC accepts notice

CAC rejects notice

Notice treated as not given

10 days

U applies for CAC decision whether BU has ceased to exist or is no longer appropriate

U does not contest claim

10 days

CAC accepts notice and asks EU to comment

CAC rejects notice

10 days

CAC decides original unit still exists but is no longer appropriate

CAC decides unit no longer exists

Recognition ceases day after CAC notice, or on date originally specified by E, if later

10 days

Parties agree different BU

Parties cannot agree different BU

CAC decides appropriate BU

New BU

If same as original, CAC issues 'no change' decision

See next chart (p 149)

CAC declares new BU recognized on same (or modified) terms as before

E = Employer
U = Union
CAC = Central Arbitration Committee
BU = Bargaining Unit
day = Working Day

6

Union Recognition

148

Flow Chart: Where New Business Unit is Imposed by CAC

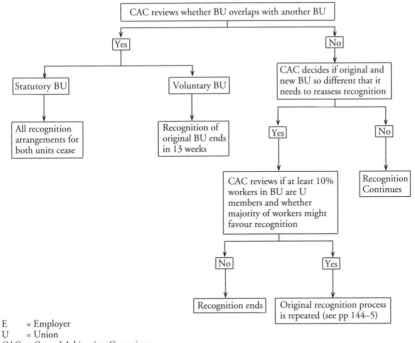

E = Employer
U = Union
CAC = Central Arbitration Committee
BU = Business Unit

H. De-recognition

(See flow charts at pp 152–3)

6.19 What happens once the three-year period of compulsory statutory recognition has passed? Once more than three years has passed, either the employer or the workers in the unit can apply to end a statutory recognition arrangement. There are three different routes for ending a statutory recognition:

(a) employer application if fewer than 21 workers (see (TULR(C)A 1992, Sch A1, paras 99 to 103 and para **6.20** below);

(b) employer's request to end arrangements (see (TULR(C)A 1992, Sch A1, paras 104 to 111 and para **6.21** below);

(c) workers' application to end arrangements (TULR(C)A 1992, Sch A1, paras 112 to 116 and para **6.22** below).

There are no special procedures for terminating voluntary recognition agreements.

6.20 What happens if the employer and any associated employer employ less than 21 workers?

(a) If the employer believes that it and any associated employer(s) employed fewer than 21 workers on average in any 13-week period ending at least three years after the recognition was declared, he may give the union, copied to the CAC, a notice:
- identifying the bargaining arrangements;
- specifying the relevant 13-week period;
- giving the date of the notice;
- stating that the employer, taken with any associated employer(s), employed an average of fewer than 21 workers in the specified period of 13 weeks (to find average: add together the number of workers employed for all or part of each week and divide by 13);
- stating that the bargaining arrangements are to cease to have effect on a date specified in the notice at least 35 working days after that on which notice is given;
- giving the notice within five working days after the last day of the 13-week period.

However, the notice will be invalidated if another notice has been given on the same basis in the previous three years, or on the basis of the employer or workers wishing to end the recognition arrangement (TULR(C)A 1992, Sch A1, paras 99 and 99A).

(b) Once the CAC has validated the notice, which it must do within 10 working days, the bargaining arrangements will cease on the date set out in the notice unless the union makes an application in the correct form supported by requisite documents, copied to the CAC (TULR(C)A 1992, Sch A1, paras 100 and 101).

(c) The CAC has 10 working days to decide if the union's application is valid. If it is, it will give employer and union an opportunity to put their views on the questions:
- whether the 13-week period specified by the employer ends after three years of statutory recognition; and/or
- whether the employer and associated companies have employed fewer than 21 workers on average over that 13-week period.

(TULR(C)A 1992, Sch A1, paras 102 and 103)

(d) If the answer to either of these questions is no, then statutory recognition continues. If the answer to both questions is yes, then recognition will end on the date set out in the employer's notice or, if later, the day after the CAC releases its decision (TULR(C)A 1992, Sch A1, para 104).

What happens if the employer requests that the recognition period end? **6.21**

(a) After the end of the three-year compulsory recognition period, an employer may write to the union:
- identifying the bargaining arrangements;
- stating that the letter is made under Schedule A1 of the Trade Union and Labour Relations (Consolidation) Act 1992; and
- requesting the union to agree to end the bargaining arrangements.
- If recognition was granted by CAC automatically (ie without a ballot, on the basis that a majority of workers in the bargaining unit were members of the union), the employer's notice must also assert that fewer than half of the workers in the unit are now union members.

(TULR(C)A 1992, Sch A1, paras 104 and 127)

(b) The union may:
- agree to the request within 10 working days, in which case recognition ends;
- inform the employer it does not accept the request but is willing to negotiate, in which case the parties have 20 working days within which to agree;
- inform the employer within 10 working days that it does not agree to the request but is willing to negotiate and may also, within a further 10 days, propose that ACAS be requested to assist. If the employer rejects or fails within 10 working days to agree to ACAS assistance, the de-recognition process must end. Otherwise, there is the same 20-day negotiation period as above;
- not respond, or refuse the request, in which case the employer may apply to CAC for a de-recognition ballot.

(TULR(C)A 1992, Sch A1, paras 105 to 107)

(c) If an employer asks the CAC for a de-recognition ballot it must do so in due form with relevant documents giving notice and a copy of the application and documents to the union. CAC will accept the application if it decides:
- (a) that at least 10 per cent of the workers in the bargaining unit want to end bargaining arrangements; and
- (b) a majority of workers in the unit would be likely to want to end the arrangement;
- (c) where automatic recognition applies (see para **6.20(a)** above), whether fewer than 50 per cent of workers in the unit are still union members.

If the answer to any of these questions is no, the recognition agreement remains in place.

(TULR(C)A 1992, Sch A1, paras 108 to 110)

6

Flow Chart: De-recognition

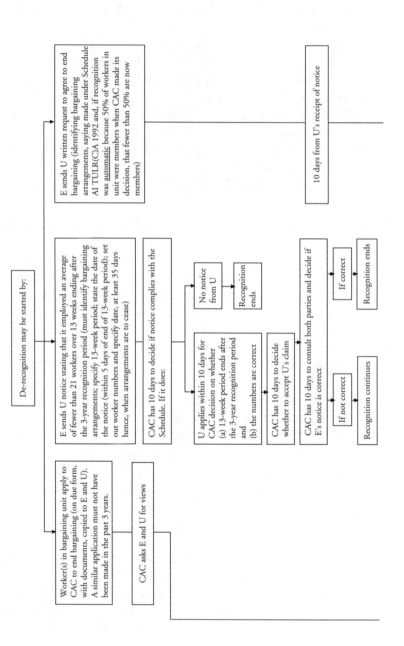

De-recognition may be started by:

Worker(s) in bargaining unit apply to CAC to end bargaining (on due form, with documents, copied to E and U). A similar application must not have been made in the past 3 years.

E sends U notice stating that it employed an average of fewer than 21 workers over 13 weeks ending after the 3-year recognition period (must identify bargaining arrangements; specify 13-week period; state the date of the notice (within 5 days of end of 13-week period); set out worker numbers and specify date, at least 35 days hence, when arrangements are to cease)

E sends U written request to agree to end bargaining (identifying bargaining arrangements, saying made under Schedule A1 TULR(C)A 1992 and, if recognition was automatic because 50% of workers in unit were members when CAC made its decision, that fewer than 50% are now members)

CAC asks E and U for views

CAC has 10 days to decide if notice complies with the Schedule. If it does:

No notice from U → Recognition ends

U applies within 10 days for CAC decision on whether
(a) 13-week period ends after the 3-year recognition period and
(b) the numbers are correct

CAC has 10 days to decide whether to accept U's claim

10 days from U's receipt of notice

CAC has 10 days to consult both parties and decide if E's notice is correct

If correct → Recognition ends

If not correct → Recognition continues

152

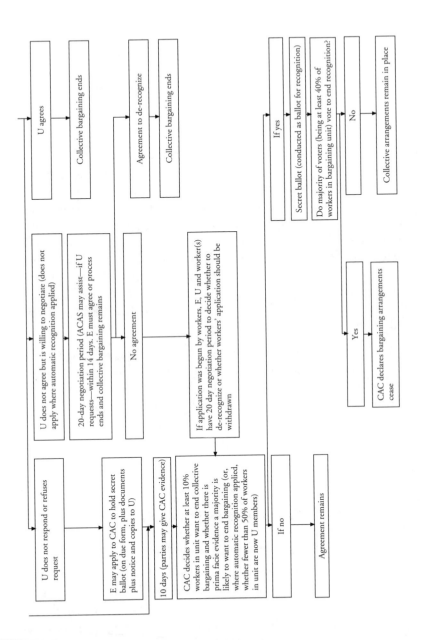

Union Recognition

6

(d) If CAC accepts the ballot application it proceeds to a secret ballot (after an additional 20-day negotiation period if the process was begun by a workers' application, see para **6.22** below). The secret ballot is conducted as a ballot for recognition (see para **6.13** above). The question for the ballot to determine is whether a majority of the voters (being at least 40 per cent of workers in the bargaining unit) vote to end recognition. If they do, then CAC declares bargaining arrangements cease. If they do not, then the collective agreement remains in place (TULR(C)A 1992, Sch A1, paras 117 to 121).

6.22 What happens if the workers request that the recognition period end?

(a) Once three years have elapsed since CAC declared the existence of a recognition agreement, a worker or workers within the bargaining unit may apply to CAC, in due form, with relevant documents, to have the bargaining arrangements ended. Notice of the application and a copy of it and relevant documents must be given to the employer and union. CAC will consider any evidence submitted by the workers, the employer, or the union within 10 working days of receipt of the application, and will then decide whether:

- at least 10 per cent of workers in the bargaining unit wanted to end bargaining arrangements; and
- the majority of the workers in the unit would be likely to favour derecognition.

(b) If the answer to either of those questions is no, then the application fails. If the answer to both questions is yes, then CAC will proceed to conduct a secret ballot in accordance with the procedure set out in para **6.20(d)** above (TULR(C)A 1992, Sch A1, paras 112 to 116).

Flow Chart: De-recognition

(See flow charts at pp 152–3)

I. Victimization/Dismissal

6.23 Is a worker protected from detriment or dismissal on an individual basis?

(a) If a worker believes he has been subjected to detriment by any act or omission on the part of his employer short of dismissal, as a result of his reasonable actions or omissions in support or opposition of any recognition or de-recognition claim, he may bring a complaint to the employment tribunal (TULR(C)A 1992, Sch A1, para 156). The complaint must be made within three months of the date of the act or omission (or if a series, on the date of the last act or omission). A grievance must be brought prior to the claim where detriment is alleged (EA 2002, s 32 and Sch 4 and see paras 7.81–7.83). The burden of proof is on the employer to show why he acted or failed to act. An employment tribunal may award just and equitable damages having regard to the infringement and any direct loss to the worker (including expenses and loss of benefit). The compensation award may be reduced if the worker has failed to mitigate his loss, or if he has contributed to the loss (TULR(C)A 1992, Sch A1, paras 158 to 160).

(b) If an employee is dismissed or selected for redundancy wholly or mainly as a result of his reasonable actions or omissions in support or opposition of any recognition or de-recognition claim, this will be automatically unfair dismissal (TULR(C)A 1992, Sch A1, paras 161 and 162). This would be the case even if the employee has been employed for less than one year.

(c) If a worker who is not an employee has his contract terminated wholly or mainly as a result of his reasonable actions or omissions in support or opposition of any recognition or de-recognition claim, this will be regarded as victimization and will be subject to the same maximum basic and compensatory award limits as for unfair dismissal (see TULR(C)A 1992, Sch A1, para 161 and para 7.124).

J. Appeal

What right of appeal will the parties have? The only method of appealing a decision of CAC is by making an application for judicial review of the decision to the High Court. However, intervention by the court is likely to be limited (*Fullarton Computer Industries Ltd v Central Arbitration Committee* [2001] IRLR 752). **6.24**

7

DISMISSALS

A. Introduction

All employees have the right not to be wrongfully or unfairly dismissed. These **7.01** rights are distinct but overlapping. Wrongful dismissal occurs, in essence, when a person is dismissed in breach of the contract of employment, normally when dismissed without being given notice or paid in lieu of notice. No minimum period of employment is necessary. A claim can be brought in the Employment Tribunal, but the claim is limited to £25,000. If the value of the claim is higher than £25,000, the claim should be brought in the High Court or county court.

7.02 Statute gives employees the right not to be unfairly dismissed. The right only applies to employees, not to workers. With a few exceptions, such as those dismissed for asserting a statutory right or for 'whistle-blowing', employees must have at least one year's service before they can bring a claim. A claim will be defeated if the employer can show that an appropriate procedure was followed before the dismissal, and that the employee was dismissed for a legitimate reason. Legitimate reasons are misconduct, incapability to perform the role, retirement, redundancy, illegality, unsuitable qualifications to carry out the role, or some other substantial reason justifying dismissal. Save in all but a few exceptional cases, there is a cap on the total compensation that can be awarded to someone who has been unfairly dismissed (£72,900 for those dismissed between 1 February 2008 and 31 January 2009 and £76,700 for those dismissed between 1 February 2009 and 31 January 2010).

B. Wrongful Dismissal

CHECKLISTS

Grounds for Wrongful Dismissal: Initial Hurdles

7.03 Who has the right not to be wrongfully dismissed? The principles set out here for wrongful dismissal apply to workers as well as to employees (see paras **1.01** and **1.02** and thereafter for the distinction between employees and workers).

7.04 Has the employer, without cause, terminated the employee's contract of employment without:

(a) allowing the employee to work out all his notice; or
(b) paying the employee in lieu of his salary and benefits for all of his unworked notice period; or
(c) paying the employee in accordance with a clause allowing the employer to terminate the employment immediately on making a payment in lieu of the salary due for the balance of the notice period?

If so, the employee has been wrongfully dismissed.

7.05 Has the employer paid the employee in lieu of notice, where there is no contractual provision allowing payment in lieu? If so there may still be a technical breach of contract and hence a wrongful dismissal but the employee is unlikely to have suffered any financial loss. This breach is generally only relevant if the employer subsequently seeks to rely on post-termination restrictions. In these circumstances the employer will normally not be able to enforce any covenants in the employment contract which prevent the employee from competing with the employer for a period of time.

Has the employer dismissed the employee for cause but ignoring any contractual **7.06** procedural requirements such as disciplinary and warning procedures which are expressly or impliedly incorporated into the employee's contract of employment (for example, because expressly referred to in the contract, staff handbook, or collective agreement)? If so, this will be wrongful dismissal (*Gunton v Richmond upon Thames LBC* [1980] ICR 755) but there are likely to be only two remedies:

(a) damages limited to the period between actual dismissal and the date dismissal should have taken place had proper procedures been followed; or

(b) (very rarely and only if sought promptly enough) an injunction preventing the employer from terminating the employment until proper procedures are undertaken (*Robb v London Borough of Hammersmith and Fulham* [1991] ICR 514, HC).

Has the employer acted so badly that the employee is entitled to accept the **7.07** conduct as constructive dismissal and resign (see also para **7.68**)? If so, and the employee resigns, this will be constructive dismissal. Examples of constructive dismissal are set out at para **7.76**.

Has the employee suffered a psychiatric illness as a result of the employer's actions **7.08** (provided that those actions are not part of the dismissal process)? If so, there will be a constructive dismissal, and damages can include personal injury damages for psychiatric illness (eg where an employee was unreasonably suspended for a long period on implausible but very serious charges: *Gogay v Hertfordshire County Council* [2000] IRLR 703, CA (see also paras **7.320–7.340**).

Has the employer acted so badly (eg by conducting a fraudulent business) that his **7.09** employees suffer a stigma which prevents them gaining alternative employment? If so, the employees may be able to recover damages beyond the notice period. However, this will be very rare, for the employees will have to show they were refused jobs because of the stigma of having worked for their previous employer (*Malik v BCCI* [1997] IRLR 462, HL).

Has the employee suffered a loss? He might not have—for example, if he imme- **7.10** diately moved on to another job on the same or improved financial terms. If no loss, no damages will be recovered (see paras **7.20** and **7.307**).

The Employer's Defence

Has the employee committed a material breach of contract entitling the employer **7.11** to terminate the contract? A breach of contract may be a breach of an express term of a contract or staff manual or it may be that the employee has shown himself to be so incompetent or to have conducted himself so badly as to entitle the employer to terminate the contract. In essence, the tests to be applied as to whether the employee's incompetence or misconduct are sufficiently serious to justify dismissal are the same as those which apply in unfair dismissal (see paras **7.154–7.181**). If the employer dismissed the employee for cause, it has a full defence to a wrongful dismissal claim.

7.12 Does it matter whether the employer did not know of the breach of contract before the dismissal? No. The court will examine all of the employee's conduct before dismissal, whether or not the employer knew of the conduct before it terminated the contract (*Boston Deep Sea Fishing and Ice Company v Ansell* (1888) 39 Ch D 339).

7.13 Has the employer given the employee proper notice of the termination of his contract of employment before the date of dismissal which the employee is to work out? If yes, there is no wrongful dismissal.

7.14 Has the employer paid the employee a proper amount of compensation in lieu of notice amounting either to the value of salary and benefits for the period between the actual date of dismissal and the earliest date any notice could have expired, or to salary during the notice period if there is contractual provision allowing the employer to terminate the contract immediately on payment of salary in lieu of notice? If yes, the employee has suffered no loss. An employee is not entitled both to work out his notice period and to be paid in lieu of notice following the expiry of that notice period. For the appropriate length of an employee's notice period, see para **7.16**.

Consequences and Damages

7.15 What is the remedy for constructive dismissal? If an employee succeeds in demonstrating to the court that he has been wrongfully dismissed because:

(a) his contract of employment was terminated without notice;
(b) his contract has terminated without a payment in lieu of notice; and
(c) in either case there was no just cause for this

he will be entitled to recover damages. For detailed calculation of damages, see para **7.322**. The amount of damages will be the value of the employee's salary and benefits (possibly including any bonus payable during the notice period) after deduction of tax and national insurance contributions, for the balance of the outstanding notice period, less various deductions and then grossed up for any tax payable at the time of payment.

Quantification of Damages

7.16 What is the employee's notice period? This is the notice the employer must give the employee to terminate the employment. This is normally set out in the contract, but if not it will be statutory notice (essentially a week for the first year, then an additional week per completed year of employment, up to a maximum of 12 weeks) (ERA 1996, s 86) or, for more senior employees, a longer period of implied notice (see also paras **1.107–1.109**).

Is the employee on a fixed-term contract that cannot be terminated before the **7.17** end of the term? If so, the 'notice period' will be the period between the actual date of termination and the end of the fixed term.

Is the employee on a fixed-term contract that can be terminated by the employer **7.18** giving the employee a shorter notice period? If so, the 'notice period' will be the shorter of the notice period the employer can give to terminate the employment, and the period between the actual termination date and the end of the fixed term (eg for a two year fixed-term contract that either party can terminate at any stage upon giving three months' notice, the notice period will be three months, or the period between actual termination and the end of the two-year period, if shorter).

What is the employee's benefits package during the notice period? The aggregate **7.19** of all salary and benefits payable during the notice period is calculated. This may include the following:

(a) Salary. If a contractual salary review date falls during the notice period, the employee might be able to persuade the court that he should be credited with a suitable salary uplift for the period from the review date until termination even if any rise is discretionary (*Clark v BET* [1997] IRLR 348, HC).

(b) Bonus. An employee can always recover any contractual bonus that was due to be paid during any unworked notice period. He may also recover any discretionary bonus he might have been paid during the period, if the employer acted totally unreasonably in failing to pay him any bonus or in paying him one which was unjustifiably low (*Clark v Nomura International plc* [2000] IRLR 766, HC). However, the Court of Appeal has narrowed the occasions where this can be applied where the bonus is discretionary, saying (a) that it would take an overwhelming case to persuade a court to find that the level of bonus payment was irrational or perverse where much of the exercise of discretion depends upon judgement and fluctuating market and labour conditions; and (b) that a clause in a contract which says that no bonus is payable if, on the date payment is due, the employee is no longer employed or has given or received notice will generally be upheld (*Commerzbank AG v Keen* [2007] IRLR 132, CA (see para **1.121**)).

(c) Commission. An employee rewarded by commission can normally recover damages for the commission he should have earned during the notice period.

(d) Car or car allowance, with maintenance, insurance, and private petrol.

(e) Pension (either employer contribution into a personal pension plan, or the value of a non-contributory scheme—a difficult calculation, but a reasonable rule of thumb is 10 per cent of salary per annum).

(f) Insurances (eg private health insurance, permanent health insurance, death in service benefit).

(g) Provision of housing.

(h) Other benefits such as club membership, newspaper allowance, home provision of electronic equipment.

(i) Share options or other employee long-term incentive schemes (note: such schemes normally contain valid provisions preventing employees from obtaining damages for loss of rights under share option schemes. These are known as Micklefield clauses, after the case of *Micklefield v SAC Technology Limited* [1990] IRLR 2180, HC (see para **1.119**).

(j) Other compensatable rights. These may include the foreseeable consequences of any loss of benefits. If the employee should have been entitled to benefits which were to be granted during the period when notice should have been given and has suffered loss as a result (for example by having to pay for medical treatment in the absence of contractual medical insurance), then the employee can seek to recover these costs from the employer. He may claim damages for the value of the loss (eg if an employee on three months' notice is only entitled to permanent health insurance (PHI) after he has been employed for a year, and his employment is unlawfully terminated without notice after ten months, and he then falls ill, so that he would have received benefits under the PHI policy, he may recover those benefits from the employer as damages) (see also para **1.115**).

7.20 Are there any reasons to reduce the salary and benefits package? These are:

(a) Mitigation of loss. Has the employee taken all reasonable steps to find alternative employment?

- If yes, did he obtain a new job (whether temporary, permanent, or self-employed) during the unexpired portion of the notice period? If so, he must give credit to the employer for the sums he has received for the weeks of his new employment as a result of his mitigation of loss (if he is paid more than previously, the additional payments do not go towards reducing loss for any period during which the employee was unemployed).

- If no, it is reasonable for the employee to hold out for a position comparable to his earlier one for three to six months, but after a reasonable time he should lower his sights. If the employee has not been actively seeking work, or has unduly limited the scope of his search, damages will be reduced to the extent the court decides that the employee should have obtained paid employment during the notice period.

(b) Discount for accelerated payment. This is, in effect, reverse interest. If an employer pays an employee, upon termination of his employment without notice, money representing the salary the employee would have earned over the notice period (say, six months), the employer is entitled to reduce the total payment on the basis that the 'present value of the money' is actually greater than the aggregate of the salary payments over the six-month period: the rationale is that the employee could, if he so wished, place the money in a deposit account immediately and earn interest upon all the sums in his account even though in the normal course of events he would not have received all the salary payments immediately.

(c) Any social security payments received should be deducted.

(d) Permanent Health Insurance (PHI); if the employee is in receipt of permanent health insurance or other insurance during the period, whether this shall be deducted will depend on the terms of the insurance policy. If the employer is bound to account to the insurers for any sums recovered in relation to the period, then the employer should not deduct insurance benefits from the total amount due.

Other issues include: **7.21**

(a) *Tax treatment*: Sections 401 and 403 of ITEPA 2003 provide that the first £30,000 of any payment made in consideration of, in consequence of, or otherwise in connection with the termination of an employee's contract of employment, or in respect of loss of office, is tax free. Payment under enhanced redundancy schemes will automatically come within this exemption, as will payments of compensation in respect of a breach of contract. However, payments made where there is a contractual provision requiring them, such as a payment in lieu of notice provision (PILON) in a contract of employment or made in part to secure the employee's agreement to new post-termination restrictions do not qualify for the exemption and are taxed as normal.

(b) *Failure to follow disciplinary procedure*: if an employer ignores contractual procedural requirements before implementing any dismissal, in addition to general damages the employee may be entitled to damages representing the salary he would have received had proper warning procedures been undertaken, up to the date when the employer could properly have terminated the contract having carried out the relevant procedures. Damages under this head will normally be in the region of two weeks' salary and benefits, although in one case damages of five months were awarded.

(c) *Effect on post-termination restrictions*: if the employer wrongly terminates the employee's contract of employment (eg by terminating the contract without giving full notice, unless the contract allows him to do this by having a PILON clause), then the contract ceases to be effective from that date and, if the employee formally accepts the employer's breach, post-termination provisions such as restrictive covenants cease to have any effect (*General Billposting Co Ltd v Atkinson* [1909] AC 118, HL). This will not prevent the employee enforcing the rest of the contract against the employer.

(d) *Additional damages: psychiatric injury and stigma*: in very rare cases, employees may be able to receive additional damages, eg because they have suffered psychiatric injury because of an employer's action (other than one leading up to dismissal), or because they cannot get another job because of the stigma of working for their previous employer (see para **7.09**).

(e) *No damages for loss of statutory rights*: if an employee is dismissed without notice, but would have been in continuous employment for a year had he been dismissed with notice, so that he would have been able to claim unfair dismissal, he cannot seek to recover what he would have earned as unfair dismissal compensation by claiming damages for the loss of opportunity to bring any unfair dismissal claim (*Harper v Virgin Net Ltd* [2004] IRLR 390, CA).

7.22 Where should the employee bring wrongful dismissal proceedings?

(a) If the claim is worth £25,000 or less, the claim can be brought in the employment tribunal, so long as it is made within the three months after the effective date of termination of the contract (see para **7.59** for definition of the effective date of termination). (Employment Tribunals Extension of Jurisdiction (England & Wales) Order 1994 and Employment Tribunals Extension of Jurisdiction (Scotland Order 1994—'the 1994 Orders')). While the employee is not bound to lodge a grievance under the statutory grievance procedures (see para **7.83**) before bringing such a claim, if he does not do so, the value of any successful claim will be reduced by 10 to 50 per cent, at least for all dismissals taking effect before the statutory grievance procedures are repealed, which is likely to take place in April 2009 (Employment Act 2002, s 31).

(b) If the claim is for more than £25,000, the employee would be better advised to start proceedings in the High Court or county court. An employee cannot sue for a substantial wrongful dismissal claim in the employment tribunal and then seek to recover any sums in excess of £25,000 in a higher court (*Fraser v HLMAD Ltd* [2006] IRLR 687, CA (see para **7.36**)).

7.23 When should the employee bring proceedings? During the three-month period after the EDT of the employee's contract (see para **7.59** for the definition of EDT). If not, it will be out of time (1994 Orders, art 7) and a claim should be brought in the High Court or county court).

Differences between Wrongful and Unfair Dismissals

7.24 Can an employer rely on actions unknown to it at the time of dismissal?

(a) An employer's defence to a claim for *unfair dismissal* will only succeed if the employer can demonstrate to the employment tribunal the actual reason for the dismissal, and then show that this dismissal was fair. Breaches of contract on the employee's part discovered after dismissal may only be relied upon to reduce the damages ultimately payable.

(b) When defending a claim for *wrongful dismissal* an employer will be able to rely upon any prior breach of contract by the employee to justify a summary dismissal, whether or not the employer knew of the breach at the date of dismissal.

Does it matter if the employer fails to follow fair procedures? **7.25**

(a) If an employer fails to follow contractual or general procedural requirements, any dismissal will generally be *unfair*. If it fails to follow the statutory dismissal procedure requirements, for so long as they continue to exist (they are likely to be repealed in April 2009), the dismissal will automatically be unfair (ERA 1996, s 98A). Provided that the statutory procedures are followed, the only exception to this rule is when the employer can show that procedural steps, such as the conduct of a disciplinary meeting, could never have made any difference.

(b) An employer will not be penalized in any action for *wrongful* dismissal if it fails to follow fair procedural requirements, except where contractual warning procedures have been totally ignored, when the position is as set out in para **7.21(b)**.

Must everyone in a similar position be treated the same? **7.26**

(a) An employer will be held to have *unfairly* dismissed an employee if it treated more leniently another employee who behaved in a similar fashion to the dismissed employee.

(b) For *wrongful* dismissal, the court will look only at whether the employee's conduct has been sufficiently serious to amount to a breach of contract which would justify dismissal. Precedent is immaterial, save that employees treated more leniently without reason may be cited by the employee as an example to illustrate that the conduct in question could not have been sufficiently serious to justify dismissal.

What are the time limits to bring claims? **7.27**

(a) An employee who believes that he has been *unfairly* dismissed must bring a complaint before the employment tribunal within three months of the date of termination of employment.

(b) An employee who wishes to claim damages for *wrongful* dismissal must bring proceedings in a High Court or county court within six years of the date of termination of employment, or within three months from the date of dismissal if he wishes to sue in the employment tribunal.

7.28 Is there a limit on compensation?

(a) The amount of compensation for *unfair* dismissal to which an employee is entitled is limited by statute.

(b) There is no limit in respect of damages for wrongful dismissal claims brought in the High Court or county court, but claims brought in the employment tribunal are limited to £25,000.

7.29 Can the employee ask to be re-instated?

(a) In relation to *unfair* dismissal, the employee can claim the remedies of reinstatement or re-engagement. However, even if the remedy is sought in such cases, it is not often granted.

(b) It is only in the very rarest circumstances—generally when the employer is a public authority or other large body with alternative departments in which the employee could be employed—that an employee will be 'reinstated' in a *wrongful* dismissal claim.

7.30 Who can bring claims?

(a) Only employees can claim damages for unfair dismissal.

(b) Consultants, freelancers, and other individuals engaged under contracts as well as employees may claim damages for *wrongful* dismissal. Only employees can sue for wrongful dismissal in the employment tribunal. Other individuals must sue in the High Court or county court.

Commentary

Basic Test

7.31 An employee is wrongfully dismissed if, without cause, he is dismissed without full notice or without money in lieu of notice. The notice period is either: that set out in the contract; the appropriate implied notice; or is determined in accordance with the statutory minimum period calculated in accordance with the employee's length of service.

7.32 An employer may legitimately terminate an employee's employment without notice or money in lieu of notice if the employee has committed gross misconduct or some other serious breach of his contract of employment such as dishonesty, disobedience, or serious incompetence. The test whether an employee has committed a sufficiently serious breach of contract is similar to the test whether an employee's conduct or capability is such that he can be fairly dismissed (see sections 7.F and 7.G (paras 7.154–7.200)).

Wrongful Dismissal Damages

If an employer, without legitimate reason, summarily terminates an employee's **7.33** contract, the employee is entitled to compensation for his notice period. This is quantified by calculating the net payments he should have received during the balance of his notice period. The first £30,000 of the total of all termination payments paid to employees (whether compensation for infringing a statutory right or damages for wrongful dismissal) is normally tax free (Income Tax (Earnings and Pensions) Act 2003, ss 403–406), unless paid pursuant to a contractual provision such as 'payment in lieu of notice' clause in an employment contract, and any balance above £30,000 is grossed up at the employee's marginal tax rate to arrive at the final figure.

In addition, if procedural requirements such as disciplinary and warning proce- **7.34** dures are incorporated into contracts of employment, but are ignored, this could give rise to a claim by the employee for damages representing the salary he would have received had proper warning procedures been undertaken, up to the date when the employer could lawfully have terminated the contract. In extreme cases, an employer who suspends an employee without any contractual right to do so, or who dismisses an employee without going through contractual disciplinary procedures, may be ordered to reverse the decision if the employee applies to the High Court for an injunction. If an employer dismisses an employee without notice, and by doing so deprives the employee of the benefit of statutory rights which would accrue if the notice period were worked out (eg by summarily dismissing someone whose notice period was three months after they had been employed for 50 weeks, thereby depriving them of the opportunity to claim unfair dismissal) no damages will be awarded for the loss of opportunity to bring any unfair dismissal claim (*Harper v Virgin Net Ltd* [2004] IRLR 390, CA).

Court Jurisdiction in Wrongful Dismissal Cases

Because the right to damages for wrongful dismissal is a common law right rather **7.35** than a statutory right, the limitations and restrictions imposed by statute do not apply. For example, there is no minimum service requirement before one can claim damages for wrongful dismissal. In addition, an employee is not entitled to damages for wrongful dismissal merely because an employer has not followed fair procedural requirements, or because any serious breach by the employee of the contract of employment was only discovered subsequent to dismissal and was not cited as the reason for dismissal.

It used to be the case that a claim for wrongful dismissal could only be brought in **7.36** the county court or High Court, but not in the employment tribunal. However, it is now possible for employees whose employment has terminated to bring a claim in the employment tribunal instead, although the amount of any award is subject to a maximum of £25,000 (1994 Orders) and no interest can be awarded until 42 days after the judgment. The limit on these claims has not been increased from £25,000 since the introduction of the legislation in 1994. High-earning employees would be ill-advised to bring such a claim in an employment tribunal: once the tribunal has given judgment or the case has been dismissed, the issue will be *res judicata* and similar proceedings cannot then be brought in the High Court. Although the compensation for wrongful dismissal and unfair dismissal overlaps to a certain extent, a wrongful dismissal claim will give the employee a useful additional weapon subject to two provisos: first, if a claim for wrongful dismissal is brought in either the employment tribunal, the High Court or county court the employer can counterclaim for losses it considers it has suffered as a result of the employee's breach of contract (other than where those losses have arisen as a result of a breach of the duty of confidence/fidelity by the employee) subject again to a maximum of £25,000 (1994 Orders, art 4)—no such counterclaim can be brought in the employment tribunal if the claim is only for unfair dismissal; and second, an employee with a potentially large unfair dismissal claim who succeeds in such a claim in the employment tribunal, where damages are limited to £25,000, cannot seek to recover any excess in High Court proceedings (*Fraser v HLMAD Ltd* [2006] IRLR 687, CA). An employee does not have to bring a grievance before making any breach of contract claim against an employer in the employment tribunal, but should he not have done so any award will be reduced by 10 to 50 per cent (EA 2002, s 31), at least until the statutory proceduces are repealed in April 2009.

WRONGFUL DISMISSAL/BREACH OF CONTRACT FLOWCHART

A

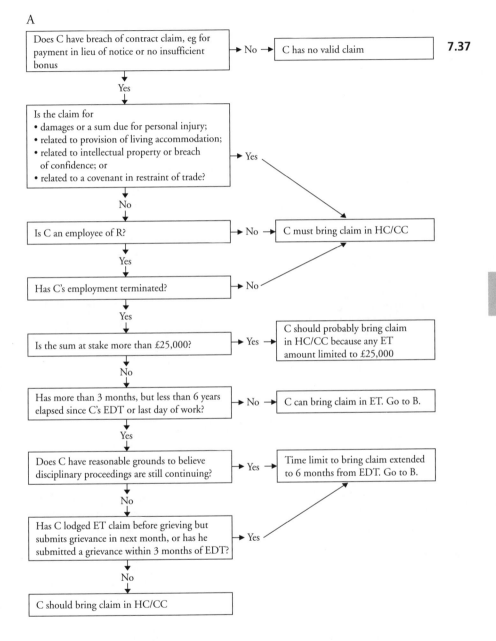

B

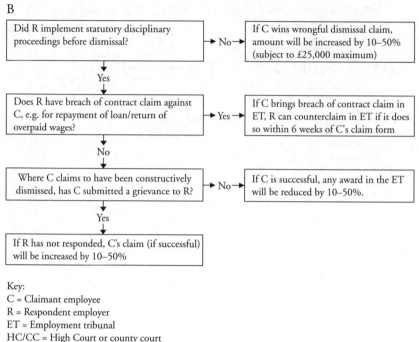

Key:
C = Claimant employee
R = Respondent employer
ET = Employment tribunal
HC/CC = High Court or county court
EDT = Effective date of termination of C's employment

C. Unfair Dismissal

CHECKLISTS

GENERAL CHECKLIST

Issues

7.38 Is the individual an employee? If not, he has no unfair dismissal right.

7.39 Has the employee been dismissed, either directly by the employer or as a result of constructive dismissal (see paras **7.67**–**7.85**)? If not, he has no unfair dismissal claim.

7.40 Is the employee in one of the categories which prevents him from bringing a claim for unfair dismissal (see para **7.61**)? If he is, he cannot bring a claim.

Has the employee brought his claim in time, within three months from the date **7.41** his employment actually ended? If not, he is unlikely to be allowed to pursue his claim unless:

(a) the employment tribunal considers it was not reasonably practicable for the case to have been brought earlier; or

(b) when the three months expired, the employee reasonably believed that the formal statutory procedure (including the appeal) was still being followed in relation to the dismissal (Employment Act 2002 (Dispute Resolution) Regulations 2004, reg 15) in which case there is an automatic three-month extension; or

(c) the employee believes he was constructively dismissed and either files his ET1 within three months of the EDT (see para **7.59**) but before or within 28 days of lodging a grievance with his employer, or has lodged a grievance within time, in which case time may be extended to six months from the EDT (EA 2002, s 32; Employment Act 2002 (Dispute Resolution) Regulations 2004, reg 15).

Has the employee got the necessary continuity of service—essentially one year— **7.42** unless special situations apply (see paras **7.56–7.58**)? If not, in the absence of one of the special situations, he will not be able to maintain his claim.

Does the employee believe he has been constructively dismissed? If yes, see paras **7.43** **7.67–7.80**).

Does the employee believe he has been dismissed for trade union, health and **7.44** safety, or whistle-blowing reasons? If so, he may apply for interim relief (see paras **7.86–7.90**).

What is the reason for dismissal? Is it a fair reason (see paras **7.92** and **7.93**)? If **7.45** yes, the employee's claim will not succeed. Is it for an automatically unfair reason (see para **7.94**)? If yes, the employee's claim will succeed. If the employer has not made it clear why the employee is being dismissed, any employee continuously employed for one year or more (unless she is pregnant, when there is no qualifying period) should request written reasons for his dismissal (see para **7.141**).

Has the employer followed the correct procedure (see sections **7.J** (statutory pro- **7.46** cedures), **7.G** (incompetence), **7.H** (ill health), **7.K** (misconduct/some other substantial reason), and **7.146–7.153** (retirement))? If the statutory procedures are not followed, then for so long as they are in place (they are likely to be repealed in April 2009) the dismissal will be automatically unfair. If the statutory procedures are followed, but other general procedures are not, dismissal may be unfair (see para **7.281**).

Consider remedies. Does the employee want to be reinstated or re-engaged? Is **7.47** this practicable? If not, what compensation/damages are due (see section **7.N**)?

Factual Issues to be Covered

7.48 It is prudent for an employer and employee facing a dispute to obtain as much as possible of the following information:

(a) identity of the employer, and any associated employer;

(b) length of service of the employee;

(c) contractual terms—value of salary/wages and benefits, plus general contractual obligations and entitlements, for example, duties, hours worked, etc. Documents should evidence contractual terms, for example, letter of appointment, contract, amendment letters, staff handbook, collective agreement, etc. Custom and practice may also be relevant in the absence of express written terms;

(d) any relevant disciplinary procedures;

(e) the reason for any termination of employment. Whether the stated reason is the true reason;

(f) what enquiries the employer made into the allegations against the employee;

(g) whether the employee retains any company property. If he does, this should be returned;

(h) what warnings were given earlier to the employee;

(i) what warning, consultation, and disciplinary meetings were held relating to the dismissal;

(j) all correspondence and notes of meetings relating to the enquiries, disciplinary meetings, and dismissal;

(k) whether there was an appeal. If there was, all relevant documents and notes of meetings relating to the appeal and the reason why the person hearing the appeal allowed or rejected the appeal;

(l) the efforts the employee has made to find a new job. Has he retained details? He should, to show that he properly mitigated his loss;

(m) whether it is practicable to reappoint the employee in his old or any similar job;

(n) whether the employee received any settlement payment. If he did, whether a legally enforceable settlement agreement was completed?

(o) whether there are any post-termination restrictive covenants in the contract. Do these apply? Is the employee breaking them, and if so will the court enforce them?

General Considerations in Bringing Tribunal Proceedings

7.49 What is the position on legal costs?

(a) Normally, in the employment tribunal and EAT, each party pays its own legal costs whatever the outcome;

(b) If one party has been particularly vexatious or unreasonable, or if bringing or defending a claim is misconceived, that party (or on occasion his representative in court) may be asked to pay a proportion of or all of the other party's costs;

(c) In the High Court or county court, in the absence of any formal settlement offer which beats the amount the court has arranged, the unsuccessful party normally pays a proportion of the winner's legal costs;

(d) Legal aid is not available for employment tribunal claims (save for initial advice), though it is for appeals to the employment appeals tribunal (EAT) and for claims in the county court and High Court;

(e) Some lawyers may be prepared to take on a claimant's case on a 'no win no fee' basis;

(f) An employee may obtain assistance from his trade union, Citizens Advice Bureau, or the Free Representation Unit.

7.50 When should proceedings be brought? Employment tribunal proceedings normally come to court within three to nine months (shorter cases being heard more quickly), High Court and county court proceedings normally come to court within six months to two years (depending upon their length and complexity).

7.51 How are cases proved? All facts relied upon must be proved by reference to documents, by oral witness evidence, or by agreement between employer and employee.

7.52 Might the parties settle the action before going to court? If there is any prospect of settlement, it should be explored to save costs, management time, possible adverse publicity, and uncertainty. ACAS or other mediation specialists offer a mediation service. If the claimant is receiving job seekers allowance or Income Support, then if the case proceeds to tribunal the recoupment provisions apply. In essence, these mean that if the employee wins a claim against the employer, the employer is required to remit direct to Jobcentre Plus any benefits the employee has received during the period for which the employer has been ordered to compensate him. This only has happend after a tribunal judgment. It may therefore be sensible for both parties to settle a case where the employee has been receiving the state benefits, taking into account the fact that the employee will then not have to give up any portion of the agreed damages.

7.53 If both unfair and wrongful dismissal cases are to be brought, which should be brought first? If proceedings for unfair and wrongful dismissal are brought, where they are both brought in the employment tribunal they will be heard together, along with any counterclaim by the employer. If proceedings are brought in both the High Court or county court and the employment tribunal, the parties should each consider which court they would wish to hear the application first.

Employers generally prefer actions to be heard first in the High Court or county courts, and employment tribunals will normally stay their proceedings pending the outcome of any wrongful dismissal case. Findings of fact in one court will generally bind the other.

Who Can Bring a Claim?

7.54 Is the claimant an employee? Individuals who are not classified as employees (see para **1.04**) are not entitled to bring claims for unfair dismissal.

7.55 Is the claimant an agency worker? A recent case has made it difficult for agency workers to claim that they are employed by the end user of their services—such a relationship will only exist where it is necessary to imply an employment relationship between the two. Generally, this is hard to prove where agency relationships are genuine (*James v London Borough of Greenwich* [2008] IRLR 302, CA). Thus, where express contracts between the agency and the worker, and between the agency and the end-user are consistent with the nature of the working relationship, the individual is unlikely to be held to be employed by the end-user. Unless Parliament changes the law, an agency worker is unlikely to be able to claim an employment relationship with the end user unless the agency relationship itself is regarded as a sham, or where there have been direct negotiations on terms and conditions between the end-user and the agency worker. If an individual starts off as an employee, and then, at the request of the employer, changes to work via an agency, the court may be willing to regard the new arrangements as a sham, and conclude that the individual remained an employee. When deciding whether arrangements are a sham, if a tribunal is going to override express contractual terms in an agreement, it must conclude that the real agreement was different from the written one and that the contractual terms were included to create a misleadingly different impression (*Consistent Group Ltd v Kalwak and Others* [2008] EWCA Civ 430, CA) (see also paras **1.14** and **1.15**).

Period of Employment

7.56 How long must the claimant have been employed? Unless one of the exemptions applies (see para **7.60**) an employee must have been employed for at least a year before the effective date of termination to be able to bring an unfair dismissal claim (ERA 1996, s 108(1)). To check this:

(a) establish start date (para **7.57**);
(b) ensure the employment is deemed continuous and that there are no weeks not worked which break continuity (para **7.58**);
(c) establish the effective date of termination (para **7.59**);
(d) ensure at least one year has elapsed between the start date and the effective date of termination.

When did the employment begin? The period starts on the date the employment **7.57** commences, by virtue of the contract of employment, and not necessarily upon the date when the employee's duties began. For example, an employee who is told in his contract that his employment will begin on Friday 1 January, but who does not present himself for work until Monday 4 January, will nevertheless be treated as though his employment started on 1 January.

How do you measure continuous employment? For an employee's employment **7.58** to count towards the calculation of his continuous employment there must be a contract of employment in existence throughout the relevant period.

(a) If a contract of employment subsists for even only one day during any week that whole week (Sunday to Saturday) will count. Thus, if an employee works the Monday of week one, and the Friday of the following week, he will be able to count two weeks towards his continuity.

(b) Bridging rules: notwithstanding the fact that there is no contract of employment during any period, the employee may still be counted as having continuous service where:
   • the employee is absent through sickness or injury;
   • the employee is on holiday (*Vernon v Event Management Catering Limited* [2007] EAT 0161/07);
   • the employee is absent on account of a temporary cessation of work, for example, as a result of a lay-off or a natural break in the work available (such as a school holiday where the employee works in a school);
   • the absence is by arrangement or custom, where it is understood, before the absence begins, that the employee will be taken back following the absence (for example, a secondment or sabbatical);
   • the employee is absent from work through pregnancy or on maternity, paternity, parental, or adoption leave;
   • the employee is absent as a result of having taken part in industrial action or because of a lock-out, though the number of weeks of industrial action is disregarded in deciding the total number of weeks the employee has worked;
   • an employee is reinstated or re-engaged following any dismissal, when the period when he was in fact not working for the employer is still regarded as part of his continuous service;
   • an employee's employer changes as a result of a transfer of undertaking, when the employee's employment with the new employer is deemed to have commenced on the date the employee started working for the old employer;
   • the employee's job is transferred from his employing company to that of an associated employer (ie a company of which the other, directly or indirectly, has control, or a company which is under the ultimate control of the same

person who controls the original employer), when employment is deemed to have commenced on the date when the employee started working for the first employer;

- a personal employer dies and his personal representatives maintain an employee's employment, when the employment will be deemed to have begun when the first employment began;
- there is a change in the partners, personal representatives, or trustees who employ an employee, when the employment will be deemed to have begun when the first employment began.

7.59 When is the effective date of termination (EDT)? The EDT may be:

(a) The date any notice period given expires or (if notice is less than the notice period to which the employee is statutorily entitled, the date statutory notice (see para **7.59(b)**) would have expired (ERA 1996, s 97(1)(a)).

(b) If no notice is given, and employment is not legitimately terminated for gross misconduct, the EDT is the date on which statutory notice would have ex-pired, had it been given on the date the employee was actually or construc-tively dismissed (ERA 1996, s 97(2) and (4)). Statutory notice is essentially one week after the employee has been employed for a month, and one week per completed year of service after that, subject to a maximum of 12 weeks (ERA 1996, s 86) (see para **1.108**). This is so even if payment is given in lieu of notice but dismissal takes effect immediately. Thus, if someone is dismissed after 360 days' employment, the EDT will be on day 367, so the person will be deemed to have continuous employment for over a year and hence be able to bring an unfair dismissal claim even if the employee waives his right to notice (*Secretary of State for Employment v Staffordshire County Council* [1989] IRLR 117, CA).

(c) The date the term of a fixed-term contract expires (unless the parties agree that the contract should continue after that date) (ERA 1996, s 97(1) (c)).

(d) If the employee is dismissed with notice, but is not required to work during the notice period (garden leave), the EDT is the date of expiry of the notice period (ie at the end of the garden leave period), even if the employee is immediately given pay for the full notice period at the start of the garden leave.

(e) The date an employee is summarily—and legitimately—dismissed for gross misconduct (ERA 1996, s 97(1)(b)).

(f) If summary dismissal is communicated by letter, the date of termination is the date when the employee read the letter or first had the opportunity to read the letter, which is normally later than the date upon which the letter was sent (generally, letters sent by first class post are deemed to take two days to arrive) and the EDT is this date *plus* (save where dismissal is legitimately for gross misconduct) the statutory notice period.

(g) If the employer serves notice on the employee to terminate a contract and the employee subsequently serves a counter-notice terminating the contract on an earlier date, the EDT is nevertheless the date when the employer's notice would have expired.

(h) If an employee resigns and rightly claims constructive dismissal, the EDT is the date of resignation plus the period of statutory notice to which the employee would have been entitled.

(i) If an employee is told to resign or be dismissed, the EDT is the date the resignation takes effect plus the period of statutory notice to which the employee is entitled.

(j) The date the employer and employee agree the employment will terminate. This is the case even if the employee has already received notice of his dismissal but then agrees an earlier termination date (*Palfrey v Transco plc* [2004] IRLR 916, EAT).

[Note: any appeal in any disciplinary procedure following dismissal is to be ignored for the purposes of estimating the EDT unless there is an express contractual provision which states that the contract will remain in force during the appeal.]

Dismissals When Employee Need Not Have One Year's Employment to Bring a Claim

Is the reason for dismissal one of the exceptions to the general rule, where there is **7.60** no qualifying period and the employee does not have to have one year's continuous employment to bring a claim? They include dismissals:

(a) for trade union reasons (TULR(C)A 1992, s 154) or reasons connected with union recognition (TULR(C)A 1992, Sch A1, para 162);

(b) for a health and safety reason (ERA 1996, s 108(3)(c));

(c) because of the employee's actions or proposed actions as the trustee of a relevant occupational pension scheme (ERA 1996, s 108(3)(e)) or as an employee representative for TUPE or redundancy collective consultation (ERA 1996, s 108(3)(f));

(d) for asserting a statutory right (ERA 1996, s 108(3)(g));

(e) for a pregnancy or other parental leave-related reason (ERA 1996, s 108(3)(b)) (see para **7.112**);

(f) for asserting rights under the Working Time Regulations 1998 (ERA, 1996, s 108(3)(dd)) or for a National Minimum Wage (ERA 1996, s 108(3)(gg)) or under the Tax Credits Act 1999 (ERA 1996, s 108(3)(gh));

(g) for making a protected disclosure (ERA 1996, s 108(3)(ff));

(h) for activities as a member of a European Works Council (ERA 1996, s 108(3)(hh));

(i) for asserting rights as a part-time worker or fixed-term employee, or for supporting someone else to do so (ERA 1996, s 108(3)(i) and (j));

(j) for exercising rights to accompany, or be accompanied by, workers at grievance and disciplinary hearings (Employment Relations Act 1999, s 12(4), Employment Equality (Age) Regulations 2006, Sch 6, para 13);

(k) for taking part in legitimate industrial action after a properly conducted ballot, provided that at least twelve weeks have elapsed since the employee started to do so (TULR(C)A 1992, s 238A);

(l) because he is a protected shop-worker who refuses to work on a Sunday (ERA 1996, s 108(3)(d));

(m) on grounds of age (ERA 1996, s 108(3)(n));

(n) where the employee is selected for redundancy where the principal reason was really one of those set out above (ERA 1996, s 108(3)(h)).

[Note: in all these exceptions, the key factor is the motive for dismissal: the courts will not look at whether the employee actually has the relevant right, or whether or not that right has actually been infringed.]

7.61 Which employees are *not* entitled to bring claims for unfair dismissal?

(a) Those who have less than one year's continuous employment (see para **7.58**) unless they fall within one of the exemptions to this rule (see para **7.60**).

(b) Those who are not employees but who are employed under contracts for services such as freelance workers or independent contractors (*Carmichael and Another v National Power plc* [2000] IRLR 43, HL; *Ready Mixed Concrete (South East) Ltd v Minister of Pensions and National Insurance* [1968] 2 QB 497; *Redrow Homes (Yorkshire) Ltd v Wright* [2004] ICR 1126 (see para **1.10**)).

(c) Agency workers (see paras **7.55** and **1.14–1.18**).

(d) Those working under illegal contracts, though if an employer persuades an employee to accept an illegal contract (for example, one which enables the employer to defraud HMRC) it may still be enforceable by the employee. If the employee genuinely does not realize that the contract is illegal when he enters into it, he will still be able to rely upon the contract (*Colen v Cebrian (UK) Ltd* [2004] ICR 568). On the other hand, an employee who worked under a contract for the supply of services, under which she had not paid income tax or National Insurance contributions, who then claimed she was in fact an employee during the period failed in an unfair dismissal claim because the EAT held that her contract was tainted with illegality (*Daymond v Enterprise South Devon* [2007] EAT 0005/07—the key issue here was that the sophisticated structure in place might be held to be a misrepresentation to HMRC). If there has been full disclosure of the position to HMRC, so that there is simply an error of categorization when HMRC treats the individuals as self-employed, claimants are unlikely to be prevented from pursuing employment tribunal claims (*Payne v Enfield Technical Services Ltd* [2008] All ER (D) 300, CA).

(e) Employees who are constructively dismissed but who fail to make use of the grievance procedure before bringing their claim (Employment Act 2002, s 32—see paras **7.81–7.83**). [Note: this provision is likely to be repealed when the statutory procedures are repealed in April 2009.]

(f) Those engaged on a fixed-term contract of one year or more who agreed before 25 October 1999 in writing to exclude their right to claim unfair dismissal, and whose employment is terminated on the expiry of the fixed term. The expiry of any fixed-term contract entered into after 25 October 1999 will amount to dismissal.

(g) Employees who have entered into a valid compromise agreement with their employer, following advice from a solicitor, union official, or similar trained person, settling their unfair dismissal claims (ERA 1996, s 203). To be binding, the agreement must be carefully worded and include a full description of the statutory claims to be settled and must follow exactly the provisions of ERA, s 203 (*Hinton v University of East London* [2005] IRLR 552, CA). In *Palihakkara v BT plc* [2006] EAT 0185/06, discrimination claims were not excluded because the compromise agreement did not conform to SDA, s 77 or RRA, s 72, and settlement of 'all claims past or future arising out of the termination of employment' only settled claims that arose from the termination itself—it did not settle earlier claims.

(h) Those whose contracts of employment are frustrated by some circumstance unforeseen when the contract was entered into which renders performance of the contract very different from what was originally contemplated—for example, because the employee is severely incapacitated for a very long time as a result of sickness or because the employee is imprisoned (*Williams v Watsons Luxury Coaches Ltd* [1990] ICR 536, EAT).

(i) Those older than 65 (or the 'normal retiring age' for that category of employee employed by the particular employer, if lower) (ERA 1996, s 109(1)); [Note: this only applies to dismissals before 1 October 2006. The age limit is removed by the Employment Equality (Age) Regulations 2006.]

(j) Those who resign, in the absence of any situation of constructive dismissal, unless they have been told by their employer to 'resign or be sacked', in which case the resignation will be treated as a dismissal.

(k) Where it is not clear to the employee whether he has been dismissed or not. In this situation, if the employment tribunal finds that in fact the employer's words or actions did not dismiss him, he will be treated as having resigned and so will not succeed in a claim for unfair dismissal. Equally, if the employee is not given a definite leaving date there will be no dismissal. Both of these points are, however, subject to the rules which apply when the employee leaves in circumstances of constructive dismissal (see para **7.67**).

(l)   Those employed in the police service; certain Crown employees, particularly those in the armed forces; and share fishermen and people employed on board ships registered outside Great Britain (ERA 1996, ss 191–200). [Note: those working on ships registered in Great Britain will be eligible to claim compensation for unfair dismissal unless they are wholly employed or resident outside Great Britain.]

(m) Those who are not employed in Great Britain (*Lawson v Serco Ltd* [2006] IRLR 289, HL) but peripatetic employees based in Great Britain or expatriate employees working for a business carried on in Great Britain, such as a foreign correspondent of a British newspaper, may be entitled to bring claims. An example of the interpretation of these provisions is *ADT Fire & Security plc v Speyer* (EAT/0125/06) where an employee recruited in UK who worked in Asia (but not the UK) for the last seven and a half years of his employment, reported only to Asian-based managers for the last six years of his employment, and whose pay was determined by his Asian managers (although payment was administered from the UK) was not regarded as having a sufficient connection with UK to allow him to bring a claim in an employment tribunal here.

Commentary

7.62   In addition to wrongful dismissal claims, most employees are entitled to claim compensation for unfair dismissal. Such a claim must generally be brought within three months of the EDT (see para 7.59 for definition of EDT) although this may be extended if a tribunal accepts it was not reasonably practicable to have done so within time or because the employee reasonably believes the statutory procedure was still ongoing (see para 7.41(**b**)). Only employees are able to bring unfair dismissal claims. An employee may include someone supplied to an employer by an agency—the Court will examine whether it is necessary to imply an employment relationship between the end-user or the agency and the individual (*James v London Borough of Greenwich* [2008] IRLR 302, CA). Generally the court will look at the business reality considering two main issues: is the end-user obliged to provide the individual with work and is the individual obliged to attend and do the work under the end-user's direction and control (*Carmichael v National Power plc* [2000] IRLR 43 HL; *Ready Mixed Concrete (South East) Ltd v Minister of Pensions and National Insurance* [1968] 2 QB 487, HC)? See also paras 1.14–1.18 and 7.55. To bring a claim for unfair dismissal, an employee has to overcome certain hurdles. The most important hurdle is that, in order to be entitled to complain of unfair dismissal, generally employees must have been employed continuously for one year or more by the EDT. It does not matter how many hours a week they work during this period if they have one year's continuity.

Certain categories of employees are excluded from bringing unfair dismissal **7.63** claims. They include those who have resigned rather than been dismissed, those who have been constructively dismissed but have not followed the appropriate grievance procedures, and those working abroad.

The Act of Dismissal

CHECKLIST

An employee cannot bring a claim for unfair dismissal unless he has actually been **7.64** dismissed. Dismissal occurs by:

(a) Direct dismissal (see para **7.65**);

(b) Expiry of a fixed-term contract (see para **7.66**);

(c) Constructive dismissal (see paras **7.67–7.85**).

Direct dismissal

Has the employee been told to leave? If yes, he has been dismissed. **7.65**

(a) Words of dismissal, whether oral or written, should be unequivocal and should set a date for the termination of employment.

(b) Words spoken in the heat of the moment (for example, 'get out and never come back' said at the end of a fierce argument) generally do not amount to a dismissal unless they are repeated subsequently or confirmed in writing. Equally, an employer should allow an employee apparently resigning in such circumstances a couple of days to cool off and reconsider.

(c) Once given, notice to dismiss cannot be withdrawn unless the employee agrees.

(d) An employee told that unless he resigns or otherwise agrees to his departure he is to be dismissed will be regarded as dismissed (*Sandhu v Jan der Rijk Transport Ltd* [2007] ICR 1137).

(e) If an employee resigns without being forced to, this will not amount to dismissal (*Riordan v War Office* [1959] 3 All ER 774).

(f) If an employee has resigned and is working out his notice, and the employer subsequently terminates the employment and pays the employee in lieu of the balance of the notice period, this cannot be an unfair dismissal—the cause of termination was the employee's resignation (which cannot be unilaterally retracted), not the employer bringing forward the ultimate departure date (*Tom Findlay & Co Ltd v Devlin* [2008] EAT 0071/06).

Expiry of a fixed-term contract

7.66 Has a fixed-term contract expired and not been renewed? If so, this will be a dismissal (unless it was entered into before 25 October 1999).

Constructive dismissal

GENERAL CHECKLIST

7.67 If the employee believes he has been constructively dismissed:

(a) Has the employer committed a breach of contract which goes to the root of the employment relationship (see para **7.76** for examples) or a series of breaches culminating in a breach which is effectively the last straw (see paras **7.69** and **7.75**)?

(b) Did the employee resign as a result of this breach (see para **7.70**)?

(c) Did the employee act promptly in resigning following the breach or last straw, so that he could not be said to have waived his rights in relation to the breach?

(d) Has the employee lodged a grievance in time (see paras **7.81–7.83**)? (For extensions of time for lodging employment tribunal applications where the grievance is not complete within three months from the termination of employment, see also para **7.41(c)**.)

If the answer to any of these questions is no, or if the employer has a defence to the claim (see paras **7.78–7.80**), the employee will not succeed in demonstrating that he has been constructively dismissed. However, if an employer is to contest a claim on the basis that no grievance has been filed, it must tick the relevant box on his ET3 (formal response to a claim) noting the employee's failure to follow the grievance procedure, or must write a covering letter at the time of submission of his ET3 stating his wish to pursue the point (see para **7.81**).

7.68 Has the employer committed a repudiatory breach of contract? If not, there will be no constructive dismissal. The employer's breach of contract must be sufficiently important to justify the employee resigning, or must be the last in a series of less important incidents. The employer's conduct must amount to a fundamental breach of contract (*Western Excavating (EC(C) Ltd v Sharp* [1978] QB 761). Unreasonable behaviour not amounting to a breach, for example, delaying the date on which salary payment is made, is not sufficient. The employer's actions will not amount to a constructive dismissal, however unreasonable, if there is an express contractual term allowing him to take that action. For example, a provision in a contract—or in a collective agreement or staff handbook, if its terms are incorporated into the contract of employment—that an employer is entitled to vary shift patterns, will enable the employer to do so. However, the employer has a duty not to conduct himself in a manner, without reasonable or proper cause, likely to destroy or seriously damage the relationship of trust and confidence between the parties. Thus any change in shift pattern could not be wholly unreasonable, and would require reasonable prior notice (*United Bank Ltd v Akhtar* [1989] IRLR 507, EAT).

An employee may rely on constructive dismissal citing a pattern of actions, the **7.69** most recent of which is the 'last straw'. The last straw need not itself be a breach of contract so long as it is more than trivial and is capable of contributing to a breach of the implied term of mutual trust and confidence and has been preceded by blameworthy or unreasonable conduct in the past. This is an objective, not a subjective test (*Omilaju v Waltham Forest LBC* [2005] IRLR 35, CA). Examples of what might constitute the last straw could include a reduction in the number of hours worked, or a requirement to move to some workplace way away, even if the contract allows such changes to be made, provided this has been preceded by previous unreasonable behaviour toward the employee (see also para **7.75**).

The employee must leave in response to the breach. In any resignation letter an **7.70** employee would be wise to set out the employer's breach on which he relies in resigning and claiming constructive dismissal. If the employee has indeed breached the contract, it can still be a constructive dismissal even if the employee had an ulterior motive for resigning (*Shipperley v Nucleus Information Systems Ltd* [2007] UKEAT 0340/06).

The employee must act promptly in resigning following the breach or he may **7.71** be deemed to have waived the breach and agreed to vary the contract. What is 'prompt' will vary according to circumstances, but will normally be within at least one or two months. In *Quigley v University of St Andrews* (UKEATS/0025/05) a two-month delay was sufficient to affirm the contract preventing the employee from arguing that he was constructively dismissed, even though he had claimed the gap was caused by the length of time it took him to consult his solicitor.

The employee may rely upon the conduct of anyone employed by the employer **7.72** in a supervisory capacity, and not only upon the conduct of the particular person who has the power to dismiss the employee.

Deliberate misconduct or bad faith is not a necessary prerequisite for the obliga- **7.73** tion of mutual trust and confidence to be destroyed (*Post Office v Roberts* [1980] IRLR 347, EAT).

A common argument in constructive dismissal cases is that the employer has **7.74** acted in such a way that it has breached the implied term of trust and confi- dence that should exist in the employment relationship. To establish breach, the employee must show conduct by the employer 'which, objectively considered, is

7

Dismissals

likely to seriously undermine the necessary trust and confidence in the employment relationship' (*Baldwin v Brighton & Hove City Council* [2007] IRLR 232, EAT; *Woods v WM Car Services (Peterborough) Ltd* [1981] 347, CA). Where breach of the implied term is raised in relation to a single act, the employment tribunal should ask itself the following questions:

(a) what was the conduct of the employer that is complained of;

(b) did the employer have reasonable and proper cause for that conduct including consideration of whether its action was within the range of reasonable responses; and if not

(c) was the conduct complained of calculated to destroy or seriously damage the employer/employee relationship of trust and confidence (*Fairbrother v Abbey National plc* [2007] IRLR 320, EAT)?

7.75 However, where the employee is relying on the 'last straw' doctrine (see para **7.69**) the relevant principles are:

(a) the final straw act need not be of the same quality as the previous act relied on as cumulatively amounting to a breach of the implied term of trust and confidence, but it must, when taken in conjunction with the earlier acts, contribute something to that breach and be more than utterly trivial;

(b) where the employee, following a series of acts which amount to a breach of the term, does not accept the breach but continues in employment, thus affirming the contract, he cannot subsequently rely on the earlier acts if the final straw is entirely innocuous;

(c) the final straw, viewed alone, need not be unreasonable or blameworthy conduct on the part of the employer. It need not itself amount to a breach of contract. However, it will be an unusual case where the 'final straw' consists of conduct which viewed objectively as reasonable and justifiable satisfies the final straw test. In 'last straw' cases, one does not need to review whether the action was within the range of reasonable responses (*GAB Robbins (UK) Ltd v Triggs* [2008] IRLR 317, CA);

(d) an entirely innocuous act on the part of the employer cannot be the final straw, even if the employee genuinely (and subjectively) but mistakenly interprets the employer's act as destructive of the necessary trust and confidence (*Omilaju v Waltham Forest* [2005] IRLR 35, CA).

EXAMPLES

7.76 Examples of constructive dismissal include the following actions if taken without the employee's consent or without an express contractual provision entitling the employer to do so (unless that provision is wholly unreasonable—for example, requiring an employee to change job location to a considerable distance from his home, or imposing material shift patterns, without reasonable notice):

(a) imposing a salary reduction (*Industrial Rubber Products v Gillon* [1977] IRLR 389, EAT);

(b) materially reducing benefits (*Gillies v Richard Daniels & Co Ltd* [1979] IRLR 45, EAT; *French v Barclays Bank plc* [1998] IRLR 646, CA);

(c) reduction in status (*Lewis v Motorworld Garages Ltd* [1985] IRLR 465, CA; *Coleman v S & W Baldwin* [1977] IRLR 342, EAT);

(d) change in hours or shift patterns;

(e) removing the most enjoyable or central aspect of a person's job if this reduces job satisfaction or prestige (*Hilton v Shiner Ltd* [2001] IRLR 727, EAT);

(f) requiring someone to go on garden leave if there is no contractual provision entitling the employer to do so (*William Hill Organisation Ltd v Tucker* [1998] IRLR 313, CA). This principle has been watered down slightly, in *SG&R Valuation Service Co v Boudrais and ors* [2008] IRLR 770, HC, when garden leave was enforced, even though there was no relevant contractual provision, for employees who intended to damage their employer's business, and seriously demonstrated they were not willing or ready to work;

(g) suspending a person, when there is no contractual right to do so;

(h) imposing new restrictive covenants on an employee without going through proper procedure (*Willow Oak Developments Ltd t/a Windsor Recruitment v Silverwood and Others* [2006] IRLR 607, CA);

(i) failing to bring an employee's attention to a right he holds which is about to expire, when the right has been negotiated collectively on behalf of employees, and the employee could not reasonably have been expected to be aware of the right (*Scally and Others v Southern Health and Social Services Board and Others* [1991] IRLR 522, HL);

(j) moving someone from a hands-on role to a managerial one (*Land Securities Trillium Ltd v Thornley* [2005] IRLR 765, EAT);

(k) behaving without reasonable and proper cause in a manner likely to destroy or seriously damage the mutual relationship of trust and confidence which should exist (between employer and employee), for example, by:

- conducting a fraudulent business (*Malik v BCCI* [1997] IRLR 462, HL);
- giving an employee no or a low salary rise or bonus out of all proportion to colleagues, without any justification (*Clarke v Nomura International plc* [2000] IRLR 766, HC);
- allowing a bullying or harassing environment to persist, or failure to investigate allegations of harassment (*Bracebridge Engineering Ltd v Darby* [1990] IRLR 3, EAT);

7

Dismissals

- non-trivial bullying or harassment of the employee by another employee ((1) Reed, (2) Bull Information Systems Ltd v Stedman [1999] IRLR 299, EAT);
- offering an employee who has been on long-term absence from work through stress a new job in his old department, when the employee had maintained that his health problems would be exacerbated by a return to that department. There is an implied contractual term that the employer will safeguard its employee's health and safety at work. If it does not do so, it will be in breach of contract. When examining whether the employer's conduct is fair, the tribunal will look at whether, before requiring a return to the same department, the employee obtained medical reports and consulted with the employee on the medical position and on alternatives (Thanet District Council v Webster, [2003] IDS Brief 728, p 6);
- a senior executive acting in a high-handed and aggressive manner towards employees (Horkulak v Cantor Fitzgerald International [2004] ICR 697, QBD);
- rudely and unjustly criticizing an employee in front of others (Isle of Wight Tourist Board v Coombes [1976] IRLR 413, EAT);
- accusing an employee, without foundation, of inability to do his job (Courtaulds Northern Textile Ltd v Andrew [1979] IRLR 84, EAT);
- suspending an employee (even if pursuant to a contractual right) without reasonable and proper cause (Gogay v Hertfordshire County Council [2000] IRLR 703, CA);
- maintaining suspension of an employee even though the employer has already concluded that one of two charges against the employee is unfounded (Camden and Islington Mental Health and Social Care Trust v Atkinson [2007] EAT 0058/07);
- giving an unjust and unmerited warning or other disciplinary sanction out of all proportion to the offence (Stanley Cole (Wainfleet) Ltd v Sheridan [2003] IRLR 52, EAT);
- giving a bad reference without checking that it is fair and reasonable (TSB Bank plc v Harris [2000] IRLR 157, EAT);
- requiring an employee to relocate, without giving reasonable notice (United Bank Ltd v Akhtar [1989] IRLR 507, EAT);
- imposing a disciplinary suspension without pay, unless the employer has the power to do so under the contract of employment;
- laying off employees without pay, in the absence of an express contractual provision allowing the employer to do so (D & J McKenzie Ltd v Smith [1976] IRLR 345, CS);
- failing to give an employee the necessary support to perform his functions and duties properly (Associated Tyre Specialists (Eastern) Ltd v Waterhouse [1976] IRLR 386, EAT);

- failing to cooperate with an employee in his attempts to achieve sales targets which allow him to obtain benefits under a bonus scheme (*Takacs v Barclays Services Jersey Ltd* [2006] IRLR 877, QBD—interim decision of the High Court);
- failing to provide a satisfactory working environment to enable the employee to work, for example, requiring people to work in an unpleasantly smoky atmosphere (Waltons & Morse v Dorrington [1997] IRLR 488, EAT);
- requiring the employee to work in unsafe conditions (*Marshall Specialist Vehicles Ltd v Osborne* [2003] IRLR 672, EAT);
- causing psychiatric damage by volume or character of work (*Walker v Northumberland County Council* [1995] IRLR 35, DC);
- in the absence of a written contractual provision entitling the employee to do so, failing to pay full wages to an employee during periods of sickness absence (*Secession Ltd t/a Freud v Bellingham* [2006] IRLB Issue 788, p 17);
- failing adequately to investigate a grievance, for example failure properly to address a complaint of overworking, which accompanied a complaint of alleged bullying, when looked at cumulatively in the context of earlier unreasonable actions (*GAB Robbins (UK) Ltd v Triggs* [2008] IRLR 317, CA);
- refusing to provide work (in the absence of a reasonable contractual power to do so) for the employee if the employee's job is such (for example he is a scientist or doctor) that his skills constantly need exercising to avoid atrophy;
- refusing to provide work where a significant proportion of the employee's remuneration is based upon commission;
- not making reasonable adjustments to a disabled employee's job which would allow him to continue working (*Greenhof v Barnsley Metropolitan Council* [2006] IRLR 98, EAT);
- making public remarks about an employee which are highly damaging to his reputation (*Clements v RDF Media Group Ltd* [2008] IRLR 207, HC).

7.77 Examples of actions which have been held not to amount to constructive dismissal include:

(a) Appointing to an interview panel someone who was perceived by the interviewee to be biased against transsexuals, when the employer had not been aware of the interviewee's gender reassignment (*Baldwin v Brighton and Hove City Council* [2007] ICR 680, EAT).

(b) An employer's failure to follow an allegedly appropriate grievance procedure in considering a grievance. The EAT held that conduct breaches the implied term of trust and confidence only if there is no reasonable and proper cause for it. Here, the conduct did not fall outside the range of reasonable responses available to the employer (*Abbey National plc v Fairbrother* [2007] IRLR 320, EAT).

(c) An employer's breach of a statutory duty (eg abuse of an employee's trade union rights) may not necessarily be a constructive dismissal (*Doherty v British Midland Airways Ltd* [2006] IRLR 90, EAT).

(d) Where the act in question was not performed by the employer but by someone over whom it had no responsibility (*Yorke v Moonlight* [2007] EAT 25/06).

Employer's Defence

7.78 Once an employee has shown there is a substantial breach going to the root of his contract of employment, the burden of proof turns to the employer to show, on a balance of probabilities, whether his breach of contract was a reasonable response in all the circumstances, so that any 'dismissal' will be fair.

7.79 What must the employer prove? The employer must show that it has not acted in substantial breach of contract. Conduct which will usually *not* amount to an event of constructive dismissal includes:

(a) minor alterations to the employee's contractual terms;

(b) changes allowed by the contract of employment (for example pursuant to flexibility provisions—*White v Reflecting Roadstuds Ltd* [1991] IRLR 331, EAT);

(c) a delay in payment of wages, if not substantial;

(d) lack of consultation over the appointment of a subordinate;

(e) telling an employee he will be dismissed at some time in the future (this is not constructive dismissal because the employer may intend to give due notice, which would not be a breach of contract); or

(f) introducing adverse changes to employees' contracts brought on in response to a necessary reorganization as the only perceived alternative to dismissing the employees (*St John of God (Care Services) Ltd v Brooks* [1992] IRLR 546, EAT).

7.80 The employer may also succeed where it can show:

(a) there is a reason for the acts to which the employee has taken exception, and this reason falls within one of the potentially fair reasons set out in ERA 1996, s 98(2) or is some other substantial reason; or

(b) it acted reasonably in acting in breach of contract (*Cape Industrial Services Ltd v Ambler* [2003] IDS Brief 728, p 9); or

(c) before it committed a repudiatory breach of the employment contract, the employee had himself committed a repudiatory breach (*Clements v RDF Media Group Ltd* [2008] IRLR 207, HC).

Grievance Procedure

7.81 Can the employee bring a claim without lodging a grievance? If the employee claims to have been constructively dismissed, he must lodge a grievance against his employer at least 28 days before bringing a claim (EA 2002, s 32) or his claim will not be accepted by the Employment Tribunal. [Note: this requirement may be removed when the statutory grievance procedures are repealed in April 2009.] The grievance should be in relation to the whole claim; if it is only in relation to one aspect of it, yet in the claim form the employee relies upon a series of events to show constructive dismissal, the Tribunal may not have jurisdiction to hear all the claim (*Cyprus Airways Ltd v Lambrou* [2007] UKEAT 0526/06 EAT, *Highland Council v TGWU* [2008] IRLR 272). If the employer is going to take the point that the claim is invalid because no grievance has been lodged in time, this must be specifically pleaded (*Plummer v DMC Business Machines* [2006] UK EAT 0381/06; *Hall v South Kent College* [2007] UKEAT 0087/07 and see para **7.67** for minimum pleading requirements).

What constitutes a grievance? **7.82**

(a) a document in writing which identifies the complaint. Unless the modified procedure is used (see para **7.83**(**d**), when the basis for the claim must be set out in the grievance letter), the document must simply identify the complaint—it does not need to be a sophisticated outline of the complaint;

(b) the document containing the grievance may contain other information as well;

(c) there is no need specifically to state that the document is a grievance;

(d) the grievance must relate to the subsequent claim, but the wording of the grievance and the claim form do not need to be anywhere near identical, provided the general nature of the grievance is substantially the same as the matters which are contained in the ET1 tribunal document: different descriptions or a difference by way of precise ingredients or particulars do not affect statutory compliance;

(e) the grievance can be contained in a variety of forms, eg a solicitor's letter, but not in a tribunal claim form (*Ward v The University of Essex* [2008] EAT 0391/07).

What are statutory grievance procedures? They are: **7.83**

(a) *Step 1: statement of grievance.* The employee must set out the grievance in writing and send it to the employer. He must set out the basis for the grievance. This may be made without the use of the term 'grievance', for example by a solicitor's letter threatening to bring a claim or in a letter of resignation (*Mark Warner Ltd v Aspland* [2006] IRLR 87; *Shergold v Fieldway Medical Centre* [2006] IRLR 76; and *Galaxy Showers Ltd v Wilson* [2006] IRLR 83). The detail of the grievance need not be set out so long as the employer, on a fair reading of the statement, having regard to the context in which it was made, would have appreciated that the particular complaint was being raised (*Canary Wharf v Edebi* [2006] IRLR 416, EAT). The grievance must be made within a reasonable time, but the employer's timetable need not be strictly adhered to (*Martin v Class Security Installations Ltd* [2006] UK EAT/0188/06).

(b) *Step 2: meeting*. The employer must invite the employee to attend a meeting to discuss the grievance, at a date which gives the employer reasonable opportunity to consider its response to the information. The employee must take all reasonable steps to attend the meeting.

After the meeting the employer must tell the employee its decision in response to the grievance and notify him of his right to appeal. Notification of the right to appeal can be oral, rather than in writing (*Aptuit (Edinburgh) Ltd v Kennedy* [2007] UKEAT 057/06).

(c) *Step 3: Appeal*. If the employee appeals, the employer must invite him to a further meeting, normally with a more senior representative of the employer. The employee must attend the meeting and the employer must tell the employee, following the meeting, its final decision.

(d) A *modified procedure* applies, amounting to step 1 followed by an employer's written response, if the employee's employment has ended before the grievance starts and both the parties agree. In these circumstances, the employee's grievance letter needs to be more detailed than a simple statement of the objection, to give the employer a proper opportunity of investigating the complaint.

Commentary

7.84 It may sound obvious, but in order to succeed in an unfair dismissal claim, the employee must have been dismissed, or his fixed-term contract must have ended without being renewed. Normally, this is easy to prove, for example because the employee has been told in no uncertain terms that he must leave. However, if the communication is ambiguous, the court will have to review the exchange to see if it actually amounted to a dismissal. It is also classified as dismissal where an employee is told he must resign or he will be dismissed, and he resigns as a result.

7.85 If the employee believes that the employer has seriously breached the contract of employment, he may resign and claim constructive dismissal. The employer's conduct must have been very serious, going to the root of the contract, unless there have been a series of serious events, in which case something more trivial which the employee regards as the last straw may be sufficient. Typical acts of constructive dismissal include giving the employee reduced pay or benefits, or reducing his status in some way. More recently, the concept has been developed that there is an implied term in every contract of employment that there must be a relationship of trust and confidence between employer and employee, and if this relationship is broken by the employer, this will amount to constructive dismissal. Employment tribunals will not allow a claim for constructive dismissal to be brought unless the employee has first submitted a grievance, and has allowed at least 28 days to expire before lodging the claim. However, this requirement is likely to be repealed in April 2009.

D. Application for Interim Relief

CHECKLISTS

Does the employee believe he has been dismissed for: **7.86**

(a) trade union reasons (see para **7.121**);

(b) most health and safety reasons (see para **7.106**);

(c) acting as trustee of his employer's occupational pension fund (see para **7.118**);

(d) acting as an employee representative in redundancy or TUPE consultations (see para **7.120**), or a Working Time Regulations representative;

(e) making a protected disclosure (whistle-blowing) (see paras **7.95–7.105**);

(f) activities to do with union recognition (see para **7.124**); or

(g) asserting rights to accompany or be accompanied by someone facing disciplinary or grievance proceedings (see paras **7.119**)?

In these cases, he may apply to an employment tribunal for interim relief (ERA 1996, s 128). The application must be presented to an employment tribunal within seven days of the EDT (see para **7.59** for definition of EDT).

Where dismissal is for trade union activities, what steps must the trade union **7.87** take? An authorized official of the employee's trade union must within seven days of the EDT present a certificate to the tribunal stating that the employee is, or proposed to become, a member of the trade union, and that there appear to be reasonable grounds for supposing that the principal reason for the dismissal was the one alleged in the employee's complaint.

What is the test for succeeding in a claim for interim relief? An employment tri- **7.88** bunal must decide, before making an order for interim relief, that the employee has a 'pretty good chance' of succeeding in his claim that he has been dismissed for one of the reasons set out in para **7.86** (*Taplin v C Shippam Ltd* [1978] ICR 1068, EAT). The tribunal will normally call evidence on the issues, but will tend to shy away from giving a definitive account of the material facts. If an employee has ostensibly been dismissed for redundancy, the tribunal may still order interim relief if it believes the employee may well succeed in an argument that the redundancy was fabricated to obscure the fact that dismissal was really for one of the specified reasons, such as his trade union activities (*Bombardier Aerospace v McConnell* [2008] IRLR 51, CA).

7.89 What can the tribunal order if the tribunal decides the employee's claim is likely to succeed?

(a) that the employer should reinstate or re-engage the employee; or

(b) if the employer refuses, or if it offers to do so, but the employee reasonably refuses the offer, that the employee be suspended on full pay until the hearing.

Commentary

7.90 Where an employee has been dismissed for one of seven reasons (most commonly, for trade union activities, or making a protected disclosure ('whistle-blowing') he may, provided he does so within seven days of his dismissal, apply to the employment tribunal for interim relief. If the dismissal is for participation in trade union activities, the relevant union must endorse the application. If the application is successful, because the employee persuades the panel that he has a pretty good chance of succeeding in his claim, the employee will either be reinstated or will receive full pay until the hearing.

E. Grounds for Dismissal

CHECKLIST

Reason for Dismissal

7.91 What must the employer show? In any dismissal action, the burden is on the employer to show the reason for dismissal. In a case of wrongful dismissal, the employer must then show that the reason is sufficiently serious to have justified the employer terminating the contract, whether he knew of the reason at the date of termination or otherwise. For unfair dismissal, the employer must show:

(a) what the reason for dismissal was;

(b) that it was the actual reason why the decision to dismiss was taken; and

(c) that it was a fair reason.

Potentially Fair Reasons

7.92 These are set out in ERA 1996, s 98, and are:

(a) That the employee was incapable (measured by reference to skills, aptitude, health, or any physical or mental quality) of performing the work of the kind he was currently employed by the employer to do (see paras **7.182–7.219**);

(b) That the employee lacked the qualifications required to perform work of the kind that he was currently employed by the employer to do (see para **7.228**);

(c) Misconduct (see para **7.154–7.181**);

(d) Redundancy (see Chapter 8);

(e) That if the employee were to continue to be employed in the position he held, either he or the employer would be in breach of some statutory provision (see para **7.230**);

(f) Some other substantial reason which will justify dismissal (see paras **7.233–7.235**).

Automatically Fair Reasons

When will the dismissal be automatically fair? This will happen if the principal **7.93** reason for dismissal is:

(a) Dismissal of an employee to safeguard national security. This applies whether or not the employee is a civil servant or member of the armed forces. He may, for example, be an employee of a defence contractor; or

(b) Dismissal of an employee while he is taking part in an official strike or industrial action and has been doing so for at least twelve weeks when all those taking similar action are also dismissed, or of any employee taking part in unofficial strike action (see para **7.143** and **5.44**);

(c) Retirement provided the correct procedures are followed (see paras **7.146–7.153**).

Automatically Unfair Reasons or Procedures

When will dismissal be automatically unfair? This will happen when the principal **7.94** reason for dismissal is one of those on the list below:

(a) because the employee had made a whistle-blowing allegation (see para **7.95**);

(b) to do with health and safety (see para **7.106**);

(c) because the employee asserted a statutory right (see para **7.107**);

(d) because of family-related reasons (see para **7.112**);

(e) because the employee is asserting rights to work flexibility in order to look after children or care for adults (see para **7.113**);

(f) because the employee is asserting rights as a fixed-term or part-time employee (see para **7.114**);

(g) connected to TUPE transfers (see paras **7.115** and **9.32**);

(h) because the employee is or is about to be entitled to the minimum wage, or is trying to enforce his right to the minimum wage (see para **7.116**);

(i) because the employee is or is about to be entitled to tax credits or is asserting his right to tax credits (working tax credit or disabled person's tax credit) (see para **7.117**);

(j) to do with the fact that the employee was a trustee of the employer's occupational pension scheme (see para **7.118**);

(k) because of the employee's activities as a companion in disciplinary or grievance proceedings (see para **7.119**);

(l) because of the employee's activities in being a representative for redundancy or TUPE consultations (see para **7.120**);

(m) to do with the employee taking part or not taking part in trade union activities (see para **7.121**);

(n) to do with union recognition (see para **7.124**);

(o) because of the employee's activities in connection with a strike or other industrial action (see para **7.125**);

(p) because of the employee's actual or proposed activities on a European or British Works Council (see para **7.126**);

(q) because the employee is asked to go on or is absent because of jury service (see para **7.127**);

(r) to do with Sunday working (see para **7.128**);

(s) that the employee has some criminal convictions that are 'spent' (see para **7.129**);

(t) because the employer has failed to follow the statutory disciplinary and dismissal procedures unless dismissal is because the employee is one of at least 20 to be made redundant, when the collective consultation provisions apply, (see para **8.43**). This will only apply for so long as the procedures exist (they are likely to be repealed in April 2009) (see para **7.130**); or

(u) if the employee is being dismissed for retirement, but the employer has failed to follow the statutory procedures regarding notification of retirement (see para **7.132**).

Automatically unfair grounds: whistle-blowing

7.95 If the principal reason for the dismissal is that the employee made a protected disclosure, this will be automatically unfair (ERA 1996, s 103A).

7.96 When will there be a protected disclosure (ERA 1996, ss 43A–K)? When:

(a) information is of a particular protected category (see paras **7.97–7.98**);

(b) it has been made to an appropriate person (see para **7.99**); and

(c) the disclosure is the principal reason for dismissal (see para **7.100**).

7.97 Is the information protected? Information may be protected if the employee believes the information tends to show that:

(a) a criminal offence is, has been, or may be committed;

(b) a person is in breach of, has breached, or is likely to breach a legal obligation [Note: this is the most widely used ground and could even refer to an allegation by an employee that his own contract of employment has been or is likely to be breached: *Parker v Sodexho* [2002] IRLR 109, EAT];

(c) there is or may be a miscarriage of justice;

(d) an individual's health and safety may be endangered;

(e) the environment has been, is or is likely to be damaged; or

(f) information about any of these issues may be covered up.

[Note: so long as it is reasonable for the employee to believe that the factual basis of what was disclosed was true, assessing the facts as known by him at the time, it is immaterial whether the allegations were actually factually correct (*Darnton v University of Surrey* [2003] IRLR 133, EAT). It is also sufficient for the employee to believe that what he was disclosing fell within one of the whistle-blowing categories, eg the commission of a criminal offence, even if it does not do so; so long as their belief in the underlying facts is genuine, employees are not expected to have an encyclopaedic knowledge of the law (*Babula v Waltham Forest College* [2007] IRLR 346, CA).]

An employee will not be protected if: **7.98**

(a) he is not acting in good faith in making the disclosure;

(b) the employee would be committing an offence (eg under the Official Secrets Act) by making the disclosure;

(c) the information is privileged information, ie the employee has it only because it has been obtained for or prepared by lawyers giving advice on a subject;

(d) the dismissal relates not to any disclosure itself, but to misconduct designed to prove the employee's suspicions (*Bolton School v Evans* [2007] IRLR 140, CA where hacking into a student's computer to point out weaknesses in the IT system merited dismissal).

Is disclosure made to an appropriate person? Even if about a legitimate topic (see **7.99** para **7.97**), information will only be protected if it is made by the employee, in good faith, to:

(a) his employer; or

(b) a person who has legal responsibility for the behaviour in question (if not the employer's behaviour), in good faith (eg a building contractor, where the whistle-blower works for a sub-contractor); or

(c) his legal adviser (see eg *Kirwan v First Corporate Shipping Ltd* [2008] EAT 0066/07); or

(d) a Minister of the Crown (if the employee is a civil servant); or

(e) various listed regulatory bodies, such as the Charities Commission, the Financial Services Authority, or the Commissioners of the Inland Revenue concerning possible breaches of rules which are relevant to that body (Public Interest

7

Dismissals

Disclosure (Prescribed Persons) Order 1999) provided that the employee reasonably believes the information to be substantially true;

(f) other people, such as the media, but only in the most stringent circumstances where:

- the employee, in good faith, reasonably believes the allegations to be substantially true, and does not make the disclosure for purposes of financial gain; and
- when he makes the disclosure, the employee has: either made the disclosure to his employer (using relevant internal procedures, if any) or relevant regulator and nothing has been or is likely to be done; or has not made this disclosure only because he reasonably believes he will be subject to some detriment (eg dismissal or demotion) or evidence will be destroyed if he tells his employer; or
- it is nevertheless reasonable to make the disclosure to the individual, bearing in mind issues such as the identity of the recipient of the information, the seriousness of the allegations, whether they are continuing or likely to occur in future, and whether disclosure of the information puts the employer in breach of his obligations to another person;

(g) to someone else if the allegations are exceptionally serious, provided that the employee:

- acts reasonably and in good faith (including regarding his choice of person to whom he makes the disclosure);
- reasonably believes the allegation to be substantially true; and
- does not make the disclosure for personal gain.

7.100 Was the protected disclosure the principal reason for dismissal? A tribunal will need to analyse the employer's conscious and unconscious mental processes.

(a) If the disclosure caused or influenced the employer to dismiss, the dismissal will be automatically unfair.

(b) If all the employee can show is that 'but for' the disclosure, the dismissal would not have occurred, or that the disclosure and dismissal were merely 'related to' each other, the dismissal will not be automatically unfair on whistle-blowing grounds (*London Borough of Harrow v Knight* [2003] IRLR 140, EAT).

(c) If, even though the employee has made a protected disclosure, the employer can show that the reason for dismissal was unrelated, the dismissal will not be automatically unfair (*Kirwan v First Corporate Shipping Ltd* [2008] EAT 0066/07—where the EAT concluded that the employee had not suffered any detriment as a result of the disclosure because the reason for the dismissal was persistent lateness to work). It is for the employer to prove that the reason was not related to any disclosure (*Kuzel v Roche Products Ltd* [2008] EWCA Civ 380, CA (but see **7.102 (d)**)).

What was actually the reason for dismissal? In deciding whether the reason **7.101** for dismissal is that the employee has made a protected disclosure, the correct approach is:

(a) has the employee shown that there is a real issue as to whether the reason put forward by the employer for the dismissal was not the true reason: has he raised some doubt as to that reason by advancing a public interest disclosure reason under ERA, s 103A?
(b) if so, has the employer proved its reason for dismissal?
(c) if not, has the employer disproved the s 103A reason advanced by the employee?
(d) if not, dismissal is for the s 103A reason.

In answering these questions, it follows: **7.102**

(a) that failure by the employer to prove the potentially fair reason relied on does not automatically result in a finding of unfair dismissal under s 103A;
(b) but rejection of the employer's reason, coupled with the employee having raised a prima facie case that the reason is a s 103A reason, entitles the tribunal to infer that the s 103A reason is the true reason; but
(c) it remains open to the employer to satisfy the tribunal that the making of a protected disclosure was not the reason or the principal reason for dismissal, even if the real reason found by the tribunal is not the one advanced by the employer; and
(d) it is not at any stage for an employee with one year's qualifying service to prove the s 103A reason (though if the employee has less than one year's service, the onus will be on him to prove that the reason fell within s 103A— *Kuzel v Roche Products Ltd* [2008] EWCA Civ 380, CA).

Is there a clause in the employment contract preventing the employee from **7.103** making the disclosure? Any provision in a contract preventing an employee from making a whistle-blowing disclosure is void.

Must the disclosure have been made recently? The protected disclosure can **7.104** have been made at any time in the past (but obviously the longer ago it was made the more difficult for the employee to show that the disclosure was the main reason for dismissal *Stolt Offshore Limited v Miklaszewicz* [2002] IRLR 344, CS).

What if the individual is not dismissed but is detrimentally treated as a result of **7.105** the disclosure? The individual can still bring a claim in an employment tribunal for compensation for his detrimental treatment. These provisions apply not only to employees but also to workers such as sub-contractors, those working for sub-contractors, freelancers, casuals, and those doing work experience.

Automatically unfair grounds: health and safety dismissals

7.106 If the principal reason for a dismissal is that the employee is a health and safety representative or otherwise takes action because of the inadequacy of health and safety provisions, the dismissal will be automatically unfair (ERA 1996, s 100). In particular, a dismissal will be automatically unfair where the employee is dismissed because:

(a) his dismissal is in relation to the performance of his duties as a designated health and safety representative or appointed representative of workers in relation to matters of health and safety or as a member of a health and safety committee;

(b) where there is no such representative or safety committee, he brought matters to the attention of his employer which he reasonably believed were harmful or potentially harmful to health or safety; or

(c) in circumstances of danger which he reasonably believed to be serious or imminent because of inadequate health and safety, he left or prepared to leave or refused to return to his place of work or prepared to take appropriate steps to protect himself or other persons from the danger.

[Note: there is no statutory maximum ceiling for compensation for dismissals on health and safety grounds (ERA 1996, s 124(1A)).]

Automatically unfair grounds: assertion of a statutory right

7.107 Dismissal will be automatically unfair if the principal reason for the dismissal is that the employee either brought proceedings against the employer to enforce a relevant statutory right or alternatively alleged that the employer had infringed such a right (ERA 1996, s 104).

7.108 What are the relevant statutory rights for these purposes? They are limited to:

(a) rights under ERA 1996 (for example, the right to written particulars of terms and conditions of employment; the right to statutory minimum notice). This would include dismissal for the principal reason that the employee complained that her salary had not been paid on time, on the basis that she was asserting her statutory right not to have unlawful deductions made from her wages (*Elizabeth Claire Care Management Ltd v Francis* [2005] IRLR 858, EAT);

(b) various trade union-related rights including the right not to have action short of a dismissal taken on trade union-related grounds and the right to time off for union duties and activities;

(c) the right to retain employment terms and rights under a TUPE transfer; and

(d) rights conferred by the Working Time Regulations 1998 such as time off work and holiday entitlement.

Other statutory rights: In addition, it is automatically unfair to dismiss someone who: **7.109**

(a) refuses to comply with an obligation the employer is trying to impose in breach of the Working Time Regulations;

(b) refuses to enter into an agreement waiving his rights under the Working Time Regulations (ERA 1996, s 101A).

What statutory rights are not included within this provision? They include any **7.110** complaint that someone has been discriminated against.

Must a statutory right have been or be about to be infringed? So long as the **7.111** employee makes his claim to rights in good faith, it is irrelevant whether he actually has the right in question or whether it has been infringed.

Automatically unfair grounds: family-related reasons

Dismissal of a woman where the principal reason for the dismissal is because **7.112** she is pregnant or for a reason connected with pregnancy, or if it relates maternity leave, adoption leave, antenatal leave, paternity leave, parental leave, compassionate leave, or taking time off for dependants (ERA 1996, s 99; see paras **3.34**, **3.55**, **4.31**, **4.41**, **4.58**, and **4.68**). For example, dismissal of a woman, allegedly for misconduct but in fact, the tribunal found, because she wanted to adopt children and would therefore require increased time off to do so, was automatically unfair (*Coulombeau v Enterprise Rent-a-Car UK Ltd*—2600296/06, an employment tribunal case). To succeed in arguing that the sole or principal reason for dismissal relates to paternity leave, the employee must probably show that the dismissal was caused by the paternity leave—this is a stronger test than just showing that the dismissal was associated with taking paternity leave *(Atkins v Coyle Personnel plc* [2008] EAT 0206/07, EAT).

Automatically unfair grounds: flexible working request

It will be automatically unfair to dismiss someone for the principal reason that he: **7.113**

(a) made or proposed to make an application to work flexibly. Such an application can be made by someone with at least six months' service who has parental responsibility for a child under six (or under 18, if disabled) or who has caring responsibilities for an adult who is a spouse, partner, family member or fellow resident, to change hours, times, or place of work (see para **4.58**);

(b) appealed or proposed to appeal against a rejection of a request for flexible working;

(c) sued or threatened to sue the employer for compensation for breach of the flexible working procedures (ERA 1996, s 104C).

Automatically unfair grounds: part-time and fixed-term workers

7.114 It is automatically unfair to dismiss employees who have or who the employer believes are about to have:

(a) brought proceedings under the Part-Time Workers (Prevention of Less Favourable Treatment) Regulations 2002 or the Fixed-Term Workers (Prevention of Less Favourable Treatment) Regulations 2003, or requested a statement of reasons for any less favourable treatment;

(b) given evidence or information to assist a worker bringing proceedings under the Regulations;

(c) alleged the employer is in breach of the Regulations (unless the allegation is false and made in bad faith); or

(d) refused to forego any right under the Regulations (Part-time Workers (Prevention of Less Favourable Treatment) Regulations 2000, reg 7 and Fixed-Term Employees (Prevention of Less Favourable Treatment) Regulations 2002, reg 6.

Automatically unfair grounds: dismissal connected with a transfer

7.115 Dismissals for reasons principally connected with a transfer of undertaking will be automatically unfair unless they are for an economic, technical, or organizational reason entailing changes in the workforce (essentially redundancy) (TUPE 2006, reg 7) (see para **9.32**).

Automatically unfair grounds: minimum wage

7.116 It is automatically unfair to dismiss an employee for the principal reason that:

(a) the employee takes or proposes to take action, for himself or on behalf of a colleague, to enforce a right to a minimum wage (so long as the employee genuinely believes there is a minimum wage right and it has been breached, it is immaterial whether or not this is in fact the case);

(b) the employer was prosecuted for depriving the employee of his minimum wage rights; or

(c) the employee is about to or does qualify for a minimum wage or an increased minimum wage (ERA 1996, s 104A).

Automatically unfair grounds: tax credit rights

7.117 Under the Tax Credits Act 1999, an employee entitled to working tax credit (formerly working families' tax credit) or disabled person's tax credit is to receive the payment through the payroll, and must be provided with information about it, for example through an itemized pay statement. It will be automatically unfair to dismiss someone if the main reason for doing so is that:

(a) the employee sought to enforce tax credit rights, for himself or on behalf of a colleague (so long as the employee genuinely believes there are rights under the Tax Credits Act 1999 and that they are being infringed, it is immaterial whether or not this is in fact the case);

(b) the employer was prosecuted for depriving the employee of his tax credit rights; or

(c) the employee is entitled to or will be entitled to working tax credit or disabled person's tax credit (ERA 1996, s 104B).

Automatically unfair dismissals: trustees of occupational pension schemes

A dismissal will be automatically unfair if: **7.118**

(a) the employee is a trustee of a relevant occupational pension scheme or a director of a trustee company; and

(b) the principal reason for the dismissal is that he performed or proposed to perform any functions as such a trustee (ERA 1996, s 102).

Automatically unfair grounds: companion at disciplinary/grievance hearings

Dismissing an employee because he reasonably requests to be accompanied by a **7.119** fellow worker or union official at a grievance or disciplinary hearing who can address the hearing on his behalf and confer with him during the hearing; or acts or agrees to act as such a companion, will be automatically unfair (ERA 1999, s 12).

Automatically unfair grounds: employee representatives

A dismissal will be automatically unfair where the principal reason is that: **7.120**

(a) the employee is or is standing as a candidate to be an employee representative for the purposes of statutory consultation in relation to a proposed redundancy programme or a transfer of an undertaking; and

(b) the reason for his dismissal is the performance of his functions in that role; or

(c) the employee took part in an election for employee representatives (ERA 1999, s 103).

Automatically unfair grounds: trade union membership or activities

Dismissal of an employee mainly for one of the following reasons will be unfair **7.121** (TULR(C)A 1992, s 152):

(a) because he is or is not a member of any or any particular trade union. There can be no closed shop, and in general no policy whereby the employer refuses to employ union members;

(b) because he proposes to or has taken part in trade union activities involving his current employer at an appropriate time (ie outside working hours or within working hours with the employer's consent) (see para **7.122**);

(c) because he had or proposes to make use of trade union services at an appropriate time;

(d) because he had failed to accept an inducement not to be a member of a trade union, not to take part in trade union activities, or to de-recognize a trade union.

7.122 Examples of legitimate trade union activity for which it would be automatically unfair to dismiss an employee are:

(a) the employee recruiting other employees to the union during a meal break;

(b) shop steward fairly representing the union's and the employer's position to his members during the course of a dispute.

7.123 Examples of activity where dismissal of union representatives has been held not to be automatically unfair are:

(a) the dismissal of a union member for constantly complaining about health and safety issues when he was not the health and safety representative or a union official;

(b) the dismissal of a person acting in defiance of union policies;

(c) the dismissal of a person who, while doing something which would normally be part of his union duties (eg organizing a strike ballot) does so maliciously or dishonestly (eg by giving members false information about the issues in dispute).

Automatically unfair grounds: union recognition

7.124 Dismissal of an employee who reasonably does any of the following will be automatically unfair:

(a) acts with a view to obtaining or preventing union recognition;

(b) indicates that he is in favour of or against such recognition;

(c) acts to ensure or prevent continuation of compulsory recognition rights or indicates that he is in favour of or against such continuation;

(d) influences or tries to influence other workers to vote in a particular way or to abstain in any ballot; or

(e) votes in a ballot (TULR(C)A 1992, Sch A1, para 161).

Automatically unfair grounds: dismissal of those taking part in industrial action

7.125 Dismissal of an employee for taking part in lawful, official industrial action (ie industrial action taken for a legitimate reason once all ballot and notice requirements have been complied with) is automatically unfair if:

(a) the dismissal takes place within twelve weeks of the start of the industrial action; or

(b) the dismissal takes place after twelve weeks from the start of the industrial action, but the employee had personally stopped taking part in the action during the first twelve-week period; or

(c) the dismissal takes place after twelve weeks from the start date of the industrial action, the employee had not stopped taking part in the action during the first twelve weeks, but the employer fails to take such procedural steps as would have been reasonable for the purposes of resolving the industrial dispute, irrespective of the merits of the dispute (eg not arranging or refusing to attend meetings with the union to discuss settling the dispute, or not complying with procedures set out in the relevant collective agreement) (TULR(C)A 1992, s 238A(2), (3)).

[Note: if none of these conditions applies, an employer may lawfully dismiss employees taking part in lawful industrial action, provided he dismisses all those members of the workforce taking part—see para **5.44**.]

Automatically unfair grounds: Works Councils

It will be automatically unfair to dismiss employees who are: members of a **7.126** European or British Works Council or special negotiating body; information and consultation representatives; or candidates for any of these roles for the principal reason that they:

(a) performed functions in pursuance of their duties (save unreasonably disclosing confidential information); or

(b) asked for time off to perform the duties, with pay; or

(c) proposed to do either of the above; or

(d) have brought or threatened proceedings in the employment tribunal, EAT, or CAC to enforce consultation rights; or

(e) acted in a variety of ways with intent to bring about and pursue (or alternatively to defeat any action to bring about) Works Councils or equivalent bodies (Transnational Information and Consultation of Employees Regulations 1999, reg 28; Information and Consultation of Employees Regulations 2004, reg 30).

Automatically unfair grounds: jury service

If an employee is dismissed because he has been summoned for jury service or has **7.127** been absent from work on jury service then, unless the employee's absence would cause substantial harm to the employer's business and this has been drawn to the employee's attention but unreasonably ignored, the dismissal will be automatically unfair (ERA 1996, s 98B).

Automatically unfair grounds: Sunday working

Employees who have been continuously employed by the same employer as a **7.128** shop worker since 26 August 1994 or as a betting worker since 3 January 1995 who opted out of agreeing to do Sunday working will be automatically unfairly dismissed if they refuse or indicate they will refuse to work on a Sunday (ERA 1996, ss 101 and 36–43).

Automatically unfair grounds: spent convictions

Dismissing someone because they have a spent conviction or because they have **7.129** failed to disclose a spent conviction is an automatically unfair ground for dismissing

someone from any office, profession, occupation, or employment or for prejudic-
ing him in any way. There are exemptions in relation to sensitive professions (for
example, the police, childcare) (Rehabilitation of Offenders Act 1974, s 4(3)(b)).

Automatically unfair grounds: failure to follow statutory disciplinary procedures

7.130 Employers must (at least until the procedures are repealed which is likely to happen in April 2009) go through minimum disciplinary procedures before dismissing
an employee. If the employer fails to follow these minimum requirements, the
dismissal will be automatically unfair (ERA 1996, s 98A(1)). The requirements are,
for most circumstances, that the employer must:

(a) write to the employee setting out details of his complaint, requiring the
employee to attend a meeting;
(b) give the employee sufficient information to enable him to understand the
complaint;
(c) allow the employee a reasonable opportunity to consider his response to the
letter;
(d) hold a disciplinary meeting at a reasonable time and place, allowing both
sides to state their case;
(e) tell the employee the result and inform him of any right to appeal;
(f) if the employee appeals, hold an appeal meeting at a reasonable time and
place and then inform the employee of the result of the appeal (Employment
Act 2002, Sch 2 (see paras **7.242–7.248** for more detail).

7.131 If the employee has committed a very serious offence and is dismissed on the
spot, there is a modified procedure which requires the employer only to give
details of the misconduct, the basis for thinking the employee was guilty of it, and
a right of appeal. This procedure will only apply in the rarest of cases.

Automatically unfair dismissal: retirement procedures

7.132 If an employee is dismissed on grounds of retirement, but the employer has not
gone through the appropriate procedures, the dismissal will be automatically
unfair (ERA 1996, s 98ZG).

7.133 The appropriate procedures are: notifying the employee it proposes to retire him;
considering any request by the employee not to be retired; and considering any
appeal by the employee against a retirement decision (see para **7.146**).

General points regarding automatically unfair dismissals

7.134 There is no minimum period of employment for the employee before he can bring
a claim of unfair dismissal under these heads except for a dismissal for a reason
connected with a transfer (see paras **7.115** and **9.32**), an application for flexible
working (see para **7.113**), for failure to follow minimum disciplinary procedures

(see para **7.130**), or for retirement (see para **7.132**) where the employee must have at least one year's continuity of employment.

It is most unlikely that the employer will ever admit that the reason for dismissal **7.135** could possibly be connected with any of the matters set out above but it will be for an employment tribunal to examine whether the reason for dismissal given by the employer is the correct one, or whether the employee has established that the real reason was connected with one of the automatically unfair reasons.

If the employee is selected for redundancy for a reason which would make a **7.136** dismissal automatically unfair, statute expressly provides that the redundancy dismissal itself will be automatically unfair (ERA, s 105).

Time for Assessing the Reason for Dismissal in Unfair Dismissal Cases

A dismissal must be fair, based upon the facts known to the employer either at **7.137** the date the employee was given notice of his dismissal or, if there is an appeal, at the date of the announcement of the appeal decision.

Subsequently Discovered Conduct

While conduct discovered after notice of dismissal or announcement of any **7.138** appeal cannot be used to justify the dismissal in any unfair dismissal proceedings, it may be taken into account in the following circumstances:

(a) It may be relied upon to show the employer was reasonable in reaching any decision it did, before dismissal, about the employee's performance or conduct.

(b) It may affect remedies. If subsequently discovered conduct is very serious, it could lead to a finding that it was not just and equitable for the tribunal to make any compensatory award at all because of the employee's conduct (see para **7.308(d)**) (but see para **7.138(d)**).

(c) If new facts arise between the notice of dismissal and the termination date which show that the employer's conduct was unwarranted, this can be relied upon by the employee to show that the ultimate dismissal was unfair and vice versa. For example, if an employer gives an employee notice of termination of his employment as a result of misconduct but, before the termination date, discovers that it was another employee who committed the acts of misconduct in question, then if the employer still upholds the original employee's dismissal, this will be unfair.

(d) The employer can rely upon information relating to the original reason for dismissal received during the course of any appeal procedure even where the appeal takes place after the dismissal, though it may not use such information to introduce a fresh reason for dismissal. In these latter circumstances, if the employer wishes to rely upon the new information as a reason for dismissal, the original dismissal should be revoked upon appeal and further disciplinary proceedings instituted.

(e) It may be relied upon to justify a wrongful dismissal (see paras **7.11–7.12**).

Burden and Standard of Proof

7.139 Who must prove what the reason for dismissal is? The employer must show that the reason for dismissal is a potentially fair one. It is then for the tribunal to determine whether the employer has acted reasonably in all the circumstances in treating the reason for dismissal as a sufficiently serious one to dismiss the employee (ERA 1996, ss 98(1) and (4)). The tribunal will look at what the operative reason for dismissal was: even if the employee has committed an act of misconduct, if relying on the misconduct as the reason for dismissal was a sham device from an employer who had other reasons to wish to terminate the employment, dismissal may still be unfair (*ASLEF v Brady* [2006] IRLR 576, EAT).

7.140 Can the employment tribunal substitute its own reasoning and opinions for those of the employer? No (*Foley v Post Office*; *HSBC Bank plc v Madden* [2000] IRLR 827, CA). The matter must be judged by the objective standard of the way in which a reasonable employer in that line of business of that size in those circumstances would have behaved. The tribunal must ask the question: 'Was dismissal, as a sanction, one within the range of reasonable responses to the conduct which a reasonable employer might reasonably have imposed?' It is irrelevant whether other employers (or indeed the members of the employment tribunal hearing the case) might have behaved more leniently towards the individual.

Written Reasons for Dismissal

7.141 Can the employee require the employer to disclose the reason for dismissal at an early stage? Yes, if the employee has been continuously employed for one year or more he has the right to request written reasons for his dismissal. No such continuity qualification applies if the employee is pregnant at the time of the dismissal or if she is dismissed during her maternity leave. The employer must respond to such requests within 14 days (ERA 1996, ss 92 and 93). If the employer unreasonably fails to give reasons, he is liable to pay the employee two weeks' pay and make a declaration of what the reasons for dismissal were (ERA 1996, ss 92 and 93).

7.142 Is the employer bound by the stated reason? An employment tribunal is not bound to accept the employer's stated reason or reasons for dismissal if it finds that the reasons given conceal the true reason, but in any tribunal proceedings the employer is bound by the facts given in support of any dismissal, though not necessarily by the legal label given to those facts. When considering the reasons the tribunal will seek to ensure that they are genuinely held by the employer. If the employer relies on more than one reason, he may have to prove all of them to show a fair dismissal. If the tribunal decides that the stated reason for dismissal, even where misconduct has been committed which would potentially justify a dismissal, is not the true reason, the dismissal may be unfair (*ASLEF v Brady* [2006] IRLR 576, EAT).

Commentary

In respect of all qualifying employees, an employer must show that the reason for dismissal is one of the statutorily fair reasons set out in ERA 1996, s 98. These are incapability, lack of qualifications, misconduct, redundancy, retirement (from 1 October 2006), or breach of statutory provisions. There is also a catch-all ground of 'some other substantial reason which would justify dismissal'. It is *automatically fair* to dismiss someone to safeguard national security, to dismiss someone for retirement provided the statutory procedures are followed (ERA 1996, ss 98ZA–98ZG), or to dismiss someone while they are taking part in an official strike or industrial action which has lasted for over 12 weeks when all those in a similar position are dismissed, or while taking part in unofficial action (TULR(C)A 1992, ss 237–238A) but even so the employer must show that appropriate steps were taken and dismissal was within the range of reasonable responses (for example, that there were no suitable redeployment options, *B v BAA plc* [2005] ICR 1530, EAT). **7.143**

If dismissal is for a number of reasons (eg taking part in trade union activities, whistle-blowing, asserting statutory rights) dismissal will be *automatically unfair* (see para 7.94 for the full list). In these circumstances, except where dismissal is for reasons connected with a transfer, an application for flexible working, failure to follow minimum statutory disciplinary procedures, or retirement the employee does not have to have been employed for at least a year in order to bring an unfair dismissal claim. **7.144**

In examining the reason for dismissal, the tribunal will look at the facts known to the employer at the time of the dismissal. Subsequently discovered facts may be relied on to reduce any compensation, or to defend a wrongful dismissal claim, but cannot be used to defend the allegation that any dismissal was unfair. An employee employed for at least a year also has the right to demand that the employer sets out the reason for dismissal in writing. Once this is given, it is hard for the employer to depart from it. **7.145**

7

Dismissals

Special Provisions Relating to Retirement Dismissal

7.146 If the employer claims the employee was dismissed by reason of retirement:

(a) Is the employee aged at or above the normal retirement age? If there is no normal retirement age, is the employee 65 or older? If not, the dismissal will not be fair for retirement reasons.

(b) Has the employer notified the employee 6–12 months in advance of his intended date of retirement and told him of his right to request not to retire? If not, the dismissal will be unfair except in the circumstances set out in para 7.146(c).

(c) Has the employer notified the employee 2–26 weeks in advance of his intended date of retirement and his right to request not to retire? If yes, the dismissal may be fair, taking into account
 • the length of notice
 • whether the employer properly considered any right to request not to retire (see para **2.129**)
 • whether the retirement was the genuine reason for dismissal;

(d) Following para 7.146(c) if the tribunal considers dismissal was not for retirement, return to normal tribunal procedures.

(e) Has the employer properly considered any request not to retire? If not, the dismissal is likely to be unfair, and the employment may continue for remedy purposes.

7.147 Retirement dismissals after 1 October 2006 are not subject to the normal test of fairness of procedure set out in ERA 1996, s 98(4). Instead the provisions of ERA 1996, ss 98ZA–98ZG apply. This has a number of consequences:

(a) Dismissal of an employee below the age of 65, in the absence of a normal retirement age below 65, is not for retirement.

(b) Dismissal of an employee aged 65 or older, in the absence of a normal retirement age, or at the normal retirement age, is on the ground of retirement provided the employer has notified the employee that he proposes to retire him and told the employee of his right to request not to retire (Employment Equality (Age) Regulations 2006, Sch 6, para 2). The dismissal takes effect on the intended date of retirement. If the normal retirement age is lower than 65 it must be objectively justified.

(c) Dismissal of an employee below the relevant normal retirement age is not for retirement.

7.148 What happens if the employer has not warned the employee at least six months in advance of his proposal to retire him? If an employee has not complied with the duty to notify the employee of his intended date of retirement at least 6–12 months in advance, and of his right to request not to retire, whether or not the decision is fairly for the reason of retirement will be decided taking into account:

(a) whether or not the employer notified the employee two weeks to six months in advance of his intended date of retirement and his right to request not to retire (Employment Equality (Age) Regulations 2006, Sch 6, para 4);
(b) how long before dismissal the notification was given;
(c) whether the employer followed or sought to follow the duty to consider procedure set out in the Employment Equality (Age) Regulations 2006, Sch 6, paras 5 to 9 if the employee has requested not to retire.

A dismissal for retirement will be fair if steps para **7.146(a)**–**(c)** are followed and if the employer has properly considered any request to postpone retirement (see paras **7.150**–**7.152**) provided that in reviewing these factors the tribunal determines that the real reason for dismissal was indeed retirement.

7.149 If the tribunal reviews the three factors at para **7.146(a)**–**(c)** and decides that the failures were sufficient to render the decision not for retirement, then the dismissal will be considered under normal unfair dismissal principles. However, the employer may have difficulty then convincing a tribunal that such a dismissal was fair because he will have to show the reason for the dismissal was for some other potentially fair reason and that the statutory dismissal procedures were followed.

7.150 What must the employee do if he does not want to retire? If the employee requests not to retire on the intended date of retirement, he must do so

(a) within three months of any notification to retire, if the notification is given to him 6–12 months before the intended date of retirement;
(b) before the intended date of retirement, in any other circumstances.

7.151 If the employee requests not to retire, what must the employer do? The employer must meet the employee (who has the right to be accompanied by a colleague or trade union official) to consider the request (or, if not practicable to do so, must consider any written representations), and must then decide whether:

(a) to extend employment indefinitely;
(b) to extend the employment to a specified date; or
(c) to reject the request.

If (b) or (c) applies, the employee must be given the right of appeal.

7.152 What happens if the employer does not follow the steps in para **7.151**? If the employer dismisses the employee before considering the employee's request not to retire on the proposed date then (except for the purposes of deciding on what date the employee was dismissed for the purposes of bringing employment tribunal proceedings) the employment will be deemed to continue until the day after the employer gives notice of his decision.

7.153 [Note: in December 2006 the High Court referred to the ECJ the issue whether imposing a default retirement age of 65 properly implements the EC Equal Treatment Framework Directive (*The Incorporated Trustees of the National Council for Ageing (Age Concen England) v Secretary of State for BERR*, Case C-388107). The Attorney-General, whose opinion is frequently followed by ECJ, has said that a rule permitting employees to be dismissed at 65 can in principle be justified). The ECJ's decision is likely to be announced in 2009. In similar but not identical circumstances, the ECJ decided that a retirement age of 65 in Spain was justified (*Palacios de la Villa v Cortefiel Servicios SA* [2007] IRLR 989, ECJ).]

F. Potentially Fair Reason: Misconduct

INTRODUCTORY CHECKLIST IF THE EMPLOYER CLAIMS THAT THE
EMPLOYEE WAS DISMISSED FOR MISCONDUCT

7.154 Was the conduct sufficiently gross that dismissal was within the range of reasonable responses available to the employer (for examples, see paras **7.173–7.180**). If yes, the dismissal will potentially be fair. Go to para **7.145**. If not, the dismissal will be unfair unless there have been previous warnings (see para **7.156**).

7.155 If the employer had an exhaustive list of matters which constituted gross misconduct, was the conduct of a type on the list? If not, any summary dismissal will be unfair. This is not necessarily the case if the list is not exhaustive.

7.156 If the employee's misconduct is not so gross that it justifies dismissal, has the employee previously been given warnings telling him that dismissal may be an option if there is further misconduct (see para **7.169** for examples of minor offences)? If not, the employee will have been unfairly dismissed.

7.157 Is there another employee who has committed similar misconduct who was not dismissed, and did not have mitigating circumstances which would militate against dismissal? If so, dismissal will probably be unfair (see para **7.273**).

7.158 Was the misconduct known to the employer at the time of the dismissal? Did it form the real reason for the dismissal (see paras **7.91**, **7.137–7.140**)? If the answer to either question is no, the employee will have been unfairly dismissed, but his award may be reduced on the basis that it is not just and equitable to award compensation in these circumstances (see para **7.308(d)**).

Did the employer follow a statutory procedure giving the employee written details **7.159**
of the relevant circumstances, inviting him to a meeting, and offering an appeal
(see paras **7.242–7.248**)? If not, the dismissal will automatically be unfair and any
financial award must (save in exceptional circumstances) be increased by 10–50
per cent (but still subject to any relevant statutory cap).

After the dismissal and disciplinary procedures have been repealed: **7.160**

(a) did the employer follow the ACAS Code? If yes, the dismissal may be fair. If
no, then the award is likely to be increased by 0–25 per cent, depending upon
the severity of any failure to follow the Code;

(b) did the employee fail to follow the ACAS Code? If yes, dismissal may be
unfair, and then the award is likely to be decreased by 0–25 per cent, depending on the severity of the failure to follow the Code.

However, at the time of writing these procedures are still subject to consultation.

Did the employee fail to participate in the statutory disciplinary procedure, for ex- **7.161**
ample by failing to appeal (see para **7.244**)? If yes, and if the employee is found to
have been unfairly dismissed, his award must (save in exceptional circumstances)
be reduced by 10–50 per cent.

Did the employer conduct a proper investigation into the misconduct prior to the **7.162**
dismissal (see paras **7.252–7.256**)? If not, was there an appeal and was the failure
remedied prior to the appeal decision? If the answer to both questions is 'no',
the employee will have been unfairly dismissed. If it is yes to either question, go
to para **7.163**.

Was the conduct of the disciplinary meeting fair (see paras **7.264–7.269**)? If not, **7.163**
the dismissal will be unfair if the process outlined in paras **7.264–7.269** is not
followed, and may otherwise be unfair unless any lapses would not have affected
the outcome of the decision (see para **7.281**). If it was, go to para **7.164**.

Having conducted a reasonable investigation (see paras **7.162** and **7.163**) did the **7.164**
decision-maker genuinely believe, on reasonable grounds, that the employee was
guilty of the misconduct (see paras **7.270–7.273**)? If no, the employee will have
been unfairly dismissed. If yes, go to para **7.165**.

Was dismissal, given the conduct in question and the decision-maker's state of **7.165**
mind, within the range of reasonable responses available to the employer? If yes,
the dismissal will be fair (see para **7.274**). If no, it will be unfair.

If the procedure pre-appeal was insufficient, was the failure remedied by an **7.166**
appeal (see paras **7.276–7.280**)? If yes, the dismissal may be fair. If no, it will be
unfair.

Disciplinary Code

7.167 Where might you find a disciplinary code? A disciplinary code may be expressly incorporated into the employee's contract of employment. If it is, its provisions should be adhered to. In the absence of an express disciplinary code, any employment tribunal will, at least until they are repealed in April 2009, decide whether the employer has followed the statutory disciplinary procedures (see para 7.242) and will have regard to the ACAS disciplinary Code of Practice (see paras **7.168**– **7.169**). It will also expect any contractual disciplinary code to be along similar lines.

7.168 What is best practice? The ACAS Code of Practice on Disciplinary and Grievance Procedures provides that facts should be established promptly following any disciplinary matter and an individual should be interviewed and given the opportunity to state his or her case and be advised of any rights under the procedure before a decision is made. The Code is in the process of being revised at the time of going to press. When the statutory dismissal and disciplinary procedures are repealed (likely to take effect in April 2009) it is likely that employers will be penalized by having up to 25 per cent added to any compensation payable to an employee if they fail to follow the ACAS Code.

Minor Offences

7.169 When should the employer give a warning? The ACAS Code of Practice states that in the case of minor offences the individual should be given a formal oral warning or, if the issue is more serious, a written warning setting out the nature of the offence and the likely consequence of further offences. Further misconduct might warrant a final written warning, which should contain a statement that any one occurrence could lead to suspension or dismissal. Minor offences include lateness, taking meal breaks which are too long, minor acts of insubordination or rudeness, and so on. Appeals should be available at every stage.

7.170 Should absence be dealt with as misconduct? No. Frequent short-term self-certified absences should be dealt with under the procedure set out at para 7.210, and not as misconduct.

Gross Misconduct

7.171 When can the employer dismiss an employee? Any single act of gross misconduct (ie serious breach of contract) will be sufficient to justify immediate dismissal without notice, money in lieu of notice, or compensation. Employers should be consistent (*Cain v Leeds Western Health Authority* [1990] ICR 585), and impose similar sanctions for similar offences; if not, the employee given the tougher sanction may be unfairly dismissed so long as the circumstances are truly comparable

(*Levenes Solicitors v Dalley* [2006] EAT/0330/2006). Misconduct involves some deliberate or reckless act or omission. Negligence or carelessness will generally be regarded as incapability (see para 7.192).

When can warnings be taken into account? If the employer has a disciplinary **7.172** procedure which specifies that minor acts of misconduct are subject to progressively more serious warnings and ultimate dismissal, this should be followed. In the absence of such procedure, the employer should follow the ACAS Code. Normally, spent warnings cannot be relied on as part of the cumulative process (*Diosynth Ltd v Thomson* [2006] IRLR 284, SCS), but this is not a hard and fast rule where the employee has committed gross misconduct (*Airbus UK Ltd v Webb* [2008] IRLR 309, CA—where five employees were watching television during working hours. One had a spent warning, the other four had clean disciplinary records. The fact that the employer viewed the clean records as a mitigating factor converting dismissal to a final warning for four of the employees did not make dismissal of the fifth employee unfair, where the employer viewed him differently because he had previously been subject to a final written warning, even though that warning was spent.)

Examples of Misconduct

Refusal to obey a lawful order

Refusal to obey a lawful order is misconduct. The nature of the refusal and the **7.173** importance of the order will determine whether the misconduct is minor or gross (*UCATT v Brain* [1981] IRLR 224, CA). To determine what is lawful, one must look at the contract and any other incorporated documents such as a collective agreement or staff handbook, and at custom and practice. If the instruction is not lawful, that fact is not necessarily decisive when deciding whether any resulting dismissal was reasonable (*Farrant v Woodroffe School* [1998] ICR 184).

Examples of refusals include: **7.174**

(a) refusal to comply with safety requirements;

(b) refusal to move location if the contract provides that the employee can be required to move to a proposed new site;

(c) refusal to perform a task which the employee is contractually obliged to perform;

(d) refusal to work reasonable overtime if the contract provides that the employees must work overtime, so long as the employee is not being asked to work hours or at times that would involve a breach of the Working Time Regulations 1998;

(e) refusal to comply with an instruction to abide by new terms of employment (*Robinson v Tescom Corporation* [2008] EAT 0567/07, where the employer restructured its workforce and only accepted under protest new terms of employment under which he was to be responsible for a wider sales area than before. He then refused to cover the wider area. While he could possibly have resigned and claimed constructive dismissal, the fact that he chose to stay but refused to cooperate with the management instructions meant that dismissal was a reasonable response for the employer to take.)

7.175 Examples of refusals which would not amount to misconduct under this head:

(a) refusal by employees to work in dangerous conditions (and indeed a dismissal on this basis may be automatically unfair);

(b) refusal to obey an unlawful order, for example, to falsify accounts;

(c) refusal to work overtime if the employee is not contractually obliged to do so;

(d) refusal to accept change in terms and conditions of employment. However, if the employer can show that the changes are justifiable because of pressing business need, the dismissal may be for some other substantial reason and so the employer would be justified in dismissing the employee.

Breaches of discipline

7.176 If an employer is considering disciplining an employee must the offence be listed in the employer's disciplinary code? If the employer's disciplinary code sets out an exhaustive list of disciplinary offences, no additional offences omitted from the list may be relied upon. If the disciplinary code sets out examples only of breaches of disciplinary procedure, then items which are not set out in the list may nevertheless, if sufficiently serious, be categorized by the employer as misconduct. To justify summary dismissal, the conduct must completely undermine the trust and confidence inherent in the employment relationship (*Neary v Dean of Westminster* [1999] IRLR 288).

7.177 Examples of breaches of discipline are:

(a) drunkenness at work;

(b) being unfit to work as a result of drug abuse;

(c) theft of employer's, colleagues', clients', or suppliers' property (*Trusthouse Forte Hotels Ltd v Murphy* [1977] IRLR 186, EAT);

(d) physical violence or fighting;

(e) threatening behaviour;

(f) bad language;

(g) rudeness;

(h) fraud, for example, falsifying timesheets, or giving false information on a curriculum vitae (for example, not disclosing a past, unspent conviction);

(i) gross insubordination;

(j) failure to comply with legitimate management instructions, eg a director flouting his managing director's express instructions not to attend a particular meeting (*Annis v Eclipse Energy* [2007] All ER (D) 73, HC);

(k) failure to comply with important company policy—eg an employee with an otherwise exemplary work record breaching a smoking ban (*Smith v Michelin Tyre plc* [2007] 100726/07—an employment tribunal case) or failure to disclose and seek formal approval for work performed for third parties, even though the employee had mentioned the work to her employers (*Guernina v Thames Valley University* [2008] EWCA Civ 34, CA);

(l) working for or assisting a competitor whilst still employed (*Davidson and Maillou v Comparisons* [1980] IRLR 360, EAT) (although merely seeking alternative employment even before the termination of the present contract is not unlawful: *Harris & Russell Ltd v Slingsby* [1973] IRLR 221, NIRC) and, in the absence of a contractual provision to the contrary, preparing to compete by developing a competitive product in one's spare time may not be a breach of fiduciary or other duties: (*Helmet Integrated Systems v Tunnard and others* [2007] IRLR 126);

(m) misusing or unlawfully disclosing confidential information;

(n) unauthorized use of or tampering with a computer (*Denco Ltd v Joinson* [1991] IRLR 63, EAT);

(o) taking industrial action (but see para 7.125);

(p) taking bribes or secret commissions;

(q) serious breach of codes of relevant professional or governing bodies.

Criminal offences

Can an employee be dismissed for having committed any crime? Criminal offences **7.178** should only merit dismissal if they relate in some way to the employee's duties, for example, because they show that the employee is unsuitable for performing that type of work, or the offence renders the employee unacceptable to other employees.

Examples of criminal offences which justify dismissal are: **7.179**

(a) dishonesty (fraud, theft, etc): this will normally justify dismissal unless, for example, the employee has been actively employed (ie not just on suspension) for a period;

(b) sexual offences: these will justify dismissal if the employee's duties often put him in contact with women or children, especially vulnerable ones, for example, where the job is in the education or health sectors (*X v Y* [2004] IRLR 665; *P v Nottinghamshire County Council* [1992] IRLR 362, CA).

When do criminal offences not justify dismissal? These include minor drugs or **7.180** traffic offences which will not usually justify dismissal unless, for example, drug addiction affects the employee's capability or the employee's job requires a clean driving licence.

7.181 For appropriate procedure where misconduct is alleged, see paras 7.249–7.280.

G. Potentially Fair Reason: Incompetence

INTRODUCTORY CHECKLIST IF THE EMPLOYER CLAIMS THAT THE EMPLOYEE WAS DISMISSED FOR INCOMPETENCE

7.182 Had the employee had a prior warning of incompetence? If not, was the incompetence one of those very rare occasions when it amounted to such gross negligence that the employer could not reasonably be expected to continue to employ the employee (see para **7.199**)? If yes, the employee may have been fairly dismissed. Go to para **7.185**. If no, the employee will have been unfairly dismissed.

7.183 Has the employee been given a warning telling him that unless there is an improvement in his performance, he may be dismissed? Is that warning still current and unexpired (see para **7.288**(**b**))? Has sufficient time expired to allow the employee to demonstrate an improved performance? If the answer to all questions is yes, the employee may have been fairly dismissed. Go to para **7.184**. If the answer is no, unless para **7.182** applies, the employee will have been unfairly dismissed.

7.184 Can the employer demonstrate that it is reasonable to conclude that the employee has been incompetent, for example does he have samples of poor quality work, or details of particular incidents (see paras **7.192–7.193**)? If yes, the employee may have been fairly dismissed—go to para **7.185**. If no, the employee will have been unfairly dismissed.

7.185 Did the employer follow a statutory procedure giving the employee written details of the relevant circumstances, inviting him to a meeting and offering an appeal (see paras **7.242–7.248**)? [Note: these procedures are likely to be repealed in April 2009.] If not, any financial award must (save in exceptional circumstances) be increased by 10–50 per cent (but still subject to any relevant statutory cap).

7.186 Did the employee fail to participate in the statutory disciplinary procedure, for example by failing to appeal (see paras **7.242–7.248**)? [Note: these procedures are likely to be repealed in April 2009.] If yes, and if the employee is found to have been unfairly dismissed, his award must (save in exceptional circumstances) be reduced by 10–50 per cent.

After the dismissal and disciplinary procedures have been repeated: **7.187**

(a) Did the employer follow the ACAS Code? If yes, the dismissal may be fair. If no, then the award is likely to be increased by 0–25 per cent, depending upon the severity of any failure to follow the Code.

(b) Did the employee fail to follow the ACAS Code? If yes, then the award is likely to be decreased by 0–25 per cent, depending on the severity of the failure to follow the Code.

However, at the time of writing, these procedures are still subject to consultation.

Was the conduct of the pre-dismissal meeting fair (see paras **7.264–7.268**)? If **7.188** not, the dismissal will probably be unfair unless any failures were minor. If it was fair, go to para **7.189**.

Are there any mitigating circumstances (for example, previous good record of long- **7.189** standing employment) which would militate against dismissal in favour of a further warning (see para **7.198**)? If yes, dismissal may be unfair. Go to para **7.190**.

Was dismissal, given the incompetence in question, the conduct of the disciplin- **7.190** ary meeting, and any mitigating factors within the band of reasonable responses open to the employer? If yes, the dismissal will be fair (see paras **7.270–7.274**). If no, it will be unfair.

If the procedure pre-appeal was insufficient, was the failure remedied by an appeal **7.191** (see paras **7.276–7.280**)? If yes, the dismissal may be fair. If not, it will be unfair.

Evidence of Incompetence

The employment tribunal must rely to a large extent on the evidence of the **7.192** employee's superiors in deciding whether or not an employee has been incompetent. An employer should have specific examples of incompetence, for example:

(a) failure by the employee to perform part of his duties;

(b) complaints by colleagues or customers about the actions of the employee;

(c) inaccuracies committed by the employee;

(d) delays in finishing work by the employee;

(e) inflexibility and lack of adaptability on the part of the employee (*Abernethy v Mott Hay & Anderson* [1974] IRLR 213, CA);

(f) slovenliness or persistent carelessness on the part of the employee; or

(g) negligent acts or omissions on the part of the employee.

Discrete and dissimilar acts of incompetence may cumulatively be relied upon by **7.193** the employer. The employee is to be judged by the standards to be expected of someone in his present job, even if he has been over-promoted by the employer: the employee cannot demand to be returned to his former position, though in these circumstances a prudent employer would seek to establish whether there are any lower grade jobs to which the employee could be transferred.

Procedure

7.194 Before dismissing the employee for incompetence, what procedure will the employer normally need to adopt? The employer would be well advised to go through the following steps:

    (a) appraising the employee, pointing to areas of poor performance (see para 7.195);

    (b) warning the employee of the consequences of my failure to improve (see para 7.196); and

    (c) giving the employee the opportunity to improve (see para 7.197).

7.195 *Appraisal*: The employer should discuss with the employee the criticisms he has of the employee's performance. The employer should maintain a system to monitor the employee's progress. Dismissals for poor performance are unlikely to be fair if the employee has been given positive appraisals immediately prior to the dismissal.

7.196 *Warning*: The employer should write to the employee telling him where his performance is deemed to be sub-standard, inviting him and a representative to come to a meeting to discuss his concerns, and giving him an opportunity to express his point of view and explain why he might have been performing badly. If the explanation is not satisfactory, the employer should warn the employee of the consequences of a failure to improve. This should, preferably, be in writing. The warning should set out:

    (a) where the employee has failed to meet the required standards;

    (b) the time within which the employee must improve;

    (c) the standard the employee must meet;

    (d) the fact that if the employee fails to improve, a further warning will be necessary (or, after the second warning, dismissal may be invoked).

7.197 *Opportunity to improve*: The employer must give the employee a reasonable period within which to improve. In establishing what is reasonable one must bear in mind the nature of the job, the employee's length of service, status, and past performance. The employer should give the employee the necessary support and assistance (which can include training) to enable the employee to improve. Normally, employees should receive at least two warnings before being dismissed for poor performance (but see para 7.199).

7.198 Are long service employees treated the same as recent joiners? An employee of previously good standing and long service will require special attention by the employer before any dismissal is made. He should be given reasonably substantial periods within which to improve unless there are very obvious reasons why an employee has suddenly become incapable, for example:

(a) the employee's capacity to do the job is altered, for example, because of ill health;
(b) the employee's job functions have altered, for example, as a result of new technology;
(c) the employee has failed to heed past warnings.

When are warnings for incompetence not necessary? In the following **7.199** circumstances:

(a) gross incompetence or unsuitability;
(b) incompetence which has had serious physical consequences, for example, where a pilot has incompetently landed a plane causing actual or potential injury to passengers and/or expensive equipment (*Alidair Ltd v Taylor* [1976] IRLR 420, EAT);
(c) incompetence which has serious economic consequences, for example, deliberate or reckless incompetence leading to loss of a whole production batch;
(d) incompetence where the employer reasonably believes that a warning would make no difference, for example, where an employee refuses to admit that there is any need for him to improve;
(e) the incompetence of a senior employee, who should appreciate what standards are required of him and whether he matches up to those standards. The employee must, however, be in a position to know (whether from his own experience or because he has been told his work is unsatisfactory) that he may be dismissed unless his work meets the required standard.

If an employer has dismissed the employee for incapability, care should be taken **7.200** in drafting any reference so that the reference does not indicate that the employee was a perfectly satisfactory worker (for references, see para 1.114). However, references should not refer to any acts of misconduct which have not previously been brought to the employee's attention.

H. Potentially Fair Reason: Ill-health

INTRODUCTORY CHECKLIST IF THE EMPLOYER CLAIMS THE
EMPLOYEE WAS DISMISSED BY REASON OF ILL-HEALTH

Has the employer made full inquiry (which would normally include meetings with **7.201** the employee, obtaining a medical report, and examining the sickness record) about the employee's state of health (see para **7.213**)? If not, the dismissal is likely to be unfair.

7.202 Has the employer considered whether the employee is disabled and if so whether there are any reasonable adjustments he should make to allow the employee not to be under a disadvantage? If the employee is disabled and if the employer has not made reasonable adjustments (see para **2.107**) the employee may have been both discriminated against and unfairly dismissed (see paras **7.211–7.212**).

7.203 If the employee has been persistently absent, is there any medical excuse for this (see para **7.210**)? If yes, go to para **7.204**. If not, treat the problem as misconduct. Go back to para **7.154**.

7.204 Has the employer considered all relevant factors before deciding whether or not he wishes to dismiss the employee (see para **7.215**)? If he has, and if there are no other steps (such as alternative employment) which he could take, the employee may fairly be dismissed. Go to para **7.205**.

7.205 Did the employer follow a statutory procedure giving the employee written details of the relevant circumstances, inviting him to a meeting and offering an appeal (see paras **7.242–7.248**)? [Note: the statutory procedures are likely to be repealed in April 2009.] If not, any financial award must (save in exceptional circumstances) be increased by 10–50 per cent (but still subject to any relevant statutory cap).

7.206 After the dismissal and disciplinary procedures have been repeated, did the employer follow the ACAS Code? If yes, the dismissal may be fair. If no, then the award is likely to be increased by 0–25 per cent, depending upon the severity of any failure to follow the Code.

7.207 Did the employee fail to participate in the statutory disciplinary procedure, for example by failing to appeal (see para **7.244**)? [Note: the statutory procedures are likely to be repealed in April 2009.] If yes, and if the employee is found to have been unfairly dismissed, his award must (save in exceptional circumstances) be reduced by 10–50 per cent.

7.208 Is the employee benefiting from permanent health insurance cover which will be withdrawn if dismissed (see para **7.215(m)**)? If he is, then unless there is a clause in his contract of employment which nevertheless allows the employer to dismiss in those circumstances, any dismissal is likely to be unfair.

7.209 If the procedure pre-appeal was insufficient, was the failure remedied by an appeal (see paras **7.276–7.280**)? If yes, the dismissal may be fair. If not, it will be unfair.

Absenteeism

Is the employee taking frequent short-term, self-certified absences? If so, the **7.210** employer should:

(a) review the employee's attendance record and the reasons given for it;

(b) give the employee the opportunity to explain his attendance record (*International Sports Co Ltd v Thompson* [1980] IRLR 340, EAT);

(c) if the employee does not give a satisfactory explanation, but claims his absences are on grounds of ill-health, or if there is any reason to suspect that the absences are caused by any disability, ask him to see a doctor to consider whether medical treatment is necessary. Any genuine illness must be treated with sympathy and under normal illness procedures (see paras 7.213–7.217). However, the fact that someone is disabled does not of itself prevent the employer from dismissing him for absenteeism (*Royal Liverpool Children's NHS Trust v Dunsby* [2006] IRLR 351), though an employer should consider whether it might be a 'reasonable adjustment' to disregard disability-related absences;

(d) if there is still no satisfactory explanation for the absences, give the employee a misconduct warning that further unwarranted absences are likely to result in dismissal;

(e) interview the employee after any subsequent absence to ascertain its cause;

(f) if there is no improvement in the attendance record, and still no valid reason for the absences, the employer may dismiss the employee.

Disability

Did the employer know, when it engaged the employee, of the existence **7.211** and extent of a disability? If it did, it is most unlikely to be able to dismiss the employee fairly by reason only of the disability; if it does, this is likely to be discrimination under the terms of DDA 1995 (*Williams v J Walter Thompson Group Ltd* [2005] IRLR 376, CA, see paras **2.97** et seq). In those circumstances the standard of work required of the employee will be that of a disabled person to do the particular job in hand.

What happens if the employee becomes disabled during the course of his **7.212** employment? He should be treated in the same manner as employees suffering from other illnesses but subject always to the provisions of DDA 1995, in particular in relation to the making of reasonable adjustments to the workplace (see para **2.107**).

Illness

7.213 Before taking any action regarding the employee's illness then, provided the employee is not disabled within the definition of DDA 1995 (see para **2.99**) the employer should take the following steps:

(a) consult the employee about the situation and ask the employee for his own views on his health and abilities (*East Lindsey District Council v Daubney* [1977] IRLR 181, EAT);

(b) where appropriate, obtain a medical opinion. This medical opinion should be more detailed than a mere expression of opinion that the employee is unfit to work, and should deal with the likelihood of an improvement in health and attendance. The employee cannot be compelled (in the absence of an express contractual term) to undergo medical examinations;

(c) examine the sickness record;

(d) discuss the position again with the employee;

(e) review whether there is any alternative employment which might suit the employee. If the employee is disabled within the definition of the DDA 1995, but the employer is contemplating dismissing the employee, for example because of incompetence or absenteeism, the employer must review whether any reasonable adjustments might improve the position, for example by giving training or adapting the working environment (in the case of incompetence) or changing the working hours (in the case of absenteeism), and if there are any he should make them. Failure to do so would render a dismissal a breach of DDA 1995, s 4(2)(d) (see para **2.107**).

7.214 What happens where the absences are unconnected and intermittent, or where otherwise there will be no apparent benefit from a medical review of the position? In these circumstances there will be no obligation to obtain medical evidence (*Lynock v Cereal Packaging Ltd* [1988] IRLR 510, EAT).

7.215 What facts should the employer consider, once it has formed a reasoned opinion of the employee's medical state?

(a) the nature of the illness;

(b) the likelihood of it recurring;

(c) the length of absences likely and the intervening spaces of good health;

(d) the requirements of his business;

(e) whether the employee's tasks can smoothly be done by colleagues or temporary employees while the employee is absent;

(f) the impact on colleagues of the employee's absence;

(g) the employee's length of service;

(h) the need for the employer to have employees of this nature in rude health (for example, deep-sea divers, heavy manual workers);

(i) whether the ill-health might cause potential problems at the workplace (for example, an epileptic may be thought not to be able to work with dangerous machinery or in a nightclub);

(j) whether continuing to employ the individual in his former job, or any suitable available employment, could give rise to injury for which the employer could be liable, if medical opinion is disregarded and the employee returns to work (*Liverpool Area Health Authority (Teaching) Central & Southern District v Edwards* [1977] IRLR 471, EAT);

(k) alternative employment (for example, a desk job for the employee, even if at a reduced rate of pay). The employer is not however expected to create a special job for the employee but only to look to see whether he has any suitable vacancies (*Merseyside & North Wales Electricity Board v Taylor* [1975] IRLR 60, HC);

(l) whether it is possible to make adjustments to the workplace so that the employee could return to work;

(m) the employer's sick pay scheme. The employer should generally not dismiss an employee who is still entitled to benefits under the scheme, especially if by doing so, the employee is unable to benefit from the scheme in the future. Even if the employer has an express contractual right to dismiss, the courts are likely to strive to stop the employer blocking an employee's rights under, for example, a permanent health insurance scheme (see para **1.115**).

(n) whether the employee could be retired on the grounds of ill-health under his pension scheme. If he could, an employer must consider this option before determining to dismiss him for long-term sickness (*First West Yorkshire Ltd and Haigh* [2008] IRLR 182, EAT).

See generally, *Spencer v Paragon Wallpapers Ltd* [1976] IRLR 373.

Is it clear, after consultation with the employee and his representative, that: **7.216**

(a) the employee will not within a reasonable time be able to resume his duties satisfactorily;

(b) there are no alternative available jobs which the employee could be offered; and

(c) for disabled employees, no reasonable adjustments can be made to improve the position?

Then it may be reasonable for the employer to dismiss the employee. This may be the case even where the employer's behaviour caused or contributed to the relevant incapacity, if there is no prospect of the employee being sufficiently well to return to work and the employer acted reasonably in all the circumstances (*Mcldie v Royal Bank of Scotland* [2006] All ER (D) 393, EAT).

7.217 Does the employee have very serious ill-health, which will either mean he cannot in future carry out his old role or will be absent for long periods of time (at least more than the period when the employer's sick pay scheme operates)? This can in rare circumstances mean that the contract terminates by frustration, and there is, therefore, no dismissal.

AIDS

7.218 Is the employee HIV positive? An employer will generally not be able to dismiss an employee who is HIV positive unless AIDS has manifested itself and prevents the employee from working properly. The employer must consider the issues set out at paras **7.213–7.216** above and the provisions of DDA 1995 (see paras **2.96–2.116**) in the normal way. The employer should seek to allay unreasoned fears of any of the employee's colleagues. A person who is HIV positive (as with those with cancer or multiple sclerosis) is now automatically regarded as disabled (DDA 1995, Sch 1, para 6A).

Responsibility for Absences

7.219 When considering whether the employee was unfairly dismissed on grounds of ill-health, the cause of the ill-health is immaterial. An employer who caused the ill-health may still dismiss an employee after going through the steps in paras **7.213–7.215**, but may face High Court or county court proceedings for a personal injury claim.

I. Other Potentially Fair Reasons for Dismissal

7.220 Other potentially fair reasons are:

(a) lack of appropriate qualifications;
(b) that it is illegal for the employer to continue to employ the employee;
(c) some other substantial reason justifying dismissal.

INITIAL CHECKLIST IF THE EMPLOYER CLAIMS THE EMPLOYEE HAS BEEN DISMISSED BY REASON OF LACK OF RELEVANT QUALIFICATIONS, OR ILLEGALITY

7.221 Can the employer demonstrate why ownership of the qualifications has become necessary (see para **7.228**)? If not, the dismissal will be unfair. If yes, go to para **7.223**.

Can the employer demonstrate why the employment is now illegal (see para **7.222** **7.230**)? If no, the dismissal will be unfair. If yes, go to para **7.223**.

Were there any alternative positions into which the employee could have been **7.223** placed? If there were, and they were not offered to the employee, the dismissal is likely to be unfair.

Did the employer follow a statutory procedure giving the employee written details **7.224** of the relevant circumstances, inviting him to a meeting and offering an appeal (see paras **7.242**–**7.248**)? [Note: the statutory procedures are likely to be repealed in April 2009.]

If not, any financial award must (save in exceptional circumstances) be increased by 10–50 per cent (but still subject to any relevant statutory cap).

Did the employee fail to participate in the statutory disciplinary procedure, for **7.225** example by failing to appeal (see para **7.244**)? [Note: the statutory procedures are likely to be repealed in April 2009.] If yes, and if the employee is found to have been unfairly dismissed, his award must (save in exceptional circumstances) be reduced by 10–50 per cent.

After the dismissal and disciplinary procedures have been repeated: **7.226**

(a) Did the employer follow the ACAS Code? If yes, the dismissal may be fair. If no, then the award is likely to be increased by 0–25 per cent, depending upon the severity of any failure to follow the Code.
(b) Did the employee fail to follow the ACAS Code? If yes, then the award is likely to be decreased by 0–25 per cent, depending on the severity of the failure to follow the Code.

Note, at the time of going to press, these provisions are still subject to consultation.

If the procedure pre-appeal was insufficient, was the failure remedied by an appeal **7.227** (see paras **7.276**–**7.280**)? If yes, the dismissal may be fair. If no, it will be unfair.

Lack of Qualifications

When can this ground apply? Generally, an employer has an opportunity to assess **7.228** a prospective employee's qualifications before employing him. There are therefore only limited circumstances where this ground can be relied upon, for example:

(a) where someone employed as a driver loses his driving licence; or
(b) where regulations, or new and profoundly sensible employer practice, require an employee carrying out work which the original employee had previously been doing to have particular qualifications, which the original employee does not possess.

7.229 Where an employer proposes to dismiss for lack of qualifications, he should still look to see whether there are any alternative vacant jobs in which he can place the employee.

Illegality

7.230 Is it definitely a breach of the law for this employee to continue in employment? If an employer is to dismiss an employee under this head the employment must genuinely be in breach of the law. If the employer erroneously believes it is, then the dismissal may be fair for some other substantial reason but not under the heading of illegality (*Kelly v University of Southampton* [2008] IDS Brief 846). Examples of illegality include:

(a) the employee losing a work permit (*Hounslow v Klusova UK* EAT/0325/06, [2006] IDS Brief 819);

(b) the employee being disqualified from driving if driving is an essential part of the job;

(c) the employee no longer having relevant professional qualifications (for example, an employed solicitor or doctor who is struck off their respective professional register).

7.231 Before dismissing on the ground of illegality the employer should consider whether it has any alternative vacancies which it could offer the employee that the employee would not legally be disqualified from performing. The employer does not have to create a suitable position if none is available.

7.232 If it is illegal for an employer to continue to employ an employee, the employee can be dismissed without the employer having to follow the statutory disciplinary and dismissal procedures. However, it is sensible, for so long as the procedures remain in force, for an employer contemplating dismissing for illegality to follow the statutory procedures in case it is wrong in its assumption that it would be illegal to continue to employ.

Some Other Substantial Reason

7.233 This is a catch-all fair ground for dismissal. Examples include:

(a) An unreasonable refusal by the employee to accept changes in the terms and conditions of his employment whose imposition is necessary for sound business reasons (*Willow Oak Developments Ltd v Silverwood* [2006] IRLR 607, CA; *Catamaran Cruisers Ltd v Williams and Others* [1994] IRLR 386, EAT).

(b) Where a genuine business reorganization dislodges an employee: the employer must show there is economic necessity for the reorganization and be prepared to produce supporting financial accounts (*Banerjee v City &*

Eastern London Health Authority [1979] IRLR 147, EAT). If the reorganization is not genuine, but a pretext for getting rid of an old employee, it will be unfair (*Oakley v The Labour Party* [1988] IRLR 34, CA). When reviewing the employer's decision, the tribunal should conduct a balancing act, taking into account the advantages to the employer of its business reorganization and the disadvantages to employees—the employer does not have to go so far as to show that the changes are vital for the survival of the business (*Glasgow City Council v Deans and others* UKEATS/006/05).

(c) A personality clash, if it disrupts the workplace: an employer should first try to establish whether the position is remediable, for example, by moving one of the employees to another department.

(d) The dismissal of the employee at the request of a third party (*Dobie v Burns International Security Services (UK) Ltd* [1984] IRLR 329, EAT): the employer must take into account, however, the potential injustice to the employee before acting on the third party's request. This will only be a fair dismissal in exceptional cases, for example, if a valued customer requires the employer to dismiss the employee (which the employer will have to prove— for example, by having a letter from the customer). This ground will not help any employer who, for example, gives in to union pressure to dismiss the employee. The tribunal will consider the extent of any injustice caused to the employee by the dismissal (such as reviewing length of service, work record, whether the employee could have been assigned to other duties, difficulties in obtaining new employment) before deciding whether it was reasonable for an employer to give in to third party pressure (*Greenwood v Whiteghyll Plastics Ltd* [2007] EAT 0219/07).

(e) A breakdown of trust and confidence between employer and employee (*Perkin v St George's Healthcare NHS Trust* [2005] IRLR 93, CA, when behaviour at the disciplinary meeting was appropriately taken into account).

(f) Imprisonment of the employee.

(g) The wish of a small employer to appoint his child to do the relevant job.

(h) The protection of the employer's business, for example, where the employee refuses to sign a reasonable restrictive covenant (*Willow Oak Developments Ltd v Silverwood* [2006] IRLR 607, CA).

(i) The dismissal of an employee who refuses to agree a new shift pattern which would have resulted in him losing substantial overtime earnings (*Scott and Co v Richardson* [EAT 0074/04], IDS Brief 786).

(j) A dismissal arising following a transfer of undertaking for an economic, technical, or organizational reason entailing changes in the workforce (*McGrath v Rank Leisure Ltd* [1985] IRLR 323, EAT).

(k) The non-renewal of a contract where the employee has been told in advance it is temporary and why (for example, because it replaces someone on maternity leave (ERA 1996, s 106(2)) or someone who is suspended on medical grounds). The employer should have told the employee at the outset that he is being employed to replace such a person and the employment will cease when the person returns to work.

7.234 The following have been held not to justify dismissal:

(a) a rumour that the employee would leave to start up a rival business;
(b) the fact that a relation of the employee has been convicted of dishonesty;
(c) the fact that the employee is looking for alternative employment.

7.235 No employee should be dismissed for some other substantial reason unless appropriate warning and consultation procedures are first carried out (see paras 7.249–7.285).

Retirement

7.236 Check first if the employer claims the employee was dismissed by reason of retirement (see paras 7.146–7.153).

7.237 Is the employee aged at or above the normal retirement age? If there is no normal retirement age, is the employee 65 or older? If not, the dismissal will not be fair for retirement reasons.

7.238 Has the employer notified the employee 6–12 months in advance of his intended date of retirement and told of him of his right to request not to retire? If not, the dismissal will be unfair except in the circumstances set out in para 7.239.

7.239 Has the employer notified the employee 2–26 weeks in advance of his intended date of retirement and his right to request not to retire? If yes, the dismissal may be fair, taking into account:

(a) the length of notice;
(b) whether the employer properly considered any right to request not to retire (see paras 7.146–7.153);
(c) whether the retirement was the genuine reason for dismissal.

7.240 Following para 7.239, if the tribunal considers dismissal was not for retirement, return to normal misconduct or incompetence tribunal procedures (see paras 7.154 and 7.182).

7.241 Has the employer properly considered any request not to retire? If not, the dismissal is likely to be unfair, and the employment may continue for remedy purposes.

Redundancy

See Chapter 8.

J. Statutory Disciplinary Procedure for All Dismissals

CHECKLIST

Is the employer contemplating dismissing the employee? If so, then until they are **7.242** repealed [likely to take place in April 2009] the employer must follow the statutory procedures, unless any of the exceptions in para **7.243** apply.

Is the employee: **7.243**

(a) likely to be retired;

(b) employed for less than one year, in circumstances where it is certain that none of the automatically unfair grounds for dismissal which do not require one year's service before a case is brought apply (*Scott-Davies v Redgate Medical Services* [2007] ICR 348, EAT);

(c) one of at least 20 employees likely to be made redundant at the same establishment within a period of 90 days or less, so that the employer must collectively consult with a recognized trade union or staff representatives before effecting any redundancies;

(d) in a category or of a description where all employees of that category or description are dismissed and then re-engaged;

(e) on strike or taking other industrial action where the action is unofficial or has been lasting at least 12 weeks;

(f) employed in a business which has suddenly ceased to function because of an event which could not have been foreseen by the employer so that it is impractical for the employer to employ anyone;

(g) going to be employed illegally if he continues in employment?

If so, the statutory procedures will not apply (Employment Act 2002 (Dispute Resolution) Regulations 2004, reg 4). However, an employer should be particularly cautious when deciding to ignore the procedures, particularly if there is any prospect that the employee could argue that the circumstances set out above do not in fact apply. If they do not do so, yet the employee is dismissed, the dismissal will be automatically unfair, and the employee will be entitled to an uplift of 10—50 per cent on any compensation awarded.

What are the minimum procedures which must be followed? There are three **7.244** stages, or 'steps'. Each step must be taken without unreasonable delay.

7

Dismissals

(a) *Step 1* The employer must write to the employee setting out the circumstances which lead it to contemplate dismissing the employee and inviting the employee to a meeting to discuss it. The information needs to be sufficient to enable the employee to understand and prepare for the complaints he has to meet. The tribunal will not be unduly pedantic in reviewing whether the case has been precisely set out, so long as the employee knows enough to be able to answer the allegations as best he can (*Sahatciu v DPP Restaurants Ltd* [2006] EAT 177/06). Nevertheless, it is sensible for this information to include:

- the reasons why dismissal is being contemplated (for example, for poor performance, one should detail specific lapses, or for misconduct, one should set out exactly what conduct is complained of, though great detail may be unnecessary if, when viewed in context, the employee would clearly have understood what the misconduct was (*Draper v Mears Ltd* [2006] IRLR 869, EAT));
- any evidence supporting the allegations, for example documents, witness statements, or notes of relevant conversations (see para **7.263**).

(b) *Step 2* The employer should invite the employee to a meeting to discuss the position before any decision to dismiss is taken. The timing and location of the meeting must be reasonable, and the meeting must be conducted in a manner that enables both employer and employee to explain their cases (EA 2002, Sch 3, Part 3). The employee may be accompanied by a colleague or a trade union official (ERA 1999, s 10; TULR(C)A 1992, s 119) (see para **7.267**). Following the meeting the employer must inform the employee of the decision and notify him that he has a right of appeal. This notification does not have to be in writing (*Aptuit (Edinburgh) Ltd v Kennedy* [2007] UKEATS 0057/06).

(c) *Step 3* If the employee exercises the right of appeal, the employer must invite the employee to an appeal meeting. Where possible, the appeal should be conducted by a more senior manager than the one who conducted the dismissal meeting. The employee may be accompanied at the meeting, as in step 2 above. After the meeting, the employer must notify the employee of the decision.

7.245 When can the employer avoid the procedures?

(a) See para **7.243** for details of when the procedures do not apply.

(b) In very rare cases, where an employee has reasonably been dismissed on the spot for gross misconduct, a *modified procedure* can be used consisting of, in place of steps 1 and 2, a written document sent by the employer to the employee describing what misconduct the employee was dismissed for committing, why the employee was thought guilty of the misconduct, and his right of appeal. An employer should be very wary of adopting this route.

(c) The procedures need not be started or completed if either party has reasonable grounds to believe there may be a threat to any person or property; or that, having been harassed, he reasonably believes he will be harassed again; or that it was not reasonably practicable to begin to comply with the procedure within a reasonable period (Employment Act 2002 (Dispute Resolution) Regulations 2004, reg 11).

See also the ACAS Code of Practice on Disciplinary and Grievance Procedures. It **7.246** is not yet obligatory to follow this, but while the disciplinary and dismissal procedures still apply, a failure to do so may be taken into account by an employment tribunal. However, when the disciplinary and dismissal procedures are repealed (likely to be in April 2009), the law is likely to require an employer to comply with the provisions of the ACAS Code. Failure by a party to comply with the Code is likely to result in an increase or decrease to any compensation award of up to 25 per cent.

What happens if the employer does not follow the procedure? If the employ- **7.247** ee wins the claim, the dismissal is automatically unfair (ERA 1996, s 98A). The amount of compensation (except in exceptional circumstances) must be increased by 10 per cent and may be increased by up to 50 per cent (in all cases subject to the statutory maximum award that may apply to the claim—£66,200 for dismissals occurring during the year beginning 1 February 2008 and £66,200 for dismissals during the year beginning 1 February 2008). When considering the extent of any increase, the tribunal must focus on only the circumstances surrounding the failure to complete the procedures—other issues, for example that the employer is a large company which behaved shoddily, must be ignored (*Aptuit (Edinburgh) Ltd v Kennedy* [2007] UKEATS 0057/06). If the employee fails to comply with the procedure (for example by unreasonably failing to attend a meeting) or does not appeal, but wins the claim, the award must (again, save in exceptional circumstances) be reduced by 10 per cent and may be reduced by up to 50 per cent (EA 2002, s 31).

Additional Commentary

There are minimum procedures required before an employer can dismiss an **7.248** employee, irrespective of the reason (Employment Act 2002 (Dispute Resolution) Regulations 2004, regs 3 and 4(1)(b); EA 2002, s 30). While these are discredited, and the Government has announced they will be removed in new legislation to be brought before Parliament shortly, they are likely to remain in force until at least April 2009. These are an irreducible minimum. Good practice (and often, the employment tribunal) requires that further procedures should be followed as well.

K. Fair Procedure Generally

7.249 Before dismissing an employee, an employer is expected to:

(a) conduct a proper investigation into what has gone on (see paras **7.250–7.259**);

(b) make sure the employee understands the case against him (see para **7.263**);

(c) allow the employee to be accompanied at any disciplinary meeting by a colleague or trade union official (see paras **7.263(a)** and **7.267**);

(d) hold a meeting, giving the employee a fair opportunity to respond, whether it is to deny the allegations, put forward mitigating circumstances which should be taken into account, or both (see paras **7.264–7.268**);

(e) make a decision, imposing an appropriate sanction on the employee (see paras **7.270–7.274**);

(f) notify the employee of the decision (see para **7.275**);

(g) give the employee the opportunity to appeal;

(h) conduct an appeal, which may be used as an opportunity to correct any procedural defects which took place at the original disciplinary meeting (see paras **7.276–7.280**).

Investigation

7.250 What should the investigation consist of?

(a) The employer should review any documentary evidence (eg showing incompetence if that is what is being alleged);

(b) The employer should consider what other evidence may be necessary (eg clocking cards, if it is an issue whether the employee was on site at a particular time, phone records, or emails). [Note: if reviewing phone records or emails, the employer should make sure it has notified employees that phone records or emails may be checked. Care should be taken not to invade the employee's privacy by reviewing obviously private communications, or communications between the employee and his legal representatives (Data Protection Act 1998 and see Chapter 10).];

(c) Statements should be taken from witnesses (see paras 7.256–7.258).

7.251 Who should conduct the investigation?

(a) larger employers: the investigation should where possible be undertaken by someone who is not making the decision to dismiss or likely to conduct any appeal;

(b) smaller employers: if the investigation cannot be conducted as in (a), then it can be conducted by the person who is to take the decision. If at all possible, the person who might hear any appeal should not be involved.

How rigorous should the investigation be? The investigation should be con- **7.252**
ducted in accordance with paras 7.253–7.257. The employment tribunal
will examine whether the relevant provisions of the ACAS Code of Practice:
Disciplinary and Grievance Procedures have been followed.

Is the employee accused of criminal behaviour? Where charges which are crimi- **7.253**
nal in nature have been made, and where the consequence of the dismissal may
result in loss of reputation, loss of job, and possibly the prospect of securing
future employment in the chosen field, a careful, conscientious, and full investigation is necessary (*A v B* [2003] IRLR 405, EAT). In particular:

(a) if the employee refuses to take part in the disciplinary process for fear of
    prejudicing his defence in the criminal proceedings, the employer should
    consider whether he has sufficient evidence to justify dismissal without
    hearing the employee;

(b) there should be an investigation, and where doubts remain it may be appro-
    priate for the employer to postpone the decision until he can interview the
    employee (*Ali v Sovereign Buses (London) Ltd* [2007] EAT 0274/06);

(c) the employer should be responsible for the conduct of any investigation and
    should not rely on any parallel police investigation. It is also preferable not to
    have police present during any disciplinary meeting, particularly if the employee
    does not consent (*Read v Phoenix Preservation Ltd* [1985] IRLR 93, EAT).

Is the alleged conduct so serious, or are there genuine fears that the employee **7.254**
may disrupt the investigation or the work place if he remains in post? The employer should consider whether to suspend the employee (with pay unless the
contract provides otherwise) during the course of any investigation. Generally,
there should be at least a preliminary enquiry before suspension (*Gogay v Hertfordshire County Council* [2000] IRLR 703, CA). If there is no contractual right
to suspend, the employee may claim that suspension is an act of constructive
dismissal or in rare circumstances, where suspension is likely to be a breach of
contract and unduly harsh in its effect on the employee, may obtain an injunction requiring the suspension to be lifted (*Mezey v SW London and St George's
Mental Health NHS Trust* [2007] IRLR 244, CA).

Is the employee a trade union official? No disciplinary action against a trade **7.255**
union official beyond an oral warning should be taken without first discussing
the matter with a senior trade union representative or full-time official.

Witnesses should ideally be asked to deal with the following points (*Linfood Cash **7.256**
& Carry Ltd v Thomson* [1989] IRLR 235, EAT):

(a) the date, time, and place of any observation or incident;

(b) whether the individual had an opportunity to observe clearly what happened;

(c) the details of the event;

(d) any additional facts which have a bearing on the event;

(e) any circumstantial evidence giving credence to the key recollections;

(f) whether the individual has any reason to be biased against the employee.

7.257 Where witnesses do not wish to be identified, because they are frightened of reprisals from the employee under investigation, the employer should:

(a) take statements, ignoring the fact the witness wishes to be anonymous;

(b) cover the items set out at para 7.256, plus whether the witness has suffered at the hands of the accused, or has any other reason to fabricate;

(c) seek further evidence to corroborate/undermine the statement;

(d) make tactful inquiries as to the probity of the witness;

(e) if the witness is still not prepared to be named, decide whether the fear is justified and whether to proceed with the disciplinary action;

(f) where possible ask the people taking the decision to interview the witness;

(g) provide the statement, with any elements identifying the witness removed, along with any other relevant statements and documents, to the employee and his representatives. However, even this may not be required where it would be within the range of reasonable responses not to disclose the statements, even in anonymized form (*Surrey County Council v Henderson* UK EAT/0326/05, where the employee was alleged to have threatened serious violence against individuals, but they did not wish to be identified for fear of reprisals by the employee);

(h) if the accused raises any issues which need to be put to the witness, consider adjourning to allow further investigation;

(i) make full and careful notes (*Linfood Cash & Carry Ltd v Thomson and Another* [1989] IRLR 235, EAT).

7.258 [Note: there is still a risk that confidential witness statements may be disclosed to the employee if a court decides that doing so is necessary for the fair disposal of the case (*Arqiva Ltd v Sagoo* [2007] UKEAT 0135/06), but the employer may be able to provide copies of statements in redacted form, omitting confidential or sensitive information (*Defoe v HM Prison Service* [2007] UKEAT 0451/06)].

7.259 After the investigation, if it believes there may be grounds for disciplining the employee, the employer should write to the employee setting out the case against him, and enclosing any relevant documents which the employee has not already been given. For content of letter, see para 7.263.

Commentary

7.260 Before taking disciplinary actions, and in particular before step 1 in a statutory disciplinary procedure preparatory to possible dismissal, the employer should conduct a reasonable investigation into the issue (*British Home Stores Ltd v Burchell* [1978] IRLR 379, EAT—see para **7.271**). While the statutory procedures are in force (they are likely to be repealed in April 2009), if there is a minor failure to follow appropriate procedure in relation to the dismissal, then so long as the minimum statutory procedure is followed (see paras **7.242–7.248**) this shall not be regarded, by itself, as making the decision to dismiss unreasonable if the employer can prove it is still 50 per cent likely that it would still have decided to dismiss the employee had it followed the proper procedure (ERA 1996, s 98A(2), overturning *Polkey v A E Dayton Services Ltd* [1988] AC 344, [1987] IRLR 503, HL, on this point). For example, employers are not generally obliged to allow those who have complained about an employee's behaviour to be cross-examined by that employee. However, there may be exceptional occasions where a proper investigation requires complainants to make their statements before the employees (*Dolan v Premier International Foods Ltd* [2005] All ER (D) 152, where the complainants, who were making allegations of harassment, included the employee's immediate supervisor).

The employer should always make proper investigation of all the circumstances. **7.261** The tribunal will consider whether the employer's investigation was within the reasonable range of inquiries which should be made: it must not substitute its own view of exactly what it would have done (*Sainsbury's Supermarkets Ltd v Hitt* [2003] IRLR 23, CA). The employer should take all necessary witness statements and examine all relevant documents. Even if the employee has been caught red-handed committing an act of gross misconduct, it is still not sensible to dismiss the employee on the spot if any anxiety about possible harm to the employer or its employees can be dealt with by suspending the employee and then pursuing the minimum statutory procedures (Employment Act 2002 (Dispute Resolution) Regulations 2004, reg 3(2)).

Disciplinary Meeting—General

Following internal investigation, the employer should hold a disciplinary meeting. **7.262** If the employer has a written procedure about the conduct of the meeting, it should be followed.

Notice of Meeting

Once the employer has conducted its internal investigation it should ask the **7.263** employee to attend a disciplinary meeting. In order to comply with the statutory procedure, the notification should be in writing (see para 7.244(a)). The employee should be told the following before the meeting:

(a) The time and place of the meeting (which should give him reasonable time to consider his response to the allegations). [Note: if the employee's chosen

7

Dismissals

companion is not available for the hearing at that time and the worker proposes a reasonable alternative time within the next five working days, the employer must postpone the hearing to the suggested time (ERA 1999, s 10(4) and (5)), failing which the employer is liable to pay the employee up to two weeks' pay subject to the statutory maximum pay (ie up to £700 at the rates current from 1 February 2008 and £700 at the rates from 1 February 2009) (ERA 1999, s 11(3)).]

(b) The fact that the meeting will be a disciplinary meeting.

(c) The topics which will be discussed at the meeting.

(d) The fact (if it be the case) that the employer is considering dismissal as an option.

(e) The right of the employee to be accompanied by a colleague or (if appropriate) trade union representative. [Note: it is sensible, but not obligatory, to include this in the letter.]

(f) The evidence against the employee and all key documents (for example any investigatory report) which will be relied on. [Note: it is preferable to provide the evidence before any meeting, but where the meeting may lead to dismissal this must be provided and the employee must be given sufficient time to consider it.]

Conduct of Meeting

7.264 Who should be present at the meeting?

(a) the person who is to take the decision;

(b) the employee;

(c) any companion the employee chooses to bring—the employee has the right to be accompanied by a colleague or a trade union official. He can only be accompanied by any other person (eg a family member or a legal representative) if the employer consents;

(d) the person who conducted any investigation;

(e) a note taker;

(f) any witness who is to give oral evidence or who it has been agreed will be cross-examined (see para 7.266).

7.265 The meeting should be chaired by the person who will be responsible for taking the decision to warn or dismiss. If possible, this should not be a witness or a complainant in the case. Ideally, he should conduct the meeting in the following manner, though failure to adhere to this plan will not automatically render a dismissal unfair (see para 7.260):

(a) Identify those present.

(b) Explain the purpose of the meeting.

(c) Outline the structure at the meeting and inform the employee and any representative that they may ask questions or make observations at any stage, and that when the employer has set out the allegations, the employee will have the opportunity to respond to those allegations either by calling evidence or by argument, and to put forward any explanation or mitigating circumstances.

(d) If appropriate, arrange representation for the employee. The employee should have the opportunity to be accompanied by a colleague of his choice or, in some circumstances, a trade union representative. However, the employer is not obliged to allow the employee to be represented by a solicitor.

(e) Inform the employee of the allegations being made.

(f) Describe the evidence to the employee (if it has not already been provided). (This may be done by the person who conducted the investigation, if he is present at the meeting.) If the evidence is in writing, the employee should have been given the documents or witness statements. If this has not happened, either give the employee the documents, allow him a short adjournment so he can read them, then ask him if he needs more time to consider them and, if he does, adjourn the meeting to another date. If for some reason it is wholly and reasonably undesirable for the employee to be given any particular item of written evidence, it should have been described to the employee before the meeting and at the meeting its contents should be explained in detail. If the evidence is oral, witnesses should be called or at least their evidence should have been described in detail to the employee before the meeting.

(g) The employee and/or his representative should then have an opportunity to put the employee's case, both relating to the allegations themselves and to any facts in mitigation. [Note: if the employee is facing criminal prosecution, the employer must not prejudice a trial but should only give the employee the opportunity to make any statement he may volunteer: no pressure should be put upon the employee to admit guilt.]

(h) If the employee asks to bring a witness to support his case, this should generally be allowed.

(i) The employee should be asked whether there is any further evidence or inquiry which he considers could help his case.

(j) If an employee asks for additional questions to be put to witnesses an employer would be wise to adjourn the meeting to make further inquiries, or to ensure that those questions are put to the witnesses subsequently.

Can the employee or his representatives cross-examine witnesses? A disciplinary **7.266** procedure is not a court of law. An employee is not normally entitled to cross-examine witnesses. If the employee wishes to do so, the employer must consider the following:

(a) The chair should consider whether it would be fair and reasonable to allow him to do so taking into account issues such as what cross-examination would achieve, whether the result could be achieved another way, and the likely effect on witnesses (especially in a harassment or bullying case).

(b) If there is a stark difference of evidence on fact, and this fact goes to the root of the disciplinary allegation, the chairman should only refuse to allow cross-examination if he has good reasons to do so (for example, because the witnesses, having been asked if they will attend the disciplinary hearing, have refused to do so on the basis that it would be far too stressful—perhaps because they claim to have been bullied by the employee under investigation, or because the witnesses are not employees and cannot therefore be compelled to attend).

(c) The chair would be wise to give reasons for any decision refusing to allow cross-examination.

(d) If cross-examination is refused, the employer should go back to the witnesses after the disciplinary hearing and put to them any allegations made by the employee which have not already been addressed (*Santamera v Express Cargo Forwarding* [2003] IRLR 273, EAT).

(e) If the employee does not ask to cross-examine witnesses, the employer will not be at fault in failing to suggest it (*Horn v Voluntary Hostels Group*, 14 February 2003, EAT).

7.267 Role of any companion. If the employee is accompanied, the companion:

(a) may (unless the employee has indicated he does not wish the companion to do so) address the hearing by putting the employee's case, summing up that case, and responding on the employee's behalf to any view expressed at the hearing;

(b) may confer with the employee during the hearing;

(c) may not answer questions on the employee's behalf;

(d) may not act in such a way that either the employer is prevented from explaining his case or any other person is prevented from making any contribution to the hearing (ERA 1999, s 10(2)).

7.268 Has the employee or his representative raised potentially valid points that have not been explored by the initial investigation? It may be necessary for the chair to initiate further inquiries should the employee have raised fresh issues. For example where an employee is himself suspended and has been denied the opportunity of being able to contact potentially relevant witnesses, the employer needs to make sure that it focuses as much on any potential evidence that may exculpate or point towards the innocence of the employee as on the evidence directed towards proving the charges (*A v B* [2003] IRLR 405, EAT).

Those hearing the disciplinary proceedings should then consider what decision **7.269** to make. The tribunal must be satisfied that the sanction the employer has imposed is fair in all the circumstances.

Standard of Proof

How convinced must the decision-taker be of the employee's guilt? The standard **7.270** of proof is a reasonable suspicion, amounting to a belief in the guilt of the employee of that misconduct at that time.

What must the employer establish: **7.271**

(a) the fact of his belief in the guilt of the employee;
(b) that the employer had in his mind reasonable grounds on which to sustain that belief;
(c) that the employer had carried out an investigation which was reasonable in all the circumstances (*British Home Stores Ltd v Burchell* [1978] IRLR 379, EAT).

What if suspicion genuinely points to one or other of two employees? Both may **7.272** be dismissed (*Frames Snooker Centre v Boyce* [1992] IRLR 472).

What if there has been a similar event before, or if two people are accused of the **7.273** same misconduct? All employees should be treated the same. If the employer has not acted consistently (for example, because employees had been led to believe that particular categories of conduct would be overlooked, or met with only a mild disciplinary sanction (*Hadjioannou v Coral Casinos Ltd* [1981] IRLR 352 EAT) or because in truly comparable cases one employee is dismissed while another has not been (*Securicor v Smith* [1989] IRLR 356, CA)) then the dismissal is likely to be unfair. This is because it will not have passed the test in ERA 1996, s 98(4) that the tribunal must have regard to 'equity and the substantial merits of the case'.

What sanction should the employer impose? When reviewing the employer's **7.274** decision to dismiss, an employment tribunal will look at whether the decision to dismiss is within the band of reasonable responses which a hypothetical reasonable employer might have adopted in the circumstances. The employment tribunal must not substitute its own decision for that of the employer (*Iceland Frozen Foods Ltd v Jones* [1982] IRLR 439, EAT and *Foley v Post Office*; *HSBC Bank plc v Madden* [2000] IRLR 827, CA).

Notification of Decision

7.275   The employee, and any representative, should be notified of the employer's decision, preferably in writing. The employee should also be told of his right to appeal. An employee has the right to be accompanied to that appeal by a colleague or trade union representative, but not a solicitor. There is no obligation on the employee to be informed of that right, but it is good practice to do so. The employer should clearly specify any time limit within which the appeal should be lodged. It makes sense for notification of the right to appeal to be contained within the document recording the decision, but it is acceptable for the employee to be told of the right to appeal orally (*Aptuit (Edinburgh) Ltd v Kennedy* [2007] UKEATS 0057/06).

Appeals

7.276   If possible, the appeal body should be composed of different and more senior people from those who made the decision to dismiss (EA 2002, Sch 2, para 13(3)).

7.277   Can new evidence be introduced? Appeals may take into account additional facts learnt since the decision to dismiss. It used to be thought that an appeal could not provide justification for unfairness at a lower level unless the appeal is a comprehensive rehearing. However, this is no longer the case, provided that the employee is given a proper opportunity before the appeal hearing to understand the case against him and respond appropriately. However, producing information for an employee at appeal cannot cure any breaches of the statutory dismissal and disciplinary procedures if it should have been provided to the employee before the decision to dismiss (*Davies v Farnborough College of Technology* [2008] IRLR 14, EAT—a case involving failure to supply information regarding reasons for the employee's selection for redundancy). In these circumstances, the appeal should be allowed and statutory procedures should begin again.

7.278   When should the appeal be heard? Appeals should be heard speedily (EA 2002, Sch, 2, para 12)—three months from the decision to dismiss may be so long a gap that the dismissal is automatically unfair because it is in breach of the statutory dismissal and disciplinary procedures (*Khan v Home Office* [2006] UKEAT 0026/06). Conversely, an employer should not reject an appeal simply because the employee did not comply with the contractual time limit for bringing the appeal, so long as the employee appeals within a reasonable time—to do otherwise would be automatically unfair dismissal (*Masterfoods v Wilson* (UK EAT/02022/2006).

7.279   Normally, a dismissal or resignation cannot be unilaterally withdrawn. However, by appealing, the employee impliedly consents to an employer's withdrawal of the dismissal. Therefore, if the appeal is upheld, the employee cannot claim to have been dismissed (*Brock v Minerva Dental Ltd* [2006] UKEAT 0356/06).

7.280 Consequences of a failure to appeal. If an employee fails to exercise his right of appeal, then for so long as the statutory disciplinary and dismissal procedures are in force (they are likely to be repealed in April 2009) the employer may be able to argue that there should be a reduction in any compensation paid because the employee has failed to mitigate his loss. A dismissed employee who does not take up an invitation to appeal will, save in exceptional circumstances, have any compensatory award reduced by 10–50 per cent (see para 7.247).

Consequences of Unfair Procedure

7.281 Where there is failure to follow a proper procedure, then the tribunal will consider whether the employer has shown that the employee would have been dismissed had a fair procedure been followed. For so long as the statutory disciplinary and dismissal procedures are in force (they are likely to be repealed in April 2009), there are five possible outcomes.

(a) The employer may show that it complied with the statutory procedures, and that it is at least 51 per cent likely that if a fair procedure has been complied with, the dismissal would have occurred in any event. It will then be fair under ERA 1996, s 98A(2).

(b) The employer may persuade the tribunal that there was a chance of dismissal but it was less than 50 per cent, in which case the dismissal will be unfair but compensation should be reduced on *Polkey* principles (see para 7.281(c)). The Court must attempt the task, however speculative, of evaluating the evidence on what might have happened had a proper procedure been followed (*Software 2000 Ltd v Andrews* [2007] ICR 825, EAT) unless evidence on this point is particularly sparse (*Clarke v Governing Body of Hastingbury School* [2008] EAT 0373/07 and 0374/07).

(c) The principles are set out in *Polkey v AE Dayton Services Ltd* [1987] IRLR 503, HL. In brief, in addition to the principle set out in para 7.281(b), they are that a dismissal will be unfair if inadequate procedures are followed, unless at the time the decision was taken and bearing in mind the facts the employer actually knew, a reasonable employer could have known that conducting a procedure (in this case, there was no consultation with individual employees before they were selected for redundancy) would be useless. The tribunal must consider the action of the employer in treating the reason as sufficient to dismiss as part of its review of the manner of dismissal. It is not sufficient, to pass the *Polkey* test, for the employer to show that the result would have been the same had a proper procedure taken place.

(d) The tribunal may decide that the employment would have continued but only for a limited period, in which case compensation for loss of earnings should be restricted to the remuneration the employee would have received during this period.

(e) The tribunal may decide that the employment would continue indefinitely, in which case compensation will be assessed on normal principles. This decision should only be reached where the evidence is so scant or unreliable that it should be ignored because, even with a certain amount of legitimate speculation, it is impossible to reconstruct what might have happened. (*Software 2000 Ltd v Andrews and Others* [2007] IRLR 568, EAT).

7.282 When the statutory minimum disciplinary and dismissal procedures are repealed, it is likely that the Government will require employers to follow the ACAS Code of Practice on Disciplinary and Grievance Procedures, and that if this Code is not followed, a tribunal will have the discretion to increase or decrease any compensation award by up to 25 per cent. The position described in para 7.281(a) will cease to apply, and the Court will review the position simply in line with the *Polkey* principles described in para 7.281(b) and (c).

Additional Commentary

7.283 The general principle is that no employee should be dismissed without being able to understand why it is that the employer is contemplating dismissal and having a fair chance to put his side of the case, either to rebut the allegations or to plead that there are mitigating circumstances which should reduce the sanction from dismissal to, say, a warning. The employee should also be given the opportunity to present his case in the best possible way by being allowed to be accompanied by a colleague or trade union representative. There is no right to be accompanied by a lawyer, and this will only be allowed if the employer consents.

7.284 Tribunals now lay great emphasis upon the employer following a fair procedure before warning or dismissing an employee. Though it is not true that, provided the statutory minimum disciplinary and dismissal procedures are followed while they continue to be in force, any procedural irregularity renders a dismissal unfair, it is one of the factors that is taken into account when deciding whether the employer has acted reasonably in dismissing the employee. While the procedures are in force then, so long as they are complied with, any other procedural irregularity will not render a dismissal unfair if it is at least 50 per cent likely that the employer would still have dismissed the employee had a fair procedure been followed. When the statutory procedures are repealed, tribunals are likely to revert to the *Polkey* principle that applied before. This is that tribunals will expect a fair procedure to be implemented unless the employer *knows* at the time it decides not to have any disciplinary or consultation procedure that any meeting, no matter what explanation or suggestion the employee may advance, could not make any difference to the decision to dismiss.

If more than minor inadequate procedures are followed, but the result would have been the same, this might affect the employee's remedy: it will not affect the unfairness of the dismissal.   **7.285**

L. Warning Procedure

Should a warning be given instead of dismissal? Except for gross misconduct, dismissal should not be the sanction for a first offence. The ACAS Code of Practice on Disciplinary and Grievance Procedures lays down, for minor offences, a three-stage warning process before dismissal: oral warning, first written warning, and final written warning, and then dismissal. The number of warnings may however be reduced either because of practicalities or because an offence is of a more serious nature.   **7.286**

Is the misconduct a 'first offence'? Dismissal will not normally be a valid response to a first act of misconduct, unless the misconduct is potentially serious. Generally, the employer should give the employee a first (perhaps oral) warning for minor offences, and a written warning for more serious offences or subsequent offences.   **7.287**

When can successive warnings be given?   **7.288**

(a) *Successive warnings* need not relate to the same subject matter.
(b) *Lapsed warnings*: in the absence of an express provision regarding the lapse of warnings, it is generally assumed that oral warnings should lapse after six months and written warnings after 12 months. It is unreasonable to take a lapsed warning into account when deciding whether to dismiss someone for gross misconduct: if it influences the decision, the dismissal will be unfair (*Diosynth Ltd v Thomson* [2006] IRLR 284). However, the absence of lapsed warnings may be a mitigating factor where several are disciplined for the same offence (see para 7.172).
(c) *A warning subject to appeal* can still be relied upon when taking action regarding a fresh offence, though the employer must, when deciding what weight to attach to the earlier warning, bear in mind that it is subject to appeal.

Have other employees behaved in a similar way to the employee being disciplined, yet not been sanctioned? Warnings are especially important where rules   **7.289** have recently been disregarded in practice. For example, it would be unfair to dismiss a man for sleeping on a night shift where in practice his colleagues had been doing the same, to management's knowledge, for some time and management had not told employees that in future on-shift sleeping would be regarded as serious misconduct. If management had not known of the custom, dismissal would have been a reasonable sanction, provided it was applied consistently.

7.290 When is a warning not necessary? In the following circumstances:

(a) where the employer's rules clearly and reasonably spell out that a particular action will result in instant dismissal;

(b) where the employee's conduct is likely to endanger safety;

(c) where a warning would make no difference, for example, because the employee refuses to accept he has done anything wrong;

(d) where the employee knew that he was putting his job in jeopardy.

M. Stress Issues Prior to Investigatory/Disciplinary Meetings

CHECKLIST

7.291 If an employee who is subject to a disciplinary or performance procedure goes off work and claims he cannot attend the procedure on the grounds of stress, the employer should postpone the procedure until the employee returns or do the following:

(a) Check the staff handbook to see if it contains procedures to follow in these circumstances. If it does, these should be followed. If not, proceed as below.

(b) Obtain the employee's consent to his GP giving the employer his opinion on:
   • whether the employee is fit to attend the disciplinary procedure;
   • if not, when he is likely to be; and
   • whether there are any steps which could be taken to enable the meeting to take place.

(c) If concerned about the GP's response, seek the employee's consent to them being seen by a medical practitioner chosen by the employer, who should be asked similar questions.

(d) An employee is not obliged to give consent to sharing medical information, even if his contract of employment states that he must undergo any medical examinations that the employer reasonably requests. However, if this contractual term is in place and the employee refuses to see a doctor or to allow the employer to know the doctor's opinion, the employer can proceed carefully, making his own assumptions. If the employee allows his GP to give his opinion, but refuses to undergo a second opinion, the employer is effectively stuck with the first opinion.

(e) Make sure that all the allegations against the employee are set out clearly, and sent to him, together with copies or (where appropriate) summaries of witness statements and documents which will be relied on.

(f) Extend the time limit for any responses.

(g) Consider providing written questions to which answers will be sought in advance of the meeting, perhaps inviting written replies and/or representations.

(h) Consider permitting the employee to be accompanied by a relative or friend in substitution for any colleague from work or union representative.

(i) Hold the hearing at a neutral venue, preferably close to the employee's home.

(j) Where possible, appoint someone with little or no prior involvement with the employee to chair the meeting and make the decision.

(k) Follow any recommendations from the medical practitioners on how the meeting should be held and conducted.

(l) Offer the employee breaks during the meeting.

(m) Send the employee and his representative a copy of written reasons for the decision.

(n) Allow an extended time for appeal.

N. Remedies

INITIAL CHECKLIST

If the employee has been unfairly dismissed, consider remedies. Does the employee want to be reinstated or re-engaged? If he does, the tribunal must consider whether this is practicable and whether the employee has contributed to his dismissal so reinstatement or re-engagement would not be just or equitable. If it is practicable, the employment tribunal may well exercise its discretion to make the necessary order. For details of the consequences, see paras **7.295** and **7.296** and for details of the consequences if the employer fails to reinstate or re-engage, see paras **7.300–7.302**. **7.292**

If compensation is the appropriate remedy, consider the following: **7.293**

(a) What is the actual loss the employee has suffered to date? Calculate the loss of salary and benefits.

(b) For how long is this likely to last in future? Does the employee have another job? If the salary is the same or more than with the employer, the employer's liability will cease from the moment the employee gains a new and ostensibly permanent job. If less than the old salary, how long will this continue? If there is no new job, when is the employee likely to find one and at what salary? Further details are set out at paras **7.306–7.307**.

(c) Would the employer have been dismissed fairly by the employer in the near future in any event or if a fair procedure had been followed? If yes, but the statutory procedures have not been followed, then the period for which the employee will be compensated will end when he would otherwise have been dismissed, although any basic award will still be payable (*Polkey v A E Dayton Services Ltd* [1988] AC 344, HL). If there is doubt whether, had a proper procedure been followed, dismissal would have resulted, but dismissal was at least 50 per cent likely then the dismissal will not be rendered unfair because of the procedural lapse (ERA 1996, s 98A(2)). If dismissal was less than 50 per cent likely the dismissal will be unfair, but the award can be reduced to reflect this chance (see para **7.281**).

(d) Has the employee mitigated his loss by finding another job? If the employee has failed to take appropriate steps to find another job, would he have found alternative employment had he taken those steps? If the answer to either question is yes, there will be no further compensation to cover the period from which the alternative employment was or should have been obtained. The only caveat to this is that if the new job carries a lower salary and benefits package, the employee may recover damages representing the difference between the old and the new for such time as the tribunal decides this discrepancy will last. For further details, see para **7.308**(a).

(e) Did the employee contribute to his own dismissal? If there is an element of contributory fault, the compensation payments payable to the employee will be reduced by an appropriate percentage (see para **7.308**(d) and (e)). [Note: conduct arising after the dismissal or which did not cause or contribute to the dismissal, cannot be taken into account (*Mullinger v Department of Work and Pensions*) [2007] UKEAT 0515/05).]

(f) Has the employer made any ex gratia payment to the employee? If so, it will be taken into account in reducing the award—see para **7.308**(b).

(g) How much compensation should be awarded for the employee's loss of statutory rights (particularly because he will have to work for a year at his new employer before he is generally entitled to claim he has been unfairly dismissed and for two years before he is entitled to a redundancy payment)? Generally an award in the region of £250 is made here.

(h) In what order should any deductions from the compensation award be made? See para **7.310**.

(i) Should the employment tribunal add to the award on the basis that the employee has been deprived of the money due to him for a period? The tribunal is entitled to make an allowance for loss caused by delayed payment and interest is a measure of the loss (*Melia v Magna Kansei Ltd* [2006] IRLR 117, CA). However, interest of itself cannot be awarded.

Remedies I: Reinstatement and Re-engagement

A person who is dismissed may be entitled to any of the following remedies: **7.294**

(a) reinstatement (see para 7.295);
(b) re-engagement (see para 7.296);
(c) compensation (see paras 7.303–7.323);
(d) injunction.

The most common redress is compensation.

Reinstatement

An employee who is reinstated should be treated as if he had not been dismissed. **7.295**
He is restored to his old position, with full continuous employment, and treated
as if he had held that position throughout the period since his dismissal. He will
receive an amount equivalent to the salary and benefits he would have
earned during the intervening period. If he would, during the interim, have
received additional benefits, for example, a non-discretionary Christmas bonus
or a pay increase, he will be deemed to benefit from this. In making any reinstatement award the tribunal must spell out the relevant terms and conditions which
will apply to the employee and the date by which reinstatement is to take effect
(ERA 1996, s 114).

Re-engagement

An order that the employee is to be re-engaged means that he must be offered **7.296**
another job by the employer or associated employer with full continuity of service. This job may be different from his original position provided it is comparable and suitable. The employment tribunal must be specific about the nature of
the job, the remuneration, and any payment to which the employee will be entitled, and should take into account lost salary, benefits, rights, and privileges,
which should be restored to the employee. The tribunal should also specify the
date by which the changes must take effect. These terms are at the discretion of
the tribunal. The employee will normally be awarded full pay and benefits in the
interim unless he has caused or contributed to his dismissal (ERA 1996, s 115).

Making reinstatement or re-engagement orders

When are reinstatement or re-engagement orders often made? They are only **7.297**
ordered if the applicant so wishes. The following steps are looked at:

(a) Does the employee want to be reinstated or re-engaged?
(b) Is it practicable for the employer now to comply with a reinstatement or
     re-engagement order?

7

Dismissals

(c) If the employee caused or contributed to some extent to his dismissal, would it be just to order reinstatement or re-engagement? If re-engagement, on what terms? They should not be significantly more favourable than those applying to his old job.

7.298 When is reinstatement or re-engagement not ordered? When clearly it would not be practicable for the employer to comply with the order. This has been held to apply:

(a) if it would lead to serious industrial strife;

(b) if the atmosphere at the workplace has been poisoned by the employee;

(c) if the employee indicates he has no trust or confidence in the employer;

(d) if there is insufficient work for the employee to carry out, particularly if the employee was originally dismissed for redundancy or if redundancies have occurred since the dismissal. This ground will not assist the employer who has engaged a replacement for the employee unless *either* it was not possible for the employer to arrange for the dismissed employee's work to be done without engaging a permanent replacement, *or* that replacement was engaged after a lapse of a reasonable period from the date of dismissal during which period the employee had not said he wanted to be reinstated or re-engaged and it was no longer reasonable for the employer to arrange for the work to be done except by a permanent replacement; or

(e) if the employee is not fit to return.

7.299 Reinstatement and re-engagement orders are rarely made where the employee has caused or contributed to his own dismissal or where the employer has totally lost trust and confidence in the employee.

Consequences if an employer refuses to reinstate or re-engage

7.300 If the reinstatement or re-engagement order is made and not complied with, unless the employer can show it was not reasonably practicable for it to comply with the order, the employee will receive compensation for unfair dismissal calculated on the normal basis and subject to the compensatory award maximum (£63,000 for dismissals whose EDT is on or after 1 February 2008 and £66,200 where the EDT is on or after 1 February 2009) unless the amount of back pay from the date of dismissal to the date of the tribunal order exceeds the maximum possible compensatory award. In that case the actual back pay will be awarded and the maximum ignored (ERA 1996, s 124(3)).

Refusal to reinstate or re-engage

7.301 If the employer refuses to comply with a reinstatement or re-engagement order:

(a) The tribunal will examine whether it was not practicable for the employee to comply with the order, giving due weight to the employer's commercial judgement, but ignoring any permanent replacement unless the employer can show it was not practicable for him to arrange for the dismissed employee's work to be done without engaging a replacement.

(b) If it was not practicable, the employee will receive an unfair dismissal award, calculated on the standard basis but also taking into account losses suffered because of the failure to reappoint, such as wages in the interim. This is subject to the statutory financial maxima (maximum weekly wage for basic award of £330 and maximum compensatory award of £63,000 for dismissals whose EDT is on or after 1 February 2008 and £66,200 for dismissals whose EDT is on or after 1 February 2009) (see para 7.59 for definition of EDT).

If it was practicable for the employer to comply with the order, the employee will receive: **7.302**

(a) unfair dismissal award (see para 7.304); plus
(b) an *additional award* of between 26 and 52 weeks' pay (a week's pay being subject to the statutory maximum: £330 for dismissals whose EDT is on or after 1 February 2008 and £350 for dismissals whose EDT is on or after 1 February 2009) (see para 7.59 for definition of EDT).

Remedies II—Compensation

Unfair dismissal: basic award

Normal calculation   Compensation for unfair dismissal has two elements, a   **7.303**
basic award and a compensatory award (ERA 1996, s 118). The basic award is calculated on the basis of gross pay and in the same way as the redundancy payment (see paras 8.120 and 8.137). It may be reduced in four circumstances:

(a) where the employee's conduct before being given notice was such that it is just and equitable so to do, whether o r not the employer knew of the conduct at the time of the decision to dismiss;
(b) where the employee has already received a redundancy payment (in which case, he cannot receive a basic award as well);
(c) where the employee has received an ex gratia payment from the employer expressed to include the basic award (in which case there will be no further basic award (*Chelsea Football Club and Athletic Co Limited v Heath* [1981] IRLR 73)); and
(d) where the employee has unreasonably refused an offer of reinstatement.

Minimum award in certain circumstances   The basic award is subject to a sta-   **7.304**
tutory minimum of £4,700 (for dismissals on or after 1 February 2009, and £4,400 for dismissals whose EDT is between 1 February 2008 and 31 January 2009) where dismissal is because of:

(a) union-related reasons;

(b) health and safety reasons;

(c) acting as a Working Time Regulations representative;

(d) acting as a pension scheme trustee; or

(e) acting as an employee representative for TUPE or redundancy consultation purposes.

7.305   **Minimum award where non-compliance with minimum disciplinary procedures**   Where the employer has failed to comply with statutory minimum disciplinary procedures, the basic award will be calculated as normal (subject to the statutory maximum for a week's pay—£330 for dismissals whose EDT is after 1 February 2008 and £350 for dismissals whose EDT is after 1 February 2009), but subject to a minimum of four weeks' pay, unless this would amount to injustice to the employer (ERA 1996, s 120(1)(A) and (1)(B)).

Unfair dismissal: compensatory award

7.306   This compensates the employee for the loss suffered by him as a result of the unfair dismissal, and is subject to a statutory maximum (£66,200 for dismissals whose EDT is after 1 February 2009 and £63,000 for dismissals between 1 February 2008 and 31 January 2009). It takes into account the following:

(a) loss of earnings between dismissal and the employment tribunal hearing, subject to deduction for anything earned during the period. Pay rises which the employee is likely to have been awarded had he remained employed during the period of the award can be taken into account (*Leyland Vehicles v Reston* [1981] IRLR 19, EAT);

(b) if the employee starts a new job after a while on higher wages than before, the excess wages cannot be used to reduce any loss before he started the new job;

(c) if the employee earns less than the national minimum wage, wages shall be deemed to be at minimum wage level (£3.40 per hour for 16 and 17-year-olds, £4.60 per hour for those aged 18–21 and £5.52 per hour for those aged 22 or over, with effect from 1 October 2007 (figures to rise to £3.53, £4.77, and £5.73 from 1 October 2008)) (*Paggetti v Cobb* [2002] IRLR 861, EAT);

(d) net future loss of earnings. This is speculative. The tribunal must estimate when the employee is likely to obtain a new job and the likely wage he will then receive, calculated on the balance of probabilities—this will include any possible salary increases or benefits such as bonus or commission payments;

(e) net loss of contractual benefits such as company car and petrol, health and life insurance, or subsidized/free accommodation;

(f) expenses reasonably incurred as a consequence of looking for alternative employment;

(g) loss of pension. This calculation may be based on the Government Actuary's Department table, available from HMSO. Alternatively, it may be calculated by looking at what it would cost the employee to replace his lost benefits. In essence there are two forms of pension loss: loss of pension position accrued thus far and loss of future pension opportunities;

(h) loss of employment protection rights—normally £250—because the employee will have to build up continuous service in another employment before being able to claim statutory employment rights;

(i) financial loss caused by the manner of dismissal, if the manner is in breach of the relationship of trust and confidence.

Commentary

(a) The statutory maximum increases from 1 February each year, substantially in line with inflation.   **7.307**

(b) There are no unfair dismissal damages for distress, depression, stress, humiliation, injury to feelings, damage to reputation, or loss of family life resulting from a dismissal (*Dunnachie v Kingston upon Hull City Council* [2004] IRLR 727, HL).

(c) There are no damages for loss of earnings flowing from any breach of the implied term of trust and confidence. These damages should be sought as part of a breach of contract claim. The employment tribunal can only award unfair dismissal compensation for losses suffered as a result of the dismissal itself (*Johnson v Unisys Ltd* [2001] ICR 480; *GAB Robins (UK) Ltd v Triggs* [2008] IRLR 317, CA).

Reductions in compensatory awards

How are compensatory awards reduced? The reductions which may be made and the order in which they should be made is as follows: **7.308**

(a) *Mitigation.* The employee is under a duty to mitigate his loss. He should therefore make all reasonable efforts to find alternative employment. If he does not do so, this will be taken into account in reducing the award. If he does so successfully, then remuneration from the new job will be taken into account when assessing the award, from the date when the employment starts. Example: An employee earning £300 per week is dismissed. Five weeks later he takes up new employment at £280 per week. The employment tribunal hearing is in week 15 and the tribunal estimates that the pay differential will last for a further 12 weeks. The employee will receive:

(i) for the first five weeks: 5 × £300	=	£1,500
(ii) the next ten weeks: 10 × (£300 – £280)	=	£200
(iii) for subsequent 12 weeks: 12 × (£300 – £280) =		£240
Total		£1,940

If, instead of earning a new salary of £280 per week on week 5, the employee earns £310 per week from that date, his compensation will be as (i), and will be £1,500. The fact that he has more than mitigated his loss from week 5 is not taken into account in reducing pay during the unemployed period.

In general the employee need not take the first available job, but after a reasonable period will be expected to lower his sights and take up a position with lower status and/or pay. Normally the employee will not be criticized for refusing another position with the employer who has just dismissed him. Onus of proof of lack of mitigation is on the employer.

If an employee starts up a new business which earns little at the beginning, he may still be deemed to have sufficiently mitigated his loss and the tribunal will take into account the low initial earnings.

If an employee immediately embarks on a radical change of career on a much lower salary, the employer will not be expected to compensate the employee for his reduced rate of pay.

If an employee after a reasonable period looking unsuccessfully for a new job decides to go back to college to re-train, he will not be criticized for failing to mitigate his loss.

(b) *Ex gratia payment or High Court award.* In general, an ex gratia payment or High Court award for wrongful dismissal by an employer designed to cover loss of earnings or to go towards unfair dismissal compensation will be deducted from the total award. The deduction will, however, be made before the statutory maximum ceiling is imposed. Example: if a tribunal decides that the total loss is £80,000 but the employer has already paid the employee an ex gratia payment of £5,000, the employee will be deemed to need compensation of £75,000, and the award will still be subject to the statutory maximum (£63,000 for dismissals since 1 February 2008 rising to £66,200 for dismissals whose EDT is after 1 February 2009). The compensatory award will not be £66,200 less £5,000 making £61,200.

(c) *Procedural irregularity:* Polkey *reduction.* If employment would have ceased anyway, for example, because unfair dismissal is only a result of a procedural irregularity, or if there is a percentage chance that it would have ceased, an award may be nil or only a percentage of the actual loss. If warning or consultation procedures might have lasted an additional, say, two weeks but the result would have been the same, the compensatory award may be only two weeks' pay (*Polkey v A E Dayton Services Ltd* [1988] AC 344). See para 7.**281** for current position.

(d) *'Just and equitable reduction'.* If the employer can prove to the employment tribunal that:
- the employee is guilty of serious misconduct; or
- if it had conducted a proper investigation, it would have fairly dismissed the employee for the conduct in question

any award may be reduced, probably by 100 per cent, either to reflect the gravity of the situation or (in the second case) to reflect the percentage chance that the employee would have been dismissed in any event.

(e) *Contributory fault.* The award will be reduced if the employee has caused or contributed to his dismissal by his own contributory fault (ERA 1996, s 123(6)). This will apply where the conduct was discovered before dismissal. The relevant conduct must not relate to the exercise of reasonable trade union activity. Contributory fault must generally be in the nature of misconduct or deliberate incompetence. The employee must have been blameworthy in some way and not just, for example, suffering from bad health. Where the employee has behaved so badly as to be the sole cause of the breakdown of trust and confidence between the parties, so that the employer could not bear to continue to employ the employee, damages for any dismissal which is deemed to be unfair because an inadequate procedure was followed may be reduced by 100 per cent (*Coxon v Rank Xerox Ltd* [2003] ICR 628). Any reduction for contributory fault is made before the application of the statutory maximum award. For example, if the tribunal decides that the individual has lost £100,000 but has contributed 25 per cent to his own dismissal, his compensatory loss will be 75 per cent of £100,000 or £75,000. The statutory maximum will then be applied and the award will still (for dismissals occurring between 1 February 2009 and 31 January 2010) be £66,200. The award will not be 75 per cent of £66,200.

(f) Generally, the statutory maximum should be applied as the last step in calculating the compensatory award.

(g) If the employee has received a jobseekers' allowance (formerly unemployment or supplementary benefit) or income support between the date of dismissal and the employment tribunal hearing, the Government may recoup the payments made from the award of compensation. This will not apply where a case has been settled out of court.

(h) *Employee's failure to follow the statutory procedure.* If the employee has failed to comply with the statutory dismissal and disciplinary procedures (see para 7.244) for example, by failing to attend a meeting or not exercising a right to appeal, the award will (save in exceptional circumstances) be reduced by between 10 and 50 per cent, depending on the gravity of the failure (EA 2002, s 31(2))—likely to be repealed in April 2009 and replaced with arrangements whereby the award can be increased/reduced by up to 25 per cent if the ACAS Code of Practice on Disciplinary Procedures has not been followed).

7.309 *Increases in the award.* If the employer has failed to follow the statutory dismissal and disciplinary procedures (see para 7.244) any award must, save in exceptional circumstances, be increased by 10–50 per cent, depending on the gravity of the breach (EA 2002, s 31—Note that this is likely to be repealed in April 2009 and replaced with arrangements whereby the award can be increased/reduced by up to 25 per cent if the ACAS Code of Practice on Disciplinary Procedures has not been followed).

7.310 Order of Deductions (ERA 1996, s 124A; EA 2002, ss 31 and 38):

(a) Calculate the employee's loss in accordance with ERA 1996, s 123(1) (see para 7.305).

(b) Deduct any payment already made by the employer as compensation for the dismissal other than an enhanced redundancy payment.

(c) Next deduct sums earned by way of mitigation or to reflect the employee's failure to mitigate (failure to mitigate may of course result in deciding to halt the calculation of loss at the date of the failure to mitigate).

(d) Apply any *Polkey* percentage reduction (up to 50 per cent—any greater reduction would indicate that the dismissal should be fair (ERA 1996, s 98A(2)) if dismissal would have resulted in any event even if any procedural irregularities had not occurred (see para 7.281).

(e) Increase or reduce by 10–50 per cent (unless exception applies) for failure to comply with dismissal and disciplinary procedure or grievance procedure.

(f) Increase for employer's failure to provide written particulars (EA 2002, s 38).

(g) Apply percentage reduction for employee's contributory fault (ERA 1996, s 123(6)).

(h) Deduct any enhanced redundancy payment to the extent that it exceeds the basic award (which will also have been set off under s 122(4): ERA 1996, s 123(7)).

(i) Apply the statutory cap (ERA 1996, s 124).

(j) Allow for recoupment of social security payments.

7.311 [Note: it is unclear whether a non-statutory redundancy payment should be deducted immediately before or after the statutory maximum is applied.]

No statutory ceiling or award

7.312 There is no statutory maximum ceiling on awards for dismissal where the main reason for dismissal is:

(a) a health and safety reason (see para 7.106);

(b) whistle-blowing in protected circumstances (see para 7.95);

(c) redundancy where selection is for a health and safety reason or whistle-blowing (ERA 1996, s 124(1(A)).

Damages for wrongful dismissal

Pre-dismissal damages   In addition to any damages for wrongful dismissal **7.313** for the period after dismissal, the employer should also pay the employee any pre-dismissal liabilities. These may be as follows.

(a) Any arrears of pay due from before the termination of employment.
(b) Money in lieu of untaken holiday entitlement.
(c) Any unpaid but justifiable expenses already incurred by the employee.

The sums paid under para 7.313(a) and (b) are taxable, and the employer must **7.314** deduct the appropriate tax and national insurance payments from the amount paid to the employee, and account to HMRC for those sums.

Damages for wrongful dismissal (save in a case where damages are only due **7.315** because an appropriate disciplinary procedure was not followed) are calculated as follows:

(a) quantify the net value of the salary and benefits which the employee has lost during the whole of his notice period (or part of it, if the employee is dismissed while working out his notice) (para 7.316);
(b) deduct from this sum any money he received or should have received from elsewhere during the notice period (para 7.317);
(c) apply any relevant income tax issues (para 7.318).

Calculation of damages   See para 7.323 for sample calculation. First add **7.316** together the total value of salary and benefits during the notice period:

(a) net wages lost during the notice period (taking into account any pay rises the employee would have been awarded);
(b) *plus* the net value of contractual benefits lost during the notice period. Benefits may include the following:
   • Car or car allowance (with or without general maintenance or petrol expenses).
   • Share options. If an employee has share options under a scheme which provides, as most do, that the loss of options on termination of employment, howsoever caused, shall not give rise to a claim for damages for wrongful or unfair dismissal, no loss will be suffered. If no such clause exists (either in the option scheme or the contract of employment), then one may include in the calculation of damages value for lost options if the options could have been exercised for profit during the notice period.

- Pension benefits. Normally, employers' pension contributions are valued. If none is expressed, contributions are deemed to be 10 per cent of basic gross salary (see paras **7.306(g)** and **1.119**).
- Non-discretionary bonuses and commissions. If a bonus is discretionary, the employee may nevertheless claim damages for its recovery if failure to pay it was unreasonable or capricious (for example because, even though the employee was still employed when bonuses were due and performs well, the employer had decided to dismiss the employee and so pays no bonus: *Clark v Nomura* [2000] IRLR 766, HC, but see para **7.19(b)**).
- Health insurance.
- Permanent health insurance.
- Life insurance.
- Free or reduced rate accommodation.
- Travel or goods subsidies.
- Payment of home/mobile telephone bills, newspaper bills, television or video rental etc.
- Membership of clubs or professional bodies.

7.317 Deductions   Second, make any of the following deductions:

(a) *less* any sums received by the employee because he mitigated his loss by finding alternative employment or was unreasonable in failing to mitigate (see para **7.308(a)**);

(b) *less* any discount for accelerated payment (see para **7.20(b)**);

(c) *less* any social security payments received.

7.318 Tax   Then apply tax calculation. Under sections 401 and 403 of ITEPA 2003, the first £30,000 of any payment made upon termination of employment or loss of office is free of tax. This concession does not apply:

(a) where the employment contract contains a PILON provision entitling (even if not obliging) the employer to terminate the contract immediately by making a payment in lieu of notice;

(b) to those who are approaching retirement age when their employment is terminated;

(c) to payments made wholly or in part as consideration for the employee agreeing to abide by post-termination restrictions;

(d) to any other payment made pursuant to contract.

7.319   Any payment above £30,000 is taxed at the employee's current marginal rate. Therefore, having calculated the total sum due net of tax, if it is over £30,000 that element above £30,000 must be 'grossed up' before the final payment is arrived at (see para **7.323**).

Other issues

Manner of dismissal   No damages will be awarded to reflect any pain, suffering,   **7.320**
psychological injury, or loss of reputation as a result of the dismissal, or the manner of dismissal if the disciplinary process is fully bound up with the dismissal
itself (*Johnson v Unisys Ltd* [2001] 2 WLR 1076, HL). However, where there has
been a pattern of events stretching back over a period, the courts may say that
damages may be recoverable for any psychological injury caused by the employer's
treatment. Each claim must be looked at individually taking into account matters
such as:

(a) the nature and pattern of any warnings;
(b) the consistency of the employer's conduct;
(c) whether there was a natural break in the process before dismissal became a
     practical proposition; and
(d) whether the alleged injury is attributable to the conduct complained of
     (*McCabe v Cornwall County Council* [2003] IRLR 87, CA). See also paras
     7.326–7.344.

Directors.   Before paying any director of a public company damages for wrong-   **7.321**
ful dismissal, regard should be had to sections 215–222 of the Companies Act
2006, which provide that shareholder consent is from time to time necessary;
whether or not the payment should be regarded as a related party transaction
under the rules of the London Stock Exchange; rule 21 of the City Code on
Takeovers and Mergers; the joint statement of best practice, issued by the
Association of British Insurers and the National Association of Pension Funds,
relating to compensation for departing directors of companies listed on the
London Stock Exchange; and the provisions of the Combined Code on Corporate
Governance which also provides guidance as to the amount of termination pay-
ments which should be made to directors of listed companies.

If an employee recovers damages in an employment tribunal for unfair dismissal,   **7.322**
but those damages cannot be shown to be specifically attributable to loss of
earnings for any period, the employee will not be obliged to give credit for the
compensatory award received when calculating damages for wrongful dismissal.
The employee will, however, be obliged to give credit for any ex gratia payment
already received from the employer before any court action.

7.323   Method of Calculation of Damages

(with tax rates current from 6 April 2008)

Annual value of package	Gross Value	Taxable element
Salary	a	a
Contractual benefits (as per **7.316(b)**)	b	b
Employer's pension contributions	c	-
Value of car		d^a
Total	e	f

Calculation of employee's personal allowances:

(Single person's allowance £6,035)		g
Taxable pay (f-g)		h

Calculation of tax:

1. Up to £2,030 @ 10%	i	
2. Up to £2,321–34,600 @ 20%	j	
3. H - £34,600 @ 40%	k	
Annual tax (i+j)	l	
Employee's national insurance contributions (11% income on earnings of between £105.01 and £770 per week + additional 1% earnings over £40,040))		m
Net annual pay (e-k-l)		n
Net loss during notice period (1/12m x number of months' notice due)		o

Deductions:

1. Discount for mitigation of loss	p	
2. Discount for accelerated payment	q	
3. Any social security payment	r	
Total deductions	s	
Total contractual loss (o-s)		t
Add (if appropriate) any redundancy payment (see Chapter 8)		u
Total loss (t+u)		v

Gross up (assuming marginal rate equals 40%):

u-£30,000 = v
v x 100/60 = w

Total payment due (less any ex gratia payment received)		x+£30,000

[Note: compensation for unfair dismissal, if awarded, will be added to 't'.]
[a] (based on CO_2 emissions and engine size. Sliding Scale from 15% to 35% of list price)

Commentary

An employee who has been unfairly dismissed can claim reinstatement, re-engagement, or compensation. Reinstatement and re-engagement mean, in effect, that the employee resumes his old position, or a similar position, on the same terms and conditions as before and is treated as though he had never been dismissed. In other words, the employee will receive back-pay for the period from dismissal to the date of reinstatement or re-engagement. A court will generally only make a reinstatement or re-engagement order if satisfied that it is practicable for the employer to make available a suitable job, and that the relationship of trust and confidence between employer and employee is intact. It is rare that both these elements will come together, and it is therefore rare that reinstatement or re-engagement orders are made. If an order is made and the employer refuses to comply, the employee is entitled to compensation plus an additional costs penalty of between 26 and 52 weeks' pay, the week's pay being subject to the statutory maximum (£330 for dismissals after 1 February 2008 and £350 for dismissals whose EDT is on or after 1 February 2009). **7.324**

The more normal remedy for unfair dismissal is compensation. This comes in two parts: the basic award, which is the equivalent of the statutory redundancy payment, and which is calculated by reference to age and length of service; and the compensatory award, which seeks to quantify the actual loss suffered by the employee. This award is subject to a statutory maximum of £66,200 for dismissals after 1 February 2009 (£63,000 for dismissals during the preceding year). This maximum is reviewed by the Government annually and increased in line with inflation. The statutory awards can be reduced if the employee is found to have contributed to some extent to his own dismissal. **7.325**

O. Personal Injuries Caused by Manner of Dismissal

Manner of Dismissal

Can an employee sue his employer for any psychological damage caused by the manner of the dismissal? Employers have a duty to take reasonable care to ensure their employees do not suffer physical or psychological injuries at work. The law may allow such a case to be brought if: **7.326**

(a) the employer knows that the employee has suffered from severe stress;
(b) the employee is then subject to a drawn out or unfair disciplinary procedure which culminates in dismissal; and
(c) the employee suffers an injury to his health as a result.

Right to Bring a Personal Injury Claim

7.327 If it is reasonably foreseeable that an employee will suffer psychiatric illness if subjected to particular treatment, such as bullying or an excessive workload, the employee can sue the employer for damages for any personal injury caused. However, the employee must show that the employer knew there was a real risk its actions would cause him psychological harm (*Sutherland v Hatton* [2002] IRLR 263, CA and *Barber v Somerset County Council* [2004] UKHL 13, HL). An employer is entitled to assume an employee can cope with the normal pressures of the job unless he knows something specific about the individual concerned or the job that should make him consider the issue of psychiatric injury. No jobs should be regarded as intrinsically dangerous to health.

7.328 Is the claim brought in the High Court/county court within three years of the employer's offending actions? If not, it is out of time.

7.329 Has the employer acted unreasonably in conducting a disciplinary investigation (eg by allowing the employee to remain in limbo for a substantial period while on suspension or by telling the employee it will not investigate thoroughly damaging allegations made against him)? If not, the employee has no claim.

7.330 When the employer started on this process, did it have dismissal in mind, or was it initially thinking only in terms of a less serious sanction such as a warning until it discovered later in the day that the complaint was more serious than it first thought? In reviewing this, one might examine:

    (a) the consistency of the employer's conduct and intention at different stages in the process;

    (b) the nature and pattern of any warnings;

    (c) whether there was a natural break in the process before dismissal became a practical proposition.

7.331 If the conduct of the investigation or suspension is 'part of the procedure' of dismissal, so that the employer had dismissal in mind when he took the steps the employee complains of, the employee probably has no claim.

7.332 Was the psychological injury caused by the employer's unreasonable actions? If not, the employee has no claim.

7.333 (a) Did the employer know that the employee suffered from a psychological problem such as severe stress before it took the unreasonable actions? For example, had he been signed off work—even for a short period—as suffering from stress/depression (*Barber v Somerset County Council* [2004] UKHL 13, HL).

    (b) Were the employee's working conditions such that the employer should have taken steps to remove any impending harm to health?

If not, the employee has no claim (see para 7.335(b) and (c)).

[Note: these principles are taken from the cases of *Johnson v Unisys* [2001] 2 WLR **7.334** 1076, HL; *Sutherland v Hatton* [2002] IRLR 263, CA; *McCabe v Cornwall County Council* [2003] IRLR 87, CA; and *Barber v Somerset County Council* [2004] UKHL 13, HL.]

Bringing the Claim

To succeed, the employee would need to establish the following: **7.335**

(a) Is the claim brought in the High Court/county court within three years of the employer's offending actions? If not, it is out of time.

(b) Was the employee's mental condition such that it should alert the employer that he is particularly vulnerable to stress? An employer is only under a duty to take steps to improve the position where there are signs that he, or the job, might plainly lead to impending harm to health from stress at work. Relevant factors to consider in determining whether the employee is particularly vulnerable are:

- has the employee told the employer he is at risk of suffering a psychological illness, for example by stating that his health was suffering as a result of excessive workload or stress at work (*Jones v Sandwell Metropolitan Borough Council* [2002] IRLR 263, CA)? If not, the employee is unlikely to be able to maintain a claim;
- has the employee recently taken off frequent or prolonged absences which are uncharacteristic, and is it reasonable to think these may be attributable to stress at work, for example because the employee or a colleague told management so? If so, the employee may be able to maintain a claim;
- has the employee been off work explicitly for stress at work or depression? If so, the employee may be able to maintain a claim;
- has the employee, to the employer's knowledge, had a nervous breakdown or is he otherwise vulnerable? If not, then in the absence of any other signs of potential ill-health the employee is unlikely to be able to maintain a claim;
- does the employee come across to colleagues as calm and unflappable? If so this will count against his ability to bring a claim;
- are there signs from the employee of an impending harm to health? If so, the employee may be able to bring a claim;
- has the employee not told the employer of his mental health problems (*Bishop v Baker Refractories Ltd* [2002] IRLR 263, CA; *Bonsor v RJB Mining (UK) Ltd* [2004] IRLR 164, CA)? If so, the employee is unlikely to be able to sustain a claim;

- has disclosure of a history of mental health problems been made only on a confidential basis to the employer's occupational heath department (*Hartman v South Essex Mental Health and Community NHS Trust* [2005] IRLR 293)? If so, the employee is unlikely to be able to maintain a claim. [Note: the employer is not obliged to make intensive enquiries or obtain medical reports, and is generally entitled to take what the employee tells him at face value.]

(c) Is the job unduly stressful? Indications that the job may cause stress at work, requiring the employer to check that the employee can cope or take steps to alleviate the stress (see para 7.339) include:

- the nature and extent of the employee's work: while no jobs are so intrinsically stressful that psychiatric injury is always reasonably foreseeable, more stressful jobs, coupled with the presence of some of the other factors, may tip the balance (*Melville v Home Office* [2005] IRLR 293, CA) where the employee had to recover bodies of prisoners who had committed suicide and the employer had not fully followed its policy on traumatic incidents). If so, the employee may be able to maintain a claim;
- is the employee's workload much greater than normal?
- are the demands on the employee unreasonable in comparison with others in similar jobs?
- are there signs that others doing similar jobs are suffering abnormal levels of stress?
- is there an abnormal level of sickness or absenteeism among those doing similar jobs?

7.336 [Note that the indications of impending harm to health from stress at work must be plain enough for any reasonable employer to realize he should do something about it.]

7.337 Counselling. Does the employer, to its employees' knowledge, provide a confidential counselling service for employees with referral to appropriate counselling or treatment services? If so, this will improve his position. However, this is not a panacea for an employer which could implement a satisfactory remedy by, for example, reducing the workload of someone who claims to be stressed out because of pressure of work, but who fails to take this step (*Melville v Home Office* [2005] IRLR 293, CA; *Barlow v Borough of Broxbourne* [2003] All ER(D) 208; *Daw v Intel Corporation Ltd* [2006] EWHC 1097).

7.338 Was the psychological illness caused by stress at work or was there some other cause? If not caused by the employer's actions, the employee has no claim.

7.339 Are the indications of potential psychological harm to the individual from the job so plain that a reasonable employer would realize he should do something about it? If so, he should establish what steps he could take, and take such steps as are reasonable in the circumstances bearing in mind:

(a)   the magnitude of the risk of harm occurring;
(b)   the gravity of any harm;
(c)   the costs and practicability of preventing harm;
(d)   justifications for running the risk;
(e)   the size and scope of his operation, its resources, and the demands it faces (including the interests of other employees and the need to treat them fairly, for example in any redistribution of duties); and
(f)   whether there are any steps to take which might produce some good. (If no good is likely to result, there is no need to take the steps. It may be sensible for the employer to take expert medical or other opinion at this point.) Not only may failure to take reasonable steps (for example by not transferring the employee into a department away from the cause of stress) render the employer susceptible to an unfair dismissal claim; it will also entitle the employee to resign and claim constructive dismissal for the employer's failure to provide a safe place to work (*Thanet District Council v Websper* [2003] IDS Brief 728 p 6).

Is the only reasonable and practicable step for the employer to take to dismiss the   **7.340**
employee, but the employee wants to be kept on (*Bishop v Baker Refractories Ltd* [2002] IRLR 263, CA)? If the employer retains the employee, the employer will not be in breach of duty.

Has the employee failed to take such steps as are reasonable in the circumstances?   **7.341**
If an employee has acted reasonably, bearing in mind the stress guidance at para 7.335(**b**), it is unlikely to be responsible for any ensuing personal injury; a vulnerable employee cannot be totally protected from acts which would normally lead to dismissal such as misconduct. The Court will examine whether the employer could and should have done anything differently.

Has the employer's breach of duty in failing to take any reasonable steps caused   **7.342**
or materially contributed to the employee's psychological injury? Only in these circumstances will the employer be liable to pay damages to the employee. It is not enough to show that occupational stress has caused the harm.

Damages. Damages will be calculated on a normal personal injury basis—   **7.343**
essentially a figure to reflect the damage suffered by the stress plus loss of earnings during the period before which the employee could reasonably be expected to return to an equivalent job plus medical care and other expenses.

7.344   Reducing the damages:

  (a)   does the psychological injury have more than one cause? If so, the employer is only liable for his share of the blame, unless the harm is truly indivisible (*Sadler v Portsmouth Publishing and Printing Ltd* [2004] All ER(D) 223);

  (b)   does the employee have any pre-existing disorder or vulnerability? Was there a chance he might have succumbed to a stress-related illness in any event? If so, damages should be reduced.

P. Making/Defending a Claim

7.345   When must the employee bring a claim? An employee must bring an action, on form ET1 (obtainable from any employment tribunal or job centre), for unfair dismissal by delivering the form to the local office of the employment tribunal (identified by reference to the employer's post code—a list appears in the index of the Employment Tribunal Booklet on how to bring a claim) so that it arrives within three months of the termination date (see ERA 1996, s 111(2)). [Note: this is the date employment actually ended, not the Effective Date of Termination described in para 7.59. This period may be extended by three months if, at the end of the initial period, the employee reasonably believes that the dismissal process is ongoing—for example because he believes an appeal is still underway.]

Before bringing a claim, an employee should consider whether any useful evidence might emerge if he makes a data request asking for information held about him (chapter 10). While relevant evidence should be disclosed by the employer during the course of proceedings, taking this step may widen the net and speed up the process.

7.346   The application is sent by the employment tribunal to the employer who has 28 days within which to respond. Short extensions may be granted following written requests to the Secretary of the relevant employment tribunal. The employer should set out any jurisdictional or factual defences, for example, that the complaint has been lodged out of time, or the employee was fairly dismissed by reason of his misconduct.

7.347   If the employee has alleged that he has been constructively dismissed, the employer should argue first that there was no dismissal, but alternatively that if there was a dismissal it was for a specified reason which was fair: in the absence of such a plea, if the employment tribunal decides there was a constructive dismissal, the employer will lose the opportunity to argue that the dismissal could be fair.

7.348   The employment tribunal will probably order that the parties disclose to each other all relevant documents they have, provide each other with witness statements setting out the evidence they will tell the tribunal, agree a chronology setting out the key events, and agree what documents should go in a bundle of relevant documents. It may ask the parties to provide further information to each other setting out the nature of their case, or ask the parties to attend the tribunal for a pre-hearing review on a discrete point (for example whether the applicant is an employee or has made the claim in time) which might determine the whole case, or for a case management discussion. It may also require an employee to provide the employer with a schedule of the loss he has suffered. If, on a pre-hearing review, the tribunal decides that one of the parties has no reasonable prospect of success, it may require that party to make a deposit to the court of up to £500 before it can continue. An employment tribunal can award costs against a party of up to £10,000 or can refer assessment of costs to the county court. The tribunal also has power to award costs against a party's representative who has acted vexatiously, abusively, disruptively, or otherwise unreasonably.

The employee can bring a claim for wrongful dismissal in the employment tribu- **7.349** nal but the maximum damages that can be awarded are £25,000. Such a claim must be brought within three months after dismissal. However, if the employee does so the employer may bring a counterclaim against the employee for any breach of contract. Breach of contract claims brought in the employment tribunal must have arisen or be outstanding on the termination of employment and cannot relate to provision of living accommodation, intellectual property, confidentiality, or covenants in restraint of trade.

Applications for wrongful dismissal claiming more than £25,000 or personal **7.350** injuries must be brought in the High Court (or county court if the claim is for under £50,000), using the appropriate forms. The relevant county court can be found on the website <http://www.courtservice.gov.uk> or in the phone book.

Wrongful dismissal claims must be filed within six years of the date of dismissal. **7.351** Personal injury claims must be brought within three years of the behaviour complained of and the employee must have written to the employer clearly stating his claim (pre-action protocol for personal injury claims). Defendants normally have 28 days from being served with the documents to produce a defence, but time may be extended. If one party believes the other has no possible legal case (irrespective of the facts) he may apply for summary judgment in his favour. Otherwise, the case will proceed with parties exchanging all relevant documents and the witness statements on which they will rely. Expert medical evidence will normally be required in personal injury cases. Before the trial, the parties are expected to provide the court with an agreed bundle of relevant documents, a chronology, and witness statements, and each should provide a skeleton argument summarizing the points that party will make before the court. The winning party will normally pay half to two-thirds of the losing party's costs (or more if a Part 36 Offer was not bettered—see para 7.357(**b**)).

7

Dismissals

Settlement

7.352 Must any jobseekers' allowance or income support be returned to Jobcentre Plus if there is a settlement? If a complaint is settled, the employee need not account to the Secretary of State for the return of the jobseekers' allowance, whereas if there is a trial and an award is made, the Secretary of State will seek to recover any jobseekers' allowance or income support benefit paid. These are the only two benefits that are set off against compensation in this way.

7.353 How can the employer prevent the employee from bringing a claim, even if he has agreed to settle the case?

(a) Settlement does not prevent the employee from applying to an employment tribunal for further damages unless:
  - it has been approved by an ACAS conciliation officer;
  - it has been documented in a statutory form of agreement known as a 'compromise agreement' (see para 7.354) which has been signed by the employee; or
  - the parties have already fairly agreed an appropriate compensation payment and it would be unjust or inequitable for the employer to pay any further sum. In this case an employment tribunal may not make a further award. This is likely only to apply if the employee has received significantly more than the contractual amount due to him, or if he has received considerably more than the statutory maximum. However, it will not prevent the employee from being able to bring a claim in the employment tribunal.

(b) a well-worded full and final settlement agreement, even if not approved by an ACAS officer or in the form of a compromise agreement (see para 7.354) will still prevent an employee from bringing a claim for wrongful dismissal or personal injuries in the High Court or county court.

7.354 A compromise agreement is an agreement signed by an employee referring to ERA 1996, s 203. Where the employee has been advised on its terms and their effect by a solicitor or barrister who is properly insured or by another expert such as a trade union official or a Citizen's Advice Bureau worker; ie the employee must have been told that signing the agreement will prevent him from bringing or continuing his claim for unfair dismissal and other statutory claims.

Ex Gratia Payments

7.355 Can these be taken into account by an employment tribunal when deciding what compensation to award? Yes.

Is payment expressed to include the basic award? If not, it may be deemed to cover only the compensatory element and a tribunal can award a basic award even if the sums actually paid to the employee are sufficient to cover both elements. **7.356**

Can the employer protect its position if the employee refuses to settle? **7.357**

(a) In the employment tribunal: although there is no formal payment into court mechanism in the employment tribunal, it is possible to write a 'Calderbank letter' making an offer to settle the case 'without prejudice' on terms but reserving the right to show the letter to the tribunal after the hearing when costs are to be considered. In writing any such letter, the employer would be wise to state that if the offer is accepted the employer will agree the employee was unfairly dismissed—in the absence of such a statement a tribunal has held it is reasonable for the employee to reject an offer, even if he is subsequently awarded a lower sum by the tribunal. If the employee is awarded less than the amount set out in the Calderbank letter, he may suffer a costs penalty.

(b) In the High Court or county court: a tactic when considering a claim for wrongful dismissal, is to make a 'Part 36 Offer'. This is a good idea where the employer believes that a court may award the employee some but not all of his claim, but the employee will not accept this. The amount of the payment into court should be the amount the employer considers to be due together with appropriate interest payments. Alternatively, the employee can make a Part 36 Offer, setting out the lowest sum he would settle for. If the employer is ordered to pay more than the employee has said he would accept, or the employee fails to beat the amount the employer has paid into court, he will suffer serious cost and interest penalties.

7

Dismissals

8

REDUNDANCY

A. Introduction

An employer in financial difficulty often needs to reduce the number of its **8.01** employees by making them redundant and an employee properly made redundant is entitled to a redundancy payment, calculated on a sliding scale, in accordance with age and length of service. Redundancy is potentially a fair reason for dismissal. However, an employee who is unfairly selected for redundancy will be unfairly dismissed. An employer must consult with employees before making them redundant, and, where making 20 or more people redundant within three months, must also enter into collective consultation. Most tribunal cases concerning redundancy revolve around: whether the people selected for redundancy are actually redundant; whether they have been selected for some unfair reason; whether proper individual consultation and/or collective consultation has been implemented; and the compensation to which any redundant person is entitled.

B. Overview of Practical Steps an Employer Should Take Before Implementing a Redundancy Programme

To protect themselves, employers who propose to make people redundant should take the following steps:

8.02 Identify the business need for making redundancies (see para **8.20**) and work out a plan for doing so including:

- identifying roles to be made redundant;
- number of redundancies;
- criteria for selecting those to be made redundant.

8.03 If proposing to make more than 20 people redundant in one establishment over a 90-day period, and if no union is recognized, organize an election for staff representatives, with whom the employer can consult (see paras **8.43–8.48**).

8.04 Begin consultations with staff representatives or recognized trade union representatives (see paras **8.49–8.56**). Give as much warning as possible to allow any union or affected employees to inform themselves of facts and consider alternative solutions, either for the employer or the employee.

8.05 Notify BERR on form HR1 if proposing to make 20 or more redundant over a 90-day period (see paras **8.62–8.64**).

8.06 Consider inviting volunteers for redundancy (see para **8.74**).

8.07 Establish whether there are any alternative jobs either with the employer itself or any associated employer (see paras **8.90–8.99**).

8.08 Consider whether to inform all employees who perform roles which have been identified as potentially redundant that they are at risk of redundancy (see **8.78**).

8.09 Select the employees for redundancy, fairly and in accordance with the selection criteria (see paras **8.31–8.39**). Where a union or staff representatives are involved, it is wise to seek their confirmation that the selection process has been fair and consider any representations they may make about the process.

8.10 Consult with those provisionally selected for redundancy (see paras **8.74–8.89**).

8.11 Write to those provisionally selected inviting them to a meeting when the redundancy will be discussed (see para **8.83**)(a).

[Note: this step is always good practice, but is not necessary where collective consultation has been conducted, and will no longer be an absolute requirement when the statutory disciplinary procedures are repealed (likely to be in April 2009).]

Meet those provisionally selected for redundancy, individually, to discuss all the issues. **8.12**
The individual may be accompanied by a colleague or trade union official (see **8.80**).

[Note: this step is always good practice but not necessary where collective consultation has been conducted, and will no longer be an absolute requirement when the statutory disciplinary procedures are repealed (likely to be in April 2009).]

Consider offering those selected for redundancy alternative employment, **8.13**
whether or not suitable (see paras **8.90–8.99**).

Give those selected for redundancy notice terminating their employment, requir- **8.14**
ing them to work out their notice or making them a payment in lieu, and paying
a redundancy payment to those entitled to it. The notice should set out how the
redundancy payment is calculated (see para **8.106**).

Inform the employee that he has a right to appeal (see para **8.83**). **8.15**

Allow those selected for redundancy time off to search for another job. **8.16**

Consider requiring those to be made redundant to sign a compromise agreement, **8.17**
by which they waive any claims against the employer (see para 7.353).

Keep any vacancies which may arise under review and consider offering them to **8.18**
any employees who have been told they are to be made redundant.

Conduct any appeal, and notify the employee of the result (see para **8.106**). **8.19**

Failure to follow all these steps will not necessarily mean that a redundancy is
unfair, but the more steps that are taken, the stronger the employer's position will
be (*Williams v Compair Maxam Limited* [1982] ICR 156).

C. When is a Person Redundant?

CHECKLIST

Can the employer show that it has a business need for making redundancies? Are **8.20**
there economic or practical reasons why the employer needs to reduce the workforce? If so, it may take the decision in principle that it should make redundancies.
The employer will need to explain why it believes any redundancies are necessary,
but will not be required to show that those reasons are empirically justifiable (see
para **8.27**). It will need to show one of the reasons set out at para **8.21**.

Has the employer decided that: **8.21**
(a) it has closed down or intends to close down the business where the employee
works (in which case all those employed in the business are potentially redundant); or

(b) it needs to slim down the number of employees required to carry out work of a particular kind (in which case, employees carrying out that work will be in a pool of those who are potentially redundant); or

(c) it no longer needs employees to carry out work of a particular kind (in which case all employees carrying out that work are potentially redundant) (ERA 1996, s 139)?

The employer should establish which jobs it wishes to make redundant, and whether any job functions will in future be varied to encompass different or additional tasks.

8.22 Has the employer considered whether there are any other options, such as reduction of overtime or restrictions on recruitment, which might reduce the number of those who will need to be made redundant? If it does not do so, a tribunal might decide any ensuing redundancy is an unfair dismissal.

8.23 Are there any employees working under fixed-term contracts? Employees working under fixed-term contracts will be entitled to a redundancy payment (and have the right not to be unfairly dismissed) if they are selected for redundancy either during or at the end of their fixed term.

8.24 Will the employee be replaced? Where an employee is replaced there is no redundancy (unless the replacement is a self-employed contractor: but note, this might amount to a transfer of undertaking—see Chapter 9);

8.25 Are the only items which are to change minor, for example, because hours change? If so, there is no redundancy (though the need for one more person on a day shift and one fewer on a night shift, for example, might be sufficient to amount to a redundancy).

8.26 What is the reason for the employee's dismissal? Is it because his role is redundant, or is it for some other reason? If it is for some other reason but redundancy is given as the ostensible reason, the employee will probably have been unfairly dismissed.

Commentary

8.27 An employee is dismissed by reason of redundancy if the dismissal is attributable wholly or mainly to the fact that the employer has ceased or intends to cease to carry on the relevant business at all, or business in the particular place where the employee was employed; or because the requirement of the business for the employee to carry out work of a particular kind has ceased or diminished or is expected to do so (ERA 1996, s 139, *Murray and Another v Foyle Meats Ltd* [1999] IRLR 562, HL). The commercial decision that the business needs fewer employees of a particular type rests with the employer, and the tribunal will generally not inquire into whether the employer was reasonable in taking that commercial decision. An employer selecting people for redundancy should be able to demonstrate to a tribunal that it has reviewed the number of staff it needs to maintain the business it proposes to carry on and the positions which will thereby become vacant: if it thinks in terms of which individuals it no longer requires, this may indicate that any selection process is unfair.

When a tribunal looks at the issue of redundancy it takes into consideration not only **8.28** the employing company but also, in reviewing the question whether the employee should be offered alternative employment elsewhere, any associated companies.

When a whole business or office closes down there is rarely an issue whether the **8.29** employee is redundant. If there is any question, it relates only (in a claim for unfair dismissal) to whether associated employers have appropriate alternative work for the employee.

When, however, the employer is merely reducing numbers rather than closing **8.30** the business altogether, problems can arise if it cannot actually show that its cost-cutting measures are the direct cause of a particular person's departure. Company restructuring which does not involve a reduction in numbers of employees is unlikely to involve any redundancies, though people losing their job as a result may have been dismissed for 'some other substantial reason' (see para 7.233(b)). An employee may successfully claim unfair dismissal if he can show that no proper method of selecting people for redundancy was implemented or that there is some other motive for dismissal.

D. Selection of Those Employees to be Made Redundant

CHECKLIST

Has the employer selected someone for redundancy for an automatically un- **8.31** fair reason? These are listed in para **7.94**. It will be automatically unfair for the employer to select for such a reason.

Are all the employees performing a particular role going to be made redundant? If **8.32** not, but the number is to be reduced, the employer should adopt selection criteria which can be applied objectively. It should, where possible, seek to agree them with authorized representatives (see paras **8.53–8.56**).

What are the selection criteria (see para **8.40**)? Fair criteria include: **8.33**

(a) suitability to perform the tasks that will be required;
(b) ability/experience/qualifications/efficiency;
(c) conduct/attendance record (taking into account reasons for poor conduct or attendance).

8.34 Are the selection criteria unfair (see para **8.41**)? Unfair criteria include:

(a) age or 'last in first out'—these used to be used as selection criteria from time to time. It is now no longer wise to do so, as this could amount to age discrimination (see para **8.40**);

(b) selection for taking part in trade union activities;

(c) selection on an automatically unfair ground—eg because the employee has done something (such as whistle-blowing, complaining about health and safety issues, or trying to enforce a statutory right) which would make any resultant dismissal unfair. Automatically unfair grounds are listed in para **7.94**.

8.35 Are the criteria given equal status? They may be weighted by giving some, say, marks out of five and other more important criteria marks out of ten.

8.36 Could selection be perceived to be on a subjective basis? If so, the selection would not be reasonable. For example, 'those whom the relevant managers believe are necessary to make the company viable' is too subjective.

8.37 Is the pool of employees from which selection will be made clearly defined? If individuals whose jobs are to go are capable of performing the work carried out by people in other departments, or if they can be contractually required to carry out such work (and vice versa), serious consideration should be given to including people in those other departments in the pool for selection. This is not a hard and fast rule, but if it is to be rejected, adequate reason should be given in the event that the issue is raised in tribunal proceedings.

8.38 Have any employees been 'bumped'—ie dismissed to make way for another employee whose job was redundant? If, as a result of creating a large pool, A from one department which is not losing any jobs is made redundant so that B, whose job had ceased to exist, can move across to A's job, this 'bumping' will be a legitimate redundancy provided the selection criteria and all other procedures are followed (*Safeway Stores plc v Burrell* [1977] ICR 523, EAT (see paras **8.42** and **8.99**)).

8.39 Can the employer show it has applied the criteria objectively and reasonably? This is best done by documenting the way in which the criteria are applied. Glaring inconsistencies, even if made in good faith, cannot be justified (*Northgate HR Ltd v Mercy* [2008] IRLR 222, CA).

Commentary

8.40 The employer must choose his own selection criteria, which must be reasonable (*Williams and Others v Compair Maxam Ltd* [1982] IRLR 83, EAT). Most fair criteria would include one or more of the following factors: the type of skills and capabilities for which there is a continuing employment need, and the suitability for the individuals to perform those tasks: competence, attendance, and conduct. In the past, age and 'last in first out' have been applied as criteria, although their use has been declining. Now, it may be unwise to adopt these as criteria because this may disadvantage younger employees who will not have had the opportunity to build up substantial years of service, and it is therefore challengeable as indirect age discrimination (but see *Rolls-Royce plc v Unite the Union* [2008] EWHC 2420 (QB) where including length of service as one of six selection criteria was not discriminatory—the process had been agreed with the Union, it promised a peaceable and fair selection, and respected the loyalty and experience of the older workforce, protecting them from being put on to the labour market in difficult economic times). The criteria should be capable of being objectively checked, but can be weighted in favour of particular criteria.

The employer must not use as his principal reason for selecting a person any facts **8.41** relating to the individual's membership of or participation in the affairs of a trade union, or any other automatically unfair reason (see para **7.94** for automatically unfair reasons).

In addition, the pool from which the employee is to be selected for redundancy **8.42** needs to be ascertained. The pool which the employer chooses from which to select those to be made redundant must be within the band of reasonable choices for the employer; there may be more than one appropriate pool (*Hendy Banks City Print v Fairbrother*, 21 December 2004, UK EAT/0691/04). If, for example, the employer decides that he needs two fewer employees in one department, yet there are employees in another department who perform similar tasks and who, by their contract of employment, could be required to work in the first department, then those other employees could also be subject to the same criteria for selection. This 'bumping' rule is sound practice to follow, though it is not a hard and fast rule in every case (see *Lionel Leventhal Ltd v North* EAT 0265/04, IDS Brief 778 where on the facts of the case the employer should have considered bumping a more junior employee, even though the potentially redundant employee had not requested it: factors to consider are how different the two jobs are, the difference in remuneration, and the qualifications of the potentially redundant employee).

E. Consultation

Collective Consultation

CHECKLIST

Are 20 or more employees potentially to be made redundant at the same estab- **8.43** lishment within 90 days or less? (TULR(C)A 1992, s 188) (see para **8.66** for the meaning of establishment)? If 20 or more employees are potentially to be made redundant (or redeployed—see *Hardy v Tourism South East* [2005] IRLR 242, EAT) during this period, the employer will need to undertake collective consultation, either with a recognized trade union, or with special employee representatives. Any election for employee representatives must be fair (TULR(C)A 1992, s 188A) (see paras **8.46–8.48**). For the meaning of establishment, see para **8.66**.

8.44 What if the number to be made redundant changes during the process? If the original intention was to make 20 or more employees redundant, there must still be collective consultation. This is the case even if the number ultimately reduces—perhaps because in the event fewer are made redundant or because some employees take voluntary redundancy/early retirement packages (*Optare Group Ltd v TGWU* [2007] EAT 0143/07).

8.45 Is there an independent trade union which the employer recognizes to bargain on behalf of individuals who are members of the class who may be made redundant? If so, the employer must consult with the union (TULR(C)A 1992, s 188(1B)).

8.46 If there is no recognized trade union, are there any elected employee representatives? They must be employees when elected, but may be either:

(a) general representatives (eg on staff committees) so long as they have authority from the employees to receive information and to be consulted on redundancies; or

(b) ad hoc representatives, elected for the purposes of the present consultations (see paras **8.47** and **8.68**).

If there is no existing staff representative body, the employer must arrange for the election of representatives before it begins the consultation process (see para **8.68**). (See para **8.72** where the employer has formally established works councils.)

8.47 Does the employer choose to elect representatives specifically for the purposes of the proposed redundancies? If so, it must ensure that:

(a) the arrangements are fair;

(b) the number of representatives are sufficient to represent the interests of all employees affected by the proposals;

(c) all affected employees are entitled to participate in the vote for employee representatives and to vote for any candidate who stands for election (either for the whole workforce or, if relevant, for a particular class of employees);

(d) before the election, the term of office of the employee representatives is determined (which should be long enough to cover the required period of consultation);

(e) the candidates for election are individuals who are affected by the employer's proposals;

(f) no employees are unreasonably excluded from standing for election;

(g) any election is conducted to ensure that voting is (as far as reasonably practicable) done in secret and that the votes are counted accurately;

(h) the elected representatives have access to the affected employees (and are given accommodation and any other facilities—for example, office space, computers, printers, reasonable time, etc).

(TULR(C)A 1992, s 188A) (see para **8.68**)

Have the employees not elected any representatives? Where an employer has **8.48** invited employees to elect representatives and they have failed to do so within a reasonable time, the employer's only obligation will be to provide all employees affected by the proposals with the information outlined below (TULR(C)A 1992, s 188(7B)). In all other cases, failure to appoint representatives will mean that the collective consultation process is invalid (see paras **8.57–8.58**).

Timing of Collective Consultation

Is it planned for there to be 19 or fewer redundancies at the relevant establishment **8.49** within a period of 90 days or less? If so, there is no obligation to consult collectively.

Is it planned for there to be between 20 and 99 redundancies over a period of **8.50** 90 days? If so, consultations should begin in good time (in essence, when a specific proposal has been formulated) though ideally representatives should be given an opportunity to comment during the planning stage when redundancies are realistically likely to be implemented, but at least 30 days before the dismissal takes effect (ie from the date notice is given) (see para **8.69**).

Is it planned for there to be 100 or more redundancies over a period of 90 days? **8.51** If so, consultations should begin in good time as above but at least 90 days before the first dismissal takes effect (ie from the date notice is given) (TULR(C)A 1992, s 188(1) and (1A)).

Are there any special circumstances which make it not reasonably practicable for **8.52** the notice periods set out in paras **8.50** and **8.51** to be given? If so, the employer's duty is still to consult as soon as reasonably practicable (TULR(C)A 1992, s 188(7)).

Information to Representatives

What should the employer disclose to the union/representatives? Within the **8.53** relevant time limits, the employer should disclose the following in writing to the appropriate representatives:

(a) the reasons for its proposals;

(b) the numbers and descriptions of employees whom it is proposed to dismiss as redundant;

(c) the total number of employees of any such description employed by the employer at the establishment in question;

(d) the proposed method of selecting the employees who may be dismissed;

(e) the proposed method of carrying out the dismissals, with due regard to any agreed procedure, including the period over which the dismissals are to take effect;

(f) the proposed method of calculating any enhanced redundancy payments.

(TULR(C)A 1992, s 188(4))

8.54 What does the employer have to consult about? Consultations with representatives should be full and frank (ie not misleading) and should take place with a view to reaching agreement about:

(a) ways and means of avoiding collective redundancies;

(b) ways of reducing the number of employees to be dismissed;

(c) ways of mitigating the consequences of the dismissals.

(TULR(C)A 1992, s 188(2))

8.55 Does the employer have to consult over the reason why redundancies are proposed, including the economic/business reasons behind the decision to reduce the workforce? Yes—for example, it should be prepared to discuss alternatives to factory closure (*UK Mining Ltd v National Union of Mineworkers (Northumberland Area) and Another* [2007] IDS Brief 841).

8.56 Must the employer reach agreement with the union/representatives? No, but any suggestions put forward by the representatives (for example, about alternative solutions to the employer's problems or finding alternative employment) should be considered and, if not taken up, the union/representatives should be informed why their suggestions have not been accepted. The consultations do not have to conclude with agreement on any issue.

Failure to Inform and Consult

8.57 Was there a failure to:

(a) inform (see para **8.53**);

(b) consult (see paras **8.54–8.56**); or

(c) where such an election is necessary, to hold a fair election of employee representatives (see **8.46–8.48**)?

If there is no or inadequate consultation, a claim may be brought in an employment tribunal against the employer for a protective award of up to 90 days' pay per affected employee (TULR(C)A 1992, s 189).

8.58 Who can bring the claim?

(a) in the case of a failure relating to the election of employee representatives, any affected employee;

(b) in the case of any other failure, any employee representative (or trade union official where relevant) to whom the failure related; and

(c) in any other case, any of the affected employees.

Can anyone else bring a claim for a protective award? No. The guidelines in para **8.58** are strict. Therefore, if representatives have been elected, only one of them can pursue a claim, and a disgruntled employee cannot (*Northgate HR Ltd v Mercy* [2008] IRLR 222, CA). **8.59**

What is the scope of the award? If the tribunal finds the complaint well founded, it can make a protective award of up to 90 days' remuneration in respect of each employee who has been dismissed as redundant or who is proposed to be dismissed as redundant. This is intended to be punitive rather than compensatory (TULR(C)A 1992, ss 189–190); the general principle is that the award should be for the full 90 days and it should only be reduced if there are reasons to do so, rather than vice versa (see para **8.73**). **8.60**

Who can enforce the award? If a union has obtained a protective award, it can only be enforced by employees in respect of whom the union was recognized. It cannot even be enforced by other members of the same union whose jobs lie outside the collective bargaining arrangements (*TGWU v Brauer Coley Ltd* [2007] ICR 226, EAT). **8.61**

Notification to Department of Business, Enterprise and Regulatory Reform

Has the employer notified the Department of Business, Enterprise and Regulatory Reform (BERR) of its proposals regarding redundancies? **8.62**

It must do so, on Form HR1:

(a) in the case of more than 20 but less than 100 redundancies at any establishment, at least 30 days before first dismissal takes effect; or

(b) in the case of 100 or more redundancies at any establishment, at least 90 days before first dismissal takes effect;

(c) where special circumstances exist which render it not reasonably practicable for the employer to notify the BERR, the employer remains under an obligation to take all such steps to ensure such compliance as is reasonably practicable in those special circumstances.

Where must the form be sent? The form must be sent not only to BERR, but also to any authorized representative (TULR(C)A 1992, ss 193–194). **8.63**

What is the sanction for failing to notify BERR? It is an offence not to notify. The employer could be convicted and fined up to level 5 on the standard scale in a magistrates' court (TULR(C)A 1992, s 194(1)) (though prosecution is rare). **8.64**

Commentary

8.65 Consultation over the redundancies should take place on two levels, both the collective and the individual.

8.66 Where 20 or more employees at any one establishment may be made redundant, the employer must consult with 'appropriate representatives'. The word 'establishment' is broadly defined. For example a production unit can be an establishment if it, say, has a head of production and a substantial and specialized workforce, and is a stand-alone operation, even if it does not have any legal, economic, financial, administrative, or technological autonomy (*Athinaikim Chartopoiia AE v Panagiotidis* [2007] IRLR 284, ECJ).

8.67 The representatives may be representatives of a recognized trade union, if there is one, or if not they must be employee representatives. Those whom the employer plans to redeploy elsewhere in the business must be included in the headcount of those potentially redundant (*Hardy v Tourism South East* [2005] IRLR 242, EAT), as must those who voluntarily accept redundancy (*Optare Group Limited v Transport and General Workers Union* [2007] EAT 0143/07).

8.68 If there is already a group of employees who have been appointed or elected to represent colleagues in general in circumstances such that they have authority to receive information about and be consulted about proposed redundancy dismissals, then, in the absence of a recognized union, this group can be consulted with. If no such group exists, or if the employer does not wish to consult with this group, he must consult with a group who has been specially elected by the affected employees in an election. The election must be held in the following way:

(a) The employer must make such arrangements as are reasonably practicable to ensure that the elections are fair;

(b) It is for the employer to decide:
- how many representatives there should be, but they must be sufficient to represent all employee interests, having regard to the number and classes of affected employees;
- whether employees of different classes should be represented by all the representatives, or just be representatives of their class; and
- the length of the term of office—which must be sufficiently long to enable them to remain in place until the consultation concludes;

(c) The candidates for election must be affected employees as at the election date;

(d) No affected employee must be unreasonably excluded from standing for election;

(e) All affected employees as at the election date must have the opportunity to vote;

(f)   The employees must be able to vote for as many candidates as are entitled to represent them;

(g)   There should be a secret ballot; and

(h)   Votes should be accurately counted (TULR(C)A 1992, s 188A).

8.69 Consultations must begin in good time and at least 30 days before any dismissal takes effect where the employer proposes to dismiss as redundant between 20 and 99 employees at one establishment within a 90-day period, and at least 90 days before any dismissal where the employer proposes to dismiss at least 100 employees (TULR(C)A 1992, s 188(1) and (1A)) (see para **8.66** for the definition of 'establishment'). The dismissal 'takes effect' not on the day the employment terminates, but on the day that notice to terminate is given to the employees (*Junk v Kühnel* [2005] IRLR 310, ECJ). These time limits apply unless there are special circumstances which render it not reasonably practicable for them to be adhered to. 'In good time' does not mean 'at the earliest opportunity' and consultation may only take two weeks if that is sufficient time to produce a fair and meaningful consultation process (*Amicus v Nissan Motor Manufacturing (UK) Ltd* EAT/0184/05, IDS Brief 793). Consultation must begin when there is a real proposal to dismiss, even if the proposal is a recommendation to management which has yet to be ratified (*Leicestershire County Council v Unison* [2005] IRLR 920, EAT), though if the proposals are still at a formative stage, the fact that there is a gap between their formulation and the start of consultations will not prevent the consultation being 'in good time' so long as there is sufficient consultation before proposals are finalized (*Amicus v Nissan Motor Manufacturing (UK) Ltd* EAT 0184/05, IDS Brief 793 where constructive negotiations began several months after proposals had been announced and lasted two weeks).

8.70 Consultation must be about ways of avoiding dismissals, reducing the numbers of employees to be dismissed, and mitigating the consequences of the dismissals. The employer should undertake the consultation with a view to reaching agreement with the representatives/union (TULR(C)A 1992, s 188(2)).

8.71 The employer also has to give notice of the intention to effect redundancies to the Department of Business, Enterprise & Regulatory Reform (BERR) if it proposes to make 20 or more people redundant over a 90-day period, and must use a form HR1. This must be done within similar time limits to those required for consultation with authorized representatives.

8.72 If the employer has an agreement by which he has to inform and consult representatives under the Information and Consultation of Employees Regulations 2004, he need not discuss impending collective redundancies with those representatives if he tells them in writing that he will be consulting under TULR(C)A 1992, s 188 (Information and Consultation of Employees Regulations 2004, reg 20(1)(c)).

8.73 Failure to consult with authorized representatives renders the employer liable to a protective award of up to 90 days' pay. This is a punitive, rather than compensatory, award and tribunals are required to look at the seriousness of the employer's default. A proper approach where there is no consultation is to start with the maximum award and then reduce it only if there are mitigating circumstances which would justify a reduction (*Susie Radin Ltd v GMB and Others* [2004] IRLR 400, CA). Because the award is intended to be punitive, it applies even where employees remained employed throughout the protected period and were not dismissed or under notice until that period had ended (*Cranswick Country Foods Ltd v Beall and Others* [2006] UK EAT 0222/06).

Consultation with Individual Employees

CHECKLIST

8.74 Does the employer want to ask for volunteers? It is not essential to do so, but it is good practice. Any volunteer who comes forward will not need to match the selection criteria. The employer need not accept the volunteer's request, but should have reasonable reasons for any refusal. People who withdraw their applications for voluntary redundancy before their employment is terminated should no longer be regarded as volunteers.

8.75 Are there fewer than 20 employees likely to be made redundant from the same establishment over a period of three months?

(a) If yes, then until at least April 2009, when the statutory dismissal procedures are likely to be repealed, the employer must adopt the minimum statutory dismissal procedures (see para **8.83**). If these are not followed, then the employee will be automatically unfairly dismissed.

(b) If 20 or more employees may potentially be made redundant, then the employer will still need to consult with each employee, but if the statutory procedures are not followed, this is not inevitably an unfair dismissal.

8.76 Are some of the roles to be made redundant unique? If so, the employer will not have to apply selection criteria in relation to these roles.

8.77 Are there a number of people performing some of the roles to be made redundant? If yes, the employer will need to establish a selection procedure (see paras **8.31–8.42**). In particular, the employer will need to:

(a) establish a selection pool;

(b) establish selection criteria;

(c) consult with staff representatives (if 20 or more likely to be made redundant over a three-month period—see paras **8.53–8.56**) over the criteria;

(d) grade people in the pool in accordance with the criteria;

(e) keep a record of the application of the grading process.

When should the employer warn the employee that he is at risk of redundancy? **8.78**
Where the roles are not unique, it is best practice to notify all employees in the
pool that they are at risk of redundancy before applying the selection criteria.
Employers have been found to have unfairly dismissed employees ultimately
selected if this has not happened. However, many employers prefer not to adopt
this procedure because of its unsettling effect on the whole work force, and in
those circumstances consultation must take place immediately after the selection
criteria have been applied.

Can the employer dismiss the employees at this stage? If an employee is given **8.79**
notice terminating his employment at or before this stage:

(a) If fewer than 20 employees are likely to be made redundant within a three-
month period, his dismissal will be automatically unfair, because the statutory
procedures have not been followed;

(b) If 20 or more employees are likely to be made redundant and the employer is
collectively consulting, any redundancy is unlikely to have been fair, unless the
employer can show it knew at the time that any consultation was bound to
have absolutely no effect on the result, and to be utterly useless (*Polkey v AE
Dayton Services Ltd* [1988] AC 344, HL).

What should be said at the first consultation meeting? The employer should con- **8.80**
tact the employees in the pool where people may be selected for redundancy,
warning them of the situation and inviting them to consultation. During consultation with an employee, the employer should explain:

(a) the selection criteria;

(b) why he has (or, if the best practice suggested at para **8.78** is adopted, he has
not) provisionally been selected in accordance with those criteria. He may be
required to show the employee his grading, but will not normally be required
to show anyone else's grades (save possibly in anonymized form—see para
8.88 under Step 1);

(c) to the extent known, the likely amount and make-up of any termination
payment;

(d) what alternative jobs are available (see paras **8.90–8.99**).

What should the employer ask the employee? He should ask: **8.81**

(a) if there are any other jobs for which the individual would like to be considered
and discuss the individual's suitability for such job(s);

(b) for comments and observations, for example, on the applicability of the selection criteria to the employee, or on the availability of alternative employment.

8.82 What should the employer say about alternative jobs within the establishment in question and in any associated companies of the employer? If they are suitable for the employee (for example, they do not involve dissimilar status, pay, skills, or location, see also paras **8.90–8.99**) the employee should be offered the job, subject to a trial period of at least four weeks if the new job is not identical to the employee's previous one. The trial period can be extended by agreement, before it commences, but only for a specified period, and to allow extra time for training. If the employer tries unilaterally to change the employee's terms, at common law the trial period is a 'reasonable period' which may be longer than four weeks. If an alternative position is too dissimilar to be regarded as a suitable alternative for the individual employee, the individual should nevertheless be informed of the vacancy and should be asked whether he or she wishes to be considered for it, even if acceptance seems unlikely (eg because the other position is much lower paid).

8.83 What statutory procedures must be followed? If the employer is proposing to make redundant fewer than 20 employees at an establishment within a three-month period, he must follow the statutory dismissal and disciplinary procedures. Failure to do so will, for dismissals carried out before the statutory procedures are repealed in April 2009, render any dismissal automatically unfair (ERA 1996, s 98A (see para **8.89**)). Any damages to be awarded will, except in exceptional circumstances, be increased by 10–50 per cent (EA 2002, s 31). The procedures, which should preferably take place after the initial consultation meeting, are:

(a) The employer should write to the employee telling him that he is at risk of redundancy, and either referring to the earlier consultation meeting or setting out, briefly, the reasons why. In addition, the employer should set out the matters listed at Step 1 in para **8.88**, or should refer to the fact that those issues were covered at the earlier meeting. In the letter, the employer should invite the employee to a meeting to discuss the matter;

(b) There must be sufficient gap between the employee's receipt of the letter and the meeting for the employee to have an opportunity to consider his response to all the information he has been given;

(c) If the employee would like to bring a colleague or union official to the meeting, he must be allowed to do so;

(d) At the meeting, the employer should
  • Inform the employee of the present position regarding the number of redundancies in the relevant pool;
  • discuss any of the employee's comments on the application of the selection criteria;
  • update the employee on any alternative jobs with the employer or any associated employer (see paras **8.90–8.99**);
  • outline the proposed termination payment;

- explain that anyone made redundant will be allowed reasonable time off to seek alternative employment;
(e) The employer must consider the employee's views properly and genuinely, and reach a view (see section **8G**—paras **8.105–8.110**);
(f) After the meeting, the employer must tell the employee (preferably in writing) its decision, and that he has a right of appeal;
(g) If the employee wants to appeal, he must inform the employer;
(h) The employer must then write to the employee inviting him to attend an appeal meeting;
(i) If the employee would like to bring a colleague or union official to the meeting, he must be allowed to do so;
(j) The employee must take all reasonable steps to attend the meeting, which must be held reasonably quickly after the employee notifies the employer of his wish to appeal;
(k) The employer may dismiss the employee before the appeal takes place;
(l) The appeal meeting must take place, exploring the employee's concerns;
(m) After the appeal meeting, the employer must tell the employee its decision (preferably in writing).

8.84 If the employer is in dire financial circumstances and must act quickly, for example, to find a purchaser, must it follow the procedures? Circumstances must be particularly exceptional before no procedures are followed, because

(a) failure to follow the procedure where fewer than 20 are likely to be made redundant at an establishment during a three-month period will render the dismissal automatically unfair—there is no exemption for exceptional circumstances. However, if the circumstances are truly exceptional, the statutory uplift may not be applied to any award;
(b) where 20 or more are likely to be made redundant at an establishment during a three-month period, the appropriate collective consultation may only be set aside if there are special circumstances rendering consultation not reasonably practicable;

When the statutory dismissal and disciplinary procedures are repealed, probably in April 2009, lack of consultation may not be fatal to an employer facing an unfair redundancy claim (*Warner v Adnet Ltd* [1998] IRLR 394).

8.85 What happens if the employee unreasonably fails to participate in the statutory dismissal procedure, or has not submitted an appeal? If so, and if he wins an unfair dismissal claim, his damages will, save in exceptional circumstances, be reduced by 10–50 per cent (EA 2002, s 31).

8.86 Was the consultation process reasonable or was it a sham? If the employee can demonstrate it was a sham, for example because the employer had reached a final but not inevitable decision before the process began, he is likely to have been unfairly dismissed (*Rowell v Hubbard Group Services Ltd* [1995] IRLR 195).

Commentary

8.87 The employer must consult with each individual employee whom it proposes to make redundant before any decision is finalized. This is to make sure the individual understands why redundancies are proposed, and why he is being selected for redundancy. Even if the redundancies are subject to collective consultation, the employer should still conduct individual consultation with the employees, for example about available alternative employment. Failure to do so (at least while the statutory procedures are in place) will render any subsequent dismissal unfair (see para **8.88**).

8.88 Where an employer proposes to make fewer redundancies than the 20 which trigger collective consultation obligations (see TULR(C)A 1992, s 188(1) and (1A)), it is obliged for all redundancies which take place before the procedures are appealed in April 2009 to go through a formal dismissal procedure with each employee (Employment Act 2002 (Dispute Resolution) Regulations 2004, regs 3 and 4(1)(b); EA 2002, s 30). The standard dismissal procedure set out in EA 2002, Sch 2, Part 2 is:

Step 1

(1) The employer must write to the employee setting out the circumstances which lead him to contemplate dismissing the employee (ie that it is contemplating making the employee redundant) and invite the employee to a meeting to discuss it.

(2) The information provided before the Step 2 meeting (ie either in writing or orally) must be sufficient to enable the employee to give a considered and informed response to the proposal. It must include:

(a) reasons why there is a redundancy situation;

(b) (if relevant) selection criteria, and the employee's performance against those selection criteria. It is not necessary for the purposes of the statutory procedure to produce the performance records of other employees, although it would be sensible to have the information to hand in an anonymized format (*Alexander and Another v Bridgen Enterprises Ltd* [2006] IRLR 422). The employee must be given sufficient information to understand and challenge his selection, but there is no prescriptive rule on exactly what he must be given to enable him to do this (*Davies v Farnborough College of Technology* [2008] IRLR 14, EAT).

Failure to consult an employee who has recently moved to a commercially risky and now potentially redundant role about the possibility of moving back to her old job does not necessarily make the dismissal unfair (*Hachette Filipacchi UK Ltd v Johnson* [2006] IDS Employment Law Brief 804).

Step 2

(1) The employer should invite the employee to a meeting to discuss the position, before any notice of redundancy is given.

(2) The employee may be accompanied by a colleague or trade union official (Employment Relations Act 1999, s 10; TULR(C)A 1992, s 119).

(3) Following the meeting the employer must inform the employee of the decision (see paras **8.105–8.110** regarding making the decision), and notify him that he has a right of appeal.

Step 3

(1) If the employee exercises the right of appeal, the employer must invite the employee to an appeal meeting.

(2) The employee may be accompanied at the meeting, as in Step 2.

(3) After the meeting, the employer must inform the employee of his decision.

If the employer does not follow the procedure, and the employee wins the claim, **8.89** the dismissal is automatically unfair (ERA 1996, s 98A). This is the case even where dismissal would inevitably have resulted had the full procedure been followed (*Wareing v Stone Cladding International Limited* [2007] EAT 0498/06). The amount of the claim will (except in exceptional circumstances) be increased by 10–50 per cent (in all cases subject to any statutory maximum award that may apply to the claim). If the employee fails to comply with the procedure (for example by unreasonably failing to attend a meeting) or does not appeal, but wins the action, the award will (again, save in exceptional circumstances) be reduced by 10–50 per cent (EA 2002, s 31). For redundancy dismissals occurring after 1 April 2009, employers must follow the ACAS Code of Practice on Disciplinary and Grievance Procedures (see para **7.246**).

F. Alternative Employment

CHECKLIST

Are there any vacancies at the workplace in question or at any other workplaces **8.90** within the company or its associated companies? If so:

(a) The employer must find out what vacancies exist;

(b) The employer must give the employee the available information about the proposed salary and benefits attaching to the alternatives;

(c) The employer should consider whether any vacancies will be suitable for any of the employees provisionally selected for redundancy;

(d) The employer should consider whether the retraining of potentially redundant employees to fit any identified vacancies is a viable option and if it is, retraining should be the subject of consultation with the union or the individual.

If not, the dismissal may be unfair (*Vokes Ltd v Bear* [1974] ICR 1; *Avonmouth Construction Co Ltd v Shipway* [1979] IRLR 14; *Fisher v Hoopoe Finance Ltd* [2005] IDS Employment Law Brief 784) (see para **8.100**).

8.91 Might there be any vacancies in future? An employer with a large staff turnover should consider whether any vacancies are likely to arise in the near future. If they are, consideration should be given to postponing some or all of the redundancies. Any new vacancy must (if it is to be effective in negating any redundancy) be offered before termination of employment and must commence within four weeks of that termination.

8.92 What happens if there is a vacancy? If a vacancy arises while employees are on notice, that vacancy should be offered to a suitable employee who was the last in the relevant category to be selected for redundancy. If a new role is created by the employer, it should review whether it is suitable for any employees to be made redundant and only if it is not, should it be offered to the workforce as a whole. In addition, the selection process for the new role must at least meet some of the criteria of fairness, even if not to the same degree as a redundancy selection procedure (*Ralph Martindale & Co Ltd v Harris* [2008] EAT 0166/07).

8.93 When should any alternative job start? If suitable alternative employment is offered before the employee's employment terminates, to start within four weeks of the termination date, there will normally be no entitlement to a redundancy payment unless the employee reasonably refuses the alternative offer, either before or during a four-week trial period (see para **8.95**).

8.94 Is the alternative employment suitable (see paras **8.101–8.102**)? Employment is unlikely to be suitable if, on an objective level:

(a) it is at lower pay;
(b) it has significantly different hours or shifts;
(c) it involves a significant drop in status; or
(d) it does not allow the employee to practice the skills he uses in a particular trade or profession.

8.95 Was it reasonable for the employee to refuse any suitable job offer? If employment is suitable, the employee may still act reasonably in refusing the job (whether before or during the trial period, but not after) if, looking at the employee subjectively:

(a) it is much further away from his home than his original job and the employer makes no concessions (eg a travel allowance and altered working times to suit travel arrangements) to compensate for this;

(b) the offer of a new job is made so late that the employee has already made alternative arrangements;

(c) health and safety conditions make the new job unsafe, either in general or because of the employee's personal condition;

(d) the job could involve the employee in health or stress problems (eg offering someone a job in a department in which someone works who has previously harassed or bullied him);

(e) the job involves more expensive housing in the vicinity of the new job than near his original job;

(f) the new job involves more anti-social hours than his original job (eg making it more difficult to arrange childcare);

(g) the new job requires a change of skills.

Was it unreasonable for the employee to refuse any suitable job offer? The **8.96** employee will probably be acting unreasonably if he rejects the offer because:

(a) the new job is in a contracting or recessionary industry;

(b) the new job is not likely to last for more than 12 to 18 months.

Did the employee unreasonably refuse any offers of suitable alternative employ- **8.97** ment (see para **8.96**)? If so, he will not be entitled to a redundancy payment (ERA 1996, s 141).

How long does the employee have to try out an alternative position? Four weeks, **8.98** or any longer period agreed between the employer and employee. If the employee resigns after the trial period has ended, it will be a simple resignation (*Optical Express Limited v Williams* [2007] IRLR 936, EAT).

Was it appropriate for the employer to consider 'bumping' so that an employee in **8.99** a potentially redundant role would be given another's job (see para **8.38**)? If not, there may be circumstances where this failure makes the dismissal unfair (*Thomas & Betts Manufacturing Ltd v Harding* [1980] IRLR 255).

Commentary

The employer also has a duty, if someone is provisionally selected for redundancy, **8.100** to see whether there is any other role that might suit that particular employee, not only with the employer but also with any associated company of the employer

(*Vokes Ltd v Bear* [1974] ICR 1). If this requirement is ignored, a dismissal is normally rendered unfair. If there are jobs, even if they are of lower status or carry lower wages than those which apply to the employee's present job, the prospect of moving to the alternative employment should nevertheless be raised. It is sensible for an employer to inform the employee of the proposed salary and benefits of any alternative position—failure to do so may make the dismissal unfair (*Fisher v Hoopoe Finance Ltd* [2005] IDS Employment Law Brief 784). Employees on maternity leave must be offered any suitable alternative jobs if their normal job is to be made redundant (see para **8.109**). Failure to consult an employee who had recently moved to a commercially risky and now potentially redundant role about the possibility of moving back to her old job does not necessarily make the dismissal unfair (*Hachette Filipacchi UK Ltd v Johnson* [2006] IDS Employment Law Brief 804). If there is no consideration given to alternative employment, but the employer can show it would not have appointed the employee to the vacant position in any event, the decision to make the employee redundant might still be regarded as fair if the breaches in procedure were not so serious as to make the decision to dismiss unreasonable (ERA 2006, s 98A and *Loosley v Social Action for Health* [2007] UK EAT/0378/06).

8.101 If the employer is able to identify suitable alternative work, either within its own company or with an associated company, which is substantially similar to the employee's previous position and commands a similar wage package, it is to the employer's advantage to offer such a job to the prospectively redundant employee. The job offer, which should be made before termination, to start within four weeks of the termination of the redundant job, is then generally subject to a four-week trial period (though the trial period may be extended if the employee has further training). If the employee accepts the job offer and continues to work after the trial period, there is no redundancy. If, however, he refuses a suitable job offer (either immediately or during the trial period) he will lose his right to a redundancy payment unless he can show that it was reasonable for him to reject the offer. If the job is not suitable, or if the employee acts reasonably in refusing it (respectively an objective and a subjective test) the employee will still be redundant unless he accepts the job offer and continues to work normally.

8.102 For the offer to be suitable, it must be made (orally or in writing) by the original employer or an associated employer before the employee's employment actually terminates. The new post should start within four weeks of the ending of the old one and, if not on the same terms and conditions, it is subject to an objective test of suitability. In determining this, the tribunal will review issues such as pay, status, location, and whether the new job is within the employee's skill set. If the terms and conditions differ at all from the original contract, the employee is allowed a trial period of four weeks to assess the new role, although this period may be extended by agreement. If it is not extended, and the employee resigns after the trial period is over, this will be treated as a simple resignation, not as a redundancy (*Optical Express Limited v Williams* [2007] IRLR 936, EAT).

If the terms of the new employment are suitable and the employee unreasonably **8.103** refuses it, either immediately or during the trial period, he will not be entitled to a redundancy payment.

Whether the employee is reasonable in refusing a job offer is a subjective test, **8.104** viewed from the employee's perspective. For example, an employee might reasonably refuse a job with apparently reasonable hours if it will prevent him or her from complying with childcare arrangements.

G. Making the Decision

CHECKLIST

Has the selection process identified individuals **8.105**

(a) performing unique roles which are to be made redundant; or

(b) in a pool of employees performing a role, some of whom are to be made redundant, who performed worst against the selection criteria

for whom no alternative employment can be found? If so, once the consultation processes are complete, they may now be given notice terminating their employment by reason of redundancy.

How should notice be given? Notice should be in writing, and should set out **8.106** how any redundancy payment is calculated. If there is a collective consultation, it should be given after the conclusion of the consultation process, or following the minimum number of days required for the consultation (see paras **8.49–8.52**). If there are fewer than 20 to be made redundant at an establishment within three months, then the statutory procedures will apply (at least until April 2009 when they are likely to be repealed), and the employee must be offered the right to appeal (see para **8.83**). The notice may:

(a) require the employee to work out his notice; or

(b) terminate the employment immediately, paying money in lieu of notice. This route should not be taken if the contract does not allow for immediate termination upon a payment in lieu of notice, and the employer wants to rely on any post-termination provisions in the contract of employment (eg restrictive covenants). This is because the employer would be regarded as being in breach of the contract of employment, and therefore may no longer able to rely on any of its terms (see para **8.113**).

8

Redundancy

8.107 Was the employee neither asked to work out his notice period nor paid salary in lieu? If neither, he may have a claim against his employer for breach of contract. If the amount is less than £25,000 the claim may be brought in an employment tribunal under art 3 of the Employment Tribunal (Employment Tribunals Extension of Jurisdiction) (England and Wales) Order 1994. Otherwise, it should be brought in the High Court or County Court (see paras **7.03–7.37**).

8.108 Was the employee selected for redundancy for an automatically unfair reason? Automatically unfair reasons are set out at para **7.94**. If so, the redundancy will be automatically unfair (ERA 1996, s 105—see para **8.111**).

8.109 Was the employee absent on maternity leave? If, while she is on maternity leave, an employee's job becomes redundant, her employer, or an associated employer, must offer her alternative employment if any suitable vacancy exists. The offer must:

(a) be made before the old employment ends;
(b) start immediately after the old employment ends;
(c) involve suitable and appropriate work for the employee to do;
(d) not be on substantially less favourable terms than the old employment.

If such a vacancy exists and the employer does not comply with these provisions, the employee will be entitled to claim that she has been automatically unfairly dismissed (MAPLE 1999, regs 10 and 20 (see para **8.115**)).

8.110 Did the position regarding the potential redundancy, or any suitable alternative positions, change between the date on which notice was given and the date when the redundancy takes effect? If so, and if the employer does not take action which might allow the employee to remain employed, the dismissal may be regarded as unfair (*Dyke v Hereford and Worcester County Council* [1989] ICR 800).

Commentary

8.111 Once employees have been selected for redundancy, and all individual and collective consultation processes are complete, the employer may notify the employee that his employment is to be terminated by reason of redundancy. The selection must have been made strictly in accordance with the relevant criteria, and not for any automatically unfair reasons, or the redundancy will be automatically unfair (ERA 1996, s 105). Automatically unfair reasons are set out at para 7.94, and include reasons such as that the employee has taken part in trade union activities or has made a protected disclosure. If an employee might potentially be able to accuse the employer of having selected him for redundancy because of one of these reasons, the employer should take particular care to ensure that the reason is only performance against the selected criteria, and that this is well documented.

Where the employer is under a duty to consult representatives collectively before **8.112** implementing any redundancies, notice should not be given until the minimum consultation period has expired, unless agreement on the process has been reached before then (*Junk v Kuhnel* [2005] IRLR 210, ECJ).

An employee may be required to: **8.113**
(a) work out his notice;
(b) go on garden leave (if the contract allows); or
(c) be required to leave, say, immediately with a payment in lieu of notice.

If the employee is asked to leave immediately, the employer should check that there is a clause in the employee's contract entitling it to terminate the employment without notice, so long as a payment in lieu is made ('a PILON clause'). If there is no such provision, then terminating the contract immediately could be a repudiatory breach of contract which the employee can accept and then argue that all post-termination provisions fall away. This is a concept first posed by the House of Lords a century ago in *General Billposting Co Ltd v Atkinson* [1909] AC 118, HL. There have been many cases on the concept since, but so far, contrary to the expectation of many commentators, they have upheld the principle. If there is no PILON clause, and if the employment contract contains post-termination provisions, such as restrictive covenants, upon which the employer wishes to rely, then the employer should either place the employee on garden leave (but only if there is a provision in the contract allowing it to do so, otherwise this, too, could be a repudiatory breach of contract) or enter into a compromise agreement (see para 7.353) with the employee in which the employee expressly agrees to be bound by the post-termination provisions.

If the employer does not require the employee to work out his notice, or **8.114** make a payment in lieu of notice, it will be in breach of contract. The employee can sue for payment in lieu of notice in the High Court or County Court or, if the amount due is £25,000 or less, in the Employment Tribunal (Employment Tribunals Extension of Jurisdiction) (England and Wales) Order 1994.

When an employee on maternity leave has exercised her right to return but is **8.115** not permitted to return to work, she is treated as continuously employed until her notified date of return, and as dismissed on that date. If she is dismissed by reason of redundancy while on maternity leave, and she was not (before her old employment ends) offered alternative employment if any suitable vacancy exists, she will have been automatically unfairly dismissed (Maternity and Parental Leave etc. Regulations 1999, SI 1999/3312, regs 10 and 20).

H. Calculation of Redundancy Payment

CHECKLIST

8.116 Is the individual entitled to a redundancy payment? He is not if he:

(a) is not an employee of the relevant company;

(b) is aged 65 or over (or the normal retirement age for the job in question, if lower);

(c) is under 18 years old;

(d) has been continuously employed by the employer for less than two years (including any statutory notice period due) before the EDT (ie the termination date or, if no or inadequate statutory notice given, termination date plus this notice (ERA 1996, ss 145(5), 86, and 155) —see para **7.59**. For continuity of employment see para **7.58**). Weeks spent overseas or on strike do not count towards the total period, but do not break continuity;

(e) has not been dismissed (whether by the employer, by expiry of a fixed-term contract, or in circumstances of constructive dismissal);

(f) has been dismissed by reason of misconduct (save because of taking part in legitimate industrial action) before the employment terminates (provided that, if any notice is given or if any payment in lieu of notice is made, it is accompanied by a statement that the misconduct is so serious the employer would be entitled summarily to terminate the employment);

(g) has accepted alternative employment (whether or not suitable) offered, before the employment terminated, either by the employer or by an associated company of the employer, and has continued in that employment after any trial period (four weeks unless the parties agree a longer period) has ended (see paras **8.90–8.94**);

(h) has unreasonably refused suitable alternative employment offered before the termination of employment and begun or to begin within four weeks of the termination date, either with the employer or with an associated company of the employer (see paras **8.95–8.98**);

(i) has left the employer before the termination date is fixed;

(j) has been transferred to another employer who has acquired the business for which he was working in circumstances where the Transfer of Undertakings (Protection of Employment) Regulations 2006 apply, in which case he will be deemed to be employed by the new owner, with full continuity of service, from the date the transfer takes place (see Chapter 9);

(k) has resigned during his notice period, and the employer has required him to withdraw the notice and has warned that if he leaves the employer will contest entitlement to a redundancy payment (note in these circumstances, some redundancy payment may be due);

(l) has been notified by the employer of his entitlement, within one week of the termination date, to receive a secure pension of at least one-third of his annual pay;

(m) is abroad at the date of dismissal (unless he ordinarily worked in Great Britain in the sense that his work base was in Great Britain);

(n) normally worked abroad (unless on the termination date he is in Great Britain on the instructions of his employer);

(o) is employed by an overseas government; or

(p) is a Crown servant, member of the armed forces, share fisherman, or domestic servant where the employer is a close relation.

Amount of Redundancy Payment

A redundancy payment is the product of weekly pay, age, and length of service.   **8.117**

How do you calculate pay? To calculate the gross pay an employee is contractually   **8.118** entitled to receive for the normal working week, including the value or proportionate value of any bonus, allowance, or commission if they are non-discretionary:

(a) For weekly or monthly waged employees, it will be their standard weekly wage, without tax or other deductions. Overtime will only be added if the employer has a contractual commitment to make specific overtime payments each week.

(b) For time workers, multiply the hourly rate by the normal number of hours worked.

(c) For piece workers, multiply the normal number of hours worked by the average hourly rate of remuneration over the 12 weeks before the termination date (excluding weeks when no remuneration was earned).

(d) For shift or rota workers, multiply the average number of hours worked by the average hourly rate of remuneration over the 12 weeks before the termination date (excluding any weeks when no remuneration was earned).

(e) If the employee is paid less than the national minimum wage, the award will be calculated as if the employee were receiving the national minimum wage (£5.52 per hour for those aged 22 or over, £4.60 per hour for those aged 18–21, and £3.40 for those under 18 but no longer of compulsory school age with effect from 1 October 2007 rising respectively to £5.73, £4.77, and £3.53 per hour with effect from 1 October 2008).

How do you calculate length of service? To calculate the length of service in   **8.119** completed years of employment, adding on statutory notice periods if employment was terminated without notice:

(a) Include any period of employment with a previous employer if the identity of the employer changed as a result of a transfer of undertaking or the previous employers were associated employers;

(b) Anyone on maternity leave should be treated as having been employed until her notified date of return.

8.120 How do you calculate the actual payment? To work out the appropriate redundancy payment multiply one week's gross pay (subject to the statutory maximum which, for dismissals after 1 February 2009 is £350, and for dismissals between 1 February 2008 and 31 January 2009 was £330) by a factor depending upon age and number of completed years of service. The factor is:

(a) For every year during the whole of which the employee was aged 41 or over—1.5;

(b) For every year during the whole of which the employee was aged between 22 and 40—1;

(c) For every year during the whole of which the employee was aged below 21—0.5.

8.121 The multipliers are set out in the Ready Reckoner produced by BERR for calculating the number of weeks' pay due to the employee as a redundancy payment, which is reproduced at para **8.137** by kind permission of HM Government and which is also available at <http://www.berr.gov.uk/employment/employment-legislation/employment-guidance/page33157.html>.

8.122 If the employee is contractually entitled (either expressly or by a notorious and certain custom and practice—see para **8.123**) to an enhanced redundancy payment, this should be paid to him. To the extent that it is less than £30,000, it is likely to be tax-free.

Enhanced Redundancy Schemes

8.123 Does the employer have a contractual enhanced scheme? Some employers have contractual redundancy schemes, paying employees an additional sum on redundancy, normally by reference to length of service. These often appear in staff manuals or collective agreements with unions (see para **8.133**). If contractual, employers should pay redundant employees in accordance with the scheme. Frequently, employers make a habit of making enhanced redundancy payments. If these payments are made pursuant to a notorious and certain custom and practice, then they may assume contractual status. Factors which need to be borne in mind when considering whether a redundancy payment policy has become contractually binding include:

(a) whether the policy is 'reasonable, notorious and certain';

(b) whether the policy has been drawn to the attention of the employee, and if so was it in such a way that it indicated that the employer intended to be contractually bound by the policy;

(c) whether the policy has been followed consistently and without exception on every occasion where there have been redundancies for a substantial period;

(d) how many times the has policy been followed;

(e) whether payments have been made under the policy as a matter of course, or only as a result of specific negotiations (*Albion Automotive Ltd v Walker and Others* [2002] EWCA Civ 946);

(f) whether the nature of communication of the policy supported the inference that the employers intended to be contractually bound;

(g) whether the policy was adopted by agreement;

(h) whether the employees had a reasonable expectation that the enhanced payment would be made;

(i) whether the terms were consistently applied.

How does an employer avoid enhanced redundancy payments becoming contractual entitlements? Methods include: **8.124**

(a) expressly stating in a redundancy policy that payments are discretionary;

(b) expressly considering whether or not to make the enhanced payment at the outset of every redundancy exercise, and evidencing this in writing;

(c) making it clear during collective negotiations about redundancies that any decision to make enhanced payments applies only in this situation;

(d) expressly stating when payments are made that this is not intended to set a precedent for the future.

[Note: following a transfer of undertaking, the policy followed in the past by the transferor will be relevant in deciding whether an enhanced redundancy policy has assumed contractual status.]

Does the enhanced policy offend against the principles of age discrimination? **8.125**

(a) Is the enhancement calculated in different ways for those of different ages or lengths of service? If so, it will be discriminatory on the grounds of age;

(b) Does the enhanced element use the normal age/length of service requirements (see para **8.120**) as its base? If so, it may be legitimate;

(c) Are the only variations to the normal requirements one or more of the following:
   - that the week's pay is not subject to the statutory maximum; and/or
   - that each length of service number used to multiply the week's pay is multiplied by the same number, being more than 1; and/or
   - that the final number reached is multiplied for all employees by a number greater than 1.

If so, then the enhancement will not be discriminatory. If it contains any other elements, it is likely to be potentially discriminatory and the employer will need to be able to justify its provisions.

Practical Arrangements

8.126 The employer should give the employee a statement showing how the redundancy payment has been calculated.

8.127 The employer should calculate any money due to the employee in lieu of notice. If not paid pursuant to a payment in lieu of notice clause and if total payment to the employee is less than £30,000, the net amount due to the employee may be paid. To the extent the notice payment brings the total payment above £30,000, the excess will need to be 'grossed up' (see para **7.323**).

8.128 The employer should pay the employee the payments due. Payments made on termination of £30,000 or less will generally be free of tax unless paid pursuant to an express contractual entitlement (other than an enhanced redundancy payment scheme) or unless the employee is approaching retirement. Therefore, if the contract of employment contains a clause entitling the employer to terminate the employee's contract upon making a payment in lieu of notice, the notice payment will be subject to tax. To be consistent with this approach, employees should be paid after any P45 has been issued. It is wise for the employer to retain a receipt from the employee and to seek the employee's acknowledgement that the sums are paid in settlement of all claims the employee may have against the employer, preferably via a compromise agreement (see para **7.354**).

8.129 If the employer is insolvent, the National Insurance Fund (administered by the Insolvency Service) will pay (with maxima applying for dismissals after 1 February 2009):

(a) up to eight weeks' unpaid wages for each individual (up to a maximum of £350 per week);

(b) pay during the statutory notice period (subject to a maximum of £350 per week);

(c) up to six weeks' pay in lieu of holiday entitlement (up to £350 per week);

(d) any basic award due following an unfair dismissal claim;

(e) reimbursement of apprenticeship fees;

(f) payment of any unpaid employer's pension contributions during the 12 months prior to insolvency;

(g) a statutory redundancy payment (note, this is not payable if a sum is paid under para **8.129(d)**);

(h) a redundancy payment under a collective agreement approved under the collective contracting-out provisions (ERA 1996, s 157) (see para **8.136**).

Commentary

8.130 The redundancy payment is calculated according to a fixed formula. Provided that the employee has been employed for a minimum of two years (or would have been if given statutory notice (ERA 1996, ss 155 and 145(5)) the employee will receive a redundancy payment calculated by multiplying his weekly gross remuneration (subject to a maximum payment, which, for dismissals after 1 February 2008 is set at £330 and for dismissals after 1 February 2009 is £350) by a factor determined in accordance with age and length of service. Length of service means the period from commencement of employment to the Effective Date of Termination (see para **7.59** for the definition of Effective Date of Termination and para **8.137** for BERR's Ready Reckoner).

If the employee is paid less than the national minimum wage, the award will be **8.131** calculated as if the employee were receiving the national minimum wage (£5.73 per hour for those aged 22 or over; £4.77 per hour for those aged 18–21; and £3.53 per hour for 16 and 17-year-olds who are not apprentices and are over the school leaving age with effect from 1 October 2008 (with the equivalent figures for the year ended 30 September 2008 being £5.52, £4.60, and £3.40)).

In addition to the redundancy payment, each employee is entitled either to work **8.132** out his contractual notice period, or to be paid money in lieu of notice.

Some employers have contractually enhanced redundancy payment programmes. **8.133** These may be included:

(a) in the employment contract itself;

(b) in a collective agreement incorporated into the employment contract, even if that collective agreement had expired before the redundancy took effect (*Framptons Ltd v Badger and Others* [2006] EAT 0138/06/0906) and even if the policy expressly states it is not part of the employees' contract if the policy has been followed without exception for a substantial period to such an extent that it has acquired contractual status by custom and practice (*Peries v Wirefast Ltd* [2006] EAT 0245/06); or

(c) a staff handbook (*Keeley v Fosroc International Ltd* [2006] IRLR 961, CA).

Employers may regularly pay enhanced redundancy payments, and if these have **8.134** been consistently applied so that a custom and practice is established, future employees may have a contractual right to equivalent payments on redundancy.

Enhancing the statutory minimum redundancy payments will not be regarded as **8.135** age discrimination so long as the amount an employer offers to all the different employees is calculated in the same way, eg by applying the same multiplicand (Employment Equality (Age) Regulations 2006, reg 33). The only automatically legitimate enhancements to the basic formula, which must be applied equally to all redundant employees, are:

(a) To increase the amount of a maximum week's pay used in the calculation to a number in excess of the statutory maximum, or to actual pay; and/or

8

Redundancy

(b) To multiply the appropriate amount allowed for each year of service by a number more than 1; and/or

(c) To multiply the final figure by a number more than 1.

8.136 Where the employer is insolvent, the Insolvency Service (part of BERR) will pay individuals certain amounts due to them out of the National Insurance Fund (ERA 1996, Parts XI and XII). Employees should fill in form RP1 (available on the Internet) and send it in to their local Redundancy Payments Office.

I. Ready Reckoner for Calculating the Number of Weeks' Redundancy Pay Due

8.137 To use the table:

(a) Read off employee's age and number of complete years' service. The table will then show how many weeks' pay the employee is entitled to.

(b) The week's pay will be actual gross pay, but subject to a maximum of £350 for dismissals after 1 February 2009 and £330 for dismissals between 1 February 2008 and 31 January 2009.

Appendix: Ready Reckoner for Calculating the Number of Weeks' Pay Due (pp 301–303)

Table of statutory redundancy entitlement—Redundancies on or after 1.10.06

		Service (years)																		
		2	3	4	5	6	7	8	9	10	11	12	13	14	15	16	17	18	19	20
Age (years)	18	1	1½	2																
	19	1	1½	2	2½															
	20	1	1½	2	2½	3														
	21	1	1½	2	2½	3	3½													
	22	1	1½	2	2½	3	3½	4												
	23	1½	2	2½	3	3½	4	4½	5											
	24	2	2½	3	3½	4	4½	5	5½	6										
	25	2	3	3½	4	4½	5	5½	6	6½	7									
	26	2	3	4	4½	5	5½	6	6½	7	7½	8								
	27	2	3	4	5	5½	6	6½	7	7½	8	8½	9							
	28	2	3	4	5	6	6½	7	7½	8	8½	9	9½	10						
	29	2	3	4	5	6	7	7½	8	8½	9	9½	10	10½	11					
	30	2	3	4	5	6	7	8	8½	9	9½	10	10½	11	11½	12				
	31	2	3	4	5	6	7	8	9	9½	10	10½	11	11½	12	12½	13			
	32	2	3	4	5	6	7	8	9	10	10½	11	11½	12	12½	13	13½	14		
	33	2	3	4	5	6	7	8	9	10	11	11½	12	12½	13	13½	14	14½	15	
	34	2	3	4	5	6	7	8	9	10	11	12	12½	13	13½	14	14½	15	15½	16
	35	2	3	4	5	6	7	8	9	10	11	12	13	13½	14	14½	15	15½	16	16½
	36	2	3	4	5	6	7	8	9	10	11	12	13	14	14½	15	15½	16	16½	17

Table of statutory redundancy entitlement—Redundancies on or after 1.10.06 (Continued)

	Service (years)																		
	2	3	4	5	6	7	8	9	10	11	12	13	14	15	16	17	18	19	20
37	2	3	4	5	6	7	8	9	10	11	12	13	14	15	15½	16	16½	17	17½
38	2	3	4	5	6	7	8	9	10	11	12	13	14	15	16	16½	17	17½	18
39	2	3	4	5	6	7	8	9	10	11	12	13	14	15	16	17	17½	18	18½
40	2	3	4	5	6	7	8	9	10	11	12	13	14	15	16	17	18	18½	19
41	2	3	4	5	6	7	8	9	10	11	12	13	14	15	16	17	18	19	19½
42	2½	3½	4½	5½	6½	7½	8½	9½	10½	11½	12½	13½	14½	15½	16½	17½	18½	19½	20½
43	3	4	5	6	7	8	9	10	11	12	13	14	15	16	17	18	19	20	21
44	3	4½	5½	6½	7½	8½	9½	10½	11½	12½	13½	14½	15½	16½	17½	18½	19½	20½	21½
45	3	4½	6	7	8	9	10	11	12	13	14	15	16	17	18	19	20	21	22
46	3	4½	6	7½	8½	9½	10½	11½	12½	13½	14½	15½	16½	17½	18½	19½	20½	21½	22½
47	3	4½	6	7½	9	10	11	12	13	14	15	16	17	18	19	20	21	22	23
48	3	4½	6	7½	9	10½	11½	12½	13½	14½	15½	16½	17½	18½	19½	20½	21½	22½	23½
49	3	4½	6	7½	9	10½	12	13	14	15	16	17	18	19	20	21	22	23	24
50	3	4½	6	7½	9	10½	12	13½	14½	15½	16½	17½	18½	19½	20½	21½	22½	23½	24½
51	3	4½	6	7½	9	10½	12	13½	15	16	17	18	19	20	21	22	23	24	25
52	3	4½	6	7½	9	10½	12	13½	15	16½	17½	18½	19½	20½	21½	22½	23½	24½	25½
53	3	4½	6	7½	9	10½	12	13½	15	16½	18	19	20	21	22	23	24	25	26
54	3	4½	6	7½	9	10½	12	13½	15	16½	18	19½	20½	21½	22½	23½	24½	25½	26½

Age																			
55	3	4½	6	7½	9	10½	12	13½	15	16½	18	19½	21	22	23	24	25	26	27
56	3	4½	6	7½	9	10½	12	13½	15	16½	18	19½	21	22½	23½	24½	25½	26½	27½
57	3	4½	6	7½	9	10½	12	13½	15	16½	18	19½	21	22½	24	25	26	27	28
57	3	4½	6	7½	9	10½	12	13½	15	16½	18	19½	21	22½	24	25	26	27	28
58	3	4½	6	7½	9	10½	12	13½	15	16½	18	19½	21	22½	24	25½	26½	27½	28½
59	3	4½	6	7½	9	10½	12	13½	15	16½	18	19½	21	22½	24	25½	27	28	29
60	3	4½	6	7½	9	10½	12	13½	15	16½	18	19½	21	22½	24	25½	27	28½	29½
61*	3	4½	6	7½	9	10½	12	13½	15	16½	18	19½	21	22½	24	25½	27	28½	30

* The same figures should be used when calculating the redundancy payment for a person aged 61 and above.

8

Redundancy

9

TRANSFER OF UNDERTAKINGS

A. Introduction

9.01 When an undertaking is transferred by one party to another, the Transfer of Undertakings (Protection of Employment) Regulations 2006, SI 2006/246 (TUPE 2006) operate so as to preserve, to a substantial extent, the employee's statutory and contractual employment rights which he had before the transfer. TUPE 2006 implement Council Directive 2001/23/EC (the 'Acquired Rights Directive'). They revoke the Transfer of Undertakings (Protection of Employment) Regulations 1981 (TUPE 1981). Although they are similar to TUPE 1981, they take advantage of certain policy options conferred by the Directive. TUPE 2006 applies to any relevant transfer that takes place on or after 6 April 2006. The Government has issued guidance to accompany TUPE 2006: 'Employment Rights on the Transfer of an Undertaking—A Guide to the 2006 TUPE Regulations for Employees, Employers and Representatives' (the 'Government Guidance'). Whilst this is not legally binding, it will no doubt be referred to by the courts and employment tribunals.

9.02 The checklist below is relevant to any claims (unfair dismissal, unlawful deduction, contractual claim, discrimination, information and consultation, disclosure of employee liability information) where additional protection afforded by TUPE 2006 may be applicable.

B. Qualifying Employee?

CHECKLIST

9.03 Is the relevant individual employed under a contract of service or of apprentice-ship or otherwise? If not, for example where the individual is a worker or other-wise employed under a contract for services or a partner in a partnership, TUPE 2006 will not apply (TUPE 2006, reg 2(1) and see para **9.11** below).

9.04 Was the employee employed by the transferor or some other entity, for example, another company in the same group? If employed by another company in the group, TUPE 2006 may not apply (see para **9.12** below).

9.05 Was the employee only temporarily assigned to the organized grouping of re-sources which was transferred? If yes, TUPE 2006 may not apply to him (see para **9.13** below).

9.06 Has the employee objected to the transfer by notifying the transferor or trans-feree? If so the employee will not enjoy the protection under TUPE 2006, or may only enjoy limited protection (TUPE 2006, reg 4(7), (8), (9), and (10) and see para **9.15** below).

9.07 Was the employee employed by the transferor in the undertaking immediately before the relevant transfer took place (ie before serious negotiations began be-tween the parties leading to the transfer)? Subject to the next paragraph, unless they were, TUPE 2006 will not apply (TUPE 2006, reg 4(1)).

9.08 Was the employee dismissed prior to the transfer, because of the transfer or for a reason connected with the transfer which was not an economic, technical, or organizational reason entailing changes in the workforce? If so, TUPE 2006 will apply and liability for the individual's contract of employment will, nonetheless, be deemed to be transferred to the transferee of the business (TUPE 2006, reg 4(3) and see para **9.14** below).

9.09 Was the employee dismissed prior to the transfer for some reason unconnected with the transfer, whether or not that reason is ultimately valid, such as miscon-duct? If so, TUPE 2006 will not apply and the employee's only remedy is against the transferor (TUPE 2006, reg 4(3) and see para **9.40** below).

9.10 Did the employee carry on working for the transferor after the transfer? If so, even if the employee expressly agrees with the transferor that he would continue to work for the transferor, this will not necessarily preclude him from claiming that TUPE 2006 applies and that, in fact, his employment has or should have been transferred to the transferee (TUPE 2006, reg 18 and para **9.16** below).

Commentary

TUPE 2006 only applies to people who are employed, under a contract of **9.11** employment or apprenticeship *or otherwise* (TUPE 2006, reg 2(1)), in the undertaking by the transferor *immediately before* the transfer or would have been so employed, if he had not been dismissed in accordance with reg 7(1) (TUPE 2006, reg 4(3)). Although the definition of employee is slightly wider than the definition under other legislation, it will not apply to equity partners in a partnership (*Cowell v Quilter Goodison Co Ltd and QC Management Services Ltd* [1989] IRLR 392) or an independent contractor under a contract for services.

Also it is important to look carefully at whether the transferor and the employer **9.12** are one and the same and to check which part of the business the employees are actually working in. If the employee was employed by another group company rather than the transferor, then the court may not look behind the formal legal position so TUPE 2006 will not apply to this employee except in exceptional circumstances (*Michael Peters Ltd v (1) Farnfield, (2) Michael Peters Group plc* [1995] IRLR 190; *Sunley Turriff Holdings Ltd v Stuart Lyle Thomson and Others* [1995] IRLR 184; *Duncan Webb Offset (Maidstone) Ltd v Cooper and Others* [1995] IRLR 633; *The Print Factory (London) 1991 v Millam* [2007] IRLR 526 (although these are all cases relating to TUPE 1981)).

It is necessary to consider whether the employee works in the undertaking or part **9.13** of the business that is transferred. Factors under TUPE 1981 which would have shown that he is working in the relevant part of the undertaking are: that his contract of employment specifically assigns him to that part of the business (although this will not be decisive); that he is regarded as part of the human stock or permanent workforce of that business or part of the business, for example, he spends all his time working in that part of the business; that he values his work in that part of the business above his work in other areas; or that the cost of employing him is charged to that part of the business. If these factors are in favour of the employee being employed in the relevant part of the business it will not matter that there is a mobility clause in the contract which in theory allows the transferor to move the employee. Unless the transferor actually exercises his right to move the employee prior to the transfer he will be treated as if employed in the relevant part (*Arie Botzen & Ots v Rottersdamsche Droogdok Maatschappij BV* [1986] ECR 1119; *CPL Distribution v Todd* [2003] IRLR 28). Under TUPE 2006, the Government Guidance makes it clear that those who are temporarily assigned to the business will not transfer—and whether someone is temporarily assigned will depend on a number of factors, such as the length of time the employee has been there and whether a date has been set for the employee's return or re-assignment.

The application of TUPE cannot be avoided by dismissing the relevant employees **9.14** just before the transfer if the sole or principal reason for his dismissal is (a) the transfer itself or (b) a reason connected with the transfer that is not an economic, technical, or organizational reason entailing changes in the work force (TUPE 2006, reg 7(1)). In this situation the liabilities relating to that employee will transfer to the transferee. This confirms the position under the Acquired Rights Directive and case law pre-TUPE 2006. Whether or not the dismissal is done fairly under the terms of ERA 1996 is irrelevant for these purposes.

9.15 Further, if the employee expressly informed either the transferor or transferee that he objects to the transfer the employee will not transfer; his employment will be deemed to terminate on the transfer of the undertaking, but that termination will usually not be regarded as a dismissal by the transferor (TUPE 2006, reg 4(7) and (8)). The objection can be after the transfer in certain circumstances (for example, where the identity of the transferee is unknown to the employee prior to the transfer) and should be a clear objection but can be a resignation letter (*New ISG Limited v Vernon* [2007] IDS Employment Law Brief No. 843). The exception to this is where the transfer would involve a substantial and detrimental change to his working conditions when the employee can still be treated as if they have been dismissed (TUPE 2006, reg 4(9)). See para **9.44** below in relation to the protection afforded to the employee in these circumstances.

9.16 Finally note that an employee is generally unable to contract out of TUPE 2006 consistent with the fact that an employee cannot contract out of rights under other employment legislation (TUPE 2006, reg 18; see also ERA 1996, s 203). The exception is where TUPE 2006 makes provision for agreement that the regulations will not apply in certain circumstances (although the extent of this exclusion is unclear). Thus, even if an employee consents to continuing to work for the transferor this will not necessarily mean he has given up his rights under TUPE 2006 against the transferee. However a valid compromise agreement should be effective to exclude the employee's right to claim a TUPE-related unfair dismissal but not necessarily other rights under TUPE including rights in respect of a variation in terms and conditions of employment (*Solectron Scotland Ltd v Roper* [2004] IRLR 4) or in respect of the obligation to inform and consult. To improve the effectiveness of the compromise agreement, the transferee should if possible, always be made a party to it.

C. Qualifying Undertaking?

CHECKLIST

9.17 Is the undertaking:

(a) in the United Kingdom prior to the transfer? If not, TUPE 2006 will not apply (TUPE 2006, reg 3(1)); however, it will apply if the entity is based in the UK

but transferred so that it is based outside the UK post transfer (see para
9.20 below);

(b) a transfer of shares in a company so that the only change is the identity of
the shareholders and not the identity of the employing company? If so, TUPE
2006 will not apply, even where the share sale route is adopted to avoid the
application of TUPE 2006 (but see para **9.21** below);

(c) a transfer of assets only? For example, the sale of a building, where all the
employees of the seller continue to work for the seller in a different building. If
so, TUPE will generally not apply (TUPE 2006, reg 3(2) but see para **9.21** below
in relation to the impact of employees not transferring);

(d) an organized grouping of resources which has the objective of pursuing an
economic activity, whether or not that activity is central or ancillary, which is
sufficiently structured to amount to an undertaking and so that an undertaking has actually transferred to the putative transferee? If it is, TUPE 2006 will
apply (see paras **9.18, 9.20,** and **9.21** below);

(e) part of an undertaking only? This can still be a valid transfer (TUPE 2006, reg
3(1)(a) and see para **9.21** below);

(f) a non-commercial entity, for example, a non-profit-making body? Even if it is,
TUPE 2006 will still apply (TUPE 2006, reg 3(4)(a));

(g) a transfer of administrative functions between public administrators or a reorganization of a public administration? If so, TUPE 2006 will not apply (TUPE
2006, reg 3(5)) but other similar provisions may apply (see para **9.23** below).

Under TUPE 1981, some or all of the following factors had to be proven before **9.18**
the test set out at para **9.17(d)** above was satisfied. It remains to be seen if the
court's consideration is the same under TUPE 2006 although it seems likely. If a
similar test applies, it is necessary to consider all the factors characterizing the
transaction in question, but each is a single factor and none is to be considered
in isolation.

(a) Do the parties believe that TUPE 2006 applies? They should.

(b) Do tangible assets, such as buildings or movable property, transfer? They
should, although this is not fatal if they do not (TUPE 2006, reg 3(6)(b)).

(c) Do intangible assets, such as copyright, goodwill, customers, operational
resources, etc transfer? They should although this is not fatal if they do not
(TUPE 2006, reg 3(6)(b)).

(d) Are the majority of employees taken over by the new employer (or would they
be if the transferee was not avoiding the obligations under TUPE 2006)? They
should be.

(e) Are the activities organized and carried on in a similar way before and after
the transfer? They should be.

(f) Is there any suspension of the business or activities? There should not be, or only a short one.

(g) Is the transfer affected by a series of two or more transactions? No matter, TUPE 2006 can still apply (TUPE 2006, reg 3(6)(a) and see para **9.24** below).

(h) Do any assets transfer, or is it only people? No matter, TUPE 2006 will still apply if the undertaking is labour intensive, retains its identity, and satisfies other of the criteria (TUPE 2006, reg 3(6)(b)).

(See also the cases referred to at paras **9.20** and **9.21** below.)

9.19 Is the transfer a service provision change, that is an outsourcing, insourcing, or re-tender? If so, TUPE 2006 may apply, subject to the following points (TUPE 2006, reg 3(1)(b)):

(a) Does the service provision change involve an organized grouping of employees situated in Great Britain with its principal purpose of carrying out the activities on behalf of the client? If so, TUPE 2006 may apply (TUPE 2006, reg 3(3)(a)(i)).

(b) Is the service provision in connection with a specific event or a task of short duration? If so, TUPE 2006 will not apply (TUPE 2006, reg 3(3)(a)(ii)).

(c) Is the service provision wholly or mainly concerned with the supply of goods for the client's use? If so, TUPE 2006 will not apply (TUPE 2006, reg 3(3)(b)).

(See also para **9.22** below.)

Commentary

9.20 TUPE 2006 applies to a transfer of an 'undertaking' or business or to a part of an undertaking or business situated in the United Kingdom where there is a transfer of an economic entity which retains its identity (TUPE 2006, reg 3(1)(a)). 'Economic entity' is defined as an organized grouping of resources which has the objective of pursuing an economic activity whether central or ancillary (TUPE 2006, reg 3(2)). Case law has now established that so long as the entity is based in the UK prior to the transfer, then the regulations will apply even if the transfer means that the transferring entity ends up outside of the UK (*Holis Metals Industries Ltd v (1) GMB and (2) Newell Ltd* UKEAT/0171/CEA). Under TUPE 1981, an 'undertaking' was not expressly defined, and much case law has been devoted to determining its meaning (for example, *Sanchez Hildalgo v Asociacion de Servicios Aser* [1999] IRLR 136; *Cheeseman v R Brewer Contracts Ltd* [2001] IRLR 144; *ECM (Vehicle Delivery Service) Ltd v Cox* [1999] IRLR 559).

9.21 The test pursuant to TUPE 2006 is likely to be similar to that established by this case law and, indeed, this case law is referred to in the Government Guidance on

TUPE 2006. The Government Guidance also states that business transfers covered by TUPE 2006 are those 'where there is an identifiable set of resources (which includes employees) assigned to the business or part of the business which is transferred and that set of resources retains its identity after the transfer'. In relation to the transfer of part of a business, 'the resources do not need to be used exclusively in the transferring part of the business and by no other part. However, where resources are applied in a variable pattern over several parts of a business, then there is less likelihood that a transfer of any individual part of a business would qualify as a business transfer under [TUPE 2006].' A 'transfer' includes a sale, conditional sale, grant, transfer, or assignment of a lease or some other contract, or a transfer by way of gift. A sale of shares and a mere sale of bare assets can never be a transfer of undertaking (*Initial Supplies Ltd v McCall* 1992 SLT 67; *Brookes v Borough Care Services* [1998] IRLR 636, albeit these cases were under TUPE 1981 but confirmed in the Government Guidance). However see also *The Print Factory (London) 1991 v Millam* [2007] IRLR 526 where on the facts it was found there was a TUPE transfer alongside the share transfer. The fact that employees are not taken on does not prevent TUPE applying in certain circumstances (see, for example, the decision of the Court of Appeal in *RCO Support Services v Unison* [2002] EWCA Civ 464 and *ECM v Cox* [1999] IRLR 559).

9.22 Additionally, TUPE 2006 will apply to a 'service provision change'. This is now expressly set out in TUPE 2006 at reg 3(1)(b). A service provision change is, in effect, an initial outsourcing (TUPE 2006, reg 3(1)(b)(i)) of activities from a client to a contractor, a second round tender (TUPE 2006, reg 3(1)(b)(ii)) of those activities, or a contracting back in (TUPE 2006, reg 3(1)(b)(iii)) of the activities to the client. Prior to the service provision change the activities must be carried on by an organized grouping of employees situated in Great Britain which has the principal purpose of carrying out the activities on behalf of the client. It is not a contract for a specific event or of short-term duration and the activities must not consist wholly or mainly of the supply of goods for the customer's use (TUPE 2006, reg 3(3)). The Government Guidance makes it clear that there must be an identifiable group of employees providing the service and gives the example of a courier service which uses different employees each day as a case where this test would not be satisfied (see also *Wain v Guernsey Ship Management Limited* [2007] ICR 1350). It also makes it clear that 'service provision' can consist of just one employee.

9.23 TUPE 2006 will not apply to a transfer of an administrative function between public administrations or a re-organization of a public administration (TUPE 2006, reg 3(5)). However, the Cabinet Office's Statement of Practice 'Staff Transfers in the Public Sector' may apply separate regulations, and give employees similar rights to TUPE 2006.

9.24 A transfer under TUPE can be affected by a series of two or more transactions (TUPE 2006, reg 3(4)). The actual date of the transfer is determined by when, in fact, the responsibility as employer for carrying on the business or the unit transferred moves from the transferor to the transferee (*Celtec Ltd v Astley and Others* [2005] IRLR 647).

9.25 Under TUPE 1981, there used to be an exception to the normal rule that when a transfer takes place TUPE applies where a business is 'hived down' by a receiver or liquidator of a company, who may transfer a viable part of the business to a wholly owned subsidiary in the hope of making that part of the business more saleable to others. This exception no longer applies and this will be a transfer under TUPE 2006, provided the statutory definition is met.

D. Qualifying Claim?

CHECKLIST

9.26 Does the claim relate to one of the following which occurred before the transfer:

(a) a failure to pay wages;

(b) a dismissal for a reason connected with the transfer;

(c) discrimination which occurred before transfer;

(d) negligence by the employer against the employee;

(e) the employee's continuity of employment;

(f) share option, profit shares, bonus or equivalent shares?

If the other components of TUPE 2006 have been met, the transferee will be liable for the payment and/or will have to maintain the same terms as with the transferor save where the transfer is subject to relevant insolvency proceedings, where the obligation to pay certain payments will not transfer (see paras **9.29** and **9.31** below).

9.27 Does the claim relate to one of the following which occurred before the transfer?

(a) Criminal liability (TUPE 2006, reg 4(6)).

(b) Occupational pensions insofar as the provisions relate to benefits for old age, invalidity, and survivors (TUPE 2006, reg 10).

If so, the employee will not be able to avail himself of the protection of TUPE 2006 as it will not be covered. (However, note the minimum pension requirements referred to in para **9.30** below.)

Commentary

When an undertaking is transferred, TUPE 2006 provides that any contract of **9.28**
employment of any person employed by the transferor and assigned to the undertaking shall have effect as if originally made between the person so employed and
the transferee (TUPE 2006, reg 4(1)). More particularly, the transferee takes over
all the transferor's rights, powers, duties, and liabilities under or in connection
with the employment contracts so that after a transfer, any wrongful act or omission committed by the transferor is deemed to have been done by the transferee
and obligations owed by the employee to the transferor will become obligations
to the transferee (TUPE 2006, reg 4(2)).

The exception to this is where the transfer to the transferor is subject to relevant **9.29**
insolvency proceedings, where the obligation to pay certain amounts due to the
employee will not transfer, for example, arrears in pay, statutory redundancy pay,
payment in lieu of notice, holiday pay, or the basic award of compensation for
unfair dismissal. These sums will instead be met by the Secretary of State through
the National Insurance Fund (TUPE 2006, reg 8). A relevant insolvency procedure is defined at reg 8(6) as insolvency proceedings which have been opened in
relation to the transferor, not with a view to the liquidation of the assets of the
transferor, and which are under the supervision of an insolvency practitioner.
According to the Government Guidance on TUPE 2006, this is intended to
cover any collective insolvency procedures in which the whole or part of the business or undertaking is transferred to another entity as a going concern. It does not
cover winding up by either creditors or members where there is no such
transfer.

All aspects of the employee's contract of employment and rights connected with **9.30**
that contract of employment are transferred save for criminal liability (TUPE
2006, reg 4(6)) and the rights concerning occupational pension schemes.
Occupational pension schemes are specifically excluded from any transfer (TUPE
2006, reg 10). An occupational pension scheme is defined by reference to s 1 of
the Pension Schemes Act 1993 as a pension scheme established by an employer
for employees of a certain description for the purpose of providing benefits to,
amongst others, persons of that description. It does not include a personal pension scheme, which is broadly a scheme registered and established in accordance
with the Finance Act 2004. It is only those parts of the occupational pension
scheme which relate to benefits for old age, invalidity, or survivors which shall be
exempted from transfer; all other rights and obligations will transfer (TUPE
2006, reg 10(2)). TUPE 2006 now makes it clear that an employee will not have
a claim as a result of a failure to transfer rights under an occupational pension
scheme where that failure comes within reg 10 and took place after 6 April 2006

(TUPE 2006, reg 10(3)). However, where transferred employees were entitled to participate in an occupational pension scheme prior to the transfer, the transferee employer must establish a minimum level of pension provision for the transferred employees, which requires the transferee employer to match employee contributions, up to six per cent of salary, into a stakeholder pension or to offer an equivalent alternative (Pensions Act 2004).

9.31   Reg 4(1) and (2) has the following effect:

(a) If the transferor fails to pay the employee's wages, the employee can sue the transferee to recover the underpayment save where the transfer is subject to relevant insolvency proceedings (see para **9.29** above). Note that this may also include a claim in respect of wages which should have been paid to equalize salary in accordance with EqPA 1970 (*Sodexo Ltd v E A Gutridge and Others (1) and North Tees and Hartlepool NHS Foundation (2)* EAT/0024/08)

(b) If the transferor dismissed the employee before the transfer, where the sole or principal reason for the dismissal is the transfer, or a reason connected with the transfer which is not an economic, technical, or organizational reason entailing changes in the workplace, the employee can claim reinstatement or compensation for unfair dismissal and any other outstanding liabilities from the transferee (TUPE 2006, regs 4(3) and 7(1)). (See also para **9.42** below.)

(c) If the transferor has discriminated against an employee on grounds of sex or race prior to the transfer (even where that discrimination took place when he was employed under a previous contract of employment) liability for that discrimination will transfer to the transferee.

(d) If the transferor was negligent towards the employee prior to the transfer, the employee can claim against the transferee in respect of that negligence and, potentially, under any connected insurance (*Martin v Lancashire County Council; Bernadone v Pall Mall Services Group and Others* [2000] IRLR 487).

(e) If the employee has committed acts of misconduct for which he has or has not been given warnings, or if he has been given warnings for incapability, the transferee may rely upon such misconduct or warnings when considering subsequent stages in any disciplinary procedure affecting that employee.

(f) If the employee's contract of employment contains restrictive covenants, these will transfer, but their scope will be limited to protecting the undertaking transferred; they will not be construed as protecting the rest of the transferee's business as well (*Morris Angel & Son Ltd v Hollande* [1993] IRLR 169).

(g) The employee is generally deemed to have continuous employment so far as his statutory and contractual employment rights are concerned. These will include the right not to be unfairly dismissed, the right to redundancy or statutory maternity payments, and maternity rights.

(h) The rule applies to both express and implied contractual provisions. It will not, however, give the employee rights that he would not otherwise have (for example, a redundancy package that pre-dates their employment (*Jackson v Computershare Investor Services plc* [2008] IRLR 70)). It also applies to collective agreements (TUPE 2006, reg 5). A customary arrangement or agreed procedure for selection of employees for redundancy would be deemed to be carried over (*Whent v T Cartledge Ltd* [1997] IRLR 153).

(i) Share options, profit shares, bonus or equivalent schemes transfer, even if on a normal construction the provisions do not easily transfer. However, in that case the employee only has the right to participate in a scheme of 'substantial equivalencies, but one which is free from unjust, absurd or impossible features' (*Unicorn Consultancy Services v Westbrook and Others* [2000] IRLR 80; *MITIE Management Ltd v French* [2002] IRLR 512).

(j) In relation to liability for a protective award in relation to a failure by the transferor to inform and consult, see para **9.57** below.

E. Automatically Unfair Dismissal?

CHECKLIST

Was the employee dismissed? An employee will not be dismissed if he objects to the transfer unless there has been a substantial change in working conditions or the employee otherwise has the right to claim constructive dismissal under his common law rights (TUPE 2006, reg 4(7) to (11) and see para **9.44** below). **9.32**

Has an employee who wishes to claim unfair dismissal more than one year of continuous employment with either the transferor or transferee and has he or she been dismissed in circumstances where the transfer or a reason connected with the transfer which is not an economic, technical, or organizational reason entailing changes in the workforce is the principal or only reason for dismissal? If so, the dismissal will be automatically unfair (TUPE 2006, reg 7(1) and see para **9.40** below). **9.33**

When is a dismissal definitely connected with the transfer? It is not where there is another justifiable reason for it in which case the dismissal will not be automatically unfair under TUPE 2006. **9.34**

Is there an economic, technical, or organizational reason entailing changes in the workforce of either the transferor or the transferee, either before or after the **9.35** transfer which is the principal reason for the dismissal? If such a reason exists, which must be connected with the conduct or running of the undertaking as a going concern and must involve a reduction or functional change to the work-force, the dismissal may be fair. The employer will still need to dismiss using a fair procedure (TUPE 2006, reg 7(2) and (3) and see paras **9.41** and **9.42** below).

9.36 Does liability for unfair dismissal automatically fall with the transferee in every situation? If TUPE applies, and the dismissal is by reason of the transfer or for a reason connected with the transfer which is not an economic, technical, or organizational reason, then all liability will transfer to the transferee (TUPE 2006, reg 4(3)); the transferor will not retain any liability. However, where the transferor does the dismissing, and the principal reason for the dismissal is not the transfer or a reason connected with the transfer that is not an economic, technical, or organizational reason entailing changes in the workforce, the liability may remain with the transferor (see para **9.42** below).

9.37 Can the transferor or transferee vary the terms and conditions of employment be-fore or after a transfer? Even with the consent of the employee, if the transferor is not subject to relevant insolvency proceedings, the transferor or the transferee can only impose substantial and detrimental changes to the employee's working conditions if he can then show that the reason for the variation is not the transfer it-self or is a reason connected with the transfer which is not an economic, technical, or organizational reason entailing a change in the workforce justifying the change (for example, requiring a reduction of the workforce, or a requirement that the employee performs very different job functions). If the employer is not able to show this, the changes will be void (TUPE 2006, reg 4(4) and (5) and see para **9.45** below).

9.38 Is the transferor subject to bankruptcy, company liquidation, or creditors' volun-tary liquidation proceedings? If so, regs 4 and 7 will not apply and there will be no transfer to the transferee; the Secretary of State and the insolvent transferor will be responsible for payments to the employees (TUPE 2006, reg 8(7) and see para **9.46** below).

9.39 Is the transferor subject to other insolvency proceedings? The Secretary of State may be responsible for some pre-transfer liabilities which will not transfer (TUPE 2006, reg 8 (2) to (6)) and different rules in relation to variations of terms and conditions will apply (TUPE 2006, reg 9) (see also para **9.46** below).

Commentary

9.40 Any employee who has worked for one year for either the transferor or transferee, and whether or not in the undertaking or elsewhere, who is dismissed where the sole or principal reason for the dismissal is the transfer itself, or a reason connected with the transfer which was not an economic, technical, or organizational reason (ETO reason) entailing changes in the workforce, is deemed to have been automatically unfairly dismissed (TUPE 2006, reg 7(1)). If, however, the dismissal is not for a reason connected with the transfer, but for a justifiable reason, such as gross misconduct, it will not be automatically unfair. Under TUPE 1981, dismissals may also be for a reason connected with the transfer even where a potential transferee has not been identified (*Morris v John Grose Group Ltd* [1998] IRLR 499) and a dismissal which takes place some considerable time after the transfer (for example two years) can still be for a reason connected with the transfer (*Taylor v Connex South Eastern Ltd* [2000] IDS Employment Law Brief No 670); there is no reason why this case law would not continue to apply in relation to TUPE 2006.

There is a defence to this rule where the sole or principal reason for the dismissal **9.41** is an ETO reason entailing changes in the workforce of either the transferor or the transferee (TUPE 2006, reg 7(2)) and not the transfer itself. The reason may apply to a dismissal which takes place either before or after the relevant transfer. Under TUPE 1981, the test applied has been a stringent one which, in effect, means that the reason must be connected with the conduct or running of the business. Thus dismissals carried out by the transferor at the insistence of the transferee, or dismissals whose main purpose is to raise the sale price of the business, would not have sufficient economic reason to justify fair termination of employment. Where the aim of the dismissal is to save the business this may qualify for the defence but only where, for example, the business was overstaffed, inefficient in terms of sales, and insolvent, and there was no collusion between seller and buyer (*Thomson v SCS Consulting Ltd* [2001] IRLR 801). Further, the reason must entail changes in the workforce; that is, a diminution of number of staff or a substantial re-organization (*Berriman v Delabole Slate Ltd* [1985] IRLR 305; *Green v Elan Care Ltd*, EAT/018/01). It seems likely that this case law will continue to be good law under TUPE 2006. The Government Guidance states 'the onus lies on the dismissing employer to show that the dismissal falls within the ETO exemption to the automatic unfairness rule. Neither the Regulations nor the Acquired Rights Directive define what an ETO reason may be. The courts and tribunals have not generally sought to distinguish between each of the three ETO categories, but rather have treated them as a single concept.' See also the Government Guidance relating to what is an ETO reason in the context of a variation of contract (Government Guidance, Part 3) which reflects the above case law.

Even if a sufficient ETO reason does exist, the employer must still act fairly **9.42** towards the employee and must follow all the appropriate procedures (TUPE 2006, reg 7(3)(b)). Previously, under TUPE 1981, case law had supported the fact that liability for an automatically unfair dismissal would transfer to the transferee.However, in contrast, where the dismissal by the transferor was for an ETO reason immediately before the transfer which dismissal was then found to be substantively unfair, that liability may remain with the transferor. TUPE 2006 appears to continue this position—see regs 4(3) and 7(1); only liability for an automatically unfair dismissal under reg 7(1) transfers to the transferee. TUPE 2006 is silent as to what happens where there is an ETO reason but the dismissal is, nonetheless, unfair for procedural reasons and so again liability may remain with the transferor.

9.43 Claims for TUPE-related unfair dismissals must be brought within the relevant time limits under the substantive legislation, that is usually within three months of the effective date of termination.

9.44 An employee who has resigned in response to a substantial change in working conditions to their material detriment and whose contract is or would otherwise be transferred in accordance with reg 4(1), will be treated as if he had been dismissed and could bring a claim for unfair dismissal (TUPE 2006, reg 4(9)). However, the dismissal will not necessarily be automatically unfair; it will be for the employee to prove that it is. Also, the employee will not be entitled to any damages in respect of a failure by the employer to pay the employee in respect of a notice period which he has failed to work (TUPE 2006, reg 4(10)). The Government Guidance states that a substantial change in working conditions could be a major relocation of the work place, or the withdrawal of a right to a tenured post (page 20 of the Government Guidance). This protection is in addition to the employee's common law right to claim constructive dismissal (TUPE 2006, reg 4(11)).

9.45 An employee also has additional protection under TUPE 2006 where the transferor or, more usually, the transferee varies the terms and conditions of employment of the employee. Any variation of contract where the sole or principal reason is the transfer itself or a reason connected with the transfer that it is not an ETO reason entailing changes in the workforce shall be void (TUPE 2006, reg 4(4)). Variations for an ETO reason entailing changes in the workforce or a reason unconnected with the transfer will, however, be valid (TUPE 2006, reg 4(5)). See para **9.41** above for a discussion of what constitutes an ETO reason entailing changes in the workforce. Note, however, that the Government Guidance states categorically that a desire to harmonize terms and conditions cannot constitute an ETO reason entailing changes in the workforce. The Guidance has also been amended to reflect the fact that changes to terms and conditions which are entirely positive are not prevented by the Regulations (see also *Regent Security Services Ltd v Power* [2008] IRLR 66).

Where the employee is employed in an undertaking which, at the time of the **9.46** transfer, is subject to relevant insolvency proceedings, the protection an employee enjoys will be different, in particular in relation to variation of the contract of employment. Where the entity is insolvent by reason of bankruptcy, a company liquidation, or a creditors' voluntary liquidation, regs 4 and 7 will not apply and there will be no transfer (TUPE 2006, reg 8(7); see also the DBERR guidance Transfer of Undertakings (Protection of Employment) Regulations 2006—Redundancy and Insolvency Payments—which can be accessed at <http://www.dti.gov.uk/files/file30031.pdf>). Employees will be redundant and liabilities will be borne by the Secretary of State in accordance with the statutory redundancy scheme and the insolvent transferor. Where the entity is subject to other types of insolvency, for example administration and voluntary arrangements, some pre-transfer liabilities will be borne by the Secretary of State but otherwise regs 4 and 7 will apply as normal (TUPE 2006, regs 8(2) to (6)). In addition reg 9 will apply in relation to variations of contract. Variations to the contract will be valid where they are agreed with appropriate representatives, who are either trade union representatives or, if there are none, elected representatives (TUPE 2006, reg 9(1) and (2)). Where the representatives are not trade union representatives, in addition to agreeing the variation with the appropriate representatives, the employer must obtain agreement in writing, signed by each of the representatives and, before it is signed, provide all employees to whom it is intended to apply on the date on which it is intended to come into effect with copies of the text of the agreement and such guidance as those employees might reasonably require in order to understand it fully (TUPE 2006, reg 9(5)). For a variation to come within the scope of this additional flexibility, the sole or principal reason for it must be the transfer itself or a reason connected with the transfer which is not an ETO reason entailing changes in the workforce and it must be designed to safeguard employment opportunities by ensuring the survival of the undertakings or business (TUPE 2006, reg 9(7)).

F. Trade Unions

How does TUPE 2006 affect trade union recognition? TUPE 2006 also operates **9.47** to transfer over any recognition agreement between the transferor and a recognized independent trade union but only where the transferred organized grouping of resources or employees maintains an identity distinct from the remainder of the transferee's undertaking (TUPE 2006, reg 6(1)). See also para **9.31(h)** above in relation to collective agreements.

G. Information and Consultation

9.48   Are any employees of either the transferor or the transferee likely to be affected by the transfer? If the answer to this question is yes, the obligations relating to informing and consulting will apply (TUPE 2006, reg 13 and see paras **9.53** to **9.58** below).

9.49   Is there a trade union recognized in relation to the relevant employees, or other employee representatives? If yes, they must be provided with the relevant information and consulted. If not, elections must be held to elect representatives (see paras **9.54–9.55** below).

9.50   What information must be provided to the relevant representatives? The transferor must inform the trade union or employee representatives of the following matters:

(a) the fact that the transfer is to take place;

(b) the approximate date for the proposed transfer;

(c) the reason for the proposed transfer;

(d) the legal, economic, and social implications of the transfer for the affected employees;

(e) any measure which it is envisaged the transferor or the transferee will take as a result of the transfer or, if no such measures will be taken, that fact. 'Measure' means an action which the transferor or transferee has a present plan to implement, and does not include a vague idea for the future.

(TUPE 2006, reg 13(2); *Institution of Professional Civil Servants v Secretary of State for Defence* [1987] IRLR 373)

9.51   What must the employer consult with the trade union or employee representative about? The obligation to consult only applies in relation to any measures identified in accordance with para **9.50(e)** above (see para **9.56** below).

9.52   What remedy is available to an employee if an employer fails to comply? A claim to the tribunal for a declaration and compensation of up to 13 weeks' pay (TUPE 2006, regs 15 and 16 and see para **9.57** below).

Commentary

9.53   Both the transferor and the transferee must notify representatives of employees who may be affected by the impending transfer of certain information and, if 'measures' may be taken which could affect the employees, they also have consultation obligations (TUPE 2006, reg 13).

Representatives for these purposes are, where a trade union is recognized in relation **9.54** to the employees, representatives of the trade union, or, if not, representatives elected by the employees generally or specifically for the purposes of consultation under TUPE 2006 (TUPE 2006, reg 13(3)).

If it is necessary to hold elections for the representatives, arrangements for **9.55** elections must:

(a) be fair;
(b) ensure that there are sufficient representatives to represent the interests of all the employees;
(c) identify the term for which the employee representatives shall be in office;
(d) ensure that the candidates are affected employees and that no-one is excluded from standing;
(e) equally ensure that all employees are able to vote;
(f) ensure that the election is conducted so as to secure that so far as reasonably practicable those voting do so in secret and the votes given are accurately counted.

(TUPE 2006, reg 14(1))

If measures are to be taken by either the transferor or the transferee which may **9.56** affect the employee, the party which is to take those measures must consult with the employee representatives and consider the views expressed by the employee representatives with a view to seeking the representatives' agreement to them, before reaching a final decision to implement those measures (TUPE 2006, reg 13(6)). This means that the employer must discuss them with the representatives with an open mind and make every effort to secure the representatives' agreement to what is proposed and to accommodate their objections. The employer must consider any representations, reply to them, and if they are to be rejected, state the reasons for doing so (TUPE 2006, reg 13(6) and (7)).

If the transferor fails to inform the representatives of the material facts, or if **9.57** the representatives are not consulted about any measures which may be taken, the representatives may within three months of the transfer bring a complaint in an employment tribunal for a declaration and appropriate compensation for the failure to consult. The maximum award is 13 weeks' pay for each of the affected employees. The award is intended to be punitive rather than compensatory (*Sweetin v Coral Racing* IRLR [2006] 252). An award for failure to comply with the duty to inform and consult can be made against either the transferor or the transferee. Where an award is made against the transferor, if, after being given notice, the transferee failed to provide information on time regarding any measures it proposed to take as a result of the transfer, or failed to consult about such measures, the transferee may also be liable (TUPE 2006, regs 15 and 16).

9.58 In any case, the regulations expressly provide that the transferee and the transferor will be jointly liable for a failure to inform and consult. The transferee will be liable for its failure and will also be jointly and severally liable with the transferor for any failure by it (TUPE 2006, reg 15(7) to (9)).

H. Disclosure of 'Employee Liability Information'

CHECKLIST

9.59 Is the employer a transferor of an undertaking or service in accordance with reg 3 of TUPE 2006 (see paras **9.20** and **9.22** above) to which employees are assigned? If so, the transferor must provide to the transferee certain prescribed information (TUPE 2006, reg 11(1) and see paras **9.62–9.65** below and, in particular, para **9.63** in respect of what information must be provided).

9.60 How quickly must the transferor provide the information? The information must be notified no more than 14 days before the transfer (TUPE 2006, reg 11(6) and see para **9.64** below).

9.61 What if the transferor ignores its obligations in this regard? The transferee only has the right to bring a claim before the employment tribunal (TUPE 2006, reg 12 and see para **9.65** below).

Commentary

9.62 TUPE 2006 introduces new obligations on the transferor to produce certain information to the transferee within certain specified timeframes (TUPE 2006, regs 11 and 12).

9.63 The obligation is in respect of any person employed by the transferor who is assigned to the organized grouping of resources or employees that is the subject of the transfer (TUPE 2006, reg 11(1)). The information must be notified in writing or some other readily accessible form. The information which must be provided is:

(a) the identity and age of the employee;
(b) the statutory particulars of employment;
(c) any information in relation to a disciplinary or grievance procedure which would come within the terms of the statutory dispute resolution procedures within the previous two years;

(d) information about any actual or pending court or tribunal case within the last two years;

(e) information about any collective agreement.

(TUPE 2006, reg 11(2))

The information must date from no more than 14 days before the date it is **9.64** notified and must be notified no more than 14 days before the transfer (TUPE 2006, reg 11(3) and (6)).

If the transferor fails to provide the information in accordance with reg 11, the trans- **9.65** feree may present a complaint to the employment tribunal within three months of the relevant transfer. The employment tribunal may make a declaration and award compensation (TUPE 2006, reg 12(1), (2), and (3)). The minimum award to be made by the employment tribunal shall be £500 per employee. Otherwise, the compensation should take into account the loss suffered by the transferee and the terms of any contract between the transferor and the transferee (TUPE 2006, reg 12(4) and (5)).

9

Transfer of Undertakings

10

DATA PROTECTION AND PRIVACY ISSUES

A. Introduction

The Data Protection Act 1998 (the DPA) was introduced by the Government to implement the EC Directive 95/46/EC on the protection of individuals with regard to the processing of Personal Data and on the free movement of such data. It replaced the Data Protection Act 1984, which had provided limited protection for individuals in relation to computer records. **10.01**

The DPA came into force on 1 March 2000 but because of a transitional period most of the obligations relating to manual record-keeping only came into effect on 24 October 2001. Although the DPA covers all aspects of the use of Personal Data, this book deals solely with its impact on employers and employees (including workers), and these terms will be used rather than the data protection specific terms. **10.02**

B. DPA Basics

What are the key relevant definitions in relation to data protection? The key definitions are set out in section 1 of the DPA. A summary of them is set out below. **10.03**

(a) 'Data Controller': anyone who determines the purpose for which and the manner in which data is processed. This is a very wide definition; in addition to employers it includes employment agencies and those who provide employees' information via outsourcing arrangements (eg payroll services).

(b) 'Data Processor': includes anyone (other than an employee of the Data Controller) who processes data on behalf of the Data Controller.

(c) 'Data Subject': is the person to whom the data relates, ie the employee or worker.

(d) 'Personal Data': data in relation to an individual who can be identified from that data or other information in the Data Controller's possession. This means that companies cannot be Data Subjects.

(e) 'Sensitive Personal Data': is Personal Data about the Data Subject's racial/ ethnic origin, political opinions, religious beliefs, membership of trade unions, physical/mental health, sex life, and criminal offences (including both allegations and convictions).

(f) 'Processing': this covers nearly everything from the storage of data in any form, copying, checking, sorting, through to its deletion.

(DPA 1998, ss 1–2)

10.04 What is the purpose of the DPA? The DPA regulates the conduct of employers and other Data Processors in relation to Personal Data. It gives the employee the right to access the Personal Data held about them and imposes a requirement on the employers that they give formal notification to the Information Commissioner that they are processing Personal Data and comply with the Data Protection Principles.

10.05 What is the best source of guidance for employers in relation to the DPA? The Information Commissioner, who is responsible for enforcing the DPA, has published statutory codes for employers providing guidance in relation to compliance with the DPA, pursuant to DPA 1998, ss 51(3) and 52. The employment codes deal with Recruitment and Selection (Part 1), Employment Records (Part 2), Monitoring at Work (Part 3), and Information about Workers' Health (Part 4). There is also a lengthy document of supplementary guidance which provides additional information and more detailed examples of all of the above topics. The codes are published on the Information Commissioner's website which is at <http://www.ico.gov.uk>. This site also contains other useful information about the DPA and related legislation. However the Codes mainly deal with the Information Commissioner's recommendations as to what is necessary to ensure compliance with the DPA. A failure to comply with every recommendation will not necessarily mean an employer's acts are illegal, although, as the Information Commissioner enforces much of the DPA, they are likely to be influential. The Code and supplementary guidance are therefore very useful. They are also very detailed and what follows here can only touch on the core principles which apply—if in doubt, refer to the Codes.

C. The Employer's Obligations

What are an employer's obligations? An employer is clearly a Data Controller in relation to the information that it holds in regard to its existing employees, consultants, and applicants, and former employees or consultants. As such there are two principal obligations with which any employer must comply. Firstly an employer must register with the Information Commission (DPA, ss 16 to 26) and secondly an employer must comply with the Data Protection Principles (DPA, s 4, Schs 1 and 2). **10.06**

How does an employer register? The Information Commissioner maintains a public record of Data Controllers. Almost all employers will be required to notify the Information Commissioner that they will be processing Personal Data (there are some very limited exemptions). In order to notify the Information Commissioner the employer must: **10.07**

(a) complete a form, which is available on the Data Protection website which requires the employer to set out details including the types of Personal Data which the employer will be processing and the purposes of the processing;

(b) pay a fee, which is currently £35; and

(c) renew its registration each year by paying a further fee (this is currently £35).

What happens if an employer is not registered? An employer should not process Personal Data unless it is registered (DPA, s 17). It is a criminal offence to process data if the employer is not registered (DPA, s 21). If the Information Commissioner decides to prosecute then the employer could be subject, on summary conviction, to a fine not exceeding the statutory maximum of £5,000 or on conviction on indictment to a fine which is not subject to a maximum. **10.08**

What are the Data Protection Principles? There are eight Data Protection Principles with which employers must comply (DPA, s 4 and Sch 1). The principles are as follows. **10.09**

(a) First Principle: Personal Data must be processed fairly and lawfully and must not be processed unless a number of specified conditions set out in Schedule 2 of the DPA have been met. See below at para **10.10** for more details of what this means.

(b) Second Principle: Personal Data must only be used for specified and lawful purposes.

(c) Third Principle: Personal Data must be adequate and relevant but not excessive in relation to the purposes for which it is being processed. An employer needs to be able to justify the retention of Personal Data for sound business/administrative reasons.

(d) Fourth Principle: Personal Data must be accurate and kept up to date (where necessary).

(e) Fifth Principle: Personal Data must not be kept for longer than is necessary. Unfortunately, the DPA does not specify how long data should be kept. Employers must audit their employment records and ensure that they only retain information which they can justify keeping (eg for taxation purposes).

(f) Sixth Principle: Personal Data must be processed in accordance with the rights of the employee (ie the processor must comply with requests for access to data from employees).

(g) Seventh Principle: An employer needs to take adequate measures to ensure the security and confidentiality of Personal Data and to prevent the loss of or unauthorized/unlawful processing of Personal Data.

(h) Eighth Principle: Employers with connections in areas outside of the European Economic Area (the EEA) (including the United States) should not transfer Personal Data to such countries unless the country in question ensures an adequate level of protection for the information. Where data protection laws are less strict, Personal Data may not be sent unless it is clearly necessary for the purposes of performing the employment contract or employers have obtained employees' informed consent to the transfer beforehand.

10.10 What are the specified conditions which must be satisfied for the purposes of the First Principle? In the employment field the most relevant conditions are:

(a) the employee has consented to the processing;

(b) where the processing of data is necessary for the performance of a contract or for taking steps at the request of the employee with a view to entering into a contract. For instance, an employer would not need an applicant's consent when processing data provided in a job application form or to pay the employee under their employment contract;

(c) where the data is necessary for compliance with a legal obligation (other than one imposed by contract), ie complying with a statutory requirement;

(d) where the processing is necessary for the purposes of legitimate interests pursued by the employer, except where the processing is unwarranted in any particular case by reason of prejudice to the rights and freedoms or legitimate interests of the employee or other Data Subject.

(DPA 1998, Sch 2)

When the DPA first came into force most practitioners advised employers to use consent as the route to process Personal Data. However, although 'consent' is not defined under the DPA, under the Directive it must be a freely given, specific, and informed indication of the Data Subject's wishes. The Information Commissioner has tried to steer employers away from using consent on the basis that consent is rarely informed and freely given in the employment context. Instead the Information Commissioner has in the Codes of Practice relied on exemptions such as processing being necessary for the performance of a contract or for exercising a legal obligation.

What additional obligations apply in relation to sensitive Personal Data? The **10.11** DPA places further obligations in regard to 'Sensitive Personal Data' (DPA, s 4 and Sch 3). In addition to satisfying each one of the eight Principles above, employers wishing to process Sensitive Personal Data must satisfy one of a number of further conditions which include the following:

(a) The employer has the explicit consent of the employee to the processing of the Sensitive Personal Data. The Information Commissioner takes the view that this means the consent must be absolutely clear and practically this means in most cases the consent must be obtained at the time the processing is being undertaken;

(b) The processing is necessary to perform some right/obligation imposed by law on the employer in connection with employment, eg checking an employee's right to work in the UK; administering sick pay;

(c) The information contained in the Sensitive Personal Data was deliberately made public by the employee;

(d) The processing is necessary for legal proceedings, obtaining legal advice, or establishing, exercising, or defending legal rights; or

(e) The processing is necessary for equal opportunities monitoring in relation to race/ethnic origins.

(DPA 1998, Sch 2; see also the Supplementary Guidance, p 72)

D. The Practical Effect for Employers

What is the overall practical effect for employers? **10.12**

(a) Employers should bear in mind that their obligations apply not only to current employees but to former employees, consultants, applicants, and any other individuals whose data they process.

10

Data Protection and Privacy Issues

(b) In order to comply with the Data Protection Principles, employers will need to consider whether they can process data and what exemptions they are intending to rely on.

(c) For example, if an employee makes an allegation of sexual harassment in relation to emails which another employee has been sending her, in order to investigate, the employer will be required to process Sensitive Personal Data. The employer can usually rely on one of the exemptions described at para **10.11** above but careful thought should be given to this.

(d) Another example is if an employer is selling part of their business and a due diligence exercise is under way. The employer will again need to ensure that it complies with the Data Protection Principles and considers anonymizing the data, does not send through absolutely every piece of information that it has in relation to the employee, but considers what is necessary and obtains undertakings from the party receiving the data. In this context, there is no precise exemption, and the employer will need to argue that the processing is necessary for the purposes of legitimate interests pursued by the employer.

(e) One issue which employers commonly face is the transfer of data outside the EEA. For example, an employer has their server at their head office in the United States. All Human Resources information is routed via the United States. Technically, the employer will be processing data outside the EEA. It will be difficult to obtain the relevant informed consent from the employee unless this is done explicitly. It is also arguable that some of that information may not be regarded as *necessary* for the performance of the employment contract as this is a strict test. As a result, there is a risk that the employer is not processing data in accordance with one of the eight Data Protection Principles. Options available to the employer in this situation are as follows:
   • ensure that only information which is necessary for the performance of the employment contract leaves the EEA or that information which is transferred is anonymized;
   • certain countries are now deemed to have adequate protection of data— for example, Argentina, Canada (although this is qualified), United States (but only if the entity is on the safe harbour register), Switzerland, Guernsey, Isle of Man;
   • use a 'model contract' between the UK entity which is a Data Controller and the entity receiving the information outside the EEA. For more information on model contracts, see the Information Commissioner's website.

10.13 What should an employer do to ensure proper compliance with the DPA?

(a) Establish one person within the organization responsible for ensuring employment practices and procedures comply with the DPA and for ensuring that they continue to do so. Put in place a mechanism for checking that procedures are followed in practice.

(b) Ensure that business areas and individual line managers that process information about employees understand their own responsibility for data protection compliance, and if necessary amend their working practice in the light of this.

(c) Assess what Personal Data about individuals are in existence and who is responsible for them.

(d) Eliminate the collection of Personal Data that are irrelevant or excessive to the employment relationship. If sensitive data are collected, ensure that the sensitive data condition is satisfied.

(e) Ensure that workers are aware of the extent to which they can be criminally liable if they knowingly or recklessly disclose Personal Data outside their employer's policies and procedures. Make serious breaches of data protection rules a disciplinary offence.

(f) Consult workers and/or trade unions or other representatives about the development and implementation of employment practices and procedures that involve processing of personal information about workers (see the Codes of Practice for further detail and good practice recommendations).

E. Recruitment

How will recruitment be effected? **10.14**

(a) Ensure that all advertisements, application forms, and correspondence with potential applicants set out the name of the organization to which they are providing information, and the purposes for which such information will be held.

(b) If recruitment agencies are providing information for the employer, ensure that included in their terms of engagement is a requirement that they will comply with their obligations under the DPA.

(c) Only seek Personal Data that is relevant to the recruitment decision to be made.

(d) In relation to criminal convictions, only request information that can be justified in terms of the role offered. The Information Commissioner recommends that it is made clear that spent convictions should not have to be declared, unless the job being filled is covered by the exemptions orders of the Rehabilitation of Offenders Act 1974.

(e) If checks are going to be made then ensure that the applicant is informed of this.

(f) If it is necessary to secure the release of documents or information from a third party ensure that the applicant has signed a consent form unless consent has been indicated in some other way. If any of the checks produce discrepancies, give the individual the right to explain why there are discrepancies.

(g) If the recruitment process is going to use an automated processing system, ensure that applicants are aware of this and of their right to challenge the automated process. Ensure that this is checked by an individual so that the decision is not wholly automated.

(h) Consider how long it is necessary to keep applications and records and ensure that the applicant is made aware of this. There is specific guidance in the Code depending on the type of information involved.

(i) Advise the applicant of any pre-employment vetting at an early stage. Only carry out vetting at the latest stage possible in the recruitment process.

F. Employment Records

10.15   What rules apply to employment records?

(a) Ensure that all individuals within the organization are aware of the nature and source of any information kept about them, the reason why the information is being kept, who will have access to the information, and their right of access to the information.

(b) Ensure that all records are kept accurate and up to date, and establish guidelines on how long records will be kept for.

(c) Ensure that necessary security controls are introduced so as to minimize the risk of an employee's Personal Data being processed without their consent including where data is taken away from the workplace, whether physically or electronically.

(d) Keep sickness and accident records separately from absence records and only use the latter for checking purposes, if at all possible.

(e) Ensure that the holding and use of sickness and accident records satisfies sensitive data conditions (see para **10.11** above).

(f) Only disclose information from sickness or accident records about an employee's illness, medical condition, or injury where there is a legal obligation to do so, where it is necessary for legal proceedings, or where an individual has given explicit consent to the disclosure.

(g) Do not make the sickness, accident, or absence records of individuals available to other individuals, other than to provide managers with information about those who work for them insofar as it is necessary for them to carry out their managerial roles.

(h) Ensure that information gained for pension and insurance schemes is not used for any other purposes.

(i) Consider whether spent disciplinary warnings should be retained on an employee's personnel file.

(j) Establish a clear policy in relation to reference requests and receipts and requests for disclosure of information by a third party.

(k) In the context of mergers, acquisitions, and other business transactions, try as far as possible to ensure information is anonymized and secure assurances from those dealing with it as to their use of it.

(See also employee rights at para **10.18** below.)

G. Monitoring at Work

What rules apply to the monitoring of workplace communications?   **10.16**

(a) The DPA does not prevent an employer monitoring individuals but it does place constraints in the way that monitoring can be carried out. Generally, individuals must be informed as to what information employers are likely to be monitoring. Employers should carry out a balancing act between the needs of the business and the privacy of individuals. Great emphasis is placed in the part of the Code which covers monitoring on carrying out impact assessments to determine why monitoring is necessary and why the needs of the business outweigh the individual's rights.

(b) The Code on Monitoring establishes a number of core principles:
 • Generally it will be intrusive to monitor individuals.
 • Individuals have legitimate expectations that they can keep their personal lives private and that they are also entitled to a degree of privacy in the work environment.
 • If an employer wishes to monitor an individual, they should be clear about the purpose and satisfied that the particular monitoring arrangement is justified by real benefits that will be delivered.
 • Individuals should be aware of the nature, extent, and reasons for any monitoring unless (exceptionally) covert monitoring can be justified.
 • In any event, workers' awareness will influence their expectations.

(c) Employers should identify the monitoring which currently takes place in their organization and consider whether an impact assessment should be drawn up.

(d) Employers should ensure that individuals are kept informed of the nature and extent of any monitoring.

(e) Employers should establish a clear policy on what telephone calls, email, and Internet usage is acceptable and, if appropriate, when monitoring will take place.

(f) Remember generally that it will be impossible to justify blanket monitoring of all emails or, unless in exceptional circumstances, opening emails which are marked clearly private and confidential or personal. Similarly, covert monitoring should be used sparingly and in accordance with strict criteria.

H. Information About Workers' Health

10.17 What rules apply to the processing of information about employees' health?

(a) As information about an employee's health is Sensitive Personal Data, an employer should be able to comply with one of the following requirements to ensure the processing is legal:
- Is the processing necessary to enable the employer to meet legal requirements, such as health and safety requirements?
- Is the processing for medical purposes, eg the provision of care or treatment and undertaken by a health professional or someone under an equivalent duty of confidentiality?
- Is the processing in connection with actual or prospective legal proceedings?
- Has the worker given consent explicitly to the processing of his or her medical information?

(b) In addition, the employer should conduct an impact assessment in relation to the processing of the data to be clear either that it is under a legal obligation to process the data, for example, under health and safety legislation or that the benefits to be gained by processing the information justify the privacy intrusion or other adverse impact. In conducting this assessment, the employer should also consider alternatives to the processing and the obligations placed on it in respect of the processing.

(c) In addition, the following core principles should be borne in mind:
- It will be intrusive and may be highly intrusive to obtain information about employees' health;
- Employees should be aware of the extent to which information is held and the reasons why it is held;
- Decisions about an employee's suitability for particular work are properly management decisions, but the interpretation of medical information should be left to a suitably qualified health professional.

I. Employee's Rights

Under the DPA an employee (which includes a worker) has the following **10.18** rights:

(a) To access any Personal Data which an employer as a Data Controller holds (DPA, s 7) (see para **10.19** below).

(b) To prevent processing of Personal Data likely to cause damage or distress (DPA, s 10), or to apply for rectification, erasure, or blocking of inaccurate data held by an employer as a Data Controller (DPA, s 14).

(c) To require that no decision in relation to his performance at work is based solely on the processing by automatic means of the employee's Personal Data (DPA, s 12).

(d) To seek compensation if an employee suffers damage by reason of the employer failing to comply with its obligations under the DPA (DPA, s 13).

How would an employee access Personal Data? Previous data protection legisla- **10.19** tion had always allowed employees access to certain information. However, the DPA has extended this right with the result that subject access requests have become more frequent, especially in contentious situations. An individual who pays a prescribed fee (£10 is currently the maximum that can be charged) and makes a written request is entitled, within 40 days:

(a) to be informed by the employer whether any Personal Data relating to them is being processed by or on behalf of the employer;

(b) to a description of any Personal Data being processed, the purposes for which it is being processed, and to whom the Personal Data has been or may be disclosed; and

(c) to receive copies of any Personal Data in an intelligible form.

(DPA, s 7)

The Information Commissioner has published guidance on how to deal with **10.20** such requests, both in Part II of the Code of Practice (Employment Records) and in a separate note headed 'Data Protection Technical Guidance—Determining what is personal data'. The latter note was necessary in light of the Court of Appeal's decision in *Durant v Financial Services Authority* [2003] EWCA Civ 1746, which considered the definition of both 'personal data' and 'relevant filing system'. Should an employer wish to resist an application for information under DPA 1998, s 7, reference should be made to these sources of information, but the following are the key findings:

(a) the DPA only requires a reasonable and proportionate search to be carried out; and

(b) Personal Data is limited to information related directly to the Data Subject and his privacy and does not include all information relating to claims or complaints made by the Data Subject or investigations relating to those claims or complaints.

10.21 Are there any exemptions to this right to access Personal Data? There are a number of specified exemptions (DPA, Sch 7):

(a) Confidential references given by the employer to whom the subject access request is being made will be exempt. However, if an existing employee asks for a reference provided by a previous employer, then their current employer will arguably be required to disclose it, subject to the other exemptions mentioned below.

(b) Management forecasts, negotiations, and information which is legally privileged are also excluded.

(c) An employer owes duties in relation to other individuals under the DPA. As a result, if by disclosing data an employer discloses the identity of another individual, the employer should seek that individual's consent before disclosing the data otherwise it may be in breach of the DPA.

J. Right to Privacy

10.22 What right to privacy does an employee have? At the moment, an employee does not have a free-standing right to privacy. However, in the context of the DPA and Human Rights Act 1998 (HRA) it is clear that an employee does have some rights to privacy within the workplace. The HRA requires courts and tribunals to interpret legislation in accordance with the principles of the HRA. Article 8 of the Convention contained in Sch 1 of the HRA provides that everyone has the right to respect for his private and family life, his home, and his correspondence. However, this is qualified on the basis that it may be acceptable to interfere with the right if it is in accordance with the law and is necessary in a democratic society in the interests of national security, public safety, or the economic well-being of the country, for the prevention of disorder or crime, for the protection of health or morals, or for the protection of the rights and freedoms of others which will include the employer. This means an employee is most likely to rely on the HRA to argue that a process is tainted by unfairness or that certain evidence should be excluded. In the employment context, this is most likely to arise in the context of a dispute between employer and employee, where the employee's right to privacy will be balanced against both parties' right to a fair trial (see, for example, *De Keyser Ltd v Wilson* [2001] IRLR 234; *Pay v Lancashire Probation Service* [2004] IRLR 129; *Chairman and Governors of Amwell View School v Dogherty* [2007] IRLR 98).

11

FUTURE EMPLOYMENT LAW CHANGES

A. Introduction

This chapter is appreciably shorter than that which appeared in the previous edi- **11.01**
tion, as there are no great developments in sight—rather, the Government is
looking at consolidating existing legislation. Nonetheless, set out below are the
likely key changes between now and the next edition of the book.

B. Single Equality Act

The Government is proposing a Single Equality Act to consolidate and amend **11.02**
anti-discrimination legislation and also to extend protection from discrimination outside the sphere of employment. Consultation took place in 2007 and the
Government's response was published on 21 July 2008 and the main proposals
are as follows:

(a) review of definitions and tests in discrimination to eliminate the discrepan-
cies between different types of discrimination, for example:
  • Harmonization of the definition of indirect discrimination;
  • Harmonization of the concept of justification in cases of indirect discrimi-
    nation, direct age discrimination and disability-related discrimination, as
    a 'proportionate means of achieving a legitimate aim';

(b) extension of protection from indirect discrimination to transsexuals;

(c) extension of protection against harassment in the RRA 1976 to harassment
on grounds of colour and nationality;

(d) introduction of a 'general occupational requirement' defence across all strands of discrimination except disability and the removal of the current 'genuine occupational qualifications' in sex, gender reassignment, and race cases;

(e) removal of the requirement for a comparator in victimization cases;

(f) the Government is still considering whether to allow representative actions in discrimination law, whether to make specific provision for multiple discrimination, and whether to extend employer's liability for harassment of employees by third parties beyond the current cases which are based only on sex or gender re-assignment.

C. Statutory Dispute Resolution Procedures

11.03 The Government always intended to review the statutory dispute resolution procedures two years after their implementation and an independent review at the end of 2006 was followed by consultation during 2007. A draft bill was published on 6 December 2007 which envisages the repeal of the existing statutory dispute resolution procedures in their entirety and their replacement with the following:

(a) *Procedural fairness of dismissals*
The Government has decided to revert to the position prior to the existing statutory procedures coming into force. Thus the statutory dispute resolution procedures will be replaced by a new non-regulatory system. Therefore, where a dismissal is unfair on procedural grounds alone, the tribunal will be able to reduce the compensation payable to reflect the likelihood that the dismissal would have gone ahead anyway, even if the correct procedure had been followed.

(b) *Revised ACAS code*
The tribunal will have a much wider discretion in relation to procedural failings and, in particular, by reference to compliance or otherwise with the ACAS Code, which will be revised.

(c) *ACAS conciliation*
ACAS's duty to conciliate will be widened.

The new provisions will not come into force before April 2009.

12

TABLE OF RECENT TRIBUNAL AWARDS IN DISCRIMINATION CASES

This chapter summarizes the tribunal awards made in certain cases since 2004 where discrimination, as described in Chapter 2, has occurred.

In addition to a declaration that discrimination has taken place (SDA 1975, s 65(1)(a); RRA 1976, s 56(1)(a); SOR 2003, reg 30(1)(a); RBR 2003, reg 30(1)(a); DDA 1995, s 17A(2)(a); EEAR 2006, reg 38(1)(a)) and recommendation of action which the employer must take in respect of the discriminatory act (SDA 1975, s 65(1)(c); RRA 1976, s 56(1)(c); SOR 2003, reg 30(1)(c); RBR 2003, reg 30(1)(c); DDA 1995, s 17A(2)(c); EEAR 2006, reg 38(1)(c)), the main remedy a tribunal can award in discrimination cases is financial compensation. Such an award can comprise of the following elements:

- Compensation for the applicant's loss—this should put the complainant in the same position, so far as possible, that he would have enjoyed had the act of discrimination not occurred (*Ministry of Defence v Cannock* [1994] ICR 98, EAT). Accordingly, the amount of the award will depend on how much the complainant earns and the tribunal's view of what would have happened had no discrimination occurred. Normal principles of mitigation will also apply, as will a reduction for accelerated receipt where the compensation is for future loss.

- Compensation for injury to feelings—a tribunal will also consider an award for injury to feelings as a result of the discriminatory act (SDA 1975, s 66(4); RRA 1976, s 57(4); DDA 1995, s 17A(4); SOR 2003, regs 30(1)(b) and 31(3); RBR 2003, regs 30(1)(b) and 31(3); EEAR 2006, reg 38(1)(b) and 39(3)). This should compensate the complainant for 'anger, upset and humiliation' caused by the act of discrimination. For guidance in relation to the likely amount of compensation, see *HM Prison Service v Johnson* [1997] ICR 275. However, it should be compensatory, not punitive and correspond with damages in personal injury cases. In *Vento v Chief Constable of West Yorkshire Police (No 2)* [2003] ICR 318, three bands of injury to feelings awards were identified, £500.00–£5,000.00 (less serious, isolated, or one-off cases); £5,000.00–£15,000.00 (serious cases); and £15,000.00–£25,000.00 (most serious cases). Reference may also be made to the Judicial Studies Board's guidelines on compensation for post-traumatic stress disorder.

- Compensation for personal injury—this may be sought where psychiatric illness results from the discrimination (*Sheriff v Klyne Tugs (Lowestoft) Ltd* [1999] ICR 1170).

- Compensation for aggravated damages—these are rare, but aggravated damages will be awarded where the complainant is able to establish a causal link between 'exceptional or contumelious conduct or motive' on the employer's part and the complainant's injury to feelings. An example would be the failure to investigate the allegation of discriminatory behaviour.

- Compensation for exemplary damages—exemplary damages are also rare but will be awarded where there is oppressive, arbitrary, or unconstitutional action by the Government or where the employer's conduct was calculated to make a profit for itself which would exceed any compensation payable to the complainant (*Kuddus v Chief Constable of Leicestershire Constabulary* [2002] 2 AC 122).

The amount of compensation may be uplifted by up to 50 per cent pursuant to ss 31 and 32 of EA 2002 should an employer fail to follow the disciplinary procedure or deal with a grievance brought by the employee and where this has occurred it is noted in the summaries. There is equally a power to reduce the amount of compensation, where the process is not complied with, but this is rare and none of the cases summarized include a reduction.

If individuals are named as defendants in the proceedings, a tribunal may make an award against the individual as well as the employer, or even if the employer is not found to be liable. Interest will be awarded on the compensation award made

(Employment Tribunals (Interest on Awards in Discrimination Cases) Regulations 1996 (SI 1996/2803)).

The table below sets out recent awards (since 2004) in tribunal claims where one of the claims is discrimination as described in Chapter 2. The table is not meant to be an exhaustive list and obviously the amount of any award will be dictated by a large number of factors, not least the earnings of the individual. Also, many cases settle, particularly where the amounts involved are large and as the details of the settlement are usually confidential, they are not available to be included in the table. However, the awards should be indicative of the approach taken.

For the purposes of what follows, the key set out below has been adopted:

AD	Age Discrimination
CD	Constructive Dismissal
DD	Disability Discrimination
RBR	Religion and Belief Discrimination
RD	Race Discrimination
SD	Sex Discrimination
SO	Sexual Orientation Discrimination
UD	Unfair Dismissal
R	Respondent/employer

The summaries have been sorted by the type of discrimination and then by the level of the award made. They include both employment tribunal decisions and those of the employment appeal tribunal and Court of Appeal. Case references are not provided as the majority of the decisions are unreported, but they should be accessible via the website of the relevant tribunal or court.

12

Recent Tribunal Awards

Sex Discrimination Awards

AWARD	CATEGORY	DATE	PARTIES	CASE SUMMARY
£750.00	SD	28-Apr-06	*Andrew Moyhing v Bart's and London NHS Trust, EAT*	M, a male nurse, was not allowed to carry out routine procedures and intimate examinations on female patients without a chaperone. He claimed this did not allow him to do his job properly, and that his training was also hampered. The EAT overturned a finding by the ET that it was acceptable for the Trust to have a different chaperoning policy for male nurses, than female nurses for intimate procedures. The policy, based on the assumption that all men are sexual predators was the result of stereotyping and made M feel untrustworthy. As this was not an unreasonable reaction, the Trust's policy constituted discrimination. Award: £750.00 for injury to feelings. The ET said, 'We understand why he would have wanted to bring this claim as a matter of principle, and he has succeeded. But harbouring a legitimate and principled sense of grievance is not to be confused with suffering an injury to feelings. We think that the appropriate figure is £750.'
£1,000.00	SD	11-May-05	*Walker v BHS Limited and Another, EAT*	W was a female self-employed lingerie model. R2 another employee of R1 was also a female and employed by R1 to engage models for photographic shoots. R2 engaged W on 7 June, 23, 28 June, 16 August, and 13 September 2002. On each of those occasions the Employee made sexual advances to W. W brought a claim before the ET alleging sexual harassment and that her refusal to accede to R2's advances resulted in the loss of her career as a fashion model. It was accepted by both parties that W fell within the wider definition of an employee within s 82, SDA 1975 when engaged on shoots and that accordingly R1 would be vicariously liable for the acts of R2. The ET held that W's allegations amounted to a continuing state of affairs constituting a single act extending over a period until 13 September, the last day of discrimination alleged by W. Accordingly, the ET found that as W had presented her claim on 20 November 2002, she had presented her claim in time and suffered a single act of discrimination. W was awarded £1,000 compensation. R1 and R2 appealed claiming the ET had been wrong to find W's claim had been presented in

time. W cross-appealed claiming that the ET had been wrong to find only a single act of discrimination. The EAT dismissed the appeal, allowed the cross-appeal in part, but did not alter the level of compensation.

Award		Date	Case
£1,500.00 for injury to feelings plus other earnings-related compensation	SD + UD	18-Feb-05	*Whyte v Capital & Regional Property Management Ltd, ET*

W was employed by R as an accounts administrator from 26 April 2004 until she was dismissed on 16 July 2004. W was dismissed because of concerns about her performance, which included her sickness record and her alleged failure to keep on to top of her work. With regard to her sickness record, R was aware that half of this time off was related to W's pregnancy, and this absence contributed to her being unable to catch up with her backlog. The ET accepted that there were legitimate areas of concerns in W's performance, which began before R's knowledge of W's pregnancy. However the ET found that R was too hasty in concluding that W's problems were 'insurmountable' and in dismissing her without further chances or extension of her probationary period. Therefore the ET concluded that the dismissal at that particular time would not have taken place but for W's pregnancy and her pregnancy-related sick leave. Sex discrimination and unfair dismissal findings were made. The ET concluded that had W not been dismissed on 16 July 2005, she would have been given a three-month extension of her probationary period and R would not have been able to dismiss fairly until a departure from work on 31 October 2005. Award: £1,500.00 for injury to feelings (lowest band in *Vento*). Compensation was also awarded for pay until 31 October 2005 and the following six weeks at 90 per cent of her normal pay. For reasons unrelated to R, W was unhappy in this workplace and this was not a case where the premature loss of employment was as serious as it might be with a long-serving employee with strong ties to work.

AWARD	CATEGORY	DATE	PARTIES	CASE SUMMARY
£2,317.58	SD + UD	30-Mar-04	*Porter v Lamvale Construction Ltd, ET*	P was employed by R in a position that had previously been filled by P's stepbrother. The site works manager agreed to take P on for a trial period (but had not previously suggested a trial period for P's stepbrother). P worked on the site for 3–4 weeks and there were no complaints about her work. The engineers then said that P was 'not man enough' to carry on with the job. No other work was offered to P before she was dismissed. The Manchester ET found that P had been less favourably treated than her stepbrother in comparable circumstances. An assumption about P's strength had been made on the grounds of her gender and the dismissal constituted unlawful sex discrimination. Award: £1,317.58 (plus interest) loss of earnings and £1,000.00 (plus interest) for injury to feelings.
£2,595.36	SD + UD	09-May-06	*Cairns v Christine Windridge t/a Mahon House Cattery, ET*	C worked in a cattery/kennels and was regularly seconded to work in the kennels in line with her employment agreement. After C announced her pregnancy she requested an assessment as to the risk of toxoplasmosis, and was placed on secondment to the kennels. R requested advice from a senior environmental health officer, but requested that C went back to work in the cattery before a written response was gained as her independent enquiries had led her to believe that the risk was negligible. C refused and was dismissed. The tribunal found that the risk of toxoplasmosis was sufficient to be of concern to pregnant employees, and that R had dismissed her before the evidence showing that the risk was negligible had been disclosed. Award: £2,595.36, including £1,000.00 injury to feelings and a 20 per cent uplift for failure to follow statutory procedure.
£4,000.00	SD	17-Mar-06	*Corus Hotels v Woodward, EAT*	W applied for a job as a receptionist at an hotel. Her interview was conducted in a 'crassly sexist manner' by a man whose first question to her was 'do you have any children?' W did not get the job and brought a successful claim for sex discrimination against R, for which the ET awarded her compensation of £5,000.00 for injury to feelings. In this appeal the EAT reduced that award to £4,000.00 for two reasons. First the EAT said that tribunals must not take the size of the employer's organization into account when assessing injury to feelings. Secondly, the fact the ET expressed 'deep concern' at the 'complete failure' of R's equal opportunities policy indicated that there was a punitive element to the award. Although that failure could be taken into account when considering liability, punishment for it should not form part of a compensatory award for injury to feelings.

Award	Type	Date	Case	Details
£5,000.00 for injury to feelings plus other earnings related compensation	SD + CD	31-Jul-06	*Susan Rowley v Berwick High School, ET*	SR claimed sex discrimination after she was denied a promotion as the principal pastoral teacher at the school. SR (an experienced teacher) was told that post would not be decided on qualifications but on an interview. When her male bosses offered the job to a male colleague instead, she was devastated and left teaching. The tribunal described SR as a dedicated professional who threw her energies into her profession and that the manner in which she was treated was devastating to her self-confidence. The tribunal held the school's principal had 'watered down' the requirements of the post to suit the man who eventually won it. Award: £5,000.00 for injury to feelings. Loss of earnings was also awarded.
£5,000.00 for injury to feelings plus other earnings related compensation	SD + UD		*Rowan v System 3 (Ltd), ET*	Rowan, the Claimant (C), a female employee of R, formed a personal relationship with a male employee. When the managing director of R found out about the relationship he suspended C but not the male employee. He also required C to attend a disciplinary hearing and then gave her a final written warning in respect of alleged falsification of clocking-in records. Other employees had been given verbal warnings for such misconduct. C was then dismissed following another disciplinary hearing in respect of alleged threats she had made to another employee. The male employee also left and a severance agreement was negotiated with the male employee but not with C. The Manchester ET held that C's dismissal was wholly disproportionate to the misconduct alleged and found that the principal reason for C's dismissal was her relationship with the male employee. C was subjected to a detriment and treated less favourably than the male employee, whose circumstances were not materially different. The disciplinary procedures that took place were designed as a pretext to justify dismissal for the reason of misconduct. C was subjected to sex discrimination and her dismissal was unfair. Award: £5,000.00 (plus interest) for injury to feelings. Loss of earnings was also awarded.
£6,000.00	SD	2006	*Harwood v Sargent t/a Brewers Arms Hotel, ET*	H was employed as a waitress and bartender. She brought a claim for sex discrimination alleging that R kissed her on the lips against her wishes. The tribunal upheld her claim and awarded £6,000.00 for injury to feelings. Although this was principally a one-off incident, the tribunal took into account the fact that H was only 18 at the time and that R was her employer and much older. Therefore, this was a serious case falling within the lower part of the middle band of *Vento*. Award: £6,000.00 for injury to feelings.

AWARD	CATEGORY	DATE	PARTIES	CASE SUMMARY
£7,000.00	SD	22-August-07	*Pauleen Lane v Trafford Council, ET*	PL was the mayor of Trafford. R banned her from travelling in the mayoral car with her baby, as she was banned from breastfeeding in the car. PL alleged that this was sex discrimination, and the tribunal agreed. Award: £7,000.00.
£7,000.00	SD + UD	05-Oct-05	*Newing v Toni & Guy (Andover), ET*	N was employed from 9 October 2004 by a Toni & Guy hairdressing salon that was managed and part-owned by W. It was agreed that she would be sent on a six-week stylist course organized by Toni & Guy in London, beginning on 4 January 2005. N discovered she was pregnant and told W this. He then dismissed her. The tribunal uplifted its award of £5,000.00 for injury to feelings by 40 per cent as it concluded that the failure to follow statutory procedure was near the top of the scale of non-compliance. R failed to follow any of the three specified steps in the statutory dismissal procedure and in fact made no attempt to follow a procedure of any sort. W ignored the company's own procedures, did not consult the company handbook, and ignored advice from a director. The compensation for injury to feelings therefore increased to £7,000.00.
£7,074.00	SD + CD	09-Sep-06	*Tahera Siddika v Kwais Okanta, ET*	S, a female assistant carer in a Coventry care home alleged sexual harassment by her manager in the form of suggestive text messages and phone calls over a period of several months at a Birmingham tribunal. The harassment included sending her pornographic images and over-familiar text messages, as well as claiming that she could have the wages she was owed if she slept with him. The chairman noted that neither of the parties had impressed as witnesses but S had been more credible and awarded her £7,074.00 for injury to feelings.
£7,500.00	SD	01-Dec-05	*Sutton v The Ranch Limited, ET*	S worked as a restaurant manager and went on maternity leave on 26 April 2004 and returned to work on 8 November 2004. At a meeting on 4 November 2004, to discuss arrangements for returning to work, R informed her that it did not need her full time and could offer her part-time hours of work that would be paid at an hourly rate of £5.00. S made it clear that she found this proposal unacceptable and lodged a grievance. She subsequently sought legal advice and her solicitors wrote a formal grievance on her behalf.

She received no written response to her grievance and her request for a meeting to discuss it was refused. S wrote a further letter of grievance, which she handed to a director, but he refused to read it. Awarded £5,000.00 for injury to feelings which it uplifted by 50 per cent to £7,500.00 for the 'total disregard' shown by R for the statutory grievance procedures and the genuine complaints and concerns raised by S.

| £7,500.00 | SD + CD | 04-Mar-05 | *Eastwood v (1) JCT600 Ltd (2) Mr A N Knight, ET* | E worked as a personal assistant to R2. R2 repeatedly asked E out, asked personal questions about her private life, and touched her when walking past. E frequently showed that his conduct was unwelcome, both by her words and by her behaviour. After a few months, E spoke to R1's human resources manager, Mrs S, about R2's behaviour. Mrs S decided that because the complaint was against a senior employee she would report the matter to the managing director. A meeting took place between E, Mrs S, and the managing director. The tribunal remarked that involving the managing director at the very first formal meeting about such a sensitive grievance was entirely inappropriate. At this meeting, E was asked to put her complaint in writing. She duly did this on 5 November 2003 and soon after she went on sick leave, remaining off sick until she resigned in February 2004. Between November and February, meetings took place between Mrs S and R2 and between Mrs S and E. During this period, Mrs S also sent E several letters asking her how she wished to proceed. On 19 February 2004, R2 resigned to set up a business and in ignorance of his resignation E resigned on 20 February 2004. Despite these events, Mrs S continued her investigation into the complaint. On 17 March 2004, the managing director wrote to R2 informing him there was inadequate information to support E's allegations. The tribunal concluded that R1 had conducted a 'botched investigation' and acted as it did 'through a combination of incompetence and intrigue'. It awarded £7,500.00 compensation for injury to feelings, plus £710.00 interest. The award was made jointly and severally against R1 and R2. The tribunal took account of R2's seniority within the R1's organization and said he should bear a substantial degree of responsibility for his actions in harassing E as he was in reality her employer, rather than simply a fellow employee. |

347

AWARD	CATEGORY	DATE	PARTIES	CASE SUMMARY
£8,000.00	SD	05-Mar-04	*Brown v London Underground Ltd, ET*	B, a male employee of R, had made a complaint of sexual harassment against another employee that was proven. Later, another employee made remarks to B that explicitly referred to B's earlier complaint and which offended B. B made a written complaint. An informal, not formal, investigation was carried out. Another investigator was appointed. He found the allegation proven but recommended that no further action be taken because an apology had been made. He failed to note that an express apology had not been forthcoming. When a disciplinary charge was eventually brought, no disciplinary punishment was ordered. The London South ET found that the delay in instigating a formal investigation was on the ground of B's sex. Had B been a woman making a similar complaint, R would have taken it more seriously. The ET held that, had B been female a disciplinary charge and punishment would have been ordered. The ET dismissed the claim for victimization. Award: £8,000.00.
£8,040.15	SD	26-April-07	*Angela Hildreth v Perdu Bar, ET*	AH, financial manager of a bar in Newcastle was constructively, wrongly, and unfairly dismissed by R after she told them that she was pregnant. AH was asked to choose between her job and having a baby and was suspended from her job when she told the owners that she was pregnant two months after getting the job. She resigned after returning from suspension after suffering 'harassment, a very negative appraisal, having [her] wages docked and [her] life made a misery'. Award: £8,040.15.
£8,485.05	SD + UD	21-Oct-04	*Dixon v Motorcise (Torbay) Ltd, ET*	D was appointed by R, a women-only gymnasium, as its manager. Two months after commencing this employment, D informed C, one of the owners of the company, that she was pregnant. D thereafter refused to assist with any duties which involved lifting or stretching, or painting because of the fumes. She was sent home for a week with no pay, although there was no ostensible contractual right to do so. D informed C that she had to attend an emergency scan appointment. C protested that her absence would be inconvenient and tried to persuade her to reschedule it. C made it clear that in future D was expected to make antenatal appointments out of working hours. D also asked that a risk assessment be carried out but this was not done. D went on sick leave around a month after these events and R failed to pay her her sick leave. D considered this to be the last straw and

Award		Date	Case	Details
				resigned. The parties subsequently agreed D would return and C would issue terms and conditions, including that antenatal appointments were to be taken in D's own time. D objected to this and C then refused to allow her to withdraw her resignation and return to work. The ET held that D had been constructively dismissed, resigning in responses to two fundamental breaches of contract: the failure to pay contractual sick pay and a course of conduct that undermined trust and confidence. It found that there was pregnancy-related discrimination and also that there was no record of any disciplinary process to support R's defence that its conduct had been in response to D's 'poor performance and attitude'. Award: £8,485.05 (consisting of £4,534.03 plus interest for past loss of earnings, £1,951.02 for future loss, and £2,000.00 plus interest for injury to feelings). D had obtained alternative work a few weeks after the dismissal and there was no evidence of ongoing health difficulties or continuing upset, which accounts for the paucity of the award.
£8,500.00	SD	02-Nov-04	*Carney v Rouf and Another, EAT*	The EAT will rarely interfere with the amount awarded by a tribunal for injury to feelings. However, in this case, the EAT increased a tribunal's award of £1,500.00 (*Vento* lowest band) for injury to feelings. C worked as a barmaid and suffered persistent sexual harassment. The EAT thought the harassment suffered extended beyond the lowest band and therefore substituted an award of £8,500.00 (middle band). The EAT thought that the tribunal had erred in holding that three months of sexual harassment amounted to only a short period, and that the physical contact that C was subjected to was not of any great significance. The tribunal should also have taken into account the fact that C suffered harassment from one of the owners of the business as opposed to a junior employee. Award: £8,500.00 for injury to feelings, plus interest.
£9,000.00	SD	15-Apr-04	*Mrs Campbell v Royal London Alliance, ET*	C was a facilities manager and had been told that she was the only candidate for a new post. After giving birth to twins and unfortunately losing one of the babies, she was told that an external candidate had been selected instead of her, despite the fact that the job had not been externally advertised. Further, she had not been given the opportunity to submit a CV and was only given 24 hours notice of her interview. She brought a claim for sexual discrimination and the tribunal held she was discriminated against at the interview process. Award: £9,000.00 for 'injury to feelings' plus interest.

AWARD	CATEGORY	DATE	PARTIES	CASE SUMMARY
£9,292.75	SD	21-Oct-04	*Gately v Sainsbury's Supermarkets plc, ET*	The claimant, G, worked on price control for R at its East Dulwich store. G was in a relationship with M, an assistant manager at the store until June 2002. After the relationship had ended, M continued to seek out G at work when there was no work-related reason for him to do so. M spoke to her using personal, intimate, and occasionally abusive language. G made it clear these attentions were unwanted. Between September and November 2002, G asked two senior colleagues to speak informally to M, which they did, asking him to leave G alone. In November 2002, G found herself alone in the office with M who had joined her for no work-related reason. She went home distressed and went on sick leave until June 2003. In this time, M sent text messages, which distressed G. M eventually ceased contact on the instruction of one of R's managers, after G's mother had visited the store and lodged a grievance on her daughter's behalf. G made several attempts to return to work at a different store but resigned, as she felt unable to continue working for R. The ET found M's conduct was a continuing act that ended on 29 December 2002. G presented her employment tribunal claim 48 weeks out of time. However, the ET considered it just and equitable to extend time because G had been unwell for much of the period, she had awaited the outcome of an internal investigation and had delayed issuing proceedings until the breakdown of her attempt to return to work. The ET rejected a reasonable steps defence based on R's policies on equal opportunities and fair treatment at work, which are made routinely available to all staff. The ET had to consider the steps taken in relation to the individual discriminator, M, to prevent discrimination and not those taken in relation to employees generally. There was no evidence relating to the level of information, support, or training given to M so the defence could not succeed. The ET found R was liable for sexual harassment of G by M. Award: £4,542.75 plus interest for loss of earnings; £4,750.00 plus interest for injury to feelings. The ET rejected a claim of sex discrimination relating to the handling of the grievance. The ET accepted R's explanation that inadequacies in the initial process were matters of organizational failure, sufficient to displace any inference of sex discrimination.

| £9,855.00 | SD + CD | 27-May-06 | *Hazel Taylor v (1) Mr Chalmers (2) Mr Gannon, ET* | T was sexually harassed by her boss R2, who would hug and kiss her every day when she arrived at work. He would deliberately brush against her and made offensive and suggestive comments to her. He simulated sex when standing behind her. In August 2005 he sent several sexually explicit text messages to her and T resigned. T told R1 she was leaving, he said he sympathized but could not do anything as he was in the process of selling the business to R2. The tribunal held that H was subjected to a number of incidents of sexual harassment and although she is 'of fairly robust character and able to cope with the normal banter that would take place in a bar', the tribunal was satisfied that she was upset and humiliated by her treatment. The tribunal added that the first respondent, R1, was responsible for discriminatory acts by his employees. Award: £9,855.00, including £5,000.00 for injury to feelings. |
| £9,993.79 | SD + UD | 01-Sep-04 | *Paulsen v (1) N B Mason Entertainments Ltd (2) Ferguson, ET* | In August 2002, the claimant, P, was the manager of DeNiro's nightclub. The club was operated by R1. Prior to August 2002, DeNiro's traded as The Cube, a pub. During this time, T, manager of another club operated by R1, was based at The Cube. At all times, P held the licence to the Cube. R1 went into administration. R2, the second respondent, was one of the joint administrators. Around November 2003, R2 decided redundancies were unavoidable at the club. However, R2 left it to R1's systems manager to deal with the redundancies. The systems manager interviewed P and T. Both P and T claimed to be the front person of the club but the systems manager did not investigate these claims. For no apparent reason, the systems manager concluded that T was the manager and P was the assistant manager. On this basis, the systems manager proposed to R2 that P be made redundant. P brought a claim for unfair dismissal and sex discrimination against R1 and R2. The ET held the following: (1) At all times, P was the manager of the club and T was a displaced manager who carried out managerial functions as and when required. (2) R1 had replied to the statutory questionnaire in a deliberately misleading way. It stated P was assistant manager of The Cube, and that certain criteria had been used in the selection process for redundancy when in fact there were no formal criteria at all. |

AWARD	CATEGORY	DATE	PARTIES	CASE SUMMARY
				The ET inferred from the deliberately misleading replies and the lack of a credible explanation for those replies that R1 had committed an act of direct sex discrimination against P. (3) The systems manager had accepted T's claims at face value and rejected P's claims without investigation or enquiry. On this basis, P had been treated less favourably than T in being removed from her job. The ET also found the dismissal to be unfair. It dismissed the claim against R2 because he played no active part in the decision to dismiss P. Award: £4,993.79 plus interest for loss of earnings and £5,000.00 plus interest for injury to feelings.
£10,346.66	SD + UD	07-Apr-06	*Leigh v Express and Star Limited,* ET	A temporary telephone salesperson, L, was informed that the promised extension of her contract would not go ahead the day after she informed R of her pregnancy. She had had time off work with morning sickness and had been commented on unfavourably by a colleague. She did not return to work after informing R of her pregnancy. The tribunal found that she had been dismissed because R feared that she would have further periods of sick leave attributable to her pregnancy. The ET rejected R's claim that L had contributed to her dismissal because of previous (unrelated) absences, holding that 'the effective cause of her dismissal was her pregnancy'. Award: £10,346.66, including £5,000.00 for injury to feelings and a 25 per cent uplift for failure to follow the statutory dismissal procedure.
£10,680.88	SD + UD	16-May-06	*Woods v MJM International Limited,* ET	W worked as a call centre supervisor for R, dealing with customer complaints. She worked compressed hours while having problems with childcare, and informed her employer that she was pregnant again in 2004. Her managers informed her that her compressed hours had caused problems and had only been a trial arrangement, and that she was required to work from 9 to 6pm five days a week. This was rejected, as were three other alternative proposals. She resigned. The tribunal in Glasgow found that as her working hours had been changed unilaterally, and all the proposed alternatives reduced her salary, she had been constructively unfairly dismissed. R was unable to support its claim that her compressed hours were causing problems, and the tribunal found that W

had been less favourably treated because of her pregnancy and intention to take maternity leave, which constituted direct sex discrimination. She was awarded £5,468.08 for her unfair dismissal and £5,212.80 injury to feelings for sex discrimination. W's indirect sex discrimination claim was adjourned pending the Court of session's decision in *Ministry of Defence (Royal Navy) v MacMillan*, in which the EAT had held that refusal of part-time work was not indirect sex discrimination.

| £11,000.00 | SD | 25-Nov-05 | *X v (1) Coral Racing (2) Mr Y, ET* | X was employed as deputy manager in a branch of R1. R2 worked in X's branch one day and made a number of unwanted sexual comments and sexual advances towards her. He also touched her inappropriately and X told him she objected to his behaviour. A month later, he worked in the shop again and made lewd comments to X and sexually assaulted her. X made a complaint but an investigation concluded that without a witness that could corroborate X's account, the allegations of sexual assault or harassment could not be proven. A while later, X found out that a customer, Mr N, had witnessed the assault on her but it was decided not to interview him on the grounds that he had mistaken another employee for R2. The tribunal found that X was sexually harassed by R2 and that R1 failed to carry out a reasonable investigation by failing to interview Mr N and failed to draw a reasonable conclusion given the evidence of the other staff members. X had a letter from her doctor confirming that he had seen her regularly with symptoms of acute stress that stemmed from being sexually assaulted at work. She was also distressed by the fact that R2 had subsequently been promoted to deputy manager since the assault and was working in the 'next door' branch at a neighbouring village. She had received reports that he had allegedly made threats of violence against her and she was afraid to visit her local shops. She had raised these concerns with R1, which insisted that the company had dealt with the incident properly and refused to take action. Award: R2 to pay £2,000.00 compensation for injury to feelings as he was found to have sexually assaulted and harassed X. R1 was liable for £9,000.00 for injury to feelings. |

AWARD	CATEGORY	DATE	PARTIES	CASE SUMMARY
£11,500.00	SD	13-Apr-06	*Kinsey v (1) Lee Dickens, (2) Champs Sports Camps and (3) Champs Camps Ltd, ET*	Sixth form student, K was employed over 18 months during school holidays at a school camp run by R2 and 3. The MD, R1, subjected K to unwanted attention, said she looked like a boy and that she must be a lesbian. R1 made comments about other female students, suggested K was enjoying looking at them and again accused her of being a lesbian, teased her about not having a boyfriend and made offensive comments. K became withdrawn, stopped seeing her friends, took time off college, and grew her hair to avoid being called gay. Aged 17 at the time, K felt unable to confront R1. Her mother went to see him but he became verbally aggressive towards her. K's parents then made a formal complaint on her behalf. ET ruled all three respondents were guilty of sex discrimination. Award: £11,500.00 which included aggravated damages, injury to feelings, and loss of wages.
£13,000.00	SD + UD	20-May-06	*Slow v 2Let, ET*	Britain's first lesbian and gay estate agency R, was found guilty of sex discrimination for dismissing, S because she was pregnant. R argued it only became aware of the pregnancy the day after the dismissal, which it said was for poor performance. However, S had recently been promoted, given a £4,000.00 pay rise, and use of a car. The Brighton ET held that the dismissal was to avoid paying maternity pay and awarded £7,000.00 for loss of earnings, £5,000.00 for injury to feelings, and £1,000.00 for aggravated damages.
£15,052.22	SD	27-Aug-04	*Hauton v (1) Delta Utilities Ltd (2) Ernest Geddes, ET*	The claimant, H, was employed by R from November 2002 as a bookkeeper/personal assistant. R2 was the shareholder of R1. In June 2003, H was awarded 10 per cent of the shares and company secretaryship of HVDS, a subsidiary shelf company of R1. H had a turbulent personal life during her employment with R1. Her marriage had broken up and she had an 'on-off' relationship with a man none of her colleagues approved of. R2 had deep misgivings and was concerned about the impact of H's personal life on her work. Consequently, R2 gave someone else the company secretaryship and told H he wanted the shares back. R2 made it clear that a factor in this decision was H's problematic personal life, although he also had genuine concerns about H's failure to open a bank account. The decision humiliated H, had a dramatic impact on her self confidence, and she resigned. The ET compared H's treatment to that some years before

				of a male employee who had gone to prison for a second serious assault. That employee's job was kept open for him and he was given shares on his release from prison. The ET contrasted this lenient treatment of a male who committed a drunken assault with the humiliating treatment of an otherwise well performing female who had a problematic love life. The ET found unlawful sex discrimination. Award: £9,052.22 plus interest for loss of earnings; £6,000.00 for injury to feelings. R2 was ordered to pay 70 per cent of the compensation, with the balance attributable to R1. A number of H's allegations of sexual harassment against R2 were dismissed.
£17,618.00	SD + UD	25-June-07	*Sarah Primmer v Rendezvous Café and Others, ET*	SP worked for R as a waitress. She was subjected to bullying on account of her ginger hair, and lewd sexual taunts. She was eventually sacked from her job. She claimed that she had been discriminated against as the bullying and taunts would not have occurred had she not been female. Award: £17,618.00.
£20,000.00	SD	2006	*Goddard v Wilkinson Hardware Stores Ltd, ET*	In 2001 G, who was 21 at the time, confided in her manager, X, who was much older than her, that she was receiving treatment for general anxiety disorder and obsessive compulsive disorder. X offered her sympathy and support, and from then on sought to exploit her vulnerability for the purposes of sexual favours. In 2003 G complained to head office about X's behaviour and he was suspended. G brought a successful claim for sex discrimination against R based on X's sexual harassment. Following the *Vento* guidelines, the tribunal awarded £20,000.00 (top band) for injury to feelings, to reflect the nature of the harassment, the length of time, and the 'disturbing features', of the campaign, which included abuse of power by a manager over a subordinate; the exploitation of a young woman by an older man; and the calculated exploitation of an employee whom the manager knew to be vulnerable.

12

Recent Tribunal Awards

AWARD	CATEGORY	DATE	PARTIES	CASE SUMMARY
£21,410.00	SD + CD	25-Nov-05	*Knipe v (1) Howsons (2) James Eyre Walker, ET*	K started work with R1, a firm of accountants, in June 1994 and was subsequently promoted on. While on maternity leave, she asked to return to work part time, three days a week. K maintained that her workload after she returned to work in April 2002 on a part-time basis was not significantly less than the workload she had carried as a full-time employee. She worked full-time hours in February and March 2003 and 2004 to cover an audit and sometimes swapped her hours one day a week to be available to meet clients or the senior partner. K claimed that not a week went by without R2 criticizing her in some way about her work. She received an oral warning and written warnings. The tribunal found that the warnings were unjustified and were in relation to matters involving others rather than any failing on K's part. K said the pressure she was under made her unwell. She was signed off sick by her doctor in May 2004 and resigned in July 2004. The tribunal found that R2 was aware of the legal obligations on him and his firm 'begrudgingly observed those obligations in seeking to accommodate K's request for flexible work'. The tribunal was satisfied that there was no appreciable difference between the volume and demands of the workload that K carried before and after her maternity leave. The competitive, male-dominated culture of the firm meant she was in effect expected to carry a proportionately much higher and more demanding workload than those of her full-time male counterparts. This, coupled with the insecurity of her position, meant she suffered a detriment. The tribunal concluded that her position following her pregnancy was prejudiced both by virtue of her gender and because of her choice to work flexibly on a part-time basis. Award: £21,410.00 for sex discrimination, including £5,000.00 for injury to feelings, £9,886.00 for loss of earnings, and £6,524.00 for future loss of earnings.
£22,500.00	SD + CD	06-Apr-05	*Smith v (1) The Lodge Hotel (2) Crowe, ET*	S started doing bar work at R1 in April 2003. A few months later, R2 started as a commis chef. R2 made repeated derogatory remarks about the claimant, such as 'slut, tart, slapper, whore'. S complained to her managers but they did not take any action. In April 2004, she complained to one of her proprietors, Mr B, who did not really believe her. The remarks continued and intensified. The attitude of the hotel was that 'chefs will be chefs' and that boys together in the kitchen will use the sort of language about women

				that S complained of. S resigned. The tribunal concluded that this was a case of unfair, constructive dismissal and unlawful discrimination. In awarding damages for injury to feelings, the tribunal noted that there had been a lengthy series of insulting incidents that undermined and hurt the claimant. It stated that: 'we take it as self-evident that when someone has been subjected to this treatment over a period of time, it saps the will, it destroys self-confidence, it makes the individual feel wretched'. The tribunal said that the only reason for not awarding damages in the highest bracket of injury to feelings awards was that the treatment was carried out by young men who 'possibly did not have the wit or prescience to realize the harm they were causing'. In the interests of justice, it would err on the side of caution, because where there is doubt it should be given to the respondent, and it awarded £15,000.00 for injury to feelings plus £7,500.00 for aggravated damages.
£25,000.00 for injury to feelings plus other compensation	SD	14-Sep-05	*Gilbank v Miles, CA*	Here the CA upheld a tribunal's award of £25,000.00 for injury to feelings to a pregnant employee who had suffered sex discrimination. Once it became known that she was pregnant, there had been an 'inhumane and sustained campaign of bullying and discrimination' against G. The campaign was 'targeted, deliberate, repeated and consciously inflicted' and 'not only demonstrated . . . a total lack of concern for the welfare of the claimant herself, but a callous disregard . . . for the life of her unborn child'. The reward is at the top of the *Vento* top band, to reflect the seriousness of the case. Award: for hurt feelings: £25,000.00, £500.00 for personal injury, and £3,550.60 for their failure to pay maternity pay.
£25,000.00	SD	18-July-07	*Jane Martin v Lake House Estate, ET*	JM was employed by R as Sting and Trudie Styler's UK chef, for eight years at a salary of £28,000.00 pa. JM fell pregnant and took time off when ill during her pregnancy. When JM tried to return to work after her maternity leave, she was made redundant. The tribunal found she had been a victim of sexual discrimination and awarded her £25,000.00 compensation.

AWARD	CATEGORY	DATE	PARTIES	CASE SUMMARY
£29,294.00	SD	10-Aug-05	*Jane Giles v Cornelia Care Homes, ET*	JG, a single mother with a young child, was hired in June 2004 by R on a 16-hours-per-week contract. JG took this position as it was compatible with her childcare obligations. In January 2005, R demanded that she start working full time. JG suggested a number of reasonable flexible alternatives. R refused, insisting that she work at least 25 hours per week in the office. JG was forced to resign. R contended that its actions were necessary due to the 'rapid growth of the company' and that it would have little control over JG if she worked at home. The ET upheld JG's complaint of indirect sex discrimination. The ET increased the award by 40 per cent as R had ignored the formal grievance JG filed and the award included an extra £2,000.00 in aggravated damages for the manner in which the case was conducted by R which the ET described as adding 'insult to the injury already suffered'. Award: £29,294.00 damages.
£36,324.00	SD + UD	22-Mar-05	*Mandeir v London and Edinburgh Inns, ET*	M started work with Swallow Hotels in 1993 and was promoted twice over the years, becoming general manager of the Gateshead hotel. In September 2003 (whilst M was on maternity leave) R bought Swallow Hotels and M transferred to R's employment. In February 2004, it was decided that for economic reasons the male manager of the Stockton hotel would manage both the Stockton and the Gateshead hotels and that M would be made redundant. No other hotels were identified for joint management and no other general managers were identified as redundant. M was not warned of the decision to make her redundant. M returned to work on 1 March 2004 and was told for the first time that her post had been made redundant and that she would receive 10 weeks' notice. She was subsequently informed of positions in other towns that she could apply for. The tribunal found that M's pregnancy and/or taking of maternity leave was the main reason for her being selected for redundancy. It found that R failed to show that the selection process was not discriminatory. It noted that the decision to select M was 'entirely opportunistic' and arose from her absence on maternity leave and the decision to ask a male manager to manage two hotels during her absence. Additionally, R could

			show no good reason for its failure to warn M of the potential redundancy or to consult with her about it during her maternity leave. Award: £36,324.00, including £5,000.00 for injury to feelings, £5,000.00 for personal injury, £20,580.00 for loss of earnings, and £11,686.00 for future loss of earnings.
£40,628.00	SD + UD	*Fikerte Gizaw v Home House Ltd, ET*	17-Nov-06	G, the former financial controller of R, won a claim for sex discrimination while on maternity leave. G returned to work after maternity leave to find major changes in her department instigated by her temporary replacement. While she was away R was taken over and the new owners told her she could return to her job after her maternity leave. The changes were: reorganization of the accounting team, taking on work from sister companies, promotion for her replacement, responsibilities having been taken away from her and having to return a week later than planned as she had no desk. She was eventually made redundant after company-wide poor financial results, but her temporary replacement was not. The tribunal described the redundancy consultation process as a 'sham' and the appeal process 'deeply flawed' and it awarded G her compensation after stating that R had 'behaved unreasonably.' Award: £40,628.00 for financial loss, estimated future loss of earnings, and injury to feelings.
£46,537.00	SD + UD	*Murnane v London Irish Centre, ET*	06-Sep-07	M was employed as the director of the charity, R. All previous heads of the charity had been male priests, but M was female. R asked M to resign following allegations that she had been drunk at work, and following proof that her teenage son had misused her company phone. The tribunal found that she had been victimized and consistently undermined by senior members of staff and had been unfairly dismissed, and made an award of £46,537.00 for financial loss, injury to feelings, aggravated damages, and personal injury.

AWARD	CATEGORY	DATE	PARTIES	CASE SUMMARY
£52,000.00	SD	22-Dec-05	*Charles Shoebridge v Metropolitan Police, ET*	R was held to be guilty of victimization of CS, having influenced the decision of Sky News and ITV News not to employ CS as a media commentator on security issues. CS, a former Scotland Yard counter-terrorism officer, had been a regular contributor to news organizations but had left R in 2000 after winning tribunal claims for sex discrimination and victimization and being awarded around £300,000.00 in compensation. In the present case, the ET found that R had continued in its campaign against CS by trying to stop broadcasters employing him because he had successfully sued them. R's Chief Press Officer was one of the persons responsible. Sky bosses were told by sources at R of a 'slight question mark' against CS, although Sky's Deputy Head of News told the ET that CS was sacked because staff disliked him, one describing him as 'a creep'. The ET ordered R to investigate the matter and make sure it could not happen again, imposing a six-month deadline. Award: £52,000.00 (damages for victimization, lost earnings, and injury to feelings).
£58,697.00	SD	03-Oct-06	*Bing v Chard Borough Council, ET*	B, a female town clerk claimed sex discrimination and victimization against the mayor of Chard and R. Tony Prior (who was the mayor of Chard), invited her on holiday to 'cheer her up' during her marriage break-up, pestered her with phone calls, and leered at her breasts during council meetings, resulting in her taking a month's sick leave for stress. He then offered her money which she rejected and sent her letters attacking her work for which she reported him to the Standards Board. Exeter ET ordered him to pay £33,697.00 for loss of earnings, injury to health and feelings, and aggravated damages. Before the hearing B was awarded £25,000.00 from R in settlement of her claims, making a total sum of £58,697.00.
£64,863.00	SD + UD	17-Oct-06	*D P Marland v P&O Portsmouth (Gibraltar) Ltd, ET*	A transsexual ferry crew worker, M, who worked for R on the Pride of Bilboa ferry, was awarded £64,863.00 compensation after suffering verbal abuse at work for a two-year period. The abuse had forced her to give up work two years previously. A tribunal report stated: 'For nearly two years prior to her resignation, the claimant was forced to endure at work an atmosphere of intimidation and hostility caused by the fact that she was

undergoing gender-reassignment'. R admitted discrimination on the grounds of sex, but not unfair dismissal, claiming that M had turned down other roles that had been offered to her. The tribunal held that she had been constructively dismissed. Basic award for unfair dismissal £840.00. Compensatory award for unfair dismissal (loss of statutory rights) £200.00. Loss of earnings to date £21,891.54. Future loss of earnings £16,499.46. Injury to feelings, including an element for aggravated damages £20,000.00. Interest £5,432.00.

£93,000.00	SD + CD	*Michelle Butler v Hertfordshire Police, ET*	01-May-06

B, a policewoman who had been commended for bravery as a pregnant trainee, returned to work after maternity leave. On her return she asked to work flexible hours in order to provide child care for her child. B made repeated requests to transfer to a different department with more flexible hours, but her attempts were repeatedly blocked by her Inspector (N). The Watford ET held that there had been 'no investigation as to whether or not Miss Butler could be accommodated'. Her repeated requests to transfer were rejected by N, despite her 'exhibiting signs of exhaustion'. N was the subject of 'scathing criticism' at the tribunal, who found that he was unsympathetic to B from an early stage, and an 'unimpressive witness'. Award: £93,000.00, includes past wages and two years' future lost wages, plus £2,600.00 interest.

£112,000.00	SD + UD	*Vince-Cain v Orthet Ltd, EAT*	12-Aug-04

C was marginalized and then dismissed in October 2001 after taking two periods of maternity leave (initially from 12/12/98 to 3/3/99 and then from Christmas 2000 to end April 2001 for her second pregnancy). The EAT held that she did not have to mitigate her losses by taking another job, but was entitled to go into higher education instead when she was unable to find a job at the same seniority which was flexible enough to accommodate her childcare needs. Award: approx £112,000.00 which includes: £94,781.82 for loss of earnings, £15,000.00 for injury to feelings, £2,160.55 interest on the injury to feelings award.

AWARD	CATEGORY	DATE	PARTIES	CASE SUMMARY
£153,000.00	SD + UD	03-Aug-05	*MacKinnon v Human Resource Group, ET*	M's firm merged with R and R's chairman, P began making inappropriate advances towards M as soon as they met. P told her he was in love with her, that she was 'the most beautiful woman in the world', and made unspeakably lewd comments about her body. He offered to buy her a BMW and pay her £1,000.00 for each weekend they spent together. M claimed that when she continued to reject P, her £24,000.00 salary was cut and she was warned that her future was 'insecure' unless she had a relationship with him. She reported P to the chief executive for sexual harassment but nothing was done. She was suspended for 'gross misconduct' in July 2003 and resigned three months later. P claimed his actions were part of a 'consensual, embryonic relationship'. The ET made findings of SD, SH, and UD, highlighting the failure of the HR department to carry out a proper investigation which worsened M's injury to feelings. The ET also felt that M's colleagues gave 'poor evidence' as they feared for their jobs. Award: £153,000.00 (consisting of £123,000.00 for loss of earnings and future loss of earnings, £17,000.00 for injury to feelings, £9,000.00 for personal injury, and £4,000.00 for aggravated damages). Of this, P and R must pay half each. M was also awarded £20,000.00 in costs.
£220,000.00	SD + CD	22-Dec-05	*Laetitia Booth v Network Rail, ET*	LB resigned in January 2005, and claimed sex discrimination and constructive dismissal after being demoted and denied promotion in favour of less experienced men. She had worked in the rail industry for 14 years and had been rejected in favour of one male applicant with only 18 months' experience. The ET ruled that R had failed to follow their own procedures when allocating her to a new job and effectively demoted her on the grounds of her sex. Award: £220,000.00.

Race Discrimination Awards

AWARD	CATEGORY	DATE	PARTIES	CASE SUMMARY
£2,500.00	RD	22-Sep-06	*Matt Powell v Gloucestershire Constabulary, ET*	A Bristol tribunal held that P had been unfairly discriminated against as his application to the police force was rejected due to him being white. P was one of 108 white men whose applications were turned down in favour of people from ethnic minorities. Having reached the second round of interviews he was told he had been randomly deselected. 'We were trying to advance diversity in the force and we thought at the time that this was lawful, positive action', a spokesman said. The tribunal heard that every member of an ethnic minority that had applied had been invited to an assessment centre, while two thirds of white applicants had been turned down. Award: £2,500.00.
£3,500.00	RD	18-Oct-06	*Odimba v Cambridge Educational Associates, ET*	O, a black African of Nigerian origin, was employed by R as a catering and facilities manager. As part of her appraisal, it was noted that her communication skills were lacking and an English course was suggested. However, the course suggested was for those who spoke English as a second language. This was held to be direct race discrimination. Award: £3,500.00 for injury to feelings.
£4,000.00	RD	01-Jul-06	*Bartley v Raven Building Services, ET*	B, who is of Jamaican origin, claimed race discrimination, alleging that the foreman on the building site where he worked as a hod carrier frequently referred to him and his black colleagues as 'black bastards' and distinguished B and his black colleagues from other colleagues by referring to them in B's presence as 'your friends'. B's claim was upheld, the tribunal awarded £4,000.00 for injury to feelings. In deciding the figure, the tribunal noted that the discrimination had occurred over a period of time. However, it took into account that B generally seemed to be more concerned about his financial well-being and was prepared to overlook the obvious hurt he had suffered. Therefore in the tribunal's view, this factor brought B's claim down from the middle band in *Vento* to the higher end of the lower band. Award: £4,000.00 for injury to feelings.

AWARD	CATEGORY	DATE	PARTIES	CASE SUMMARY
£5,436.17	RD + SD	16-Mar-04	*Mackie v G&N Car Sales Ltd t/a Britannia Motor Co, ET*	M worked for R as a bookkeeper. M and the three directors of R (brothers) were all of Indian origin. M was later told by the HR manager that the directors did not approve of Asian women working for the company and that they had only employed her because she was married to a Scotsman. After a visit from the directors' father, M was dismissed and no reason was given. M found out she was replaced by a woman of South African origin. The Leeds ET found that M was treated less favourably than a hypothetical male comparator of a different racial origin by being dismissed and then denied a reason for that dismissal. She had suffered less favourable treatment on the ground of her sex and on racial grounds. Award: £2,936.17 (plus interest) for loss of earnings and £2,500.00 (plus interest) for injury to feelings.
£5,710.00	RD + UD	01-Jul-04	*Balbir Kaur v Clive Mark Schoolwear Ltd, ET*	BK was employed by R as an office assistant in January 2003. BK claimed that during an appraisal in March 2003 she was instructed by the company director not to speak Punjabi at work. BK claimed that she had only spoken in Punjabi on two or three occasions to another staff member on work-related matters. A month later she was sacked after R stated that her telephone manner was unsatisfactory. The Birmingham tribunal held that BK had been a victim of racial discrimination. R appealed and lost. Award: £5,710.00.
£7,000.00	RD	3-Jul-06	*Khan v Ealing Consortium, ET*	K brought a claim based on the fact that an individual against whom he brought a grievance based on race was subsequently on a panel assessing him for promotion. £7,000.00 was awarded for injury to feelings but nothing for loss of earnings as the tribunal did not believe that K would have been promoted.
£7,247.90	RD + UD	25-May-06	*(1) Verdi (2) Ganeva v (1) Prima IT Solutions t/a New Horizons (2) Bill Cullin (3) Carol Staples, ET*	Verdi (V) (Russian) was employed as a junior engineer at R, and G (Bulgarian) was on an extended probationary period as a training administrator due to performance issues. V overheard a colleague, R2, saying 'Bloody Bulgarian upstairs and bloody Russian downstairs . . . they should go back to their own countries.' V complained and R2 was disciplined without V being consulted

				about his complaint. V was moved away from R2 and was later dismissed due to performance issues. G was also dismissed on performance grounds. The tribunal found that G had been fairly dismissed because of her unsatisfactory performance. However, the tribunal upheld V's claim of racial harassment against R1 and R2 personally. V had been victimized because he had raised a grievance. The lack of an apology, the move and the circumstances of his dismissal did amount to victimization. He was awarded £7,247.90, being, amongst other things £5,000.00 injury to feelings and a 20 per cent uplift for failure to comply with the statutory dismissal procedure. The award was made against R and not R2 personally.
£8,000.00 plus interest	RD	31-Mar-04	*Huggins v Gwent Police Force, ET*	C was awarded £8,000.00 compensation after Gwent Police failed to act over her allegations of racial discrimination against a fellow employee. Award: £7,000.00 for injury to feelings and £1,000.00 for psychiatric illness plus £3,867.00 interest.
£10,000.00 plus interest	RD + DD	21-Jan-05	*Kanadia v Royal Bank of Scotland Group plc, ET*	K worked at R until going on sick leave in June 2002. She remained an employee on sick leave at the time of the hearing. K was disabled for DDA 1995 purposes having developed epilepsy in 1998. The ET found that, probably unconsciously, M (K's manager) was more unsympathetic to Asian staff than white members of staff. They found less favourable treatment in relation to the following matters: M curtly refused K's request to take three hours off work to take her mother to the airport; white staff had been treated more favourably; and when K tried to discuss her health with M he did not show interest or sympathy but simply told her to ring a private bank helpline for counselling. He also implemented the sickness procedure in a less sympathetic manner than he would have done for a white employee and failed to implement fully K's rehabilitation programme on her return. M suggested K resign and made it clear he did not see a role for her at his branch. The ET found that M had failed to make reasonable adjustments after sickness absence eg by arranging light duties. Award: £10,000.00 plus interest for injury to feelings (middle band of *Vento*).

AWARD	CATEGORY	DATE	PARTIES	CASE SUMMARY
£11,673.00	RD + UD	02-Sep-05	*Akhter Khan v Empower Scotland Ltd, EAT*	AK was dismissed in July 2003 after six months as a development worker at R. He had won his ET claim against R, after complaining that his manager (an Indian Sikh) told him 'you Pakistanis are all the same'. He was sacked after R concluded that his relationship with his manager had irretrievably broken down. The ET upheld his claims of unfair dismissal and victimization under the RRA 1976 as a result of him complaining of racial harassment. R appealed against this, disputing whether the above remark in the context of another remark the manager had made that 'you Muslims are all troublemakers' was capable of being RD before a finding of victimization could be reached. The EAT dismissed the appeal and decided that this was capable of amounting to RD. Award: £11,673.00.
£11,712.72	RD	14-Sept-06	*McKenzie v (1) Hulbert Press Ltd (2) Peter Spanswick, ET*	M, a black British Afro-Caribbean man, was present when R2, a co-worker, made comments, including describing himself and M as 'the new Klu Klux Klan' to a subcontractor. M complained and reacted badly when he believed the complaint was not dealt with. He was dismissed as a result. The tribunal found this to be victimization. Award: £11,712.72 including £5,000.00 for injury to feelings and a 40 per cent uplift for a failure to following the statutory grievance procedure.
£14,500.00	RD +UD	29-Dec-05	*Bhardwaj v (1) Arcwood Ltd (2) J Thurston (3) S O'Connell, ET*	B, a British Asian, was one of two bookkeepers. He was subjected to criticisms, which the tribunal found to be unsubstantiated, and then disciplined. By contrast, no investigation or action was taken against the other bookkeeper. The respondents had argued that they were incapable of committing race discrimination, because they had a large number of employees from diverse ethnic origins and had an equal opportunities policy. The tribunal concluded that '. . . the phrase "equal opportunity employer" has been used in this case by the respondents mechanically and as a cliché . . . We consider that this is a case where unconscious racial discrimination is very likely to have occurred.

As the higher courts have often said, few employers would be prepared to admit any discrimination, especially if it is unconscious.' The tribunal placed the injury to feelings compensation at the top of the lower band in *Vento*, recognizing the significant injury to B's feelings, and awarded £5,000.00. The tribunal placed the personal injury compensation near the top of the moderate bracket, because of the severity of the episode, and awarded B £9,500.00. It stated that the injury to feelings and personal injury in this case did not overlap, because of the months that elapsed before the personal injury occurred.

Award	Type	Case	Date
£16,000.00	RD + UD	*Joanna Wisniewska, Lydia Wisniewska & Sylvia Pionkowska v Glendaruel Hotel, ET*	15-May-07

Three Polish workers were unfairly dismissed after refusing to work and an argument over pay due to racial discrimination. The two sisters (JW and LW) and their friend (SP) had come to Scotland to work in the Glendaruel Hotel and were promised £180.00 a week plus free food and accommodation. However, they were called Polish 'slaves' and 'bitches' in front of customers in the public bar and forced to work more than 48 hours without pay. After one incident when they worked until 5am, they were forced to get up four hours later to clean and LW, who had recently had an operation, collapsed. The others refused to work that evening, and after a row over pay, Clive Jeffries, the hotel boss, told them to 'f*** off now'. The tribunal found that they were 'exploited to a very great degree'. Award: £16,000.00.

Award	Type	Case	Date
£20,000.00	RD	*Rosie Purves v Southampton University Hospitals NHS Trust, ET*	18-May-04

P had worked as a nurse for R for nearly 30 years. P claimed racial discrimination when P was prevented twice from taking care of a white baby after the mothers of both babies complained that they didn't want a black person caring for their baby. The ET found that R's silence and complicity in the racist demands of the mothers meant that P had been discriminated against. Award: £20,000.00.

12

AWARD	CATEGORY	DATE	PARTIES	CASE SUMMARY
£23,062.50	RD + UD	20-Apr-06	*Oluwole v (1) North East Security & Investigation Services Limited (2) Mr K S Dempsey, ET*	O (a black Nigerian man) claimed race discrimination. He was employed for 18 days as a security guard in September 2005 by R. He was summarily dismissed after complaints from the client (Mr Mathison) about pornographic images that had been accessed on the computer late at night. Other white employees who were also present were not investigated. R made a series of allegations about O, including that he had run up a £1,500.00 phone bill, fallen asleep naked on the desk at the client's premises, and downloaded pornographic images from the client's computer. Mr Mathison's evidence was secured by a witness order. The tribunal found that O had been made a scapegoat for the genuine complaints raised by Mr Mathison and that the additional allegations had been 'concocted.' O had been dismissed because of his racial origin. None of the respondent's witnesses gave oral evidence on oath. The judge inferred that the respondent had lied because it believed that O's evidence would have no credence because he was black. He was awarded £10,000.00 for injury to feelings, £5,000.00 aggravated damages, a 50 per cent uplift (under s 31(3) EA 2002) due to lack of disciplinary procedures, and interest. £4,725.75 for loss of earnings, including the 50 per cent uplift. The awards were apportioned as 80 per cent to be paid by R2 personally and 20 per cent by R.
£25,000.00	RD + UD	03-Dec-06	*Clement Lobo v London Underground, ET*	L worked for R since 1989. In September 2004 he was suspended without justification. He later found offensive graffiti had been written about him and he made an official complaint. R did not take any action and more offensive graffiti appeared with sexual and racial content. In June 2005, L was again suspended and also arrested for an assault on his manager. L was not charged or given a reason for his suspension. In July 2005, L filed claims for sex and race discrimination. In February 2006 after a catalogue of incidents he was dismissed and he claimed unfair dismissal. The ET upheld L's claims and awarded him back pay from his dismissal date and also made a rare order for reinstatement. L was awarded £20,000.00 for injury to feelings and £5,000.00 for aggravated damages in relation to the malicious accusations made against him. The ET also ordered R to pay L's legal costs because of their 'unreasonable and misconceived' conduct during the hearing.

Amount	Type	Date	Case	Details
£34,000.00	RD	17-July-07	*Pauline Taylor v Benham General Engineering, ET*	PT suffered eight years of racial abuse from colleagues and management at R (including name-calling and playing music inciting racial hatred). The tribunal awarded her £34,000.00 which included a £5,000.00 uplift for the allegation by R that PT tried to make herself look 'more black' for the hearing. R management was also ordered to attend anti-racism training.
£35,000.00	RD	23-Apr-07	*Patricia Walls v Warwick University, ET*	PW, an Irish academic applied for a post in 2005 as a research fellow with the centre for research in ethnicity and mental health, part of the university's medical school. The ET ruled that the university failed to select PW because she was Irish and they gave the post to a less-qualified candidate instead. Award: £35,000.00.
£58,776.00	RD + SD	12-Jan-05	*Shakila Ali v Jamiel Bux, ET*	A worked for the North East Centre for Diversity, a racial equality centre on Tyneside. Her boss, Jamiel Bux ('R'), made a series of bizarre demands including calling at A's home one evening and giving her a bag of live trout for her to cook for him. On other occasions, R forced A to cook him fish curries and chapatis. A had worked for the centre for 18 years, but it was only when R became a director that A started to experience problems. R even once claimed A was useless 'because she had PMT'. As a result of her treatment, A fell ill and, until the hearing, had been unable to return to work. The tribunal concluded: 'A was treated abysmally' adding that R took advantage of A because she was a Pakistani Muslim who had been brought up in a Pakistani environment until she was 23. Award: £58,776.00 (£15,000.00 for injury to feelings—borderline between the middle and top *Vento* bands; £7,500.00 aggravated damages; £10,000.00 for personal injury; an award for financial loss).

AWARD	CATEGORY	DATE	PARTIES	CASE SUMMARY
£63,176.24	RD + UD	03-Feb-04	*De Hombre, Builes, Guerreiro and Gagliano v (1) Select Service Partner Ltd (2) Mr Miah t/a Café Rajistan (3) The Splendid Restaurant Ltd, ET*	The claimants (Cs) (Spanish, Colombian, Portuguese, and Italian respectively) worked in an Italian-style restaurant operated by the R1. The tribunal found that the employment of each C transferred to R2. Each C was led to believe that their employment would continue. When they returned to work at the restaurant a lady of Indian origin had said 'You have to realize that we cannot employ them because they are not Indian'. It became clear that the Cs' employment would not continue. The London Central ET found that the Cs had suffered a detriment in that their employment came to an end. Held that each C was the subject of race discrimination and was unfairly dismissed. Awards for race discrimination (excluding interest): £29,207.00 (De Hombre); £17,539.00 (Builes); £4,560.00 (Guerreiro); £11,870.24 (Gagliano). Each award included £3,500.00 for injury to feelings.
£65,000.00	RD	06-Apr-06	*Husain v Kent Police Authority, ET*	SH, a former director of intelligence from Pakistan applied twice for the post of intelligence analyst with R, a police authority, once in 1999 and again in 2000. He was rejected on both occasions. Because of differences in the two applications, R compiled a report on SH and circulated it to other forces warning of a 'potentially fraudulent application' which led to SH being arrested and detained when he applied for a job with another police authority. The ET held that it was apparent from the differences in the two applications that SH had simply taken steps to become more familiar with the role he was applying for. The rejection of SH was direct race discrimination. Award: £65,000.00, including £25,000.00 injury to feelings; £4,000.00 aggravated damages; and £5,000.00 exemplary damages.
£75,000.00	RD + SD	23-Feb-06	*Marti Khan & Odette King v Home Office, Central London, ET*	Two interpreters, MK and OK sued the Home Office for race and sex discrimination after their interpreting tasks were outsourced to freelancers. MK and OK continued to turn up to work for 41 hours a week, but their duties comprised of basic admin and filing. They claimed that they were treated badly because they

were two ethnic minority women, and were refused access to facilities that other staff enjoyed. After 15 years they complained that despite their professional skills they were underemployed and being paid less than the freelancers, and their complaints were not dealt with under the statutory grievance procedures. After their complaints were ignored, they were signed off sick and eventually dismissed. The Central London ET found that the women had effectively been redundant since 1990, had suffered systematic race and sex discrimination, and been unfairly dismissed. The Home Office was ordered to reinstate the women in equivalent roles and the tribunal awarded them £75,000.00 each in compensation and lost earnings.

£100,000.00	RD + UD	03-Jan-07	*Wafr Jumard v Clwyd Leisure Limited, ET*

An Iraqi leisure centre worker, J, claimed race and disability discrimination after making a series of complaints about his treatment at work and the actions of his superiors. His employer had been taken over by R in 2001, prior to which he had a clean disciplinary record. He had been disciplined for not leaving the building inside one minute of a fire alarm being sounded, and been made to carry out manual labour despite having a recognized hip condition. Another complaint was about an incident in which his manager gave two white men a refund after they refused to share a jacuzzi with four Asian men, which the tribunal decided was indicative of 'the attitude of R to issues of race'. After he was dismissed for 'aggressive behaviour,' R arranged for him to be covertly filmed by two private detectives, which caused him to add a claim of victimization to his discrimination claims. The tribunal awarded him £100,000.00, which included £53,000.00 for loss of earnings as well as aggravated damages for race and disability discrimination, injury to feelings, and holiday pay.

AWARD	CATEGORY	DATE	PARTIES	CASE SUMMARY
£103,850.30	RD	16-May-06	*Miah v Shearer Darnell Recruitment Limited (default judgment), ET*	M submitted two identical applications for the same job to R, a mortgage recruitment consultancy, after suspecting that his failure to get a job, despite his copious appropriate qualifications, was the result of racial discrimination. He used his own name on one application and 'Mark Williams' on the other. Both were dealt with by the same recruitment consultant. The application in his own name received no response and M telephoned for an explanation. The consultant told M that he had left a voicemail message, which he had not. M requested proof of the message and was ignored. The recruitment consultant left three voicemails and two emails in response to the 'Mark Williams' application. The consultancy did not respond to the subsequent RRA Questionnaire or subsequent claim. A default judgment for direct discrimination upholding the claim was issued on 15 December 2005. At the remedies hearing the facts were outlined and the reasons for the high award. The experience had greatly affected M's mental and physical health and his general outlook and aspirations. The loss of earnings for mortgage advisers is considerable, given that there is a shortage of them and their average earnings are £30,000.00–£40,000.00 per year. M had only been able to find temporary work before becoming too ill to work, and he was awarded amongst other things £95,917.43 loss of earnings and £7,500.00 injury to feelings.
£104,142.00	RD	26-May-04	*Mr Mahmood Siddiqui v Royal Mail, ET*	S was a postal worker for R working night shifts in a sorting office and was systematically abused with racial taunts on a daily basis by his white colleagues for around 10 years. His ordeal included being sworn at, bullied, called 'Paki', and 'spear-chucking raghead' and receiving threats to his wife and children in attempts to make him resign or seek a transfer. As a result he was on medication for severe stress and was forced to retire through ill-health in 2002. His repeated complaints of harassment were ignored by his bosses, his immediate shift manager was said to have given 'tacit support' to the abuse and was reluctant to investigate any of his complaints. It was

only when a hidden camera caught the culprits that they were disciplined and the tribunal ruled that the company took no effective action to help him. Award: £104,142.00 damages on top of £46,400.00 awarded by the tribunal panel in an earlier hearing. He is also set to receive an award for interest and legal costs of around £50,000.00.

£145,000.00	RD and CD	23-Feb-05	*Duncan v Sandwell Metropolitan Borough Council, ET*	D applied for promotion, having been assured by her line manager that she would make a good manager. When she discovered that she was unsuccessful, her state of health began to suffer. An employment tribunal found: 'It is difficult to imagine a more serious case of race discrimination in terms of career prospects . . . D had taken time to obtain academic qualifications and was receiving support from her managers. There was then a profoundly disturbing selection process in relation to Tividale. The claimant was then victimized. She has had to leave her employment with this council to further her career progression.' Award: in addition to general loss of earnings £15,000.00 injury to feelings assessed at the highest level of the middle band in *Vento*. It concluded: 'The impact on the claimant has been devastating. She had had to fight each stage of the process, both internally and externally. She has had to engage in protected litigation in which proceedings have been vigorously defended. R . . . has not at any stage recognized the wrong done to the claimant. It has failed to apologize, even now. That must have caused considerable injury to feelings. The claimant's resignation letter has gone unanswered.' £10,000.00 of damages for personal injury was awarded, being at the lowest end of the moderately severe category. It said 'D has clearly had difficulty in coping with life and work as a result of the discrimination. This has had an impact on her whole life and she had to seek medical help. She has suffered further aggravation of a prior depressive condition.'

12

Recent Tribunal Awards

AWARD	CATEGORY	DATE	PARTIES	CASE SUMMARY
£167,768.00	RD	24-Apr-04	*Lai v Barnet and Chase Farm Hospitals NHS Trust, ET*	R employed L (of Chinese origin) as a consultant radiologist. L agreed for some of his patient reports to be checked. Even though his error rate was found to be no higher than that of anyone else, the system of dual reporting was continued. There was no evaluation of L's work or any attempt to compare his error rate with that of other radiologists. L claimed that this was a detriment imposed on him because he was Chinese. Most of the other doctors in his department were Jewish. In a second claim of victimization, D wrote to the Nuffield Hospital where L had undertaken private practice before the period of dual reporting had been imposed. R had agreed to write to Nuffield in terms that would enable L to resume private practice. However, a letter was sent raising concerns about L's abilities, despite no evidence of any concerns for patient safety being found during the period of dual reporting. L claimed that the action was taken because he had lodged a claim for RD against R. Award by Watford Tribunal: £15,000.00 for injury to feelings; £6,000.00 for aggravated damages; £74,460.00 for loss of earnings from private practice; £67,308.00 for future loss of earnings.
£171,000.00	RD	02-Feb-05	*Howard v Ministry of Defence, ET*	H, an army staff sergeant, was medically discharged with depression and agoraphobia after he had been repeatedly referred to as 'Bubba', 'nigger', 'fat', and 'hairy'. In addition, a spoof employment document questioned his nationality and contained comments about his white wife. Award: the Newcastle Tribunal awarded £171,000.00 and costs for racial harassment.
£372,357.00	RD	14-Oct-05	*David Melloy v Erlestoke Prison, ET*	DM, a white South African prison officer employed by R, suffered racial discrimination by other prison guards. He was the target of insults, one of which was written on his payslip, and was falsely accused of smuggling drugs, whisky, and Playstation games into R's premises. DM was also anonymously sent two bullet cartridges. All DM's grievances in relation to these incidents were investigated but

| £1,277,500.00 | RD | 24-Mar-04 | *The British Medical Association v Mr Rajendra Chaudhary, EAT* | C, an Indian surgeon had four years of hospital training to become a consultant but was passed over for promotion by British born doctors with the same training. C brought a claim against the NHS but R refused to assist or represent him and the case was dropped. C then claimed racial discrimination and victimization against R. The ET found in his favour and R appealed unsuccessfully to the EAT. Award: £1,250,000.00 for loss of earnings, £7,500.00 for injury to feelings for the victimization claim, and £15,000.00 for injury to health categorized as severe to moderately severe psychiatric illness. £5,000.00 aggravated damages and £75,000.00 legal costs, £6,175.00 for costs of STA appeal plus interest. |

none were upheld. DM resigned in January 2004 after having been a prison officer for over 10 years. His treatment at work led to the collapse of his marriage, a nervous breakdown, and a suicide attempt. The ET, in upholding the claim of RD, stated that 'there was evidence of name calling and racist abuse by the claimant's fellow officers [which R] failed to address. There was a specific adverse reaction to his different national origin.' In relation to injury to feelings, the tribunal considered 'the considerable emotional distress caused to the claimant by the respondent's actions. . .which took place over a lengthy period, during which his integrity was questioned and fears for his safety largely ignored'. Applying the *Vento* guidelines, the tribunal assessed the injury to feelings as being in the middle band and awarded £10,000.00. Award: £372,357.00, (including £5,000.00 for costs; £10,000.00 for injury to feelings; £5,000.00 for aggravated damages; £20,000.00 for personal injury; £23,232.00 for loss of earnings; plus an award for future loss of earnings), plus £5,084.00 interest.

Disability Discrimination Awards

AWARD	CATEGORY	DATE	PARTIES	CASE SUMMARY
£500.00	DD	19-Oct-05	*Greig v Initial Security Ltd, EAT*	This case illustrates an award at the bottom of the *Vento* lower band. The contention that the minimum award due in respect of the slightest injury to feelings is £750.00 was rejected by the Scottish EAT. The EAT dismissed G's appeal that the sum of £500.00 (awarded for injury to feelings for unlawful disability discrimination) was inadequate and should have been £2,500.00. G submitted that because the rejection of his job application had been communicated to him directly by letter, this was a discriminatory act. The EAT said that the tribunal had reached the sum of £500.00 on the basis that his claim had not been made wholly in good faith. G had admitted that he was not very well qualified for the job and there was no doubt that he did not really expect his application to be successful. Award: £500.00 for injury to feelings.
£1,500.00	DD + UD	18-Nov-05	*Wilson v Airbus UK Ltd, ET*	W had a serious accident at work and in addition to physical injury suffered post-traumatic stress disorder (PTSD). R conceded that W was disabled and admitted liability in personal injury proceedings (where the question of loss of earnings was also considered). Because of the PTSD, W did not return to work before he was dismissed. R relied on the rigid application of a 'headcount rule' which meant the number of staff could not be increased. They could not employ a replacement for W unless he was dismissed. The tribunal held that R had failed to make a reasonable adjustment, ie varying that rule to allow W to remain nominally on the books albeit unpaid until the outcome of further medical treatment was known. The tribunal awarded £1,500.00 for injury to feelings.

| £3,000.00 | DD | 19-Oct-06 | *Latif v Project Management Institute (PMI), ET* | A blind IT Project Manager, L, who studied for a Professional Management Qualification with R, was discriminated against because parts of the computer-based course were not made accessible to her. She was unable to 'read' the course guide on her text-to-speech software, and instead had to rely on paying a student to read the guide to her for six hours a week. She described this as 'painful and upsetting'. R would not agree to her request to use her own computer in the exam or to tactile diagrams (where the image is raised on the page) but did agree to give her extra time and a reader to explain diagrams and provide back-up in the event of technical problems. R argued that the tribunal did not have jurisdiction to hear the proceedings because it is a US company, but the pre-hearing Chairman stated that as R was in a position to arrange a course and exam for L in Great Britain, they were persons who moved within the jurisdiction of the legislation. The ruling is the first to find a US company with no UK presence liable under the DDA. £3,000.00 compensation was awarded for injury to feelings. |
| £6,000.00 | DD + UD | 11-Jan-07 | *David Ratcliffe v Stannah Stairlift, ET* | A stairlift company was found to have discriminated against a disabled employee, a rail designer, after refusing his request that one of its own stairlifts be installed in the office. DR had chronic back problems and walked with crutches. His request was originally ridiculed, despite the fact that he had difficulty negotiating the stairs to his second floor office and had to go to the first floor to use the toilet. His concentration was also affected by his medication. R maintained that DR had not told them how severe his back problems were when he was interviewed for the job and claimed that he had been dismissed because of grave concerns about his training and conduct. The tribunal held that R had failed to make reasonable adjustments by not allowing more than the standard two weeks for the DR's training, because of his affected concentration. Award: £6,000.00. |

AWARD	CATEGORY	DATE	PARTIES	CASE SUMMARY
£9,000.00	DD + UD	18-Oct-05	*Hodgkins v Peugeot Citroen Automobiles Ltd, ET*	H was diagnosed with blepharitis, a chronic condition. H had four absences in 12 months for which his employer, R, held a disciplinary hearing. The absences were genuine, two of them for blepharitis. At the disciplinary hearing H raised the issue of disability. Despite this, R gave H a first level recorded warning. H appealed, again raising disability and the appeal was rejected. H made a further appeal requesting that R investigate the condition. H supplied a medical report confirming his condition 'may be relevant' under the DDA 1995, suggested possible adjustments and predicted a similar level of absence for the future. The appeal was dismissed by R. The ET found that two of the four absences were disability-related. The correct comparator would be someone who had no absences within a 12-month period and would not have been warned [Note this is no longer the correct test—see para **2.105** above.] The warning would not have been upheld if those two absences had been discounted (reasonable adjustment) so the issuing of it was unjustified disability-related discrimination. The decision to uphold the warning on appeal was a further detriment and discrimination. H stayed off work until he was dismissed in August 2005. The ET accepted that H had a stress and anxiety condition for 11 months up to the hearing and awarded £5,000.00 for injury to feelings and £4,000.00 for personal injury plus interest.
£12,806.37	DD + SD	23-Mar-05	*(1) Rance (2) Jennings v (1) NCH (2) Tasker, ET*	Rance (C1) and Jennings (C2) were employees of R who formed a relationship. R2, another employee, became attracted to C2 and started sending him inappropriate emails, including derogatory statements about C1. C2 complained to his line manager; R2 was given an informal oral warning and told that the emails must stop. After further such incidents, C2 complained again but no action was taken. After yet another complaint, R2 was given an oral warning. Then C1 received a call from a colleague at another branch who made a cruel joke alluding to her cerebral palsy. This had been concocted by R2. R1 investigated but took the view that R2 should be given a chance to improve. The ET noted that the director handling the matter had failed to follow R1's procedures regarding harassment and gross misconduct. C2 resigned and claimed constructive dismissal, which the ET upheld as unfair dismissal, as well as making a finding of sex discrimination.

The ET found that R1 had failed to prevent C2's harassment. In relation to C1, the ET found that she had resigned because she wanted to seek work elsewhere. Her resignation was not as a result of R's discriminatory remark and subsequent handling of it. In relation to her disability discrimination claim, the ET found that R1 had correctly used the statutory defence—the act was isolated and not repeated. However R2 was clearly guilty of disability discrimination and C1 was thus awarded £1,000.00 for injury to feelings. Award: C1 £1,000.00 for injury to feelings. C2 £12,806.37 comprising of £7,500.00 for injury to feelings for sex discrimination and £5,306.37 for loss of earnings.

| £15,000.00 | DD | *Osborne-Clarke (as personal representative of Nigel Osborne-Clarke deceased) v Commissioners of Inland Revenue, ET* | 2006 | O-C, who had been profoundly deaf from birth and had difficulty reading complex documents, started working for R in January 2003. In October 2003 he was investigated by a line manager for an alleged incident of 'computer misuse' and admitted accessing his wife's file in breach of the R's computer policy. It was evident to his manager that O-C did not realize that he was doing anything wrong. However, because of his admission, the manager had no alternative but to refer the matter for disciplinary investigation. His manager stressed in his report the problems of understanding created by O-C's deafness and asked for the case to be expedited. Despite this, the investigating body did not contact O-C until December 2003, setting out the charge and stressing the seriousness of the matter. Two months later O-C committed suicide. The tribunal upheld the claim of disability discrimination brought on behalf of O-C by his widow. In assessing the award for injury to feelings, the tribunal noted that although it was impossible to speculate as to why O-C killed himself, it was clear that he was deeply affected by the disciplinary proceedings, and had expressed concern as to what would happen to him and his family if he lost his job. In the tribunal's view, 'the suicide demonstrates the intensity of the injury to feelings'. The tribunal held that this case fell on the borderline of the middle and top bands set out in *Vento*. Award: £15,000.00 for injury to feelings. |

12

Recent Tribunal Awards

AWARD	CATEGORY	DATE	PARTIES	CASE SUMMARY
£16,250.00	DD + UD	25-Feb-05	*Chalkley v TNT UK Limited, ET*	R refused to let C return to work on crutches, supposedly on health and safety grounds. C was told he could not return until he was '100% fit'. C's manager thought that anyone walking around the warehouse on crutches presented a health and safety hazard which could not be overcome. C asked that he be allowed to return to work or that the matter be referred to the company doctor, but these requests were repeatedly rejected. His consultant and GP both confirmed C was fit to return but R would not budge. It was not even considered that he could undertake 50 per cent of his work, which did not involve going in the warehouse. Award: £16,250.00 (consisting of £1,250.00 for psychiatric damage, £12,000.00 for injury to feelings, and £3,000.00 in aggravated damages) plus 10 months' loss of earnings and 18 months' future loss of earnings.
£16,296.31	DD + UD	04-Apr-05	*Nash v BSP Limited, ET*	N who was profoundly deaf, worked for R as a skip lorry driver. He was dismissed at a meeting that he was not told in advance was to be a disciplinary hearing. N understood that the reason for the dismissal was an abusive text message sent to another employee, X (who was related to N's boss) in response to an abusive text message from X. The ET found that X had sent daily offensive messages to N, which did not expressly refer/relate to N's disability but similar messages were not sent to other non-disabled drivers. X also treated N with less respect than other drivers. The ET held he had been dismissed because of his disability. They also highlighted the fact that no reasonable adjustment had been made to accommodate N's deafness, eg written notice of the meeting and/or an interpreter for the proceedings and to explain to N what the meeting was to be about. Award: £16,296.31 including interest (this award included £10,000.00 for injury to feelings, which did not include compensation for the bullying/harassment relied on as a background to the DD complaint).

Amount	Type	Date	Case	Details
£20,352.85	DD + UD	07-Apr-06	*Hayley Tudor v Spen Corner Veterinary Surgery and Ms S Tschimmel, ET*	T, an animal nursing assistant, had a stroke in May 2005. In June 2005, as a result of her stroke, she lost her sight. In July 2005, on phoning R to inform them that she was out of hospital and could return to her duties, she was informed that she had already been dismissed. As T's job consisted mainly of receptionist duties, it would have been easy to make reasonable adjustments for her, but her employer had simply made the assumption without seeking advice that T would be unable to perform her duties. The employer had therefore acted unlawfully and discriminated against T on the grounds of her disability. Award: £20,352.85.
£24,000.00	DD	01-Jul-06 This is the date this case was reported in the IDS Employment Law Brief 808	*Hall v Broadacres Housing Association Ltd, ET*	H, who wears a full length prosthetic in place of her right leg, brought a claim of disability discrimination against R, after they failed to act on her repeated requests to make changes to the layout of her desk so as to stop her having to turn on the right, causing her pain and discomfort due to her disability. The tribunal upheld her claim, observing that only minor adjustments to the desk were needed to help her. However, due to the 'heartless indifference' shown to her, 'she was made for years to feel like a pariah and a beggar'. In the circumstances, the tribunal thought that the award for injury to feelings should fall within the highest of the three *Vento* bands. Award: £24,000.00 for injury to feelings.
£28,900.00	DD + UD	04-Mar-05	*Talbot v (1) WAGN Railways (2) West Anglia Great Northern Railway, ET*	T was an on-train host who suffered post-traumatic stress disorder after working on a train in front of which a member of the public committed suicide. He was dismissed when he could no longer work with the public after the incident. The ET deducted £25,000.00 from the loss of earnings award because of the possibility that the attempts to find T a different long-standing role with R might have failed. Included in the loss of earnings figure was the loss suffered as a result of his undertaking a three-year university course. The ET was satisfied that T only undertook this course because he justifiably believed that he had been treated as unemployable by R, and that the only way of obtaining comparable employment would be if he could obtain further qualifications. Award: £28,900.00 plus interest (consisting of £17,765.00 for loss of earnings, £7,635.00 for pension loss, £500.00 for loss of travel subsidy, and £3,000.00 for injury to feelings (lower bracket of *Vento*)).

AWARD	CATEGORY	DATE	PARTIES	CASE SUMMARY
£70,000.00	DD + UD	21-Jan-05	*Whitten v Camden and Islington Community Health Services Trust, ET*	W, who had worked for R for 15 years, was injured in August 1999 when the strap of a heavy workbag she was carrying snapped and jolted her neck. She was dismissed in August 2000. The tribunal found that the trust, as a large employer with considerable resources, had failed in its duties under the DDA 1995 for not making a significant effort to offer W training for another job. Award: £70,000.00.
£110,352.00	DD + UD	18-Jul-05	*Godfrey v Royal Mail Group plc, ET*	G worked for R from 1984 until he was dismissed for incapability in August 2004. He had a knee problem that meant he was unable to carry out his duties as a postal delivery worker. He was diagnosed with osteoarthritis in his knee, and was told that his condition would get worse if he continued his role, walking long distances and carrying a heavy bag. G was aware that there were other positions available that could accommodate his disability. He tried to get assigned to one of these positions, offering to swap location with another employee who wanted to transfer in order to be in a position to apply for suitable posts. His request was refused. G also expressed interest in applying for a higher grade role at the office where he was based, but the post was withdrawn. G's efforts to obtain suitable positions were thwarted by R. The ET found that one manager in particular, Mr V, did everything in his power to avoid making the necessary adjustments for G. Eventually, G retired on ill-health grounds. The tribunal held that R had failed, without justification, to comply with its duty to make reasonable adjustments and had subjected G to unjustified disability-related discrimination by dismissing him. In the ET's view, R could have made reasonable adjustments which were, 'eminently practicable', with very little financial cost or disruption to R. Therefore, it was held that R had discriminated against G by failing to take any of those reasonable steps. Award: in addition to general loss of earnings, £10,000.00 for injury to feelings. The ET took the view that the discrimination was both serious and deliberate, extending over a period of 18 months. Aggravated damages: £5,000.00; £3,000.00 for personal injury; £7,923.00 for future loss of earnings.

£113,833.00	DD + UD	20-Apr-05	*Dicks v Smiths Aerospace Ltd, ET*	D, who has chronic diabetes, was dismissed on grounds of redundancy. The tribunal held that a failure to make reasonable adjustments for D's disability was the cause of his dismissal. In assessing damages for injury to feelings, the tribunal found that D has been 'severely affected by the way he has been treated after 37 years' loyal service' with R. There was no medical evidence of clinical depression, although the tribunal accepted that there was a substantial effect on D's wellbeing. It found that this was caused by D being selected for redundancy because of illness caused by diabetes, and was made worse by R's failure to acknowledge that it had a duty to make adjustments. The injury to feelings was found to fall within the middle range. The tribunal accepted that R did not act maliciously, and that there was no campaign of discrimination and awarded £12,500.00. Award: £113,833.00, including £12,500.00 for injury to feelings; £62,948.00 for future loss; £18,468.00 for future loss of pension; £13,722.00 for loss of earnings; £884.00 for pension loss; £4,885.00 for loss of private medical insurance.
£210,165.00	DD + CD	01-May-05	*Browne v Greater London Magistrates Courts Authority, ET*	B was a court usher. Her duties included work in court as an usher and dealing with paperwork in the summons office. She was 57 when dismissed and had worked at the R for over 10 years. From 1999 until her resignation in August 2002, B continually asked to be put on the rota for court for half a day only, due to problems with her feet. In April 2001, she provided R with a letter from her consultant confirming that she suffered from chronic pain in her feet and that she was advised not to be on her feet throughout the whole day. In September 2001, an occupational health worker reported to R that B's condition should be regarded as a disability and that suitable adjustments should be made at work to prevent her from standing for long periods of the day. The OHP suggested that a suitable arrangement would be to work half a day in court and spend the other half in the office. R failed to make any of the adjustments suggested and B resigned in August 2002 after she had been placed on a full working week in court.

12

AWARD	CATEGORY	DATE	PARTIES	CASE SUMMARY
				The ET found that B was disabled within the meaning of the DDA and concluded that it would have been a reasonable adjustment to vary the rota as suggested. It held that the failure to take any steps reflected B's manager's inflexibility and the reluctance of anyone more senior to take the matter in hand. Award: the ET awarded B £15,000.00 for injury to feelings. They concluded she was unlikely to find other paid work until retirement and her chances of finding pensionable employment was so small as to be nil. The ET calculated loss to be £27,451.00 and future loss to be £65,685.00 after a 10 per cent reduction to reflect contingencies. Pension loss in addition to a basic award was £28,869.00. Total award was £210,165.00.

Sexual Orientation Awards

AWARD	CATEGORY	DATE	PARTIES	CASE SUMMARY
£3,500.00	SO	2006	*Hubble v Brooks, ET*	H, a gay man in a long-term relationship, tried to apply for a job for a couple to manage a public house in West Wales. H spoke to B, who owned or controlled the pub, over the phone about his interest. However, when H revealed that his partner was male, B told him that he was looking for a male and female couple and there was 'no way' he could employ two men, because he could not afford to see the business fail. H's claim for sexual orientation discrimination was upheld by a tribunal. In considering the level of injury to feelings, the tribunal accepted that H had suffered by this treatment, but also noted that it was good to see that H was still confident enough to apply for other similar jobs. The tribunal thought it nevertheless a 'serious' and 'blatant' case. Award: £3,500.00 for injury to feelings.
£3,725.00	SO + UD	26-Jul-06	*Sean Williams v Woodhaven Residential Home, ET*	West Midlands ET found that W had been discriminated against and unfairly dismissed due to his sexual orientation. W was sacked 'without warning' and with no dismissal procedure used. R stated that the reason for dismissal was below standard work and a police caution for non-payment of a taxi fare. These arguments were rejected by the tribunal. Award: £3,725.00 including personal injury.
£4,000.00	SOR + CD	05-May-05	*Whitehead v Brighton Palace Pier, ET*	An ET found that W, having resigned after he discovered that he had been the subject of an 'exceptionally offensive' homophobic remark from a colleague, had been discriminated against. Award: £4,000.00 for injury to feelings, ET stated: 'The tribunal noted that this was a one-off incident of referring to W in an abusive manner because of his sexuality. W was, however, very upset by what he heard, exacerbated by the difficult relationship he had previously had with [his manager].'

385

AWARD	CATEGORY	DATE	PARTIES	CASE SUMMARY
£6,222.00	SO + UD	04-Jan-08	*Legg v Rubyz Limited, ET*	L, a heterosexual bouncer at a gay club, was awarded £6,000.00 after alleging that she was bullied by her employers due to her sexual orientation. L was subjected to derogatory terms on the basis that she was straight before finally being dismissed without warning after a dispute with another doorman. L's award was made up of £3,000.00 for injury to feelings and £3,222.00 for unfair dismissal. It is believed that this was the first time that a heterosexual person has made use of the Employment Equality (Sexual Orientation) Regulations 2003.
£35,345.00	SO + CD	28-Jan-05	*Whitfield v Cleanaway Ltd, ET*	W was a gay employee of R, a waste management company. He was forced to leave his job as a result of constant belittling and goading by other employees. He was nicknamed 'Sebastian' after a character in the TV series Little Britain and was repeatedly called 'dear', 'queer', 'queen', and 'someone who liked poofy drinks and handbags'. The Stratford Tribunal found that R had been lax about coming to W's aid despite previous complaints by another gay employee. The number of incidents, the repetition, and the persistence constituted enough verbal blows to find that W had been a victim of harassment and direct discrimination. Award: £35,345.00 (which included £10,000.00 for injury to feelings).
£47,345.00	SOR	11-Feb-08	*John Reaney v The Hereford Diocese and Board of Finance, ET*	JR, a homosexual Christian, was awarded £47,345.00 (including £33,000.00 for loss of future earnings and £7,000.00 damages for 'psychiatric injury') after he successfully took the R to an employment tribunal after his appointment to the role of youth worker was blocked on the grounds of his sexuality by the Bishop of Hereford, the Rt Rev Anthony Priddis. JR told the tribunal that he was questioned by Bishop Priddis on his previous gay relationship during a two-hour meeting. He had previously emerged as the outstanding candidate for the job during the interview process.

£118,309.00	SOR + UD	25-May-06	*Ditton v CP Publishing Ltd, Glasgow Employment Tribunal, ET*	D, a homosexual media sales manager, was bullied and harassed by managers at his new job and then fired after only eight days. He was called at night and informed that he was fired because he was 'psychologically imbalanced'. During his time at R he had been subjected to verbal abuse by his manager, using insults such as 'Shut it, you wee poof,' and asking him if he was from Stoke-On-Trent (rhyming slang for 'bent'). This occurred frequently in front of sales staff reporting to D. The tribunal described R's conduct as 'high-handed, malicious, insulting and oppressive'. D was awarded £10,000.00 injury to feelings and £76,937.00 for loss of earnings. Both the injury to feelings award and the loss of earnings award attracted a 30 per cent uplift pursuant to s 31 of the Employment Act 2002. This was to reflect the employer's failure to complete the statutory grievance procedure in respect of the harassment complaint and the statutory dismissal procedure in dismissing the claimant. £556.00 was awarded for unlawful deduction from wages and £133.00 for breach of contract, both sums uplifted by 50 per cent to reflect D's unexplained and inexcusable failure to complete the statutory grievance procedure. Total compensation including interest was just over £118,000.00.
£350,000.00	SO + UD	15-May-07	*Margaret Durman and Penny Smith v Barchester Healthcare, ET*	Two lesbian nurses have been awarded at least £350,000.00 after they were sacked because of their sexuality. MD and PS had been together for a year when they were sacked from Kernow House care home in September 2005. MD, a registered nurse for 35 years, had been manager of the home since 2001 and both had exemplary records. They were dismissed after they were accused of allowing the physical and sexual abuse of residents. They were both put on the Protection of Vulnerable Adults list, which meant they could no longer work as nurses. The tribunal found the allegations were groundless and that the couple had been victims of discrimination on the grounds of sexual orientation. It said that the care home had unfairly 'trawled' staff for complaints, suppressed documents, and mishandled the disciplinary procedure.

12

Religion and Belief Awards

AWARD	CATEGORY	DATE	PARTIES	CASE SUMMARY
£500.00	RBR	20-Jul-05	*Fugler v MacMillan, London Hairstudios Ltd, ET*	F, who is Jewish, worked in R's hair salon. An ET held that there was indirect religious discrimination following R's refusal to allow him to take holiday on Saturday 25 September 2004, which was Yom Kippur. F requested the holiday in early September, after being reminded of the forthcoming Jewish festival. In assessing injury to feelings, the tribunal found that F was upset on the day he left, but within days had found other employment. It said 'Yom Kippur is an important event in the Jewish calendar but it is regrettable that F did not remember to book it in good time'. Award: £500.00 The tribunal held that it was appropriate to use the minimum possible award.
£1,000.00 plus damages for loss of earnings	RBR	10-Oct-06	*Edge v Visual Security Services, ET*	E was a security guard who, as a committed Christian, made it clear that he did not want to work on Sundays for religious reasons. R agreed to try to respect his wishes but he was increasingly asked to work Sundays. He asked for a specific weekend off, was refused and said he would take it anyway. He was then sacked. The tribunal found indirect discrimination on grounds of religion and £1,000.00 was awarded for injury to feelings.
£1,100.00	RBR	20-Oct-06	*Aishah Azmi v Kirklees Council, ET*	A, a Muslim woman who worked as a bilingual teaching assistant at Headfield Church of England Junior School in Dewsbury, West Yorkshire, brought a test case against R that employed her for victimization and discrimination due to her religious beliefs. Mrs Azmi had been asked to remove her niqab (veil) whilst teaching as it was felt that it reduced her ability to teach English and communicate with the children, aged between 10 and 12. Originally, an agreement had been reached whereby A would remove her veil whilst teaching if no man was present at the time, but this agreement soon broke down after complaints from male colleagues. A refused to remove her veil and the school suspended her on full pay. A brought a claim under the Employment Equality

£8,224.00	RBR	*Mohammed Khan v NIC Hygiene, ET*	13-Jan-05

(Religion or Belief) Regulations 2004. The tribunal rejected the claims of discrimination due to religious belief, but did award £1,000.00 for injury to feelings for the way in which the case was handled. A further 10 per cent was added as statutory grievance procedures had not been complied with.

K, a Muslim cleaner, was sacked for going on a six-week pilgrimage to Mecca. K put his request for time off in writing four months before he was due to leave. R did not get back to him, but K's line manager said that he could assume his request was agreed to unless he heard to the contrary. K was suspended as soon as he returned from Mecca, then sacked for gross misconduct. The Leeds Tribunal found that he had been unfairly dismissed and suffered indirect religious discrimination. Award: £8,224.00 (including interest) for unlawful discrimination and £1,168.00 for unlawful deduction of wages.

Age Discrimination Awards

AWARD	CATEGORY	DATE	PARTIES	CASE SUMMARY
£1,000.00	AD	12-Jun-06	*Martin v SS Photay & Associates, ET*	M worked for R as a cleaner and was aged 70. There were performance issues but she was dismissed because of her health and age. 'She had fallen into the high risk category for health and safety.' R was held to be discriminatory and its acts were not justified. Award: £1,000.00 for injury to feelings in part in recognition of the manner of dismissal (by letter left in her locker) and the contents of the letter.
£1,000.00–£1,500.00	AD	25-Oct-06	*Sharma and Others v Millbrook Beds Ltd, ET*	S and others claimed when R terminated an age-related bonus scheme because R believed the bonus payment would be unlawful under EEAR 2006 but allowed younger employees to continue to receive it. It was held to be directly discriminatory and, due to the lack of consultation, not capable of justification. Three employees were awarded £1,000.00 for injury to feelings. S was awarded £1,500.00 due to the way the change was implemented while she was on holiday.
£11,108.00	AD	24-Oct-07	*Kessell v Passion for Perfume Ltd, ET*	K was dismissed ostensibly because of her reluctance to work on Saturdays. However, her manager made age-related comments about her deafness and poor eyesight and the tribunal found her manager's attitude to her age was the real reason for her dismissal. Award: £11,108.00 including £4,000.00 for injury to feelings because R's treatment of K 'severely undermined' her confidence and caused her significant distress.

| £16,081.12 | AD + UD | 04-Mar-08 | *Wilkinson v Springwell Engineering, ET* | Leanne Wilkinson, a 19-year-old, has been awarded £16,081.12 (of which £5,000.00 was awarded for injury to feelings) after a tribunal found that R had dismissed her for being too young. Ms Wilkinson, who was then 18, claimed that she suffered age discrimination when she was dismissed from her job as an administrative assistant at R in Newcastle-upon-Tyne. She claimed R had told her that she was too young for the post and that they needed an older person with more experience. The tribunal said that R had relied on a 'stereotypical assumption that capability equals experience and experience equals older age. . . age was the predominant reason for the decision to dismiss'. |

INDEX